W9-BPL-241

APR 1 8 1991

Principles
of
Visual
Perception

Principles
of
Visual
Perception

Carolyn M. Bloomer

SECOND EDITION

Design Press

To my husband,

Lynn E. Stauffer, Jr.,

this book is affectionately dedicated.

Second Edition, First Printing

Copyright © 1976, 1990 by Carolyn M. Bloomer
Printed in the United States of America
Designed by Gilda Hannah

Library of Congress Cataloging-in-Publication Data

Bloomer, Carolyn M.
    Principles of visual perception / Carolyn M. Bloomer. —2nd ed.
      p. cm.
    Bibliography: p.
    Includes index.
    ISBN 0-8306-1704-3
    1. Visual perception. 2. Composition (Art) 3. Art—Psychology.
  I. Title.
N7430.5.B57 1989
701'.15—dc20   89-33110
                                                       CIP

Design Press offers posters and The Cropper, a device for cropping artwork,
for sale. For information, contact Mail-order Department. Design Press books
are available at special discounts for bulk purchases for sales promotions, fund
raisers, or premiums. For details contact Special Sales Manager. Questions
regarding the content of the book should be addressed to:

Design Press
Division of TAB BOOKS
10 East 21st Street
New York, NY 10010

Contents

Preface to the Second Edition

In purpose, this revision of *Principles of Visual Perception* mirrors the first edition: to present an interesting, readable, interdisciplinary view of visual perception that will appeal to students and teachers of art and allied fields as well as to readers with more general interests. The emphasis is on perception as a process of constructing meaning from visual experience. In spite of its biological components, the process of perception is most significantly regulated by individual experience in tandem with varying cultural and historical worldviews. Thus, I have intentionally painted with a broad brush, interrelating everyday experiences with scientific investigations, artistic and aesthetic concepts, and historical and cross-cultural studies.

But this edition of *Principles of Visual Perception* differs from the first in several important ways. Every chapter has been extensively rewritten to address more explicitly some historical and cultural issues that were only implied in the first edition. Newer developments in art and perceptual theory are included, along with two entirely new chapters devoted to photography and electronic imaging. This edition also includes a more extensive collection of projects and experiments keyed to each chapter, with specific applications indicated for photography and computer graphics.

For viewers of art, *Principles of Visual Perception* offers a repertory of fundamental concepts for approaching the appreciation of artworks—whether historical or contemporary, Western or non-Western. Teachers will find *Principles of Visual Perception* a useful text for teaching design, composition, graphics, and art appreciation, as well as an important resource for studio art, art history, art therapy, photography, computer graphics, education, psychology, anthropology, and cross-disciplinary studies. For students in these fields, *Principles of Visual Perception* is intended to both amplify and clarify classroom study and textbook readings. While each chapter builds on those that precede it, the chapters are, in general, sufficiently self-contained that they can be read independently of each other.

Because vision is commonly assumed to be objective and unlearned, and to a great extent independent of culture, the simple question of what happens when someone looks at something is rarely addressed systematically in schools, except in specialized and highly restricted studies in biology, psychology, and aesthetics. And yet, throughout my sixteen years of teaching studio art, art history, and art education, I found that when students were armed with a basic understanding of visual perception, they not only understood their own responses more clearly, but they were able to find personal meaning in all kinds of art works, and to open their minds to other people's perceptions.

As the complexion of our world becomes more and more internationalized, it becomes urgent for us to understand the varying cultural components of perception, especially in regard to the perception of mediated imagery—in particular the mass-media images of photography and television. Indeed, at this writing I am enmeshed in just such a cross-cultural challenge as I research art in China during the period of tragedy in Tien'anmen Square. Experiencing a cultural milieu in which images are employed daily to construct an official reality in Chinese minds, I find profoundly disturbing the keen awareness that the reality being constructed simultaneously in Western minds—while radically different in content—is dependent upon virtually identical perceptual processes. I conclude that if we are to avoid disaster in the future of our shrinking planet, we must forsake the comfort of ethnocentric assumptions, and instead pursue a broader, more generous, and vastly more informed perspective on the perceptual worlds of both ourselves and other peoples. This is the larger, more idealistic (and perhaps more disquieting) perspective of the new *Principles of Visual Perception*.

Since life does not often afford us a second chance at important projects, I am especially grateful to Nancy N. Green, editor of the first edition and now Editorial Director of Design Press, for supporting and encouraging this project. A number of other people have also been essential to the realization of the present edition. These include my incredibly patient and tolerant husband, Lynn E. Stauffer, Jr., to whom this book is dedicated; Katherine Nelson, staunch friend and indomitable ally, who shouldered the burden of securing permissions, a responsibility that became unexpectedly thorny after I left for China; Eleanor Holland, who made nearly all of the new drawings for this edition, and whose cheerful spirit, inquiring mind, and technical talents have added immeasurably to the visual quality of the book. I owe special thanks to Professor Judith B. Farquhar of the Anthropology Department at the University of North Carolina at Chapel Hill, who in recent years has been a major influence on my approach to historical and cross-cultural research. Others who gave help, advice, and constructive criticism include physicist James Bradford and artist Barbara McDonald of Fairfax, Virginia; Sally Segal, Professor of Art at the University of Texas at El Paso; copy editor Stephen Gray and assistant editor Kurt Wildermuth; and Qin Jian, my research assistant at Xiamen University; and Gilda Hannah, who designed the book.

Xiamen University
Fujian Province, China
June 1989

Principles
of
Visual
Perception

1
Mind and Meaning
The First Step in Understanding Perception

Clip a half-dozen cartoons out of magazines. Cut off the captions; then place the pictures face-down in one pile and the captions face-down in another. Scramble the piles, and randomly pair each caption with a picture. Then turn over the pairs. You will have a whole set of brand-new jokes. In spite of the fact that the combinations were determined by chance, at least half of them will be funny! Try the same thing with advertisements (separate pictures from key phrases); once again, the results will be uncanny: ironic, poetic, or humorous. This simple experiment demonstrates the most fundamental process of the human mind: the attribution of meaning to things and events in the outer world. Creating meaning is an automatic process: your mind does it whether you want it to or not. How and why this happens is the subject of this book.

THINKING ABOUT PERCEPTION

Many factors influence how (or whether) we find meaning in things and events in our environment. Psychological research often creates the impression that the principles of perception are rather clearly delineated and can be scientifically measured. In comparison to laboratory experiments, however, real life (and art!) is much less predictable and much more complex, mysterious, and surprising. Although perception is subject to a number of influences that are familiar to you, you probably do not often think about these. Before going on to examine visual perception in particular (an examination that comprises the rest of the book), let us first look at perception in general. What is it? What does it do? How and why does it do it?

Projection and Expectation

The venture into creating new jokes suggests just how imaginative the human mind can be: a person instantly perceives even random or accidental events as meaningful. Even when relaxing, your mind persists in spinning out meaning—seeing identifiable images in clouds, rock formations, gnarled wood, stains on the wall. Such projections of meaning often say more about your mental processes than they do about the stimulus; this is the basis for psychologists' projective tests. The Rorschach test, for example, uses a person's responses to inkblots as a way of analyzing personality (see figure 1-1).

Projection is a part of other familiar activities such as astrology, Tarot readings, and the I-Ching (*Yi-jing*). In these, people project their own personal concerns onto established frameworks of meaning in order to discover new perspectives on their lives. Projection is also fundamental to science, even though we usually think of science as a method for avoiding projection: scientific data are meaningful only when they can be made to represent an extended projection of concepts that already exist in the minds of scientists. Because scientific concepts are constantly open to reevaluation, the same data are sometimes given different interpretations—new meanings—by subsequent investigators.

An example of projected meaning is the Clever Hans phenomenon. Hans was a horse who belonged to a retired Berlin school teacher, Wilhelm von Osten, during the early 1900s (see figure 1-2). Many people of the time, including prominent scholars and scientists, firmly believed that animals could think in human ways—if they were properly

Figure 1-1. How many different things can you see in this inkblot? (Joyce Burnham and Rachel Robertson)

Figure 1-2. Wilhelm von Osten and Clever Hans, c. 1905. (The New York Public Library)

taught. Hans was taught to answer questions by tapping a front hoof a certain number of times to indicate a particular number or letter of the alphabet. He was thought to be able to compute arithmetic problems, to read and spell, and to solve problems of musical harmony. By 1937 more than seventy dogs, cats, and horses had been taught to "think" in similar ways.

Apparently, Hans was extremely sensitive to his master's slightest movement. When the horse reached the correct number of knocks, von Osten unconsciously relaxed, giving a subtle and involuntary head motion which Hans detected. Because von Osten and others expected Hans to exhibit human intelligence, they interpreted the horse's behavior as proving the truth of their beliefs. Similar projections occur when people watch animals perform at circuses and zoos, where the context is carefully constructed to give the illusion that the animals' perceptions are the same as those of the audience. Comparable interpretations have been made of modern experiments with teaching human language to chimpanzees, gorillas, and dolphins; however, contemporary researchers are well aware of the Clever Hans phenomenon and design their studies to meet sophisticated and complex scientific criteria.

In a controversial educational study, school teachers projected their expectancies onto their pupils (Rosenthal and Jacobson 1968). The teachers were told (falsely) that test results had predicted that certain pupils were due to bloom intellectually during that school year. The teachers'

positive expectations led them to favor these students unconsciously—for example, by giving them more time to answer questions and more encouragement, praise, and help. By the same token, the teachers responded unfavorably to pupils who made intellectual gains that were not expected. The researchers named this self-fulfilling prophesy the *Pygmalion effect* after a Greek myth in which the sculptor Pygmalion fell so much in love with a statue he had created that the goddess Aphrodite brought it to life. Although the Pygmalion study has been criticized on ethical grounds, its dramatic findings brought about a greater awareness of how expectancies affect both perception and behavior in interpersonal contexts.

Memory

Researchers have long known that people memorize words much faster than nonsense syllables and forget nonsense syllables much more quickly. Patterns (for example *4589*) are recognized more easily than meaningless arrangements of the same elements (for example, *5395*). Memory-improvement techniques associate meaningful mental imagery with arbitrary series such as telephone, social security, or zip-code numbers. For example, the number *four* might be represented by a table with four legs; *five* by a hand, and *seven* by a policeman facing you with his right arm extended. To remember the number, you would first recall the meaningful image (a giant hand holding a table with a traffic policeman standing on top of it), and then decode it (*547*). Kinesthetic, auditory, and spatial types of imagery have also been favored as mnemonic devices (memory aids) since ancient times. Ideas or items to be remembered are associated with parts of one's own body, the rhythm of a sing-song chant, or with walking through a familiar place, such as a building, house, or garden. These techniques appear inefficient: they seem to demand more mental energy than does simple memorizing. However, such memory aids are common worldwide, they correspond to the multiple intelligence capacities of the human mind, and they have persisted throughout human history. In cultures with mass literacy, emphasis on memory skills tends to decline because knowledge can be stored in and retrieved from written documents instead of in people and objects. (Compare what you had to memorize in school with what was required of your parents and grandparents.) But most of all, these techniques underscore the supreme importance of meaning for the human mind.

Selectivity

Your mind cannot give equal attention to every stimulus that impinges on your senses. Conscious perception is selective; your mind pretends that some things do not exist. As a consequence, you do not experience everything in the world as equally meaningful. In fact, when you find yourself trying to pay attention to too many meaningful perceptions at once, you experience overload.

The selective aspect of perception is evident from the first day of life. Newborns prefer looking at patterned cards as opposed to plain ones. Infants also find complex patterns (such as stripes, bull's-eyes, and checkerboards) more interesting than simple patterns (such as crosses, circles, and triangles), and they direct their gaze toward spheres more often than toward flat circles. By four months of age, babies respond more frequently to patterns that resemble the human face than they do to scrambled features or featureless patterns (Fantz 1961). Even adults instantly perceive a face where it does not exist (see figure 1-3). Hence, from its earliest moments, the human visual system is involved in scanning the environment and selecting out certain stimuli (such as facelike configurations) as more meaningful than other stimuli.

Habituation

Some aspects of selective perception result from habituation: your mind tunes out stimuli that are

Figure 1-3. Decaying taillight. (Fred H. Stocking)

constant (monotonous) or repetitious and predictable (boring). For this reason, you often become aware of familiar noises (such as household appliances and city traffic) only when they stop (that is, change). If for some reason you are forced to pay attention to such stimuli (as in a factory assembly-line job, or during lengthy turnpike driving), your mind will persistently try to tune them out, and you are likely to find yourself falling asleep or daydreaming. The loss of alertness that attends monotony and boredom can have life-or-death consequences in some situations, and it is all the more problematic for being a natural response. Human perceptual systems require variation and change in order to function; when exposed to steady-state conditions, your sense receptors cease to function.

Salience

Since the stimuli you tune out remain invisible, you may feel astonished if you discover them. When your best friend is wrapped up in automobiles, art, rock music, birdwatching, or the like, you are made aware of a whole new world. Consider, too, the new-word phenomenon. A new word in your vocabulary suddenly seems to appear everywhere, as if the whole world had suddenly taken a fancy to it. But the word was always in use: you simply overlooked it before, because it was not meaningful to you. When something acquires personal meaning, it ceases to stay in the background, instead becoming a conspicuous or salient figure in the individual's consciousness.

When a different picture was shown to each eye of experimental subjects, the perceptually salient pictures were those that represented familiar objects in the subject's own culture; pictures of unfamiliar (and therefore essentially meaningless) objects from other cultures were tuned out (cited in Cole and Scribner 1974). Familiar faces, too, have a special perceptual salience; for example, notice how your own face or that of someone you know well stands out more than the faces of people you do not know (see figure 1-4). Sometimes people become painfully alert for certain stimuli, as when someone with a fear of spiders sees what appears to be a spider in a spot on the wall. This hypersensitivity is called *perceptual vigilance*.

Normalizing

In one study, the word *chack* was read as *chick* in a sentence about poultry raising, and as *check* in a sentence about banking. The readers' minds corrected the stimulus. Instead of being alert to unexpected irregularities, they tuned out or normalized the stimulus so that it could be perceived as familiar and uncomplicated. In laboratory studies, subjects usually require many repeated exposures to irregular or anomalous patterns (such as a black eight of hearts) before they begin to pick up on the anomalies; even then, their initial responses take the form of vague discomfort rather than of direct recognition. This tuning out is known as *perceptual defense*, the opposite of perceptual vigilance.

You may have experienced situations in which some part of your mind was aware of odd goings-on but another part refused to attribute unusual or threatening meanings to the situation. This is because, whenever possible, perception encourages us to experience what is probable in a situation, rather than what is possible. In this way, our perceptual systems simplify our world and keep it predictable.

Dissonance

Sometimes two or more perceptions seem to conflict with each other. You cannot tune out either one, and yet you are unable to accept them both—as, for example, when you distinctly remember placing the car keys in your pocket, but they are not there. You vacillate between two (or more) sets of possible explanations, each requiring you to reject the other(s). Such situations—particularly when your perceptions seem to be at odds with those of people around you—can be deeply upsetting. When one person intentionally creates such a condition to manipulate another, it is sometimes called *gaslighting* after a popular turn-of-the-century stage play *Gaslight* (basis for the 1940s movie) in which the husband attempted to drive his wife insane by doing such things as gradually lowering the gaslights and then denying to her that they had dimmed.

Words

Words have an amazing power to affect your perceptions of meaning. Often, simply naming a stimulus is enough (as when a doctor gives your symptoms a scientific name, or when you finally remember someone's name). Nothing has really changed, except that you somehow feel better. Identification by naming is the basis of innumerable activities, such as education, hobbies (such as birdwatching and antique collecting), medical diagnosis, and astronomy.

Words direct people's perceptions of art. Western artists and theorists often assert that an artwork should not need verbal explanations—that it should stand on its own. For this reason, some modern artists simply number their works or leave them untitled. But if art objects did indeed speak for themselves, you would not have to enroll in art history courses in order to understand them, and you would probably not be reading this book. It is a truism of perceptual experience that, the more you know, the more meaning you can perceive and the more (or less) satisfying an image becomes.

Closure

When you have successfully resolved the problem of meaning, you experience closure. The term *closure* was originally applied by Gestalt psychologists to the phenomenon of identifying a discontinuous figure as a continuous or unitary image. It is now commonly applied to the more general experience of identifying and classifying a stimulus (*Aha! I see!*)

in such a way that the observer feels free to move on to something else. Depending on the importance of the stimulus, closure is usually accompanied by feelings of relief.

Habituation, perceptual salience, normalizing, and words are ways of keeping closure unproblematic. Situations that involve perceptual dissonance make people uncomfortable because under those circumstances closure feels difficult or impossible. When closure is too difficult, people are likely to feel frustrated and, if possible, may attempt to reject the stimulus. When closure is easy, the stimulus attracts but does not hold their attention (see figure 1-5). Advertising is designed to provide instant, uncomplicated closure. As a consequence, the advertiser must constantly present fresh new images in order to entice viewers into seeking closure. Certain stimuli continue to hold interest even after repeated exposure. This is the quality people usually associate with great artworks (''Every time I look at/listen to/read it, I find something new!'')

Puzzles. Despite their need for closure, people often flirt with postponing it. Multimillion-dollar businesses exploit the public's perennial willingness to delay closure, as with crossword puzzles, jigsaw puzzles, cryptograms, mystery stories, and suspense movies. In all of these situations, however, people feel secure in anticipating that they will eventually arrive at closure: the puzzle has a solution, the writer or filmmaker will eventually clear up the mystery, and the joke's punch line will (or had better) be worth waiting for. As long as closure is promised and yet is not at hand, the audience's attention is captured.

Other People

In a now-classic series of studies, psychologist Solomon Asch (1956) observed how perceptual behavior was affected by the presence of other people. Asch devised a situation in which small groups of people were given a line and asked as a group to decide which in a series of other lines matched it. In every instance, the correct match was obvious; no subtle discriminations or measurements were required. But only one person in the group was the actual subject; unbeknownst to him or her, the others were collaborating with the experimenter. Most of the time the group reached a consensus easily, but occasionally the collaborators would insist that mismatching lines were equal in length. About

Figure 1-4. President Kennedy, 1962. (Tony Spina)

three-fourths of the time, a subject would eventually deny his or her own correct perceptions in favor of conforming to the group consensus—even though the group was clearly wrong (see figure 1-6)!

Subsequent experiments explored this phenomenon further. In one situation, an innocent subject sat in a small waiting room adjacent to an office. Smoke was piped into the room through the air-conditioning system. Immediately upon smelling the smoke, a solitary subject would alert the secretary in the office (a collaborator in the experiment) or would leave the room to look for a custodian. When other people (collaborators) were present in the room, however, the subject did nothing, even when the air became so smoky that everyone was coughing and their eyes were watering. Similarly, if a loud crash and a scream came from the adjoining office, a solitary subject immediately entered the office to investigate, but did nothing in the presence of others who were nonresponsive. When other people did not appear to share the subjects' perceptions, they tended to deny them—or at least to refrain from acting on them.

Figure 1-5. Common signs are designed to provide instant closure. Geometric and uncomplicated shapes prompt automatic recognition. Because meaning is immediately apparent, we can respond quickly and without confusion.

The findings of Asch and others suggested that the presence of other people exerts a powerful influence on individual action, suppressing behaviors that people might otherwise make in response to their perceptions. For Americans, who value individualism and personal initiative, such findings were profoundly disturbing.

Culture. Western ideology tends to assume the autonomy of the individual, but studies in evolution, primatology, and anthropology suggest that people are basically social. Since the emergence of our earliest hominid ancestors, human beings have always lived in groups. People learn their perceptions from other individuals to a much greater extent than is the case with other animals (even social species such as lions, baboons, and wolves), for whom a greater proportion of perceived meaning is genetically patterned (or instinctive).

Culture is the most prominent nongenetic influence on human perception. Other people teach you what is real: how to respond to your perceptions, and how to think about, talk about, and understand their value and significance. You learn the culturally acceptable ways to attribute meaning to your personal experience (socialization). Human infants always acquire the language, perceptions, thought patterns, and behaviors appropriate to the culture in which they are reared, regardless of who or where their biological parents may be. Culture, then, constitutes a set of collectively accepted parameters for gauging the nature of things, a perceptually shared reality, a world view.

Deviation. Marching to a different drummer can exact a high price. In our culture, individuals whose perceptions are at odds with those of others are often considered weird or even insane. People who attribute bad or good things that happen to them to plots, conspiracies, or a divine plan are said to suffer from paranoia or delusions of grandeur, and those who seem to live in their own world are considered schizophrenic. Depression and suicide are associated with an overwhelming failure to perceive the same kinds of meaningfulness as other people do. Those who do not participate in the mainstream of cultural meaning are often segregated from the general population (in prisons, mental hospitals, or ghettos). Even artists are commonly viewed as peripheral to real life. By contrast, in many other societies, the different individual is given a special role (for example, the *berdache* of the Native Americans of the Great Plains) or is thought to have special powers that are useful to the group (for example, the shaman).

Artists and Innovators. Most people tolerate a certain amount of meaninglessness in their lives: indeed, they must develop such tolerance in order to get on with things. People who expect life to be a neat package, with everything in its place, are doomed to disappointment. Certain people, however, seem to have an unusual ability to withstand—or even prefer—a larger amount of disorder and chaos than normal; this characteristic is found in artists, writers, and scientists who are mature (over 40 years old) and highly creative (Barron 1958). Western studies of these "crazy" artists and "mad" scientists suggest that they perceive unusual or new meanings in situations that are experienced as chaotic or disordered by most other people. Further, they are likely to pursue, maintain, and act on their individual perceptions—like the 25 percent of Asch's subjects who refused to go along

Figure 1-6. Drawing by Vietor; ©1978 The New Yorker Magazine, Inc.

"Wait a minute, you guys—I've decided to make it unanimous after all."

with the group consensus when it was at odds with their own perceptions. While psychologists label this trait *independence*, friends and relatives are more apt to call it *stubbornness* or *pig-headedness*. Some cross-cultural research suggests that these artistic personality characteristics are consistent from one culture to another.

Most people do not usually share an innovator's need for rethinking things; indeed, they actively avoid becoming involved with unfamiliar, discomforting, or mind-boggling ideas. For these reasons, new theories (which are based on new perceptions of meaning) often meet with strong opposition (such as Galileo's sun-centered universe, Darwin's theory of evolution, and nuclear winter). Artistic innovations often meet similar hostility: *How can you call that art? My five-year-old could do that! They could hang it upside down and nobody would know the difference!* A respected nineteenth-century critic reacted to Impressionist paintings by saying "You might as well give a monkey a paint-box!" Some present-day art critics have characterized computer-assisted art as cold and soulless.

THEN WHAT IS PERCEPTION?

The term *perception* is commonly used in a number of different ways. It can refer to responses of the nervous system to external stimulation (sensation), or to primitive awareness—as in "I perceived a sudden movement out of the corner of my eye." At the other extreme, *perception* can refer to more complex and higher-level thought processes (cognition)—as in "I perceived deep religious qualities in her paintings." Until recently, psychologists de-

fined *perception* as an intermediate step in the upward relaying of primitive sensations to higher levels of processing, in accordance with the traditional simple-to-complex hierarchy of sensation/perception/cognition (see figure 1-8). Current research in physiology, psychology, anthropology, and cybernetics, however, suggests a richer and infinitely more complex picture. Perception is thought to be less determined by sensory stimulation, and equally (or more) controlled by cognitive factors such as expectancy, normalizing, and verbal coherence. In other words, the flow runs top–down as well as bottom–up (see figure 1-8).

To review, at least four overarching processes shape perception: mental operations that affect how we attribute meaning to stimuli (for example, habituation, salience, normalizing, dissonance, and closure); the effects of words on perceived meaning; the interplay between perception and behavior (for example, the presence or absence of other people); and the framing of both perception and behavior by social or cultural context (for example, learning, socialization, deviance, creativity). In this book, visual perception is explored as a mediating process that fuses simple sensation with high-level cognition so that your experience of meaning will be unified and coherent.

Perception and Sensation

Psychologist James J. Gibson (1966, 1979) and others have pointed out that people are not consciously aware of their sensations—the excitation of nerve fibers. For example, you hear a sound; you do not feel your eardrums vibrate. As I pick up my teacup, I feel the cup, not my fingers. You are not aware of sensations themselves, but rather of the meaning-

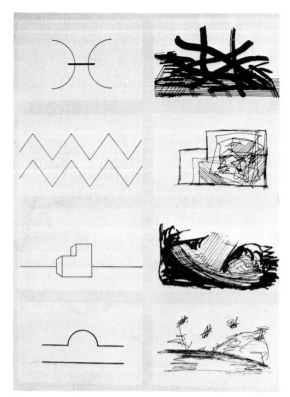

Figure 1-7. Creative personalities prefer drawings such as those on the right. "Average" preferences appear on the left. Adapted and reproduced by special permission of the Publisher, Consulting Psychologists Press, Inc., Palo Alto, Calif., from Welsh Figure Preference Test by George S. Welsh, © 1949. Further reproduction is prohibited without the Publisher's consent.

ful information that these sensations represent in your consciousness. Hence, although sensations are physiologically predictable, differences in how they are perceived can cause the same sensations to be experienced as different in significance or meaning. Familiar examples are the *Peter and Paul Goblet* (see figure 1-9) and *The Wife and the Mother-in-Law* (see figure 3-23).

At this most basic level, perception is the experience of simple closure: the act of recognizing and identifying sense stimulation in some fundamental way (as in "That's a car/a noise/Judy/my dog/money"). At this stage, perception is nonreflective: it is a seemingly automatic knowing of the nature of what we perceive. Where this knowing comes from is one of the major questions that this book explores.

Nature and Nurture

Understanding perception would be easy if it were a simple matter of biology, but such is far from the case. True, some automatic perceptions are biologically and genetically based, generated by the physiological structures and capacities of our bodies. Such perceptual processes are pan-human—that is, common to all normal members of *Homo sapiens sapiens* (and to some other species, as well). These broad perceptual capacities include such things as day and night vision, contour enhancement, and persistence of vision; differentiating figure and ground relationships; perceptual constancy; color vision; orientation to space; and the perception of motion. But other perceptions that may feel automatic are nonetheless culturally learned: for example, optical illusions; perception of depth in pictures; and the perception of reality in photographs and electronic images.

Furthermore, it is dangerous to overgeneralize from laboratory studies of perception. Such experiments are commonly conducted on Western subjects (usually college students), and do not customarily take into account individual, cultural, or subcultural differences. They usually take place under artificial laboratory conditions that do not reflect the subtleties and complexities of real-life perceiving. In the context of day-to-day living, perception is influenced by an enormous range of factors that are independent of the stimulus itself: cultural conventions (learning, experience, expectancies, beliefs, and values); physiological factors (mood, temperament, age, and health), and environmental habituations (ecological habitat). For these reasons, except at the most basic levels, human perceptions can be impressively variable and are not always predictable. Indeed, this biological capacity for perceptual variability is the hallmark of the human species.

Perception as Biological Adaptation

Each species has a genetic program for receiving and processing information critical to its survival and reproduction. Not everything needs to be perceived by every species. Frog vision, for example, only detects changes in light and dark (movement), but this suffices for obtaining food and avoiding predators. Frogs do not need to smell flowers or to see colors. Snakes are sensitive to vibrations of the earth, and they have extremely sensitive temperature sensors (infrared vision) for detecting warm-

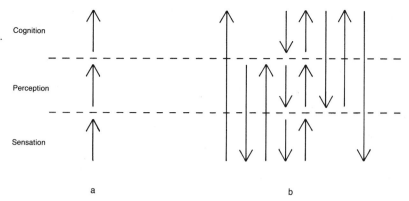

Figure 1-8. Concepts of perception:
(a) Perception as intermediate step;
(b) Perception as mediating process.

Cognition

Perception

Sensation

a   b

blooded prey; they do not need to hear birds sing or to watch ants. The colors seen by ocean fish depend on the depth of the water in which the species normally lives. This exquisite fit between a species' perceptual system and its environmental niche is part of biological adaptation and specialization.

Natural Selection. Because of normal genetic variation, not all individuals in a species are identical. Depending on environmental conditions (weather, climate, predator populations, availability of food and protective shelter, and so on) slight individual differences will be advantageous, disadvantageous, or neutral. For example, if living in tree branches becomes safer than living on the ground, individual mammals whose eyes face slightly more forward may be better able to judge near distance and so avoid falling. Under other circumstances (for example, living on open ground) this same characteristic may work against survival by decreasing the scope of side vision. Hence, genetic variation may or may not favor an individual; but the presence of variation itself is an insurance policy for the species, increasing the probability that some of its members will survive as conditions change, and that the survivors will be those who are best suited (adapted or fit) to the new conditions. When these survivors reproduce, their particular genetic variations are likely to be passed on to their offspring. The genetic characteristics of a species, then, are always a product of evolutionary changes that proved to be successful in past environments (which may or may not be the same as the present environment). Charles Darwin called this process *natural selection.*

One way to make sense of human perceptual

Figure 1-9. Reversible image: *Peter and Paul Goblet.*

systems is to consider human beings as a biologically specialized species whose characteristics evolved over a long history of natural selection. We can then better understand not only what human perception does, but why it works the way it does. What information about the environment was important for the survival of our human ancestors? How has this shaped the perceptual processes of today's human beings?

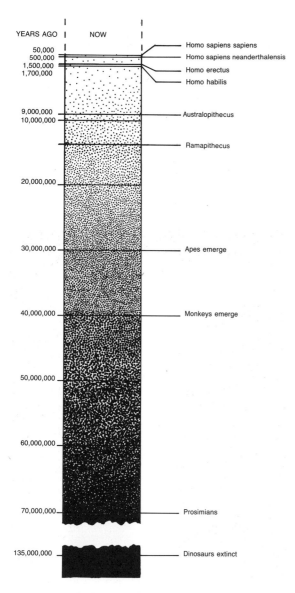

YEARS AGO	NOW	
50,000		Homo sapiens sapiens
500,000		Homo sapiens neanderthalensis
1,500,000		Homo erectus
1,700,000		Homo habilis
9,000,000		Australopithecus
10,000,000		
		Ramapithecus
20,000,000		
30,000,000		Apes emerge
40,000,000		Monkeys emerge
50,000,000		
60,000,000		
70,000,000		Prosimians
135,000,000		Dinosaurs extinct

Figure 1-10. Evolutionary time line.

Human Adaptations. The biological roots of human perception can be traced back at least 70 million years, to the emergence of certain structures of the skeleton, sense organs, and nervous system in small mammals called *prosimians* (see figures 1-10 and 1-11). Since that time, human sense organs themselves show little change. How-

ever, a great deal of change has occurred in the way sense data are neurologically processed by the brain. Human evolution is characterized by the development of additional brain space for more abstract activities such as memory, association, and speech.

Genetic evolution is a slow process. In general, it takes about 1 million years for one mammal species to diverge genetically into another species only slightly different from the first (a process called *speciation*). (Individuals of a species are capable of interbreeding with each other, but not with individuals from another species.) Although minor differences in human physiology have occurred since the appearance of *Homo sapiens* ("wise humans") 500,000 years ago, they have not been sufficient to produce further speciation. Modern humans (*Homo sapiens* var. *sapiens*, or "wise variety of wise humans") appeared about 50,000 years ago. Since then, the size, shape, and organization of the human brain appears to have undergone no change at all. Twentieth-century human beings are therefore physically and neurologically the same as the ancestors of their Ice Age ancestors. You are genetically separated by only 200 generations from the early civilizations of 5,000 years ago, from the first farmers by only 400 generations, and from the prehistoric cave artists by 600 generations. If you could trace your same-sex ancestors (that is, your mother's mother's mother's mother's mother or father's father's father's father's father) back to the beginnings of Ancient Egypt, the list of names would fit on a single page!

Beneath the trappings of modern civilization, the human body, brain, and perceptual system remain the products of natural selection for an environment vastly different from that in which most people now live. For more than 99.5 percent of human history, people lived in small foraging bands of ten to thirty individuals in natural surroundings. Like members of other species, early human beings were biologically adapted to perceiving the kinds of sense information that were critical to their survival. Contact senses (touch, taste, and smell) led them to perceive stimuli in close proximity or actually touching the body: temperature, air movement, pressure, and the chemical constitution of things ingested and breathed in. Distance senses (sight and hearing) induced perceptions related to mechanical vibrations (sound) and to small contrasts within a minute range of electromagnetic energy (light and color).

Figure 1-11. Black-and-white ruffed lemurs (*Varecia variegata variegata*) at Duke University's Primate Center: modern-day descendants of early prosimians that retain many characteristics of their ancestors. (Eleanor Holland)

The symmetrical nervous system oriented the individual to the source of the sense stimulation. Through self-referential senses, an individual perceived his or her own body orientation, posture, muscle action, and organ states. By means of memory, past perceptions were stored in the brain and could be recalled. Gesture, body language, marking, and vocalizing were used to communicate perceptions, thoughts, and memories from one individual to another.

Sense Redundancy. In a natural environment, the human senses are *redundant*; that is, they provide similar information in different forms. The perception of a predator, for example, can be derived from sight, sound, and smell. As long as the sensory information is redundant (''It *looks* like a lion, *sounds* like a lion, and *smells* like a lion.''), the perception remains noncontradictory and responsive behavior proceeds (''We should get the *@$% out of here!''). Inconsistency or dissonance in information, however, signals caution by interfering with perceptual closure (''It *looks*, *feels*, and *smells* like an edible mushroom, but it *tastes* bitter.'') Hence, knowledge of a natural environment is made up of clusters of several kinds of sense data that can be cross-referenced; vision constitutes only one aspect of this interrelated perceptual system (see figure 1-12).

Multisense information is combined into unitary perceptions because the majority of human brain neurons are involved neither with direct sense input (sensation) nor with direct output (motor activity). Instead these neurons are used for complex processing between sensation and behavior; this enables the human brain to deal with combinations (rather than with separate bits) of sense data in highly flexible and variable ways. Biologists call these mediating neurons the brain's *great intermediate net*. Because the great intermediate net synthesizes different sources of information, human senses do not need to be extremely sensitive. Early hominids did not need, for example, to detect temperature differences of 0.003 degree (as snakes can) nor to see a mouse from a distance of 3 miles (as hawks can).

Multisensory perception is part of every person's neurological legacy. An infant's perception of its mother, for example, is a synthesis of the way she looks, feels, smells, and sounds, and of the taste of the milk she gives. If the mother dons a mask, sensory dissonance terrifies the child: ''It talks like Mom, smells like Mom, and feels like Mom, but it looks like a MONSTER! WAAAAAAGH!''

Needless to say, your foraging ancestors could expect their sense perceptions to be reliable; inadequate or unreliable perceptual systems would have disappeared through natural selection. Surviving modern life, however, is a different proposition. Photography, radio, telephones, and television, for

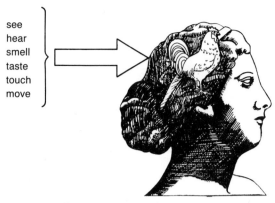

see
hear
smell
taste
touch
move

Figure 1-12. Sense redundancy. (Eleanor Holland)

example, stimulate one- or two-sense perceptions of times and places where you are not, and thus give you out-of-body perceptions. Modern life requires you to fragment sense perception, as well as to remain skeptical of much of the information you perceive.

Living in Groups. Surviving group life requires sensitivity to others. Making eye contact, recognizing individuals, being aware of others' emotional states, and communicating are essential perceptual skills for group behaviors such as sharing food, caring for and educating the young, engaging in cooperative projects, and avoiding aggression and hostility. The innate predisposition to identify and bond with other human beings is evident from earliest infancy. Analysis of videotapes and electronic sensing data has revealed that the seemingly random muscular movements of a young infant are actually whole body perceptions of the rhythms and cadences of adult voices in its immediate environment—especially its mother's.

People never outgrow this perceptual response of mirroring other people. Body language experts point out that people in conversation tend to copy each other's hand and body positions. Parents comically imitate their children's facial expressions (watch an adult spoon feed a six-month-old). Seeing the image of another person's emotional face seems to cause your own face to respond with the same expression. When spectators watch sports events, corresponding nervous activity can be measured in their own muscles. On a more disturbing level, a number of studies have shown that, after viewing violent cartoons or dramas, children's

aggressive behaviors increase, and that helping and supportive behaviors increase after viewing prosocial images, such as on *Mr. Rogers' Neighborhood*. In other species, such bonding and modeling behaviors are associated with a genetically based perceptual program called *imprinting*. Human mirroring may be a more complexly developed variation of this process.

From birth, surviving in a group is intimately involved with perceiving faces. Human infants as young as four months recognize their mother, and by five or six months they can distinguish individual faces. Adults can perceive the identity of pictured faces even when an astonishing amount of visual information has been removed. Recent primate research has found face-specific visual cells in the temporal lobes. This suggests that face perception may not be a case of simple learning (as for example, occurs in distinguishing one automobile from another), but rather is due (to an as yet undefined degree) to a biologically specialized perceptual ability.

A special aspect of face perception is eye contact. With our gaze we get in touch with other sentient beings, be they human or nonhuman: a friend, a dog, a monkey at the zoo. Eye contact leads us to perceive the other as perceiving us. We are so sensitive to eye contact that we quickly notice its absence—for instance, when someone on television reads from cue cards rather than looking directly at the camera (which creates the illusion of eye contact). People everywhere have beliefs about the power of eyes. The idea that certain individuals can cast spells by means of their gaze alone (evil eye) is almost universal.

Language and Culture. In hominid skulls as old as 2 million years (*Australopithecine*), biologist Ralph Holloway has found evidence of *Broca's area*, a part of the human brain that deals with language structure. Thus, a distinctively human propensity for structured symbolic thought is very ancient, although exactly when modern vocal capacities developed continues to be hotly debated. Speech is not essential for language: deaf and mute people engage in complex communication (as with American Sign Language, or Ameslan), and language areas in their brains also develop. Evidence for multiple intelligences likewise indicates that words, as heard and spoken, constitute only one form of complex thought. Hence, the terms *language* and *languaging* are used in this book to denote a generalized capacity for complex communication, which includes (but is not limited to) words. Capacities for symbolic communication are present in various other species, but only among human beings are languaging systems so highly and complexly developed, so flexible and variable, and so capable of sustained elaboration.

With language, perceptual experience can be shared, discussed, and elaborated; thus language enables a group to construct a common sense of reality (world view), which enables cooperative survival. Because this world view is not passed on genetically, it must be acquired anew by each person and generation born into it, through various processes of teaching and learning. The collective reality is activated and strengthened through customs, rituals, and symbolic communications (culture), which habituate each individual to familiar, predictable, and automatic forms of perception, feeling, and behavior; consider, for example, weddings, the national anthem, and graduation ceremonies.

Anthropologists often refer to culture as a *seamless web*. By this they mean that culturally learned world views appear to be naturally, universally, and unquestionably true to the people who hold them. In this sense, there are as many realities as there are cultures. And further, every cultural reality must be a reasonably correct and coherent way of perceiving the world, simply because significant error would not permit people to survive. These considerations have led most Western anthropologists to adopt an attitude of cultural relativism. By this they mean that a culture ought to be understood in terms of its own beliefs, rather than judged against another standard (such as the researcher's own culture).

Cultural relativism opposes theories of Western cultural superiority that claim to apply Darwin's biological theories to social systems. Such theories, called *social Darwinism*, were especially prevalent in the late nineteenth and early twentieth centuries. Generally, these theories assert that all cultures pass through certain universal stages such as ''savagery,'' ''barbarism,'' and ''civilization.'' As more factual knowledge about other cultures has accumulated, it has become clear that, while cultures do indeed change, these changes do not adhere to a single master pattern. Remnants of the social Darwinists' ideas and attitude are still present,

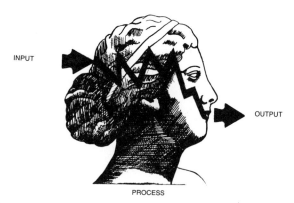

Figure 1-13. Input-Process-Output model. (Eleanor Holland)

however, when people speak of societies or their art as primitive, preliterate, underdeveloped, or advanced.

Complete cultural relativism is, of course, impossible to attain, since an observer's perceptions are meaningful only in relation to other meanings that are already present in his or her head. However, the attempt to take a culturally relative stance can be both productive and enlightening: it helps you to understand others on their own terms, and it also enables you, by means of contrast, to better understand yourself. Cultural relativism is particularly important in looking at art, because Western definitions of *realism* encourage you to see visual realism as a natural goal of artmaking. As a consequence, the art of other cultures tends to be described in terms of its so-called progress toward Western conventions. Such an attitude prevents Westerners from seeing other dimensions of meaning that are extremely interesting and profound.

Perception as Information Processing

In addition to being considered an aspect of biological adaptation, perception can also be seen as a type of information processing in which sense data are used to form internal representations (cognitive schemas or maps) of the outer world, which then assist in directing behavior. To some extent, perception can be compared to the data processing of computer technology (see figure 1-13). In this model, the physical body (eye, brain, sense organs, and so on) corresponds to the hardware that determines capabilities: the specific kinds of information (input) that can be handled, and the general opera-

STIMULUS

RESPONSE

Figure 1-14. S-R model. (Eleanor Holland)

tions that can be performed on it—the ways in which data can be processed, stored, and displayed. The sensory/motor systems can be compared to input/output devices, connected to a central processing unit, or CPU (analogous to the central nervous system, or CNS). Software, like culture, consists of specific sets of instructions or programs that tell hardware what to do with input. Machine language (the most basic instructions that the computer understands) parallels electrochemical processes in the nervous system.

Both computer programs and cultural "software" have generic characteristics. For example, all word processing programs include instructions for data entry, screen displays, editing, saving, formatting, fonts, and print files; similarly all cultures have programs involving food, sex, child rearing, illness, and death. Output (analogous to behavior) can be infinitely variable, depending on the data entered by an individual operator (person). A data disk can only be used with compatible programs; likewise, individuals plugged into an alien culture suffer various degrees of culture shock.

Caution! The computer model is attractive, but certain limitations apply. No computer hardware anywhere approaches the complexity of a single human being; no computer begins to have the number of possible interconnections typical of the circuitry in a human brain. No computer software displays the sophistication of any human culture; no computer language is as flexible as human language. No computer operations are as mercurial, imaginative, changeable, and unpredictable as human thought. But even more important, people are living organisms capable of learning, consciousness, and intention. Experience actually changes

the physical structure of the living brain, but computers do not change with use. Human beings are infinitely diverse and individual, while computer models are subject to stringent quality-control measures to ensure that they are absolutely identical. Further, human perception requires change and constant stimulation in order to function. Computers, on the other hand, rely on consistent, unvarying repetitions of limited sets of commands that would drive a human being crazy.

Analogies and metaphors help to suggest some preliminary avenues of analysis, but they are not sources of answers. Moreover, metaphors reflect the historical circumstances in which they arise. During the Renaissance, as in Ancient Greece, for example, people were thought to embody divine geometrical proportions, heavenly ratios: the human being was the measure of all things. For seventeenth-century philosophers human beings were divine mechanisms, microcosms of the perfectly orderly and mechanical macrocosm created by God, the master clock-maker. By the eighteenth century, with the rise of industrialization, people began to be seen as machines and assembly-line factories (each part of the body doing its job). Subsequently, human beings have been likened to telephone switchboards (the brain as chief operator) and to corporations (the brain as chief executive). The computer metaphor is likewise a product of its time.

Looking Backward

People rarely question the assumption that perception is triggered only by external stimuli, and yet it is a comparatively recent concept. Before the Renaissance, philosophers assumed that perception was an interactive process. Greek doctrines of *sympathy*, *empathy*, and *emanation* stressed the activity of the perceiver. Greek theories of vision, for example, conceived of the eye as emitting rays that reached out to make physical contact with an object. This idea may seem naive today, but its basic assumptions are not so different from modern thinking. Current researchers describe the visual system as scanning the environment and hunting for clarity; they describe living organisms as actively seeking out stimulation; they describe the brain as constructing perceptions and creating closure. In short, the idea that perception is an active process is once again prevalent.

The familiar stimulus-response (S-R) model is

characteristic of behaviorism, a school of psychology less than eighty years old, whose best-known contemporary representative is B. F. Skinner. The S-R model explains behavior, perception, thought, and emotion as learned responses produced by patterns of reward (*reinforcement*) and punishment. Proponents of behaviorism have sought to establish psychology as an empirical science—one in which data are considered valid only if they can be quantitatively measured and objectively replicated. The behaviorists regard consciousness as a subject for speculation appropriate to philosophy but not to science. Processing (for example, cognition, consciousness, and introspection) is considered to be scientifically unmeasurable, a so-called black box (see figure 1-14). Hence, in terms of an information-processing model, S-R psychology recognizes only input and output as relevant points of study.

Critical of trends toward reductionism and mechanistic explanations of perception and behavior in the early twentieth century, the Gestalt school maintains that the whole mind is greater than the sum of its parts (*wholism* or *holism*), and should be studied as such. The Gestaltists focus on the experiential aspect of perception and view introspection as a valid component of experimental research. The Gestalt model, then, recognizes three variables: the stimulus, events within the organism, and the response (S-O-R model; see figure 1-15).

A more recently devised approach, which also uses S-O-R thinking, is the interactive, developmental model of the Swiss scientist, Jean Piaget, who made extensive and highly detailed studies of children's perceptions, behavior, and reasoning processes. He concluded that a child constructs knowledge (that is, meaning) through active involvement with the external world, and that progressive stages of reasoning—while corresponding with timetables of biological maturation—can occur only in the presence of appropriate interactions with the environment. Piaget's theory is consistent with the idea of genetic anticipation: human physiology embodies a genetic expectancy that an environ-

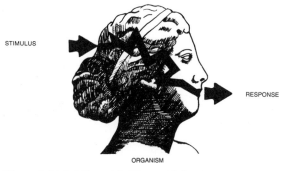

STIMULUS

RESPONSE

ORGANISM

Figure 1-15. S-O-R model. (Eleanor Holland)

ment will allow for the kinds of active behaviors needed to develop normal perception and cognition. Piaget's theories dissolve the problem of nature versus nurture or heredity versus environment by positing a process (processual model) in which the two are interdependent.

Western models of perception (and there are many more than are mentioned here) undergo continual modification. The information-processing model is especially useful for a broad exploration of perception because its general form can contain many recurrent themes: the active, thinking mind; human possession of innate capacities; the existence of internal operations (such as encoding, imaging, storage, and retrieval); and the necessity for interactive processes (such as feedback).

Perception is a complex process, inseparable from the larger considerations of human life, including considerations of biology and culture, group and individual, theory and practice. In the following chapters, various aspects of visual perception will be investigated in detail and assessed from such varied perspectives as scientific research (in biology, psychology, physiology, evolution, and anthropology), history (of art, ideas, and cultures), art (theory, practice, and analysis), and common-sense experience. For the perceptive reader, this exploration will raise some questions even as it answers others.

2

Vision
In the Eye of the Beholder

All life on earth is bathed in wavelengths of energy called *electromagnetic radiation* (see figure 2-1). What we experience as visible light is simply a tiny portion of this continuum within which typical wavelengths are about 1/50,000 inch long and travel at a velocity of 186,000 miles per second. Electromagnetic radiation of this wavelength activates the nerve cells in our eyes. Other sense cells are stimulated by other wave forms. Our skin responds to longer wavelengths, which we experience as temperature. Our ears respond to mechanical wavelengths somewhat longer than ½ inch (15,000 to 20,000 cycles per second)—stimulation that we experience as sound.

Still, most of the electromagnetic spectrum does not register upon our senses: we have no specialized cells for detecting it. Thus we are unable to perceive directly most of the radiant energy that surrounds us. Modern technology, however, has built receivers for these invisible wavelengths. These receivers (and transmitters) include radio, television, and X-ray machines, which convert the invisible energy into humanly detectable wavelengths of light or sound.

WHAT IS AN EYE?

Most forms of life depend for survival on their ability to detect the presence of light. Green plants, for example, need to find and absorb light in order to grow. Among one-celled animals, the ability to detect the presence or absence of light can warn an organism of an approaching enemy or signify the presence of food nearby. Since light waves cause chemical changes in many substances, however, an organism does not need eyes (as such) in order to detect light; a built-in biochemical reaction to light can serve the purpose.

In some organisms, light-detecting cells are dispersed throughout the body. In others, the light-sensitive cells are concentrated in a single location. A concentrated group of light-responsive cells can respond to lower levels of light and can lessen the amount of the organism's surface area that must be exposed to light in order for perception to occur. Although some one-celled animals have light-detecting areas, true eyes occur only in multicelled animals, which possess specialized groups of cells capable of performing specialized functions. Eyes are simply structures that concentrate in one place cells that are biochemically responsive to the particular zone of electromagnetic radiation we call light (see, for example, figure 2-2).

Light-detecting structures take many forms. The compound eye of an insect, for instance, is composed of thousands of separate lenses. Because each lens is set at a slightly different angle, the insect can detect movement (that is, changes in light intensity) from almost any direction. This helps explain why flies can so easily elude a flyswatter! Snails carry their eyes on the tips of retractable antennalike structures. Chameleons and other reptiles can move each of their eyes separately and can rotate each eye almost 360 degrees. Birds' eyes look to the side, which is why the pigeon in the park cocks its head to look at something. Many night-hunting predators have vertical pupils that close off surrounding images and zero in on their prey. The prey often have horizontal pupils, providing a relatively wide field of vision that is more suitable for vigilance than for attack.

Visual systems are often less complicated than you might expect them to be. For example, the

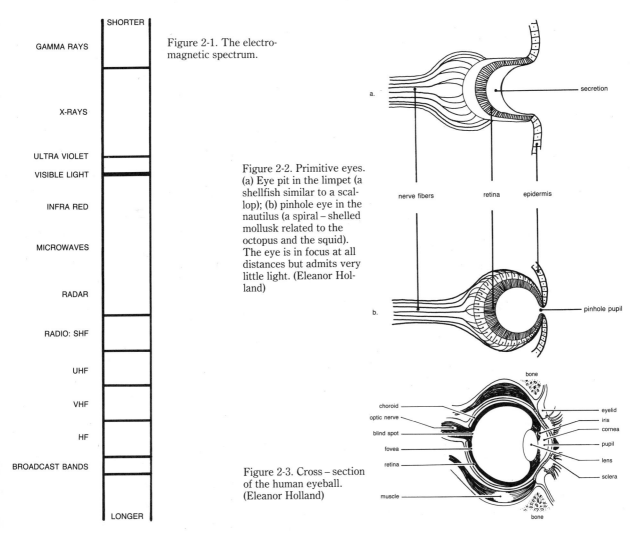

SHORTER

GAMMA RAYS

X-RAYS

ULTRA VIOLET

VISIBLE LIGHT

INFRA RED

MICROWAVES

RADAR

RADIO: SHF

UHF

VHF

HF

BROADCAST BANDS

LONGER

Figure 2-1. The electro-magnetic spectrum.

Figure 2-2. Primitive eyes. (a) Eye pit in the limpet (a shellfish similar to a scallop); (b) pinhole eye in the nautilus (a spiral – shelled mollusk related to the octopus and the squid). The eye is in focus at all distances but admits very little light. (Eleanor Holland)

a.

secretion

nerve fibers   retina   epidermis

b.

pinhole pupil

bone

choroid
optic nerve
blind spot
fovea
retina

eyelid
iris
cornea
pupil
lens
sclera

muscle

bone

Figure 2-3. Cross – section of the human eyeball. (Eleanor Holland)

frog's visual system responds only to movement: to edges and to changing light patterns. Nonetheless, this simple system has enabled untold generations of frogs to find bugs and to hop away from the shadows of approaching predators. The frog can detect something only if it generates the right kind of visual stimulus. For the frog, something that does not move (or does not make a sound) simply does not exist. For this reason, a frog will starve to death even when surrounded by perfectly nutritious dead (that is, immobile) flies, because it cannot see them!

Throughout the animal kingdom, the structures and processes of vision are selective and specialized. Like the frog's eyes, they respond only to specific stimuli. Selective vision filters out irrelevancies—information that is unlikely to be of survival value. Selective vision is embodied in specialized visual structures that represent the particularized adaptations of various species. Nature avoids wasted energy.

Human vision conforms to these principles. The structures and processes of human vision are possible because of special organs that embody a specialized biological adaptation. Moreover, human vision, like that of the frog, is selective.

HUMAN EYES

One environment that has been particularly important in the evolution of human vision is the arboreal habitat of about 70 million years ago (the Paleocene era). At that time, some small nocturnal mammals survived by jumping into the trees and clinging to branches instead of scuttling along the ground. Life in the trees demanded precise spatial judgments: an error could lead to a fatal fall. Eyes enlarged and gravitated to the front of the skull, because seeing what was directly ahead became more important to survival than seeing what was to the sides. This development also suggests that the arboreal creatures had less need to be alert for predators.

The eyes became better protected by becoming completely circled with bone (a characteristic known as *orbital closure*). As some of these animals became diurnal (active during the day), survival favored eyes that were sensitive to differences in the wavelengths of light energy (color vision). The new eyes also retained their predecessors' capability for night vision, thus effectively acting as two sets of eyes. Changes in the neurological organization of eye and brain led to binocular fusion (or stereoscopic vision), as a result of which the separate images from each eye were experienced as a single image. Stereoscopic vision improved the creatures' depth perception of objects seen at distances of less than 20 feet. Continuing primate adaptations involved anatomical changes and increases in the complexity and relative size of the brain. But the basic structure and capabilities of human eyes were set perhaps 50 million years ago.

The Eyeball

Spherical and about 1 inch in diameter, our eyeballs sit in rigid, bony sockets (called *orbits*), with only their front surfaces exposed (see figure 2-3). Each eyeball is covered by a tough white layer (called the *sclera*), which we know more familiarly as the white of the eye. Eyelashes filter out foreign matter but allow light to pass through. Eyebrows and an overhanging forehead provide a built-in sunshade and protect the eyes from falling objects such as raindrops and insects. We automatically use these protections when, for example, we squint in a cloud of blowing dust. The constant secretion of salty tears keeps the eyeball moist and disinfected. Blinking lubricates the surface of the eye and washes out foreign matter. Irritants (such as smoke, chemicals, and strong wind) and intense emotion stimulate both blinking and the flow of tears.

The Cornea

The *cornea* is a tough, transparent, protective layer which bulges out from the surface of the eyeball.

You can feel the shape of your cornea by closing your eyes and moving them while gently touching your eyelid. You can see another person's cornea when you look at the eye from the side. The cornea bends light rays inward so that they are gathered together in an area small enough to enter the inside of the eyeball through the pupil. To do this properly, the corneal surface must be smoothly curved. Irregularities in the cornea (known as *astigmatism*) cause distortions in vision that can be corrected by means of eyeglasses or contact lenses.

The cornea is made of protein and water; its transparency depends in part on the absence of blood vessels. For this reason it heals itself slowly and may develop opaque regions. Because the cornea needs a less elaborate blood supply than do most other body tissues, it can be preserved after death more easily, and when transplanted to the eye of another individual, it is more likely to be accepted. A person whose cornea has become cloudy as a result of injury or chronic infection can often regain normal vision through a corneal transplant.

The Iris

Behind the cornea is the *iris*, a circular muscle that expands and contracts to control the amount of light entering the inside of the eyeball. The *pupil* is the black opening in the center of the iris; it varies in size as the iris opens and closes. The iris thus resembles the diaphragm of a camera, which controls the amount of light reaching the film through variable-sized openings (called *apertures*). When you enter a darkened place, such as a movie theater, your irises open up to allow more light into the eyeballs, and your pupils enlarge. Conversely, when you turn on a lamp after having been in a dark room, your irises contract to screen out some of the sudden light, and your pupils become smaller. We cannot control the functioning of the iris by voluntary action; the process is fully automatic.

Certain drugs and medicines, however, do influence the functioning of the iris. Heroin and other opiates constrict the pupils, while amphetamines enlarge them. For some eye examinations, special drops are used to expand (or dilate) the pupils. Irises are also affected by emotion: your pupils may expand slightly when you look at something highly desirable to you, or when you concentrate.

The term *eye color* refers to the color of the iris, which results from the distribution of a pigment

Figure 2-4. Differences in image grain: (Left) 32.5 line screen; (right) 16.25 line screen.

called *melanin*. In skin, this same pigment causes freckles and varying shades of skin color. In the eye, the more melanin, the darker the eye. Because darker irises screen out more of the sun's rays, human eyes have evolved darker colors near the equator and lighter colors in the more northerly latitudes.

The Crystalline Lens

Behind the iris is the *crystalline lens*, which receives the light rays that have been bent inward by the cornea and bends them further so that they will converge on a small area inside the eyeball. The lens is somewhat elastic: it flattens and bulges slightly to allow the eye to focus on objects at different distances—an adjustment known as *accommodation*. The closer the object is, the more the lens must bulge in order to bring the image into focus. Accommodation is an automatic reaction; the lens responds to blur by searching out the sharpest image.

The lens's ability to accommodate lessens with age. A young child can focus on an object as close as 4 inches from the eyes, but a young adult may require 10 inches, and an aging person 16. Around the age of forty, many people become aware of a reduction in lens flexibility when they find themselves holding telephone books and other small-print material farther and farther from their eyes in order to read them. This age-related increase in focal length, called *presbyopia*, often can be corrected by wearing ''Ben Franklin'' half-glasses, which simply magnify images.

The development of opaqueness (called a *cataract*) within the lens is the single most frequent cause of blindness. The pupil of a person who has a cataract looks gray or silvery. Aging increases the likelihood of developing cataracts, but they can also be caused by diabetes, cortico-steroids, or excessive radiation. This is one reason for recent concern about the occupational safety of computer workers who receive long-term exposure to very-low-frequency (VLF) radiation from cathode-ray terminals (CRTs) or video display terminals (VDTs). Higher-level X-ray radiation is emitted by color television tubes and color computer monitors.

Blindness caused by cataracts can be dramatically reversed by surgically removing the entire problem lens! In the past, a patient suffered through a delicate recovery time and ever afterward had to wear very thick glasses to compensate for the extreme farsightedness that results when the lens is lost. The modern treatment of cataracts, however, is quite different: the natural lens is removed, and a plastic lens is implanted. The procedure can be done on an out-patient basis. To pro-

Figure 2-5. Phosphene – derived designs: (Left) a Tukano (Native Colombian) drawing phosphene patterns in the sand; (right) a wall painting on a Tukano house. When asked about these paintings, the Tukano reply, "This is what we see when we drink [the drug *Banisteriopsis*]." (G. Reichel-Dolmatoff, 1978)

tect the eye from light while it is healing, the patient wears dark glasses; but after recovery, no special glasses are needed.

The Vitreous Humor

The main cavity of the eyeball is filled with a clear, jellylike substance called the *vitreous humor* or *vitreous body*. Light waves travel through this substance on their way to the retina. Normally the vitreous humor is clear, but sometimes small particles such as red corpuscles may become trapped in it. These appear in your vision as tiny dots or gray filaments called *floaters*. You can see them if you look at something featureless, such as a blank white wall or a blue sky. You cannot focus on them; and if you try, they seem to drift away.

Sometimes, because of faulty drainage or for other reasons, pressure in the eyeball rises, producing a condition called *glaucoma*. The increased pressure can harm the optic nerve and sometimes the retina, resulting in blindness. In treating glaucoma, opthamologists reduce this intraocular pressure by means of drugs or surgery.

The Retina

About four-fifths of the inside of the eyeball is covered by several layers of cells about the size and thickness of a postage stamp. This is the *retina*—a concentration of light-sensitive cells or photoreceptors. The word *retina* means net. When you look at something, what reaches the retina is a pattern of various light wavelengths and intensities. This pattern of light stimulates a corresponding mosaic of photoreceptor activity in the retina. The photoreceptors convert the light energy into electrochemical signals, which are relayed to other neurons and ultimately to the brain. This photoreceptor activity is the basis for all our seeing of size, shape, color, texture, motion, depth, and distance.

We get a lot of information from this mosaic because the photoreceptors are extremely small and extremely numerous. As with the picture elements (pixels) in computer images, a greater number of units in the image means that a greater amount of visual information can be conveyed and that the image will have finer resolution (see figure 2-4). The units that make up the retinal patterns of the human eye are the size of the photoreceptors themselves—as small as 1 micron (1/1,000,000 meter), or 0.00003937 inch! The number of cells on one retina is over 200 million, which is more than the entire U.S. population! In addition, the photoreceptors are so sensitive that they can be stimulated by a single quantum—the smallest amount of radiant energy that exists!

Normally, the photoreceptors in the retina are activated by light, but they may be stimulated by other means as well. For example, if you simply close your eyes hard or rub them, the pressure will stimulate the retinal cells, and you will experience what appear to be flashes of light. This occurs because stimulation of photoreceptors, regardless of the source, is interpreted by the brain as light. Such sensations (which are not responses to external light) are called *phosphenes*, and they are common in all humans. Phosphene patterns can range from tiny dots of color to complex patterns in shades of glowing color. They can be induced by mechanical stimulation, pressure, blows to the head, low-voltage electrical impulses, drugs, and physiological conditions such as migraine headaches and epilepsy.

Some Native Americans of the Amazon use drug-induced phosphene experiences as a source of design motifs for decorating their house walls, domestic items, and ritual objects (see figure 2-5). With few exceptions, the whole art style of these people seems to be based on geometric phosphene patterns that occur during the first of three stages of drug intoxication. The patterns appear to be similar for all individuals in this group, regardless of age, personality, or social position. Further, these luminous images may recur for up to six months afterward, sometimes superimposed on the individual's normal daylight vision. As a result, the phosphene patterns and their cultural interpretations become more or less permanently incorporated into an individual's consciousness.

The anthropologist who studied these people (Reichel-Dolmatoff 1978) observed that artists in our own culture under the influence of hallucinogenic drugs have produced similar patterns, and that some comparable prehistoric artifacts are associated with drug paraphernalia. He suggests that some cross-cultural similarities in art may be accounted for by their having a basis in the physiological effects of drug experiences.

Rods and Cones. The human eye contains over 200 million photoreceptors. These are of two types—rods and cones—named for their shapes (see figures 2-6 and 2-7). The cones number about 7 million and are active in daylight and under good lighting conditions (for photopic vision). With the cones, we perceive color, detail, rapid changes in light, and quick movement. Each cone is individually connected to the optic nerve. The rods are much more numerous (about 130 million) and slower to respond, but they are much more sensitive to light—so sensitive, in fact, that they are overwhelmed and incapacitated by normal daylight. The rods function for night vision and in poor illumination (for scotopic vision).

Compared to the fineness of cone vision, rod vision has a coarser grain. For an analogy, look back at figure 2-4, and think of the image on the left as representing cone vision, and the image on the right

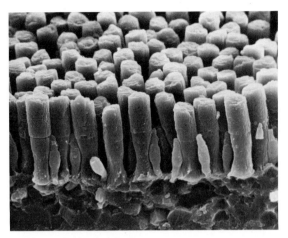

Figure 2-6. Scanning electron micrograph of rod and cone cells in a tiger salamander. (Scott Mittman and Maria T. Maglio)

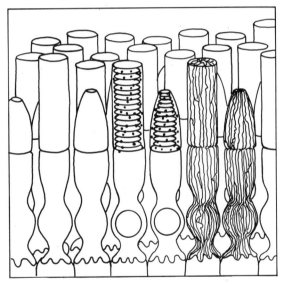

Figure 2-7. The dots represent photopigment molecules (rhodopsin in the rods; RGB photopigments in the cones). Each rod or cone terminates in a synaptic ending. (Eleanor Holland)

as representing rod vision. Because of their coarser mosaic, the rods are more sensitive to movement than to form. The greater sensitivity of rod vision to light and motion is advantageous for nocturnal animals, which account for about 60 percent of all land-dwelling vertebrates. Some of these (the bat, the owl, the loris, and the galago) have no cones at all. Although human beings are primarily

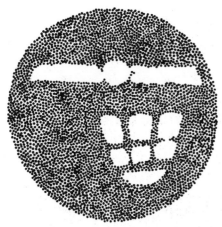

Figure 2-8. Drawing of optogram found in 1878 by the German scientist Willy Kuhne. He exposed the eye of a living rabbit to a barred window, killed the rabbit, removed its retina, and fixed the image in alum. (Redrawn from Wald 1950)

Figure 2-9. Hermann-Hering Grid. Do you see gray spots at the intersections of the white spaces? Try to look directly at one of them. What happens? Once sensitized to this effect, you will find yourself observing it in surprising places, such as plaid fabrics, gym locker grids, and paintings by Piet Mondrian.

which in turn cause electrochemical signals to move through the synaptic nerve ending to other cells in the retina. The whole process—from the absorption of light by the photopigments to the generation of a neural signal—takes place in about 3 milliseconds. In generating enough energy to trigger the nerve impulse, the photoreceptor must amplify the light energy more than a thousandfold!

A normal retina has three different sorts of cones. Each cone contains three different photopigments, making it sensitive to a broad range of wavelengths. But the particular distribution of the photopigments gives each type of cone a different peak sensitivity for blue, green, or red. This is the basis of color vision. All photopigments are composed of vitamin A molecules attached to complex proteins.

The reddish purple photopigment in the rods is called *rhodopsin* or *visual purple*. When strong light engages cone vision, rhodopsin is chemically bleached, and the rods are inactivated. Before the rods can function again, rhodopsin must be re-formed in darkness. This happens when you enter a dark room: your iris quickly expands, allowing more light to reach the retina, but the formation of visual purple (also known as *dark adaptation*) takes several more minutes. On a dark, moonless night, complete dark adaptation may take as long as forty-five minutes. In a natural outdoor environment, periods of dusk and dawn allow a gradual transition from cone to rod vision, and back again.

The discovery that visual purple was bleached by light and resynthesized in darkness was made in the late nineteenth century. It led physiologists to speculate about the possibility of finding bleached images in the retinas of recently killed animals (and in one case, in the retina of a guillotined criminal). Such images (called *optograms*) were indeed found, but they proved not to be highly detailed (see figure 2-8).

Vitamin A, together with protein, is used to replace and re-form visual purple. In as little as a month, a significant degree of night blindness (the inability to form rhodopsin) can result from a deficiency of vitamin A (or of beta-carotene, which the body uses to make vitamin A). Night driving, because of the constant on/off glare of oncoming headlights, uses up rhodopsin very rapidly. A night-blind person has a problem seeing in the dark at first and takes longer than normal to adjust to a darkened room. To such a person, a sudden bright

diurnal, we have retained the night-vision capacity of our earlier ancestors. Thus, in common with many other vertebrates, we have a duplex retina that contains rods for dim light and cones for bright light.

Both rods and cones respond to light by means of light-absorbing molecules called *photopigments* (see figure 2-7). Light striking the photopigments triggers molecular changes in the photoreceptor,

light (such as a passing headlight) is blinding. A severe and unchecked vitamin A deficiency leads to eye inflammation (conjunctivitis), dry eye tissues (xerophthalmia), and ultimately, blindness. Orange and yellow vegetables and dark leafy greens are good sources of beta-carotene. High doses (more than 5,000 IU daily) of vitamin A, taken over a long period, can be harmful (provoking hypervitaminosis A). Standard supplements in the form of beta-carotene, however, are safe.

Contour Enhancement. Vision is more complex than the simple stimulation of rods and cones by light. Photoreceptors in the retina are interrelated and interdependent. When one photoreceptor is activated by light, it stimulates some of its neighbors and represses others. Thus, whether or not a given photoreceptor responds depends on the combination of excitatory and inhibitory signals that it receives from other photoreceptors. This relationship, referred to as the *excitatory-inhibitory principle* (or *lateral inhibition*), operates in various neural, electrical, and chemical systems in which fields of positive and negative influences oppose one another. Such systems include our senses, where the effect is to sharpen perceptions such as sounds or tastes. In the retina, where different groups of photoreceptors are activated by different light intensities, the effect is to exaggerate differences, thereby maximizing the perception of boundaries between light and dark, and thus accenting contours and edges. With this heightened sensitivity, we can recognize objects in our environment more quickly. It is easy to understand why this would be an advantage in our evolutionary history. In figure 2-9, the larger white areas where the stripes intersect cause greater inhibition, and they therefore seem darker. Figure 2-10 demonstrates the Cornsweet illusion, another effect of lateral inhibition.

Figure 2-11 shows a related phenomenon, which can be observed in shadows cast in strong sunlight. In the borderline area between full sunlight and full shadow, a narrow half-shadow (or penumbra) creates the illusion that a narrow dark band borders its dark edge and that a narrow bright band borders its bright edge. These dark and light stripes are named *Mach bands* after Ernst Mach, the Austrian scientist who described them some 100 years ago. Only unusually keen observers are aware of Mach bands, since the effect simply reinforces what we

Figure 2-10. Contour contrast: the Cornsweet illusion. The only difference between these two drawings is a small area of dark-to-light shading that grades outward from the edge of the smaller circle in the figure on the right. To test this illusion, cover the edge of the smaller circle with a string.

Figure 2-11. Mach bands in shadows. (Carolyn M. Bloomer)

expect to see. Carefully rendered Mach bands can be seen in the shadows portrayed in the work of Seurat and other neo-Impressionists and Pointillists.

Scientists became interested in the contour/contrast principle only a century ago. But artists have been well aware of it for centuries. Contour enhancement can be seen in many oriental ink paintings, where the Cornsweet illusion is used to make a moon appear brighter or to accent portions of a landscape, such as mountain peaks (see figure 2-12). This illusion can be effectively created with airbrush and watercolor techniques, where a simple, soft definition of contour gives the illusion of brightness or volume. The effect is also produced by an ancient ceramic technique where an incised pattern has a sharp inner edge and a gradually graded outer edge that collects glaze during the firing process (see figure 2-13).

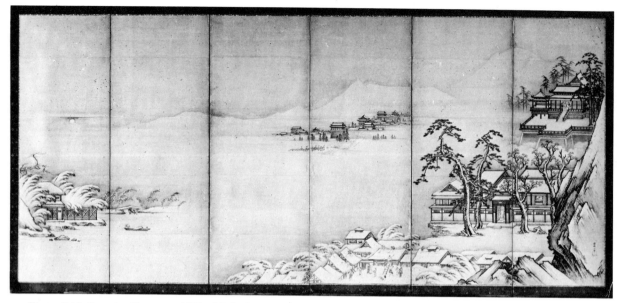

Figure 2-12. Sansetsu (Japanese, 1590–1651), *Snowscape*. Six-panel folding screen. (Museum of Fine Arts, Boston)

Persistence of Vision. After a light stimulus has been removed, the retinal nerve fibers continue to generate signals for a fraction of a second thereafter. This phenomenon is called *retinal lag.* Thus, when the eye is exposed to a rapid series of separate but similar stimuli (as with movie film and video pictures), one image will merge with the next. The separate stimulations are then experienced as a single continuous motion, through flicker fusion. How fast does this sequence have to be to seem continuous? The point at which human beings perceive a flashing light as a steady light occurs at rates of between 30 and 50 flashes per second, depending on the brightness of the light. This point is called the *critical fusion frequency* (CFF).

Without such a fusion point, we would live in a strange world. Incandescent light bulbs, for instance, are actually going on and off at a rate of 60 cycles per second, in accordance with the alternating current of household electricity. Movies are projected at seventy-two separate images per second (twenty-four images are projected three times each). Because these rates are faster than the critical fusion frequency, we perceive them as steady, continuous phenomena. Because fluorescent lights cycle at a slower rate, their flicker is often noticeable in your peripheral (rod) vision, which is sensitive to motion. But when you look directly at the fluorescent tube with cone (macular) vision, the flicker mysteriously disappears. Thus, the critical fusion frequency determines whether we will perceive movement.

Afterimage. Following the period of retinal lag—if they are not again stimulated by light—the photoreceptors return to their resting state. While this is happening, you may see an afterimage. For an example of this phenomenon, look at a TV image (which is the equivalent of staring at a low-wattage light bulb), and then look quickly at a blank wall. Afterimages are common occurrences, but we usually tune them out. Occasionally, an afterimage is so intense that it actually interferes with vision—for example, when you have your picture taken with a flashbulb. The cause of afterimages has been variously attributed to fatigue, saturation, or adaptation of the photoreceptors, to bleaching of photopigments in the cones, and to fatigue in the nervous system, which organizes and transmits stimuli to the brain.

Figures 2-14 and 2-15 enable you to experience negative afterimage—an afterimage that appears in colors opposite to those of the original stimulus. Negative afterimages occur with colors, too. Because afterimages occur on the retina, they occupy

Figure 2-13. Anonymous (Chinese, Northern Sung Dynasty), *Ting* ware dish, 11th – early 12th century. Porcelain, 10¹/₃ inch diameter. (Freer Gallery of Art, Smithsonian Institution, Washington, D.C. Accession No. 17.401)

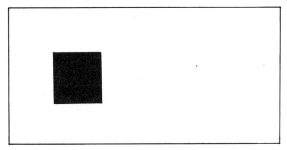

Figure 2-14. Afterimage. For at least sixty seconds, look steadily at the black square in good light. Then look at the blank area on the right. As the glowing white square fades, blinking may bring it back. To experiment with color, photocopy this figure and use markers to surround the black square with thick bands of bright color.

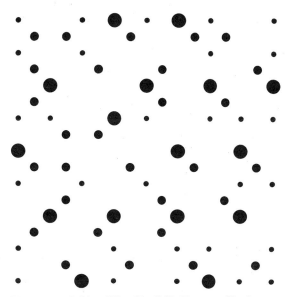

Figure 2-15. Bridget Riley (English), *Fragment No. 6*, 1965. Plexiglas print, 29¹/₄ × 29 inches. Look at this for several seconds, and you will see white circles begin to dance among the black ones. (Courtesy of the artist)

a fixed proportion of your total visual field, no matter what you are looking at. This means that, if you look at something far away, the afterimage will seem gigantic. To get this effect from figure 2-14, wait until you see the afterimage on the page, and then look up at a blank wall across the room. The afterimage which filled only a square inch on the page now appears to be several feet high! This effect is described by Emmert's law, which states that the apparent size of an afterimage varies with the distance of the surface on which the image is projected.

Another phenomenon that has fascinated people for centuries involves eidetic imagery, which is sometimes called *photographic memory*. While afterimages are indistinct and fade after a few moments, eidetic images are sharp and may persist for several minutes. They are sufficiently vivid and detailed that the person holding the image in mind can examine the picture and, for example, count the number of stripes in a cat's tail. For people who can produce eidetic images, five seconds of viewing the original picture is usually sufficient to allow recall. While an afterimage results from a single fixation, eidetic images are produced from pictures large enough to require several fixation points. And unlike afterimages, eidetic images cannot be mentally moved from the plane of the original stimulus, otherwise they disappear. Interestingly enough, eidetic images fade in chunks, much as do the stabilized images discussed later in this chapter. Consciously labeling or otherwise actively attending to parts of the original picture (a typical school behavior) interferes with the formation of an eidetic

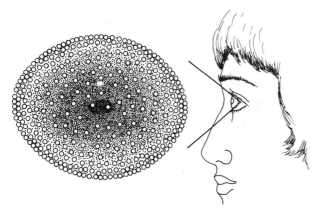

Figure 2-16. Schematic of the retinal mosaic. Dots and circles represent cones and rods, respectively. Cone density is greatest in the fovea, and the optic nerve (blind spot) is identified by the absence of photoreceptors. (Eleanor Holland)

image. Early research suggested that about half of all elementary school children possessed an eidetic capability; however, recent research using more modern methods indicates that the true figure may be closer to 5 percent—at least in contemporary American culture.

The Fovea and the Macula. The retina contains many times more rods than cones, and they are not evenly distributed (see figure 2-16). The rods are least dense in the central area of the retina, which consists almost entirely of cones. This is where our vision is clearest. In higher primates (including humans), this area is yellow and is called the *yellow patch* (or *macula lutea*). The yellow pigmentation modifies our color vision by absorbing blue-violet light.

Directly behind the lens is a shallow depression in the macula, called the *fovea centralis*. The foveal area is smaller than the head of a pin and is populated only by cones—about 25,000 of them, each connected to the brain by its own nerve fiber. The fovea is the point in the eye where vision is sharpest and clearest, the area of greatest visual acuity. Outward from the fovea, the density of cone cells diminishes, and the population of rods increases, extending the retina almost as far forward as the lens. As a consequence, while we are aware of things outside the macular area, we cannot see those things clearly. To see details of the various aspects of an object (such as a picture), we must make a series of fixations at various spots. Each

time we make a fixation, we place a part of the object in focus by directing that part to the fovea. Because the fovea contains only cones, it is blind in dim light. To see something more clearly at night, you need to look a little to one side of what you want to see; in this way you direct the image to the rods outside the foveal area. This technique is well known to astronomers and sailors, who depend on night-vision skills.

Possessing one fovea per eye is a visual specialization common to primates. Some birds have two foveas in each eye; others have a strip fovea that provides a band or horizon of clear vision. Horses have ramp foveas that allow them to see objects clearly at varying distances without changing focal point. Most vertebrates see all parts of their visual field equally well and therefore do not have to explore or scan it through a series of separate fixations. This is why some animals seem to gaze steadily at a scene, rather than looking around it as humans do.

Peripheral Vision. While an image is focused on the fovea, light is also stimulating photoreceptors in the areas outside the macula, which respond by producing *peripheral vision*. Peripheral vision extends the full visual field of a human being to slightly more than 180 degrees. This is why, even when you are looking directly at an object, you are also aware of things that surround it. Rod vision is of a coarser grain than cone vision (see figure 2-4) because 200 or more rods may connect to a single nerve cell in the brain. Peripheral vision gives us shapes and generalized forms rather than small details, and it amplifies the perception of motion. Indeed, something seen "in the corner of your eye" generates a reflex to turn your head in that direction.

This ability to be aware of the periphery of our visual field is very important, particularly in driving. People who have lost their peripheral vision are said to have *tunnel vision*, which means that they can only see straight ahead. You can test your peripheral vision by looking straight ahead and slowly moving your fingers to the sides, out of your range of vision. Just at the point when you can no longer see them, move your fingers slightly. When your fingers are at the very edge of your visual field, they will be visible when you move them, even though you are unable to see them when they are still!

The Visual Field. At any given moment, a human being's eyes can see approximately 185 degrees horizontally and 160 degrees vertically; this defines the person's visual field. Because of the varying density of cone cells in our eyes (see figure 2-16), our daylight vision has three zones of clarity: foveal, macular, and peripheral. We tend to assume that photographs and so-called realistic paintings imitate the visual field of the retina. But if this were the case, such images would represent these zones of clarity, which they do not. Instead they portray a uniform clarity across the entire image—an effect achieved in perception only after making a series of separate fixations over time from a fixed viewing position. (Objects meant to seem further from the viewer are often rendered less clearly. But this is in order to replicate the separate effect of depth of field rather than zones of clarity. Depth of field is discussed in chapter 8.)

Some artists have been sensitive to this distinction between representing a perception of the visual world and representing the visual field. Anthropologist Edward T. Hall (1966, p. 81) described his discovery of Rembrandt's portrayal of foveal, macular, and peripheral vision as follows (see figure 2-17):

Experimenting with the viewing of one of his self-portraits, my eye was suddenly caught by the central point of interest in the self-portrait, Rembrandt's eye. The rendition of the eye in relation to the rest of the face was such that the whole head was perceived as three-dimensional and became alive *if viewed at the proper distance.* I perceived in a flash that Rembrandt had distinguished between foveal, macular, and peripheral vision! He had painted a stationary *visual field* instead of the conventional visual world depicted by his contemporaries. . . . The eye must be permitted to center and *rest* on the spot that he painted most clearly and in greatest detail at a distance at which the foveal area of the retina (the area of clearest vision) and the area of greatest detail in the painting match. When this is done, the registry of the visual fields of both the artist and the viewer coincide. It is at this precise moment that Rembrandt's subjects spring to life with a realism that is startling (emphases in the original).

Figure 2-17. Rembrandt van Rijn (Dutch), *Self-Portrait,* 1659. Oil on canvas, 33¼ × 26 inches. (National Gallery of Art, Washington, D.C.; Andrew W. Mellon Collection)

Paintings by Jan Vermeer (see figure 8-4) show similar characteristics. Vermeer, a younger contemporary of Rembrandt, composed with the aid of a *camera obscura.*

The Optic Nerve. The instant that light activates the photoreceptors, a process begins in which light is transformed into electrochemical signals. Signals from the retinal cells are carried through 1 million nerve fibers that come together at the back of the retina to form the optic nerve (see figure 2-3). Once there, the signals are relayed to the brain by special neurons that make up the optic nerve. The optic nerve is the only connection between the retina and the mind. The signals that traverse the optic nerve represent the final summation of information from the eye.

The optic nerve contains no photoreceptors; consequently, the place where it enters the retina is called the *blind spot.* Normally you do not notice your blind spot, because the part of the visual field

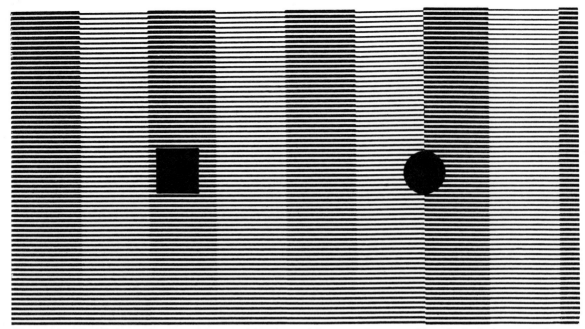

Figure 2-18. The blind spot. Close your left eye and focus your right eye on the square. Move the book alternately closer and farther away from your eyes. The circle will disappear when its image falls on the blind spot. Notice that the striped background fills in the space where the circle was. Reverse the procedure to experience the blind spot in your left eye.

that falls on the blind spot of one eye does not fall on the blind spot of the other. Moreover, the blind spot is not located in the foveal area, where you would be more aware of it. Interestingly, the blind spot does not create a ''hole'' in the image. Instead, the area of the stimulus that falls on the blind spot is filled in such that the visual field appears continuous. It is not clear whether this filling in is done in the eye or in the brain. You can experience your blind spot with figure 2-18.

Eye Movements

Three pairs of muscles move each eyeball (see figure 2-19). One pair moves the eyeball to the right or left, another pair turns it up or down, and the third pair rotates it. This makes it possible for you to direct your gaze quickly and easily around a large field of vision, without having to move your head. The muscles of both eyes must move in unison (like the front wheels of a car), since it is essential that the image falls on corresponding parts of each retina. When focusing on objects nearer than about 20 feet, the eyes must turn toward each other slightly. Otherwise, double vision (diplopia) or other difficulties will occur. Problems caused by defective

eye-muscle coordination include cross-eyes or strabismus (one eye turns toward the nose), walleyes (one eye turns too far away from the other), and lazy eye or amblyopia (inputs from the problem eye are ignored by the brain). These problems can usually be corrected by means of special eye exercises, lenses, and (in severe cases) surgery.

When you engage in activities such as reading, looking at a picture, or scanning a landscape, your eyes jump from one point to another. While your eyes are actually moving, you can see only a blur, since the visual field is registering on different sets of photoreceptors at a rapid pace. For this reason, your eyes must make frequent stops (fixations) to focus small portions of the visual field on the fovea. Since your eyes are constantly moving, your visual acquaintance with an object or scene consists of a series of sequential and selective samplings. Your perceptions, however, are of whole objects or scenes in a stationary world. For the most part, you remain unaware of the discontinuous nature of your looking process.

Laboratory observations (Noton and Stark 1971) show that, when people look at drawings and photographs, they tend to fixate on angles and sharp curves, since these features give the most informa-

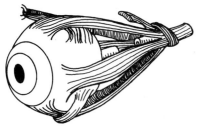

Figure 2-19. Eye muscles. (Eleanor Holland)

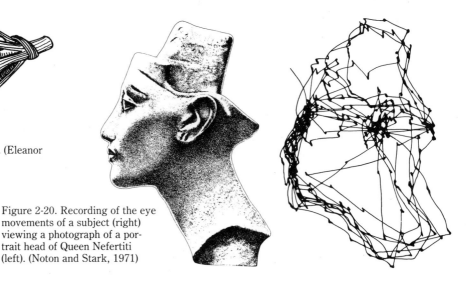

Figure 2-20. Recording of the eye movements of a subject (right) viewing a photograph of a portrait head of Queen Nefertiti (left). (Noton and Stark, 1971)

tion about the subject (see figure 2-20). Some researchers even hypothesize that a person's internal memory of an object or picture is based on a memory of the eye movements (or scan path) used in looking at it. Speed-reading techniques usually train the reader to spend less time on each fixation and to decrease the total number of fixations.

Having movable eyes makes it possible for people to fixate on objects in motion. This ability to track a moving object is called the *pursuit movement*. Such movements keep the object in foveal vision. A tracking examination is usually included in school testing for learning disabilities.

But even when you think your eyes are fixed on an object, they are still busy making several types of automatic (or involuntary) movements. One such set of movements is characterized by a drift and flick pattern, in which the eyeball first lets the image slowly drift away from the center of the fovea, and then flicks to a new fixation with a rapid movement called a *saccade*. Although saccades normally occur at a rate of between 2 and 10 per second, they take up only 10 percent of a person's overall looking time; the eyes are fixated 90 percent of the time.

At the same time, the eye makes rapid side-to-side oscillations or tremors (called *nystagmus*), which may occur at frequencies of from 30 to 150 cycles per second (authorities disagree as to the exact range); their amplitude is about one-half the diameter of a single cone. These constant movements are essential for maintaining normal vision, because an image fixed in the same place on the retina fades after a few seconds as the molecules of photopigment in the photoreceptor reach their maximum chemical reaction to the light and then return to a receptive state. Although a truly fixed image requires special laboratory equipment, you can get an idea of this fading effect by staring at a small speck on a blank surface without allowing your eyes to move. The speck will alternately appear and disappear because of this saturation effect in the retinal cells. Even bright, high-contrast images can disappear in about two seconds. Nystagmus appears to compensate for this fading effect by constantly shifting the image onto fresh molecules of photopigment. The shimmering or vibrating effects of some simple repeating patterns (see figure 2-21) may be due in part to these rapid oscillations, possibly in combination with afterimage and border contrast effects.

Laboratory experiments with stabilized images (images made to stand still on the retina by means of a device mounted on a contact lens) have established that images fade and partially regenerate in particular ways related to the meaningfulness of various areas of the image. With a drawing of a face, for example, specific features or groups of features (such as a face or the top of a head) stay visible. This suggests that both innate and learned influences affect vision, even at this automatic level.

Seeing Art. Merely looking at a work of art requires a series of eye fixations. If the work is large, you have to make many fixations across a broad area. On the other hand, if you look at a small

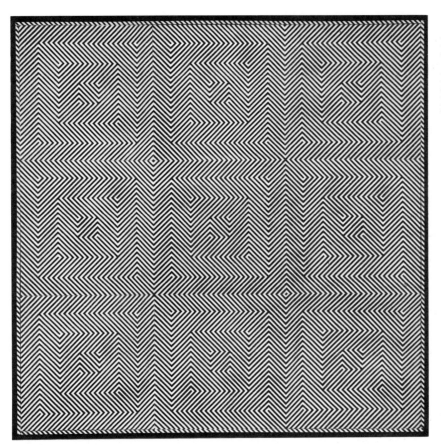

Figure 2-21. Reginald Neal (American), *Square of Three, Yellow and Black,* 1964. Mixed media, 32 × 32 inches. (Permission of the artist and New Jersey State Museum, Trenton)

artwork or at a reproduction in a book, the whole thing can often be seen with only one or two fixations. This is why the size or scale of artworks is so important. Artworks that cover entire walls, that constitute self-contained environments, or that extend across large geographical areas are experienced very differently from traditional easel paintings, which are viewed by standing in one place, with the framed edge visible in peripheral vision.

Consequently, our experience of an artwork is partly determined by our physical relationship to it; and this, in turn, is made known to us through the way we interact with it physiologically. If some researchers are right, the scan path is an integral part of our memory of the work. Bodily experience thus plays a role in the perceptual construction of meaning. This is but one reason why looking at a reproduction in a book, on a poster, or on a projected slide can never substitute for the experience of seeing the original work of art.

The visual experience of looking at easel paint-

ings is relatively recent—a product of oil painting, which (as we know it) was not technically feasible until after 1400. But by the seventeenth century, easel paintings were being bought and sold in Europe by the hundreds of thousands; they had become a commodity to be owned and collected. In the 1970s, some American artists rebelled against this collectibility of art by creating works that could not be owned by a particular person. This movement produced performance, conceptual, and environmental art, especially large-scale earthworks.

The scale of the earthwork artists' monumental creations affected people's experience of them in an interesting way. By this time, the public had come to think of art in terms of objects that could, at least in a general way, be comprehended by standing in a single location in time and space and looking at them. An earthwork, however, cannot be seen in its entirety from any single point in time or space. Christo's *Running Fence* or the Great Wall of China (see figure 2-22) have no single true view.

Figure 2-22. Earthworks, old and new: (Above) *Changcheng* ("Great Wall"), People's Republic of China, from 214 B.C. Average 25 feet high and 15 feet wide; 2,000 miles long. (Perry Kelly, Cullowhee, N.C.); (below) Christo (American, Bulgarian-born), *Running Fence*, Sonoma and Marin counties, California, 1972–76. Nylon fabric, steel poles, and cables, 18 feet high, 24½ miles long. (Photo: Jeanne-Claude; copyright Christo 1976)

Figure 2-23. Claude Monet (French), *The Houses of Parliament, Sunset,* 1903. Oil on canvas, 32 × 36⅝ inches. (National Gallery of Art, Washington, D.C.; Chester Dale Collection). To see this painting in color, turn to plate C-1. In a nineteenth-century book about paintings, no Impressionists were represented. The explanation was that their paintings could not be reproduced in black and white (color printing was not yet practical), because they would appear as meaningless blobs of gray.

It looks different from here and from there, from ground and from air, from near and from far, from high and from low, and at morning, noon, and night. Here, the idea of scale—the number of fixations required in order to see it wholly—was expanded to infinity.

ART AND THE EYE

Western artists have shown a continuing interest in the science of vision for at least 500 years. In the Renaissance, artists began to apply theories of medieval optics to the composition of pictures, leading to the system of picture construction we call *linear perspective* or *visual realism*. More recently, at least two groups of Western artists have evidenced a profound commitment to creating artforms based on aspects of the biological nature of vision.

The Impressionists

Members of this group of nineteenth-century French painters were particularly excited by theo-

ries and discoveries involving light and vision. They became obsessed with the idea of painting light instead of objects—light as it registered on the mosaic of the retina. They wanted to portray the raw sensation of seeing, uncensored by higher processes of mind (see figure 2-23). They sought to paint with a truly objective, truly innocent eye. Instead of painting compositions intellectually constructed in a studio, the Impressionists worked outdoors, attempting to record what they actually saw.

But the purportedly innocent eye, of course, is not innocent. The kind of seeing the Impressionists valued was by no means a pure mechanical process; rather, it was a highly sophisticated, carefully cultivated way of looking. An eye that sees only light—untransformed by eye and brain—is a human impossibility. Nonetheless, the Impressionists' attempt to go beyond the conventions of artistic seeing paved the way for new esthetic possibilities in painting. Although they were considered quite scandalous—even degenerate—in their time, the Impressionists maintained an artistic integrity toward the visual experience that makes them extremely popular among today's museum-goers.

Interestingly, however, viewers usually forget (or eschew) the disciplined detachment these artists so valued and instead tend to associate them with a (perhaps misplaced) romanticism.

The Optical Artists

In the 1960s and 1970s, some artists worked to create images whose effects depended solely upon the physiology of the human eye and brain (see figures 2-15 and 2-21). Whether Eskimo, French, Russian, Zulu, Chinese, or Brazilian, presumably any viewer could see these artworks in the same way. By eliminating culturally specific symbolism, the optical artists hoped to create a culture-free art independent of the influences of cultural education on the viewer's vision. These artists used a number of physiological effects, such as shimmer, after-image, vibration, and grouping. Examples in this book include works by Bridget Riley (see figure 2-15), Reginald Neal (see figure 2-21), Richard Anuskiewicz (see plate C-3), and AGAM (see figure 9-26a).

Throughout this chapter, little has been made of the commonplace analogy of the eye with a camera. This is because, at a general level, the comparison is apt to be more misleading than helpful. First, it suggests that the eye somehow takes a picture, makes a copy of some existing reality, and then sends it to the brain for processing. Second, the analogy assumes that the eye has a certain mechanical objectivity. This expresses the traditional image-copy theory of perception—part of a historical Western thesis that objectifies the human visual system as mechanical and optically precise and, more recently, as a sophisticated computer or videorecorder. One major problem with this kind of model is that, once we see the body as a machine or as a computer, we tend to look to machines and computers for answers to questions about human beings, ignoring the fact that people are not fixed-capacity machines.

Rather than replicating a fixed image, the retina is constantly engaged in generating ever-changing patterns of electrochemical activity. This little patch of cells—roughly the size of the gauze patch on a standard Band-aid—is continually trembling and jerking about. Hence, far from recording a stable picture of the physical world, the eye interprets: it predetermines which wavelengths of electromagnetic radiation you will be able to perceive, how much detail you will see, in what kind of light you will see it, what light patterns you will observe as objects, which phenomena will be defined as moving, which will be still, and so on. What you perceive as "out there" and what really is out there are two different things. (Remember that the invisible wavelengths of electromagnetic radiation are no less real for your being unable to see them.)

In short, perception is the process by which a person actively constructs reality. How you interpret your perceptual experiences depends on where and when you live and on how you deal with the values and significance your culture assigns to your experiences. In this chapter, we have begun to explore this process at the level of the eye. In the next chapter, we will consider the role of the brain in the processes of creating meaning from visual experience.

3

The Brain

It Figures

Look carefully at figure 3-1, searching for a figure that looks like . Can you see it? Now look for a figure that is identical to the first, except that it is formed by the spaces between. Practice looking first at one figure and then at the other. Do the wedges that form the figure seem to stand out? Do they appear to be even brighter than the background wedges? Can you discipline yourself to see the drawing as only a pattern of lines? Can you see it as only six contiguous shapes? As you concentrate on these different ways of seeing, the drawing seems to change subtly, but no change occurs on the page! This simple experiment demonstrates how easily the brain transforms, organizes, and interprets information from the retina. The retinal image does not change, yet your perceptions do change. Seeing is accomplished in the mind—not in the eye.

Eye and brain are linked in profound ways. Conditions in the eyes (such as blindness, eye position, and exposure to color) can affect, sometimes greatly, the electrical rhythms of the brain. In turn, activities in the brain affect the eyes. According to theories of *neurolinguistic programming*, for example, when people engage in primarily left-brain thought, their eyes typically gaze to the right; conversely, the gaze is toward the left when right-brain thinking takes place.

Stimulation of the eyes can interfere with normal brain functions. Bright lights (such as strobes), when flashing at a rate of about four to ten flashes per second, may cause people to experience strange visual patterns, headaches, and nausea. In susceptible individuals, epileptic convulsions can be triggered by flickering light from such things as television, the rotor blades of a helicopter, or flickering sunlight. Stimulating brain cells with electrodes can cause people to experience flashes of light, complete vivid scenes, or elaborate visual memories.

Conditions internal to the body also cause visual sensations. Increased blood pressure in the brain, as happens in the case of migraine headaches, can cause visual disturbances such as flashes, distortions, or spots. Abnormal electrical activity in the brains of epileptics may cause sensations of light, noise, taste, or smell. Mild drugs and narcotics such as marijuana and alcohol can heighten or depress perceptions of external reality. Intense chemical stimulation of the brain with stronger drugs such as LSD and mescaline may create visual experiences completely unrelated to external events and yet so intense that the individual cannot distinguish them from outside reality (such internally experienced events are termed *hallucinations*). When people are extremely deprived of sleep or sensory stimulation, their perception, motor coordination, and emotions are affected. Visual perception can also be affected by more common emotional states (such as anxiety, anger, or fear), which are associated with particular chemicals produced by the brain and body.

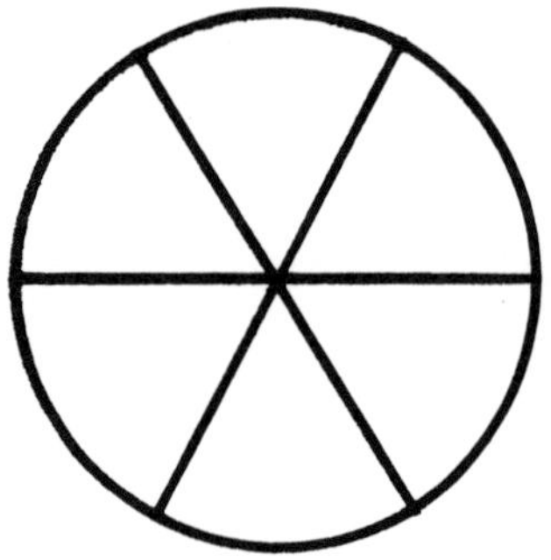

Figure 3-1. Seeing with the mind.

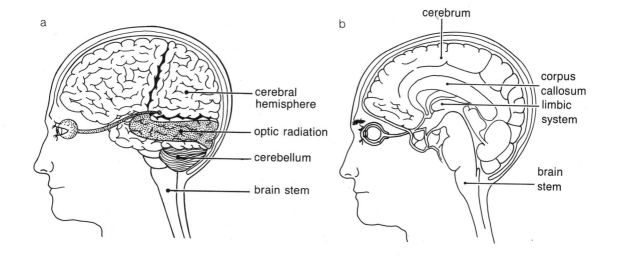

THE BRAIN

In their book *The Amazing Brain*, Robert Ornstein and Richard F. Thompson (1984, pp. 21–22) suggest a way for you to visualize your brain:

> Place your fingers on both sides of your head beneath the ear lobes. In the center of the space between your hands is the oldest part of the brain, the brainstem. Now, form your hands into fists. Each is about the size of one of the brain's hemispheres, and when both fists are joined at the heel of the hand, they describe not only the approximate size and shape of the entire brain but also its symmetrical structure. Next, put on a pair of thick gloves—preferably light gray. These represent the cortex . . . the newest part of the brain and the area whose functioning results in the most characteristically human creations, such as language and art.

In terms of evolution, the brainstem (see figure 3-2) is the most primitive part of the brain. It first appeared more than 500 million years ago in the early vertebrates, and it is commonly called our *reptilian brain* because of its striking similarity to the entire brain of a reptile. All of the nerve fibers from the cerebral hemispheres pass through the brainstem on their way to the spinal cord. The brainstem controls involuntary and automatic pro-

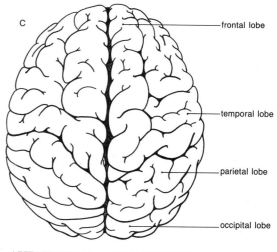

Figure 3-2. The human brain: (a) side view; (b) cross section; (c) top view. (Eleanor Holland)

cesses such as breathing, swallowing, vomiting, blood pressure, and respiration.

The cerebellum, which hugs the brainstem below the cerebrum, maintains posture and muscle coordination, and appears to play a role in the memory of simple learned processes. Above the cerebellum is the limbic system, which evolved in mammallike reptiles between 300 million and 200 million years ago. It is sometimes called our *mam-*

malian brain, and in other mammals it is the largest part of the brain. The limbic system regulates such life systems as temperature, blood pressure, heart rate, and blood sugar, and it activates physical and emotional responses associated with hunger, rage, fear, and sex. Automatic, unthinking (''gut'') reactions originate here. The limbic system is also involved in expressing and decoding nonverbal communication signals. The hypothalamus and the pituitary gland are part of the limbic system.

The cerebral hemispheres (or cerebrum) are what people usually associate with the word *brain*. The wrinkled surface of the cerebrum is actually a gray layer of folded nerve cells about ⅛ inch thick, called the *cortex* or *neocortex* (from the Latin word for bark of a tree). The convolutions or wrinkles of the cortex give the brain a greater surface area within an unchanged skull size. Hence, the wrinkled cortex contains a great many more nerve cells (called *neurons*) than it would if it were smooth-surfaced. Other higher mammals also have wrinkled cortexes, but the cortex of human beings is the most convoluted of all. The cortex is the site of functions related to thinking, planning, intentional behaviors, and creative behaviors.

The cortex evolved with the placental mammals about 200 million years ago. During the evolution of our own biological superfamily, the higher primates, brain size and brain weight increased in relation to face and body size. The brains of monkeys and apes are roughly twice as large as those of other mammals. By itself, though, brain size does not necessarily reflect intelligence. For example, an elephant's brain weighs nearly 9 pounds—about three times as much as an average human brain. But the elephant's brain constitutes only 0.2 percent of its body weight, whereas a human's brain constitutes about 2 percent of the person's body weight.

Among humans, too, bigger does not always mean brighter. The brains of tall people tend to weigh more than those of short people, but short people tend to have a higher ratio of brain weight to body weight. Among human groups, Eskimos tend to have the largest brains. The brain of the author Anatole France weighed only 2¼ pounds, while Jonathan Swift's brain weighed nearly 4½ pounds— only a few ounces lighter than the largest brain on record, which belonged to a severely retarded person with a mental age of two years. What makes a human brain distinctive is not so much its size as its neural organization, in particular the flexibility in processing that is made possible by the great intermediate net (see chapter 1).

Brain Localizations

Within the adult human cerebrum, specific brain functions are associated with specific areas. The most general division is between the left and right cerebral hemispheres (termed *lateralization*). The left hemisphere controls the right side of the body, and the right hemisphere controls the left side of the body.

In general, the left hemisphere is associated with logic, sequence, and deductive analysis; this group of processes is usually called *linear* thinking. The right hemisphere is associated with wholistic, spatial, imagistic, and metaphorical thinking; this group is usually called *simultaneous* thinking. This orientation is true for approximately 98 percent of right-handed people, and for two-thirds of left-handed people, the latter accounting for between 5 and 12 percent of the population in the Western world. For left-handers whose mothers were left-handed, brain lateralization may be exactly reversed. Some left-handed people have mixed lateralization.

Differences between left and right cerebral hemispheres have become a popular topic, and many people tend to characterize themselves or others as possessing either left-brain or right-brain personalities. Right-brain people are thought of as creative, artistic, and irrational, while left-brain people are said to be verbal, scientific, and unimaginative. Thus, scientific types are viewed as being fundamentally different from artistic types. But the situation is not so simple. Scientific progress has always depended on leaps of creative imagination, just as artistic production has always depended on the logical development of concepts and processes. Like everyone else, scientists and artists depend on having both halves of their brains working together. (For a well-developed model of creativity based on the thought modalities of left- and right-brain functioning, see Edwards 1986.)

The left and right hemispheres are connected by a 4-inch-long, ¼-inch-thick bundle of 300 million nerve fibers called the *corpus callosum*, which constitutes one-third or more of the brain's total number of nerve cells. Thus, the design of the human brain is heavily committed to communication between the two hemispheres. Truly split-brain people have had their corpus callosum surgically severed (a drastic treatment for epilepsy, which is no longer done). These commissurotomy patients show peculiar aberrations in their thought and communication processes. Split-brain research has clearly shown that normal brain functioning relies on the integration of both hemispheres.

Each cerebral hemisphere is further divided into four lobes: frontal, parietal, temporal, and occipital (see figure 3-2). The frontal lobes are involved with planning, judgment, goal-oriented behavior, movement, and some aspects of emotion. The parietal lobes compare and integrate sensory information and data about spatial orientation. The temporal lobes are occupied with hearing, perception, and memory. The occipital lobes are often called the *visual cortex*; they interpret visual inputs and send information about them to areas in the other lobes. All told, about half of the cerebral cortex is involved in processing visual imagery. The predominance of the parietal and temporal lobes is a characteristically human pattern that dates back at least 2 million years (see chapter 1).

When adults suffer brain damage from strokes, illness, or injury, the effects on thinking and behavior depend on which hemisphere and which areas have been damaged. Damage to the occipital lobe can cause blindness. Damage to the left temporal lobe usually results in a loss of language (called *aphasia*), while damage to the right temporal lobe impairs spatial abilities such as drawing and driving. Damage to the right parietal lobe interferes with visual-spatial processing. Frontal lobe destruction or removal (as in frontal lobotomy—the ''ultimate solution'' in Ken Kesey's novel, *One Flew Over the Cuckoo's Nest*) renders an individual incapable of planning complex behaviors and adapting to new situations.

This commitment of special areas of the brain to particular functions is not something we are born with. It is acquired during early childhood and appears to be a response to sensory stimulation from the environment. For example, in a newborn infant, the same brain cell may respond to light stimulation from either eye. By the time the child is six, however, each eye has established its own exclusive territory of neurons. If one eye is denied light stimulation (through infection or congenital cataract, for example) before it has staked out its territory in the brain, it will never be able to do so, and the person will be permanently blind in that

eye—even if the eye itself is restored to normal. The same is true for newborn animals such as puppies and kittens, except that the process takes place within weeks. Thus, an eye infection that keeps a kitten's eye closed (and hence unstimulated by light) may result in blindness—not because of damage to the eye, but because, without exposure to light, the closed eye could not establish its neuronal territory in the brain.

Amblyopia (or lazy eye) can also interfere with neuronal territoriality. Therapy usually includes covering the properly functioning eye in order to allow adequate opportunity for the other eye to establish its neuronal connections in the brain. Young children can successfully survive much greater brain damage than can adults, since they have uncommitted neurons that can take over for lost or injured cells.

According to psychologist Howard Gardner (1983), genetic evolution has predisposed human beings to perceive and process certain kinds of information. Different parts of the human brain and nervous system are structurally committed to performing particular kinds of mental operations that Gardner has termed *intelligences*. Because these intelligences arise from the physiological structure of the human brain, they form part of the human blueprint and to some degree are inherently present in all normal human beings (although they are subject to normal genetic variation). Gardner has identified seven of these intelligences: linguistic, musical, logical-mathematical, (visual-)spatial, bodily-kinesthetic, intrapersonal, and interpersonal. Each is characterized by localization in the brain, relative independence from the other intelligences, evolutionary continuity, expression in various cultural symbol systems, and substantiation through a solid body of supporting psychometric data.

Cultures value and develop these intelligences differently. Western-type schooling and ''intelligence'' tests (such as IQ tests), for example, focus almost exclusively on linguistic and logical-mathematical intelligence. School subjects that emphasize other intelligences (such as the arts, physical education, home economics, industrial arts, and club activities) are considered frills. But not all cultures view intelligence in this way. In many small-scale societies, interpersonal, spatial, and kinesthetic intelligences tend to be accorded the highest importance. In Western culture, too, people acknowledge

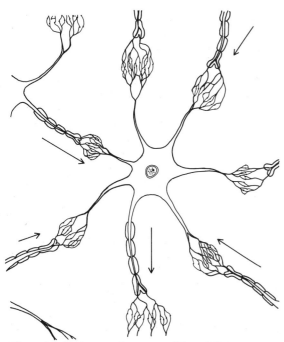

Figure 3-3. Neurons and synapses. (Eleanor Holland)

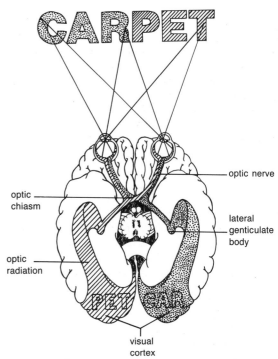

Figure 3-4. The eye-brain connection. (Eleanor Holland)

the limitations of school smarts when they distinguish having a high IQ from having common sense, or when they use phrases such as "street wise," "a way with people," "an ear for music," "a natural dancer," and "a born politician." Researchers are more and more coming to view intelligence not as an isolated ability, but rather as varying sets of skills that enable people to live successfully in their particular social and cultural setting.

Neurons and Synapses

The brain functions by means of electrical and chemical messages received and transmitted by nerve cells or neurons (see figure 3-3). The total number of neurons in a human brain has been estimated at from 10 billion to 100 billion. They are so small that the head of a pin would accommodate 20,000 of them. Furthermore, any single neuron may have as many as several thousand connections with other neurons. These numbers are difficult to comprehend. The potential is astounding, and writers have searched for vivid ways to express it:

The number of neurons in a single human brain is more than the number of human beings who have ever lived on the earth!

The total number of possible interconnections is greater than the number of atoms in the universe.

If people were scaled down to the size of brain cells: we could hold the population of the earth in our cupped hands, but there would not be enough people to make one brain!

In the human fetus: nerve cells develop and multiply to form the brain and nervous system at the amazing rate of 250,000 per minute over the nine months of development. . . .

Just to write out the number that represents the items your mind is capable of holding, you would have to write a zero a second for 90 years.

The connections between neurons in the brain are called *synapses* (see figure 3-3). In a synapse, chemical messages are carried across the synaptic cleft from the transmitting fiber (or axon) of one neuron to the receiving fibers (or dendrites) of another neuron by molecules called *neurotransmitters*. Neurotransmitter molecules have particular

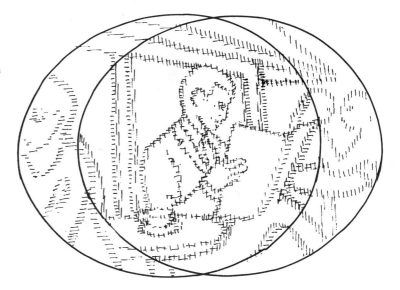

Figure 3-5. The visual fields and images seen in the right and left eyes are shown by vertical and horizontal lines, respectively. (Keith Long)

shapes that fit lock-in-key fashion into the receptor molecules on the dendrite side. They act either to excite the receiving cell, encouraging it to fire, or to inhibit the cell, discouraging it from firing. Whether or not a neuron actually fires depends on the sources and combinations of these exciting and inhibiting messages.

Receptors can be fooled by foreign look-alike molecules such as opium and nicotine. You may be familiar with the names of some neurotransmitters: *dopamine, serotonin, acetylcholine, norepinephrine, arginine, vasopressin, beta-endorphine,* and *enkephalin,* among others. The number of different neurotransmitters may number in the hundreds; their production is affected by such things as diet, ionization of the air, exercise, sleep, and emotions.

Learning and memory appear to consist of permanent changes in the synaptic connections that make it easier for the nerve impulses to follow particular neuronal pathways or circuits. These permanent structural changes are often termed *memory traces* or *engrams*. Their exact nature is still not completely understood.

From birth to adulthood, a person's brain weight more than triples. Researchers (Rosenzweig et al. 1972) have found that the number of synapses (and therefore the number of available interconnections) is related to environmental stimulation. In a series of now-classic experiments, rats raised in an enriched sensory environment had brains weighing 10 percent more than those of genetically related control groups reared in normal and deprived environments. Even the brains of very old rats grew by 10 percent as a result of living with young rats. This was especially significant, since brain weight normally decreases slightly over the course of adulthood. When the brains of the experimental rats were examined with a microscope, the dendrites of the brain cells were found to have become thicker and more dense, forming more neuronal interconnections. Similarly, in the nineteenth century, Charles Darwin observed that the cortex of domesticated animals is thinner than that of their untamed counterparts who live in a richer natural environment. The implications for human beings are profound and complex.

THE VISUAL SYSTEM

The dot pattern of the retinal mosaic (see figure 2-16) is transmitted from the eye as a series of electrical impulses traveling through the optic nerves at the rear of each eyeball. At the optic chiasm, about half of the nerve fibers from each eye cross over to the opposite side (see figure 3-4). These regrouped fibers (optic tracts) lead into an area of the thalamus (specifically, the lateral geniculate body), where each impulse is registered. The message continues through the optic radiation to the occipital lobe (visual cortex) of each hemisphere. The right and left fields of vision for each eye are relayed to

Figure 3-6. Experiments with binocular vision: (a) Cut a small hole in the center of a piece of typing paper. With both eyes open, hold the paper at arm's length in the direction of a light. Visually center the light in the hole. After you have done this, close each eye, one at a time, and compare the visual fields. Which is your dominant eye? (b) Roll up an ordinary sheet of paper lengthwise, or use a paper-towel tube. Keep both eyes open, and with one hand hold the tube up to one eye. Slowly move the open palm of your other hand toward the tube until it rests against the outside of the tube near the end. What do you see? (c) You may have done this as a child: Simply focus on something straight ahead of you and several feet away. Keep that focus while you point the tips of your index fingers toward each other until they touch in your line of vision. By moving your hands closer to and further away from your eyes—still keeping the initial focal point—you will see a phantom finger growing and shrinking. (Jane Filer)

the left and right visual cortexes, respectively. For this reason, injury to the right visual cortex will affect the left visual field of both eyes. If the damage is severe, the person will be able to see only the right half of objects and scenes.

Stimulation from the fovea and macula engages about half of the entire visual cortex. A person sees most detail in the center of the visual field, both because of the greater density of cone cells in the center of the retina (see chapter 2) and because of the greater proportion of brain cells that respond to them. Peripheral vision occupies a larger area of the retina but has a proportionately smaller neuronal territory in the brain. Finally, the nerve impulses are relayed to neurons in other areas of the brain such as in the temporal, parietal, and frontal lobes, and in the motor cortex. This complex chain of events takes place in a fraction of a second.

Binocular Vision

The brain processes the two retinal images in such a way that we normally experience them as a single image (through image fusion). The visual fields for each eye are slightly different (a condition termed *binocular disparity*), but the images are very similar and they overlap (see figure 3-5). In order for image fusion to occur, the centers of the visual fields of each eye must match in the foveas. For objects nearer than about 20 feet, this match can be achieved only if the eyes turn inward or converge (see figures 2-19 and 6-2). The closer the object, the greater the convergence required.

Fortunately, image fusion is usually easy and completely unconscious. But interestingly, the mind does not give equal weight to the images from each eye. The single image you normally perceive reflects the visual field of one eye. Because of brain lateralization, you have a dominant eye, just as you have a dominant hand. Most right-handed people are also right-eyed and right-footed. The experiment shown in figure 3-6a is often used to determine whether a person has mixed dominance. Lack of image fusion (called *double vision*) is symptomatic of abnormal conditions—for example, extreme intoxication, brain disease, brain injury, botulism poisoning, or drug side-effects.

Bizarre effects can occur when the image shown to each eye is markedly different (see figures 3-6b and c). As the brain attempts to form a solid, single image, it may alternately accept and reject parts of each eye's image. When colors are involved, the observer may see first one color and then the

Figure 3-7. This reconstruction of a Brewster lenticular-prism stereoscope was manufactured for vision training. (Collection of the author; photograph by Bruce Thompson)

Figure 3-8. Figure and ground.

other, rather than a mixture of the two. With patterns or pictures, different parts of the images phase in and out, combining and recombining in various and constantly changing ways. This phenomenon is called *retinal* or *binocular rivalry*. One way to experience binocular rivalry is to make or get a pair of 3-D spectacles (one lens is red, and the other is green or blue). Use these spectacles to look at patterns made of the same two colors.

Because human beings are extremely sensitive to even slight binocular disparities, the stereoscope (see figure 3-7) can be used to detect small differences between similar images. The stereoscope shows a separate image to each eye. When a counterfeit bill and a genuine one are viewed stereoscopically, the disparity triggers retinal rivalry, causing areas of difference to appear to vibrate. Likewise, stereoscopic viewing of microphotos of different bullets reveals whether or not they have been fired from the same gun; and stereoscopic aerial photos expose areas of camouflage that would not be evident in a single photograph. Stereoscopes have also been used in vision therapy: image fusion is used to promote eye muscle coordination. Despite these many practical applications, most people are more familiar with the stereoscope as an antique entertainment, as a children's toy (for example, the Viewmaster), or as sensational cinema (3-D movies).

Binocular vision is a factor in depth perception and is discussed further in chapter 7.

FIGURE AND GROUND

One of the most fundamental actions of the mind consists of selecting what to pay attention to and what to ignore. You usually make such decisions automatically and unconsciously. Look at the crosses in figure 3-8: even when one cross is given a square frame, the cross (and not the space surrounding it) remains the meaningful part of this simple stimulus. Gestalt psychologists have termed the relationship between a figure and its background the *figure/ground relationship*. In art, it is often referred to as *positive* and *negative space*.

In perception, figures are consistently marked by certain qualities. A figure is perceptually bright: it seems to have more intensity than the background, and it appears to stand out from it. That is why the wedges you concentrated on in figure 3-1 seemed brighter than the other wedges. A figure also has the quality of appearing as a thing that is on top of the background. The ground also has specific characteristics: it seems to be under the figure, to lack a particular form, and to be continuous (that is, it is not seen as stopping at the edge of the figure, but as continuing behind the figure). In addition, a figure suggests meaning, while a ground seems relatively meaningless.

This differentiation of figure from ground is essential to perception, and it takes place within all of your senses. For example, pause in your reading and concentrate for a moment on your body. You may become aware of your position and change it. You may feel an itch and decide to scratch it (notice the power of suggestion!). You might find a bad taste in your mouth and decide to take a break and get a drink of water. You may hear sounds—a radio

Figure 3-9. Alternating figure/ground.

ure in one situation becomes the ground in another. When you look at something—say, a bowl of fruit—you first perceive the whole thing as a figure. But as you continue to look, you notice certain parts of it—perhaps bananas. Then, as you concentrate on the bananas, they become a figure, while the apples and oranges recede into ground. The entire bowl can be a figure seen against the ground of the table, and the table can be seen as a figure against the ground of the wall. A thing becomes a figure when you pay attention to it; at that particular moment, all else dissolves into a background.

Sometimes things may become figures against your will—for example, the ticking of a clock. Ordinarily such a constant noise stays in the auditory background. But you may become suddenly aware of the ticking, perhaps just when you are trying to fall asleep. On some occasions, the ticking may remain a figure with annoying persistence: you try to push it into the background, but you cannot. The same sort of thing often happens when you feel irritable. When you have a headache, even the normal background of a household can become impossible to ignore: everything becomes an annoyance. In such a situation, people may resort to taking painkillers, tranquilizers, or other drugs to push pain or problems into the background.

Many encounter-group activities, consciousness-raising methods, self-awareness techniques, and therapies are designed to make people conscious of things they ordinarily tune out. When people form new figure/ground relationships, they perceive themselves and others with a new awareness. Gestalt therapy, for example, sensitizes people to emotional figure/ground relationships within their personalities. Meditative techniques, on the

or TV, a passing automobile, a dog barking. Previously these things were simply part of your perceptual background. Once you allowed them to become figures, however, you could pay attention to them.

Normally your mind is incredibly selective in its handling of the sensations coming in from all your senses. You cannot maintain anything like the objectivity of a machine. Consequently, you may be surprised when you play back a microphone-based tape recording: the amount of background noise you had simply tuned out is astonishing. The microphone had no ability to form figure/ground relationships; it just picked up everything indiscriminately. Cameras do the same thing. You can be so busy concentrating on the subject you are photographing that you are blind to the visual impact of the background, which you may later find annoying. In order to see what the camera "sees," professional photographers must overcome their own natural tendency to tune out background factors.

Figure/ground relationships do not exist in the outside world; they are created by the mind. A fig-

Figure 3-10. Can you identify these paintings from the shapes of figure and ground? (See page 63 for identifications.)

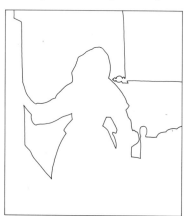
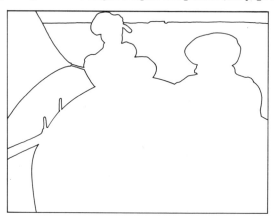
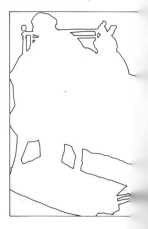

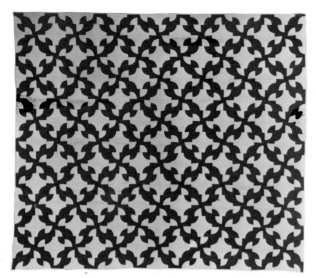

Figure 3-11. Artistic uses of alternating figure/ground: (Above) Anonymous (American), *Drunkard's Path*, n.d. Concentrate on the black and white as alternating figure and ground. Putting together this pattern is often confusing. Can you find any errors? (Photograph by Myron Miller, New York, N.Y.); (top right) for *Look Homeward, Angel*, Dawn Barrett (American), poster 1987. (Permission of the artist); (bottom right) M. C. Escher (German), *Circle Limit IV ("Heaven and Hell")*, 1960. Woodcut, 16 inches in diameter. (Haags Gemeentemuseum, The Hague)

other hand, are directed toward disengaging the self from certain kinds of figures in order to achieve a feeling of integrated unity.

Alternating Figure/Ground

Sometimes figure and ground seem to vacillate between two equally good alternatives. As you look at figure 3-9 (as well as at the familiar Peter and Paul goblet shown in figure 1-9), notice how the qualities of black and white change with each view, alternately showing the perceptual characteristics of figure and ground. When you concentrate on the white area, it seems to stand out; the black appears as a continuous space behind it. When you attend to the black area, the white seems to recede and the black stands out.

Psychologists generally agree that both views cannot be perceived simultaneously. That is, although you see different meanings in turn (creating an overall ambiguity), at any given instant you see only one meaning. This suggests limits on the number of things the brain can pay attention to at

Figure 3-12. Yin/yang symbol.

Figure 3-13. Ukiyo-e School (Japanese), *Scenes of Kyoto: The Gion Festival and Other Scenes,* late 17th century. Detail from a six-panel folding screen. Full color and gold, 1.676 × .622 meters. (Museum of Fine Arts, Boston; Bigelow Collection)

any given time. You experience ambiguity when your brain is unable to decide which meaning is preferable.

At first thought, you might expect that a figure and its ground ought to be mirror images of each other, but this is not the case. Look again at figure 3-9. The black and white shapes are surprisingly different in character. You encounter this phenomenon when confronted with jigsaw-puzzle pieces that do not look like the spaces into which they fit.

The interlocking quality of figure and ground is an aspect of artistic composition that often goes unnoticed by nonartists. Beginning artists tend to place objects in the middle of the compositional

space, ignoring the background. Most professional artists, by contrast, carefully divide the entire composition into interlocking shapes (see figure 3-10). Sometimes artists deliberately use alternating figure/ground compositions (see figure 3-11).

The experience of ambiguity bothers many people. In Western cultures, figure ("positive") has always been accorded major importance, while ground ("negative") has been defined as all factors that can be eliminated without affecting meaning. Some cultural traditions, however, emphasize that one cannot exist without the other. For example, the *yin/yang* symbol (see figure 3-12) expresses a basic concept of the ancient Chinese philosophy of

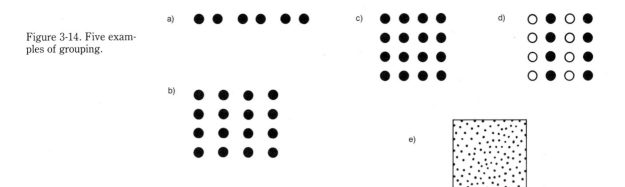

Figure 3-14. Five examples of grouping.

Taoism, according to which the two elemental forces, *yin* and *yang*, produce all things and events. *Yin* is dark, receptive, cool, and moist. *Yang* is bright, hot, hard, and dry. The successive, cyclical movements of *yin* and *yang* create orderly transformations in the world. Both nature and human life are subject to continual change as *yin* and *yang* increase and decrease.

This principle of universal order is called the Way (*Tao*). The *Tao* encompasses both contradiction and harmony, both unity and multiplicity. Figure and ground are inextricably bound together: the form of one creates the form of the other, and within each is the germ of the other. Oriental philosophies such as Taoism often unite elements that Western logic would define as paradoxical or conflicting.

You can also view such concepts as embracing the dynamic dualities of perceptual organization. For example, Oriental art has always placed great value on the use of ''empty'' space to represent meaningful parts of a picture. The Japanese screen painting (see figure 3-13) shows one historical style. From one point of view, the blank spaces appear as pieces of the picture that have been torn away. At the same time, these spaces act as opaque clouds in front of the scene. Because the houses and people are more meaningful, your mind may tend to want to perceive them as figures in front of the blank spaces, rather than as things behind them. This tension, resulting from alternation between figure and ground, actively engages your perceptual process.

Grouping and Filling In

Another way the brain forms figures is by grouping aspects of the stimulus into meaningful patterns. In figure 3-14a, for example, our tendency is to group six dots into three pairs. Figure 3-14b is seen as four rows or, if turned 90 degrees, as four columns. If they are equidistant (as in figure 3-14c), the dots can be seen as rows or as columns. In figure 3-14d, the circles and dots form separate columns. In figure 3-14e, you can pick out a line of dots. Several principles are involved in this kind of perception. Certain characteristics encourage the mind to group elements together as parts of a single unit: closeness to one another (proximity); similarity in size, shape, or color; and shared alignment. When they appear in combination, however, these effects can effectively cancel each other out.

More complex groupings occur in high-contrast photography, which reduces an image to black and white, eliminating the contours and the shades of gray you would ordinarily expect to see (see figure 3-15). At first, such an image may look like a nonsense arrangement of black-and-white fragments. Recognition usually begins when one part of the picture spontaneously appears meaningful (for example, the faces in figure 3-15). Once one part of the figure is identified, the rest of the pieces seem to fall into place. This is partly a result of what Gestaltists called *good continuation*: we tend to perceive separate lines or shapes as parts of a larger whole when the visual transitions from one element to another appear smooth (not abrupt). Good continuation, however, depends on familiarity; until the shapes can be perceived as representing something familiar, they remain nonsensical.

The human mind is so eager to fill in the blanks that it will see contours that are not physically present. These apparent edges, called *subjective contours*, result from the mind's search for a meaningful figure. In order to do this with figure 3-16a, for example, your mind groups the six angles as parts of a single but interrupted triangle, sees the circles as interrupted circles (rather than as Pac-

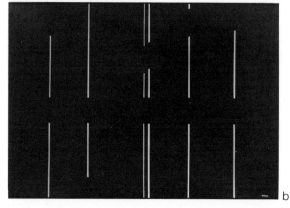

Figure 3-16. Subjective contours: (a) Subjective triangles, (b) Carolyn M. Bloomer (American), *Inside the Horsebarn*, 1971. Acrylic on canvas, 24 × 36 inches. Can you see the horizontal and diagonal supports? (Collection of the author)

Figure 3-15. High-contrast images: (Above) a photograph by Bruce Thompson; (below) some people have claimed that only true believers can see this figure of Jesus.

men), and fills in contours of superimposed triangles. This seems complicated, yet the closure itself feels simple and satisfying: the image makes sense. It makes so much sense, in fact, that it is nearly impossible to see this pattern as simply three Pac-men and three bent lines.

You continue to perceive whole images even when fully half of the visual information is missing. Figure 3-17 demonstrates a kind of venetian-blind effect, such as might occur if you looked through a picket fence or a bamboo shade.

Japanese Zen Buddhist painters apply these principles by using minimal brush strokes to convey a meaningful image. Paintings such as the one shown in figure 3-18 are composed of visual fragments—brush strokes that by themselves are abstract and meaningless. By grouping and filling in, the mind of the viewer actively combines them into a definite image. The works of the French Impressionist painters (see chapters 2 and 5) also depend on these processes.

Grouping and filling in are two ways in which the human mind perceptually organizes figure/ground perceptions from separate elements. In the exam-

Figure 3-17. Diane Greco (American), *Golda Meir*, 1979. Collage. As an exercise in a design class, 50 percent of the visual information was removed from this magazine photograph.

Figure 3-18. Kimura Nagamitsu (Japanese), *Figures and Landscape*, Kano period (15th – 19th centuries). (Museum of Fine Arts, Boston)

ples you have considered thus far, your mind has been rewarded by closures with single, meaningful figures. Some elements, however, cannot be grouped into a single meaningful figure. This is particularly true of overall patterns made up of many identical or nearly identical units. As you look at figure 3-19, interesting things happen. Many different perceptual organizations occur as your mind persists in trying to get permanent closure and be done with it. The effort is doomed, however: the pattern lends itself equally well to different possibilities. Artists sometimes make skillful use of this phenomenon (see figure 2-21).

Visual structures of this sort, composed of repeated patterns of identical or nearly identical elements that occur at regular and predictable intervals are called *periodic patterns*. When two or more such patterns are superimposed, the mind organizes additional patterns by grouping the points at which the patterns intersect. These points of intersection appear to be more intense than they physically are (see figure 3-20)—probably as an

Figure 3-19. Anonymous (American, Maine, Penobscot Bay area). *A Thousand Pyramids,* n.d. Cotton patchwork quilt. As you look at the triangles, they will seem to group and regroup themselves. You may see strong diagonals. A pattern of square boxes may suddenly appear: the dark triangles form the shadows. (Blue Hill Historical Society, Blue Hill, Maine. Photograph by Myron Miller, New York, N.Y.)

effect of lateral inhibition, which works to exaggerate the perception of differences between adjacent areas (see chapter 2).

If the angle of intersection is less than 30 degrees, the pattern is called a *moiré* pattern. This French word originally referred to a fabric made from two layers of finely striated silk that were pressed onto each other slightly out of alignment to produce a shimmering surface of watered silk. You can also see moiré patterns by looking through the folds of thin curtains or overlapping window screens. They may be observed among the wires of suspension bridges and in the finely engraved lines of postage stamps or paper money. Interestingly, something similar occurs with sound. When two tones of differing frequencies are played at the same time, a third, throbbing sound is formed out of the instants when the peaks and troughs of the sound waves coincide. As it does with visual patterns, the mind creates figures from the points at which elements in two or more patterns intersect.

Optical Illusions

Three familiar optical illusions are shown in figure 3-21. Several theories have been used to explain them. According to Gestalt psychologists, the way humans perceive a stimulus depends on the perceptual context within which the stimulus is embedded. The same visual stimulus will be perceived differently in different visual situations. Thus, your perceptions of line length and parallelism change

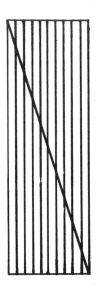
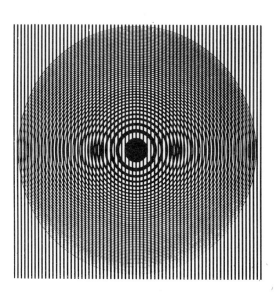

Figure 3-20. Moiré patterns: (Left) single-line moiré. (right) Fresnel-Ring moiré, a pattern formed when one set of parallel lines is combined with one set of concentric circles.

a

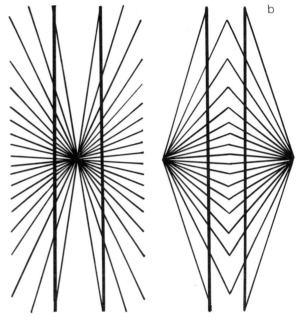

b

Figure 3-21. Optical illusions: (a) Muller-Lyer arrow illusion: the shafts of the arrows are of equal length; (b) Hering figure, or fan illusion: the vertical lines are parallel; (c) Herringbone (Zollner) illusion: the long diagonal lines are parallel.

c

when they are placed in a setting with other lines and patterns. You cannot visually separate these elements from the total figure of which they are a part. When you can do so (by covering up part of the figure, for instance), the illusion disappears.

Another explanation of these illusions involves lateral inhibition: a person's neural organization promotes an enhanced perception of certain visual characteristics such as edge, contrast, and figure (see chapter 2). In this case, some characteristics of a pattern will be exaggerated, while others will be diminished. This maximizes the perception of differences, so you experience greater contrasts than are physically present. Your visual system is not fooling you; rather, the so-called illusions simply show you aspects of normal vision that you are not usually aware of. Artificial stimuli (such as geometric illusions) isolate the effects and thereby make

you conscious of them. Another theory uses eye movements to explain optical illusions, but no theory fully accounts for these various effects.

To complicate things, most research on optical illusions has used Western subjects. An interesting question is whether people in different cultures are subject to the same illusions. Cross-cultural studies have produced confusing results. Investigators' hypotheses that "carpentered" environments, geographical habitat, or lack of pictorial traditions affect the perception of illusions have not been consistently supported by research. Some experiments have shown that dark-skinned people are less susceptible to the Muller-Lyer illusion (see figure 3-21a), regardless of where they live. Their denser retinal pigmentation has been associated with a greater ability to detect contours. Some studies have shown women to be less susceptible

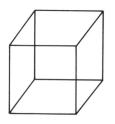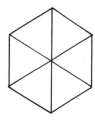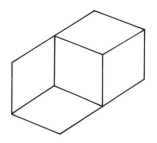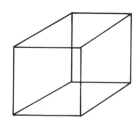

Figure 3-22. Reversible figures.

Figure 3-23. "The Wife and the Mother-in-Law."

exposing people to artificial stimuli in artificial research settings. People's perceptions of more natural objects in more natural settings might give better clues to cultural differences in perception. Such research, however, is complex to plan and analyze, and often it cannot be translated into meaningful statistical data. We need to be cautious when generalizing from experiments that ask people to make uncommon responses to uncommon stimuli.

Alternating Figures

Up to now we have been concerned with the mind's search to establish a figure. But sometimes seeing a figure only unleashes a new set of perceptual problems. In figure 3-22, each figure can alternate between (or among) two or more equally good interpretations. A certain tension results; and like a caged animal endlessly pacing its enclosure, your mind repeats the process of testing possible closures but remains unable to confirm one view as more persuasive than the other.

Look at figure 3-23. Do you see a young woman looking away from you, or do you see a toothless old crone whose chin is turned down into her fur collar? If you don't see both, keep looking. The second face usually appears quite suddenly. Unless you are familiar with this drawing or are just naturally suspicious, you probably would have been satisfied with your first interpretation. The mind tends to see only what is necessary for meaning. Once it has made closure, it does not usually continue to look for information. Mystery writers such as Agatha Christie and Arthur Conan Doyle take advantage of this tendency; they construct their stories in such a way that the reader forms misleading figures in which important clues are tuned out. With one masterful stroke, the author alters the significance of many details, and a new figure—the solution—emerges. The detective's skill lies in seeing figures that others have not seen.

than men to some illusions. People who have had Western-style schooling and extensive exposure to pictures tend to show greater susceptibility to illusions, suggesting that learning plays a role. At the same time, other research implies that children, who have had less education, are more susceptible to many illusions than are adults.

The significance of these widely varying results is unclear, but in every case the data resulted from

Figures 3-24, 3-25, and 3-26 show different ways in which artists have used the phenomenon of alternating figures. In each picture, visual evidence is given for more than one view, and your mind is unable to confirm one as more nearly correct than the others.

PREPROGRAMMING

The strategies that the mind uses in selecting and organizing stimuli are all directed toward one goal: to construct meaning from a jumble of sensory data and to arrive at closure. But why does closure occur? What mechanism in the mind says "OK, you can stop now: it computes!"?

Early theorists looked to characteristics of the stimulus for answers. They thought that characteristics inherent in the stimulus imposed certain closure patterns on the mind. More recent research in perception, however, has tended to shift emphasis from the structure of the stimulus to the structure of the mind itself. According to this newer view, closure demonstrates the reverse—that the mind has succeeded in imposing a pattern on the stimulus. In other words, the stimulus does not determine closure; instead, preexisting mental models program how the stimulus will be perceived.

Figure 3-24. Jasper Johns (American), *0–9,* 1960. Lithograph printed in black, 24 × 18⅞ inches. (The Museum of Modern Art, New York; gift of Mr. & Mrs. Armand P. Bartos)

Figure 3-25. Josef Albers (German), *JHC II,* 1963. Engraving on plastic, 20 × 26 inches. (Mr. and Mrs. James H. Clark, Jr., Dallas)

Figure 3-26. Pavel Tchelitchew (Russian), *Hide and Seek,* 1940 – 42. Oil on canvas, 78½ × 84¾ inches. (The Museum of Modern Art, New York; Mrs. Simon Guggenheim Fund)

This argument has far-reaching implications for understanding human perception. If it is correct, the human mind does not interpret stimuli with anything like an open-minded approach. Instead, people see things only in relation to categories already established in their minds. Closure does not represent objective knowledge about a stimulus, but rather the confirmation of a preexisting idea. It means that on a perceptual level people's minds are made up before the fact: they have the closure programmed before the stimulus happens!

Strong evidence supports this view. In chapter 1, we examined the Gestalt principle that the mind tends to correct stimuli and see them as more normal than they actually are. Along this line, most people have encountered difficulties at one time or another in proofreading and similar situations. (For example, can you find the problem with this this

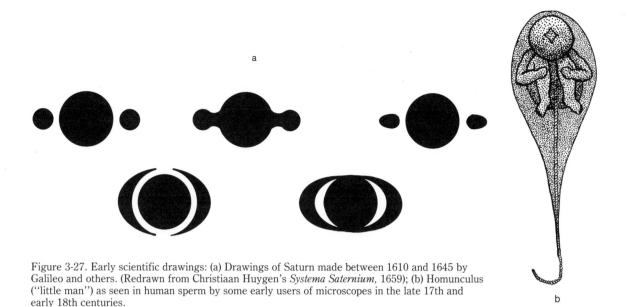

Figure 3-27. Early scientific drawings: (a) Drawings of Saturn made between 1610 and 1645 by Galileo and others. (Redrawn from Christiaan Huygen's *Systema Saternium*, 1659); (b) Homunculus ("little man") as seen in human sperm by some early users of microscopes in the late 17th and early 18th centuries.

line?) Such mental correcting can be explained by postulating that our perceptual processes clean up a stimulus in order to classify it more easily or to fit it more satisfactorily into an already-established category. Interpreting a new stimulus as a familiar gestalt is easier and more efficient than constructing a new category to account for all the minute details that make the present stimulus different from similar stimuli encountered in the past. Notice that this is also consistent with the principle of simplicity.

Some such preprogramming is necessary. You could not negotiate your way through a single day if you had to pay full attention to everything as if you were seeing it for the first time. To be efficient and practical, your brain must tune out and categorize at very basic levels. The result is that you bring an enormous number of preconceived notions to your encounters with reality.

These mental models (or paradigms) are constructed from your experiences of living—that never-ending process of trying to make sense of the world you live in. A good deal (indeed, probably most) of your mental preprogramming is determined by the culture in which you live. From the moment you are born, you learn from family, schools, friends, and media what reality is, how you should think and talk about it, and how you should behave in your world. A culture works to ensure that the people living in it share a fundamental concept of reality. Only then is communication and collective life possible (see chapter 1).

These preprogrammed responses can be termed *perceptual prejudices*. As with other kinds of prejudice, these predispose people to focus on the things that reinforce their preexisting stereotypes and to tune out inconsistencies. A classic laboratory experiment making use of playing cards nicely demonstrated this (Bruner and Postman 1949).

Interspersed among normal cards were some anomalous ones, such as a red six of spades and a black four of hearts. Subjects usually and without hesitation responded to the anomalous cards as if they were normal. Only after repeated exposures did the subjects begin to hesitate and express confusion. After identifying a few of the anomalous cards, they quickly identified the others. These subjects had readily ignored the irregularities, instead perceiving the cards as examples of their preprogrammed mental models. They tuned out visual data that were not consistent with those

In figure 3-10 the paintings are, from left to right: Jan Vermeer, *Young Woman With a Water Jug* (The Metropolitan Museum of Art); Mary Cassatt, *The Boating Party* (National Gallery of Art; Chester Dale Collection); Suzanne Valadon, *The Abandoned Doll* (The National Museum of Women in the Arts; The Holladay Collection)

models, and consequently they saw what they expected to see. Once they became aware of the anomalies, however, a new option presented itself, which they were then able to recognize easily. (These processes of tuning out and recategorizing have been termed *accommodation* and *assimilation*, respectively, by the developmental psychologist Jean Piaget.)

Knowing this, you can begin to appreciate the enormous difficulty of the search for objective knowledge about the world you live in. Probably no group of people has ever placed a higher value on objective observation than have Western scientists. The very fabric of the scientific method is woven from extreme strategies devised to ensure freedom from bias. And yet the history of science provides wonderful examples of how difficult it is to see something when you have no prior concept of its structure.

For example, scientists of the early 1600s did not conceive of Saturn as being encircled by rings. Even Galileo reported that it was a triple object. Early drawings of the planet reveal a struggle to interpret the telescopic image in a manner consistent with existing scientific paradigms (see figure 3-27a). Similar problems attended the identification in the late eighteenth century of Uranus as a planet; it was first thought to be a star, and then to be a comet. Likewise, users of early microscopes experienced considerable difficulty in assessing and describing the nature of what they were seeing: for example, sperm were observed as carrying whole little persons (*homunculi*) to the fertilization process (see figure 3-27b), and microorganisms were referred to as "little animals."

Thomas Kuhn, an historian of science, notes that Chinese astronomers recorded the appearance of sunspots and new stars centuries before Western astronomers (Kuhn 1970). Western culture had conceived of the heavens as fixed and unchanging, while the Chinese had not. Hence, the Chinese were perceptually open to discovering unusual occurrences much earlier. Kuhn suggests the anomalous playing-card experiment as a metaphor for scientific discovery. At first, only what is expected is seen, while irregularities are resisted. As anomalies become more frequent, conceptual models are adjusted and paradigms change. But as Kuhn points out, usually only people who have precise expectations are able to recognize inconsistencies.

In this chapter, we have considered some basic aspects of how the human brain organizes visual perception by constructing figure and ground relationships, grouping visual elements into unified wholes, filling in (or projecting) visual data that are not present in the stimulus, and incorporating visual experience into preprogrammed expectancies or mental models. In the following three chapters, we will explore the more complex problems of how and why the human mind generates perceptual constancy, color perception, and the perception of space.

4

Constancy
No Matter What Happens
You'll Always Be the Same to Me

When you look at yourself in the mirror, how big do you appear to be—life-size? Since you are a slight distance away, the logic of optics tells you that the mirror image is smaller than life, but how much smaller? Go to a mirror, stand your normal distance away, and close one eye; then reach out and measure your mirror image by placing your thumb on the chin and a finger on the hairline. (Alternatively, you may mark these dimensions with a squirt of shaving cream or toothpaste.)

When you look at what you have measured, it probably comes as quite a shock. My own image, for example, turns out to be a scant 4 inches high—and all my life I have been told that I have quite a long face! At this point you might recall that you can see your total height in a 3-foot "full-length" mirror. Another interesting experiment involves closing one eye, holding your head still, and with a marker tracing on a window pane the outlines of the objects you see. I guarantee that you will find the results difficult to believe. The intriguing thing here is not simply that the images are small and keep getting smaller as you move away from the window pane or mirror; more remarkable is that people remain so unaware of this extraordinary shrinkage. In fact, doubling the distance halves the image.

The same thing that happens in the mirror and on the window pane happens with all normal seeing. For example, I know that the Toyota in my driveway is smaller than my neighbor's truck, even though (from where I am standing), the Toyota's image is many times larger. When I see my friend Jane a block away, I know that she is still 5'10" and not a midget, in spite of her small image. The information pattern on the retina is telling me one thing (my compact car is bigger than a truck; Jane is a midget), but my brain seems to disregard it in favor of a different interpretation of reality.

Under normal circumstances, you have no problem accurately perceiving the actual size of things. People move toward you and away from you; you move nearer to and farther from things; and concurrently the images expand and shrink. A typical response to this paradox is "Oh well, I see far away things as small, but I know their real size." But it is not all that easy to separate seeing from knowing. Laboratory research shows that, while people may think that they see distant objects as smaller, they normally cannot accurately identify how small. The proportion of the visual field taken up by a given object is nearly always identified as being much larger than it actually is. Indeed, such errors in estimating the size of objects as they appear in the visual field constitute a major stumbling block in learning to draw according to Western standards of visual realism. Linear perspective is a drawing system that serves to counteract normal seeing.

Despite continual changes and ambiguities in the retinal pattern, your mind persists in maintaining unchanged or constant perceptions of objects. The human nervous system (like those of other species) is designed to extract the unchanging (or invariant) dimensions of the individual's experiences with the world. This function is called *perceptual constancy*, and it is an important factor in your perceptions of size, form, shape, color, and motion. The phenomenon of constancy underscores the fact that what you experience in perception is not simple sense stimulation (or sensation), but rather the product of a much more complex level of processing.

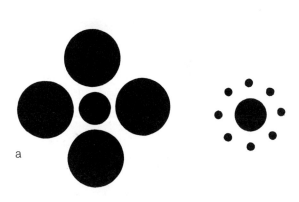

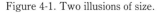

Figure 4-1. Two illusions of size.

SIZE CONSTANCY

Change in the size of an object in the retinal image is experienced as a change not in the object but in the distance of the object. In a laboratory setting, for example, subjects in a darkened room observed objects whose sizes gradually increased and decreased (for example, a balloon). They reported that the objects seemed alternately to be coming toward them and going away from them. You do not have to be in a laboratory to experience this phenomenon. Perhaps you have had the overwhelming feeling of moving through space while watching a science fiction movie. Things come toward you; you travel past planets or down raceways; they recede into the distance. You sit spellbound and anxious, your eyes glued to a flat screen, feeling as if you are whizzing past planets or falling through blood vessels—and all because a film animator has made circles get larger and smaller! Why should your mind interpret simple size changes in this way?

When the retinal image of an object changes size, two explanations are possible: either the object has changed size or its distance has changed. In most instances, it is unlikely that an object has changed size. From the earliest moments of life, your experience confirms that physical objects are likely to remain the same size, whereas your distance from them frequently changes. True, an identical retinal image can be produced by different events. (For example, an airborne balloon that appears to be gradually decreasing in size could be

either losing air or drifting away, or both.) But this is the exception rather than the rule. A more practical strategy is to assume, in the absence of contrary evidence, a difference in distance—even at the expense of tuning out and transforming certain aspects of retinal information.

Context

The context in which you see an object exerts the most important influence on your perception of its size. In everyday life, you rarely see objects in isolation. People, furniture, automobiles, trees, and houses all are seen in relation to one another. Size relationships among such familiar objects are quite consistent. In fact, filmmakers often stage gigantic catastrophes (especially storms, crashes, volcanoes, and earthquakes) in miniature. They know that, as long as the size relationships are realistic, we will not be conscious of the miniaturization.

Without context clues, laboratory subjects tend to perceive objects as smaller than they actually are. When there is no background, people seem to pay more attention to the size of the retinal image. Many research experiments that are designed to fool the eye depend for their effect on the elimination of normal information about context. Context is thus the cause of some well-known illusions. In figure 4-1a, the two center circles are actually the same size; but they look larger when surrounded by small circles, and smaller when surrounded by large circles. In figure 4-1b, three silhouettes of identical size are shown in a context of vanishing-point per-

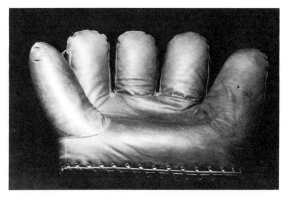

Figure 4-2. Paolo Lomazzi, Donato D'Urbino, and Jonathan De Pas (Italian), *Joe Sofa,* 1970. Polyurethane covered in leather, 33⅞ × 65¾ × 41⅜ inches. (The Museum of Modern Art, New York; gift of the manufacturer, Poltronova)

Figure 4-3. Michelangelo Buonarroti (Italian), *David,* 1501 – 4. Marble, approximately 18 feet high. (Photograph by G. E. Kidder Smith; courtesy Kent C. Bloomer)

spective. As in the case of geometrical illusions, perceptions of size (like perceptions of line length and parallelism) are affected by the visual background.

In real life, however, people hardly ever encounter problems in gauging the actual size of objects. In fact, size/distance scaling is so dependable that most adults can easily and correctly match cards in their hands with cards on a table across a room, even though one image may be thirty-six times wider than another! Children as young as six years of age can accurately estimate the sizes of familiar objects in their natural surroundings. Experiments with infants show that even babies only six to eight weeks old have a grasp of size constancy. While some particular constancy responses obviously depend on experience and learning, the process of extracting invariant information from sensory experience appears to be something the human nervous system does automatically.

When the general context of an object is eliminated, you can easily become confused about its actual size. *Joe Sofa* is a case in point (see figure 4-2). The baseball glove is actually a leather-covered couch. Even with this knowledge, though, it is difficult to imagine just how a person would fit in it. Simply including a doorway, lamp, or other familiar objects would set the viewer more at ease.

Accurate perception of scale and measurement can be of critical importance to scientists. For this reason, scientific photographs of unfamiliar objects, organisms, or artifacts often orient the reader to the actual size by including a ruler or some familiar object such as a coin. By contrast, books on art normally do not show the relative size of an artwork, even though it can be crucial to how we think about it. When we hear that Michelangelo's *David* is about 18 feet tall, we know vaguely that the statue is approximately as high as a two-story house, but abstractly reconciling that knowledge with a photograph of the statue is neither simple nor very satisfying. You can imagine the monumentality of this work much more clearly when you actually observe people dwarfed by *David*'s hugeness (see figure 4-3).

Figure 4-4. Arthur G. Dove (American), *Tree Forms,* 1932. Oil on canvas, $28^{1}/_{16} \times 20^{1}/_{8}$ inches. (The Ackland Art Museum, The University of North Carolina at Chapel Hill, Ackland Fund)

Figure 4-5. Classic advertisement. (Copyright Volkswagen of America, Inc.)

Familiarity

Familiarity with objects and their contexts is another element in size constancy. People give more attention to the size of the retinal image when gauging the size of unfamiliar objects. In his book *The Forest People,* anthropologist Colin M. Turnbull (1962, pp. 252 – 53) describes an African pygmy's first sight of the world beyond the forest:

> Then he saw the buffalo, still grazing lazily several miles away, far down below. He turned to me and said, ''What insects are those?'' At first I hardly understood; then I realized that in the forest the range of vision is so limited that there is no need to make an automatic allowance for distance when judging size. Out here in the plains, however, Kenge was looking for the first time over apparently unending miles of unfamiliar grass-lands, with not a tree worth the name to give him any comparison. The same thing happened later on when I pointed out a boat in the middle of the lake. It was a large fishing boat with a number of people in it but Kenge at first refused to believe this. He thought it was a floating piece of wood.

Likewise, the nineteenth-century German scientist Hermann von Helmholz wrote about his childhood experience of seeing people from high up in a church belfry. He thought they were dolls. In today's world of air travel, most people have had similar experiences. At altitudes of only several hundred feet, buildings and cars look like architects' models or children's toys. This suggests that, at unfamiliar or extreme distances, size constancy breaks down, at which point the viewer experiences an uncharacteristically strong awareness of the smallness of the retinal image.

Size Scaling in Art

In paintings, the manipulation of context is responsible for some interesting effects. Clues that ordinarily would orient us to object size can be removed by the artist in a number of ways: by omitting the

Figure 4-6. René Magritte (Belgian), *Tombeau des lutteurs* [*The Tomb of the Wrestlers*], 1960. Oil, 35 × 46 inches. (Collection of Harry Torczyner, New York, © 1989)

Figure 4-7. Yves Tanguy (French), *The Furniture of Time,* 1939. Oil on canvas, 45³/₄ × 35 inches. (Collection of James Thrall Soby)

usual peripheral surroundings and thus singling out objects almost never seen in isolation; by portraying unfamiliar objects; or by portraying familiar objects in unfamiliar ways. Using these techniques, Pop artists such as James Rosenquist, Roy Lichtenstein, and Andy Warhol gave a kind of ironic monumentality to common, ordinary objects such as soup cans and comic strips. By rendering familiar biological forms apart from their usual settings, the closeup compositions of artists such as Georgia O'Keeffe or Arthur Dove (see figure 4-4) become elegant and sculptural. In contrast, surrounding an object with a lot of space makes it appear small (see figure 4-5).

Another way artists can manipulate size constancy is by creating a context calculated to confuse. The Surrealist painter René Magritte often juxtaposed familiar objects in ways contrary to normal experience (see figure 4-6). Such images play with the audience's mind in much the same way as does the classic unanswerable question "If a tree falls in the forest . . ." Western viewers tend to want to pin these kinds of questions down to a single correct answer, and consequently they often find such ambiguity perplexing. They may engage in fruitless arguments about the "real" image: is it a normal rose in a doll-house, or a giant rose in a normal room? But Magritte used such images purposefully. He was reacting against a tradition in which painting was seen as a representation of the physical world. Any attempt to ascertain this artist's real intention must begin with an acceptance of the image as ambiguous.

Likewise, when an artist presents you with objects or spaces that are totally unfamiliar, you have no means of judging their size. Yves Tanguy's *The Furniture of Time* is such a painting (see figure 4-7). Depth clues represent distance between the objects, but you are given no basis to feel oriented to the scale of the objects or spaces. Are these objects supposed to be human size? microscopic? gigantic? Are they the size of chairs and couches (as a literal interpretation of the title would suggest), or is the title symbolic? This strange scene is thus a world apart from everyday physical experience—another universe, operating according to its own laws; a metaphysical vision of time.

A familiar technique for size scaling is the Renaissance compositional device known as *vanishing-point perspective* drawing—a mathematical system for determining how to size objects in a drawing or painting (see figure 4-8). The vanishing-point formulas are based on the image pattern (or optical array) of the retina. Objects at varying distances are depicted much as a camera would record them.

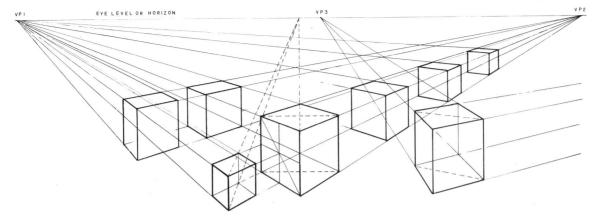

Figure 4-8. Cubes in two-point vanishing-point perspective. (After Ernest W. Watson; drawing by Keith Long)

Figure 4-9. How small is far? (Jane Filer)

Most Westerners have been taught to think that realism in artworks depends upon this type of perspective.

If you take this vanishing-point system to be a correct standard, you find that beginning artists characteristically draw objects too large in relation to one another. This mistake is a natural consequence of size constancy: it represents the normal perception of object size, rather than a perception of the diminished size in the retinal image.

To counteract the influence of size constancy, Western art students have traditionally been taught how to use vanishing points. The size of an object is determined by relating it to a set of converging lines. In figure 4-9a, for example, you can see that the far figure is drawn smaller than the near figure. But not until you study that figure out of context do you realize just how small the image really is (see figure 4-9b). Another way to measure relative image size in the scene being studied is by means of the classic gesture of the artist: pencil at arm's length, one eye closed. Sighting against the pencil, the artist can measure the relative sizes and angles of objects in the visual field.

Most people in the world do not use the retinal image as a model for constructing pictures. In fact, when shown pictures similar to those in figure 4-10, African villagers preferred versions that portrayed size constancy (figure 4-10b) over pictures that were based on the retinal image of distance (figure 4-10a). In Oriental art, too, objects are treated in accordance with size constancy. For example, the Japanese snowscape shown in figure 2-12 uses three distances: near, middle, and far. All objects in the nearer distance—the large houses, trees, and rocks—are uniform in scale, even though they are not meant to seem equidistant from the viewer.

70

a

b

Figure 4-10. Hunter, elephant, and antelope.
(Hudson 1962)

Figure 4-11. Pol de Limbourg (French), *Les Très* Riches
Heures du Duc de Berry, February page, c. 1415. (Bibliothe-
que Nationale, Paris)

Objects in the far distance—the houses at the foot
of the farthest mountains—are also uniform in
scale, even though their positions in the picture
clearly show varying distances between them. The
smallest houses (in the lower right foreground) are
servants' quarters. Their size has nothing to do
with retinal image; it reflects lower social status!

The custom of sizing people in relation to status
can be found in the art of many cultures, including
that of China, Japan, and ancient Egypt. In European medieval art (c. A.D. 476 – 1450), figures of
Mary, Jesus, and various saints are often larger
than those of the less holy persons around them.
Medieval artists were aware of size/distance relationships, but size constancy and symbolic meaning
exerted a stronger influence on their work than did
size relationships in the retinal image (see figure 4-
11).

In the Western tradition, such styles of image-
making are usually not considered realistic. But
Western realism should more accurately be referred to as *visual realism*, since ideas, perceptions, and social relations are more real for human
beings than is an instant frozen in a retina. The retinal image is merely a transient and incomplete
moment in perception. By rights, we should speak
of different representational styles as *perceptual
realism, ideational realism, sociopolitical realism,*
and even *metaphysical realism.* Modifying our
vocabulary in this way acknowledges the realities
portrayed in the art of other cultures and offers
greater insight into the significance of other modes
of visual expression. Equating the retinal image
with reality is a curious chapter in Western history—one that is discussed in chapters 7 and 8.

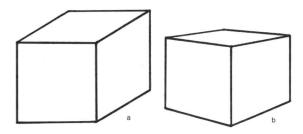

Figure 4-13. Cubes in perspective: (a) oblique perspective; (b) vanishing-point perspective.

Figure 4-12. Giovanni Di Paolo (Italian, 1402/03-1482) *Paradise*, 15th century. Tempera on canvas transferred from wood, 18½ × 16 inches. (The Metropolitan Museum of Art, New York; Rogers Fund, 1906)

So conditioned is the Western mind to reading pictures in terms of vanishing-point perspective that Westerners often suffer reverse illusions. For example, the figures in the upper half of figure 4-12 seem to be larger than the figures in the lower half, even though they are the same size. Likewise, the parallel lines of oblique perspective in figure 4-13a often give the illusion of diverging; whereas the linear perspective cube in figure 4-13b seems more normal, even though it is not consistent with the objective characteristics of a cube, since right angles and parallel sides (except for the vertical edges) are not portrayed.

Other systems for depicting objects take different approaches to size scaling. Parallel perspectives, for example, have the advantage of providing more space in which to draw the details of far objects. With vanishing-point perspective, the same area would be greatly diminished. The pictorial space of parallel perspective can extend itself indefinitely in all directions, while the pictorial space of vanishing-point perspective is finite and eventually vanishes into the vanishing points. For these reasons, scenes in parallel perspective often seem to exhibit a panoramic nature. The Japanese screen shown in figure 3-13, for example, is a scene of city life: a great many different activities are shown in equal detail, and (in keeping with size constancy) the people are all the same size.

If the artist had rendered the same scene in vanishing-point perspective, only some activities could have been shown in detail, because some people, objects, and spaces would have had to be depicted much smaller than others. This being the case, the artist would have needed to develop a hierarchy of importance—a series of judgments as to the relative significance of activities and people, which in turn would determine what should be made large and what might be reduced in size and detail (and therefore in importance). In the final artwork, however, these judgments would appear to be objective and nonjudgmental by virtue of being rendered in the visual language of the retinal image. John Trumbull's *Declaration of Independence* (see figure 4-14) is just such a constructed composition: it is based on a hierarchy of importance, yet it appears neutral and journalistic.

Even in the West, parallel perspectives are preferred for certain kinds of applications. In technical drawing, for example, these perspectives allow actual proportions and ratios to be used, thus preserving size constancy. Parallel perspective is also used in working drawings for manufacture, construction, and engineering, as well as in instructional diagrams that show consumers how to assemble toys, furniture, and other products.

Some research suggests that artists exhibit less size constancy than do other people, which would

Figure 4-14. John Trumbull (American), *The Declaration of Independence,* 1818. Oil on canvas, 144 × 216 inches. (Architect of the Capitol, Washington, D.C.)

signify an ability to break away from ordinary habits of seeing. Along these lines, a story (which may or may not be true) is told about Pablo Picasso:

Picasso had painted a portrait of a man's wife. Upon seeing it, the man complained that the painting did not look like her.

"Well, in that case," Picasso asked, "what does she look like?"

The man pulled out his wallet and removed a color photograph of his wife, thrusting it in front of the artist's eyes.

"This. This is what she looks like."

Picasso examined the photograph carefully.

"Just like this?" he asked.

"Exactly like the picture," the man nodded.

"You're absolutely sure?" Picasso persisted.

"Of course!" the man replied impatiently. "It's an exact likeness!"

Handing back the picture, Picasso commented, "Awfully small, isn't she?"

Children's art often shows a high degree of size constancy. An extreme example is the child who was given a piece of clay and instructed to make an elephant. With shocked dismay she protested "But there's not enough clay here to make an elephant!" In their drawings, children do not generally change an object's size as a way of showing distance. This is not because children cannot perceive size/distance relationships; in fact, in some circumstances children can judge distance and projected sizes even more accurately than can adults. But instead of adopting a single cameralike (view-centered or view-specific) approach, children usually apply object-centered drawing strategies. They concentrate on representing characteristics of the objects

Figure 4-15. Three projections of a drawing board.

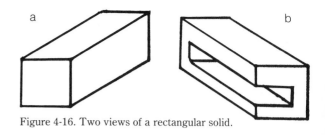

Figure 4-16. Two views of a rectangular solid.

they are drawing, rather than on depicting their appearance from a single viewpoint. Because of this, it is commonly thought that children do not intend to show depth in their drawings.

Experiments, however, have shown that even young children are usually quite systematic in depicting spatial relationships among objects—for example, inside/outside, or in front/behind. Their approach (object-centered or array-centered) to making pictures emphasizes the way objects relate to one another in actual space, rather than the way they appear in the retina of a single eye.

Object-centered approaches to picture making cannot simply be dismissed as immature because they may be associated with children. Among the world's peoples and cultures, the retinal or view-centered approach is extremely rare, and in fact it has been used only for a few hundred years in the Western European tradition. It is thus a convention of Western cultural history—not a universal or natural intention in human picture making.

Other Factors Affecting Size Perception

In the case of size perception, the mind reinterprets or corrects the immediate retinal information to conform to already established constancies. You then perceive the corrected interpretation, rather than the direct sensation that triggered it. When perception is removed in this way from direct sense information, it becomes increasingly vulnerable to further modification by other factors.

One such influence is the emotional value of the stimulus. In a classic study by Jerome Bruner and Leo Postman, children from poor homes and children from rich homes were shown coins and asked to estimate their size. A control group was asked to estimate the size of gray disks. The children who were shown the gray disks made the most accurate size estimates. All the children who were shown the coins overestimated their size—the rich children to a slight extent, and the poor children to a

great extent. This is probably consistent with your own experience. If you are very hungry, a large serving of food may not look like enough (your eyes are bigger than your stomach!). Something unexpected or threatening may appear to be larger than it is ("the wall suddenly loomed in front of me"). And the fish that got away always seems to have been especially large!

Viewpoint is another mediating influence. Objects seen from below tend to be perceived as larger than they really are, whereas objects seen from above seem smaller than they really are. This percept, too, reflects experience: normally you look up at things higher or larger than yourself, and you look down on things smaller than you are. Looking up at things is reminiscent of childhood vision and may suggest feelings of helplessness and dependency. Photographers and filmmakers take advantage of these associated feelings by placing cameras at high or low angles in order to distort apparent size and stimulate the desired emotions. Sometimes the effects are so subtle as to affect us subliminally, as when the camera in a television soap opera consistently looks up to male characters and down on female characters.

FORM CONSTANCY

Up to now we have discussed constancy in relation to perceptions of size. But the principle of constancy governs other aspects of perception as well. In the retinal image, not only do the sizes of objects change; their shapes change! A rectangular tabletop, for instance, projects onto the retina as a trapezoid. Circular objects such as plates and glasses register as ellipses.

The shape of an object as registered on the retina depends on the position of the observer. A drawing board, for example, is a rectangle when seen from the top, an extremely thin rectangle when seen from the side, and a trapezoid when seen from slightly above or below its surface (see figure 4-15). These various views are called *projections* of the object. The outside contours of an object's projection correspond to a silhouette of the object as made from a particular vantage point. An infinite number of such silhouettes can be projected for any given object. Some of these projected views are easier to recognize than others.

Your mental models of whole objects are constructed from your experiences with many objects seen from many viewpoints and in many situations. Eventually, only a partial view of an object is necessary to trigger perception of the whole object. Perception of the partial view thus becomes equivalent to perception of the whole, and our minds simply fill in what our eyes do not see. Your perceptions of objects in the physical world depend on this ability to substitute parts for wholes, because you can never see all of anything at once in a three-dimensional world. At any given moment, something is always hidden from view. The object as seen, then, plays only a small part in how you perceive it. The overall perception is created at higher levels of organization.

At the same time, the mind tunes out characteristics not relevant to the mental model, and in this way it corrects the stimulus to fit a perceptual expectancy (see chapter 3). When you see a door, for example, you expect it to open onto a closet, a room, or the outdoors. If you open it and find a blank wall, you are likely to be startled. Similarly, when you look at figure 4-16a, you probably do not suppose that its back side looks like figure 4-16b. After seeing it, though, you understand that such an appearance is possible. Once again, perception can be characterized as a process of gambling on probabilities, not possibilities.

Look at figure 4-17a. You probably see a cube— not a flat pattern composed of the three shapes shown in figure 4-17b. As a matter of fact, you will find it quite difficult to perceive figure 4-17a as a flat pattern, even though it provides outlines for only three sides of the cube you imagine you see. Your mind completes or fills in the unseen parts to fit your preexisting mental model of a total cube. Similarly, in figure 4-17c, you perceive two overlapping squares, and not an oddity such as the item shown in figure 4-17d. In fact, however, your eyes are registering one square and one L-shaped form (see figure 4-17e). Again, in order to perceive a square,

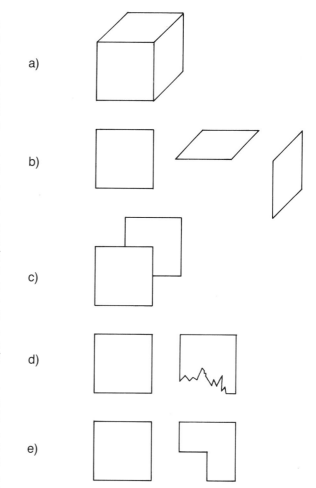

a)

b)

c)

d)

e)

Figure 4-17. Perceiving versus seeing.

you make assumptions about invisible elements. Using the familiar strategies of filling in and correcting, the mind hangs onto ideas about the forms of objects, even though the retinal projection of the object is apt to be quite changeable.

Form constancy, then, is a system of assumptions made about whole objects on the basis of simplest and most probable forms. Tuning out all but the simplest probabilities is infinitely practical for everyday perception. Imagine the problem of having to calculate all the possibilities for everything you see! The tendency to perceive wholes from parts, however, also makes it easy for people to be manipulated by such things as films and advertisements. A movie set of the main street in an Old

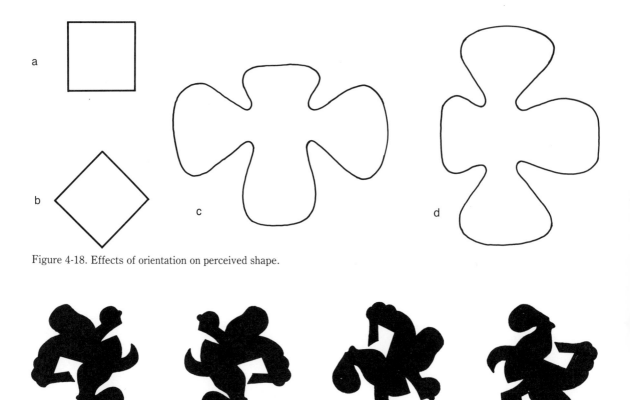

Figure 4-18. Effects of orientation on perceived shape.

Figure 4-19. The same shape in four orientations: reference position, mirror-image, turned 90 degrees to right, inverted.

West town may be nothing more than a structure of flat store-fronts. A fashion model's dress may actually be pinned and taped together in the back to give the illusion of stylish lines, and the skirt may be held out by a thin wire to give the impression of being blown by the wind. In spite of the fact that human beings are continually exposed to such trickery and illusionism, they remain amazingly gullible.

Orientation

An interesting aspect of form constancy is that changes in the orientation of a shape will change your perception of it. When dealing with shapes, your perceptual system assigns coordinates of top, bottom, and sides. When the orientation of these coordinates changes, even very familiar shapes can become problematic. Upside-down photographs of faces are difficult to recognize and often seem grotesque, as though depicting strange beings with mouths in their foreheads. Printed words and hand-

writing, when presented upside-down, can be deciphered only slowly and with difficulty. Orientation can determine whether you see a square or a diamond in two identical shapes (see figure 4-18), and it affects the perception of unfamiliar shapes as well. Figures 4-18c and 4-18d, for example, are identical figures with a 90-degree difference in orientation, yet they look different.

The first explanation that comes to mind involves relating the orientation of the image to the retina. But perceptions of shape remain constant even when the viewer's head is tilted. Hence, the mind appears to take into account changes in eye, head, or body position. For organisms that move about, perceptions of the visual world must remain accurate despite movements of body and sense organs. Thus, top and bottom are perceived in relation to the visual environment of the shape; and when you tilt your head, the shape continues to have the same relationship to its surroundings. When top/

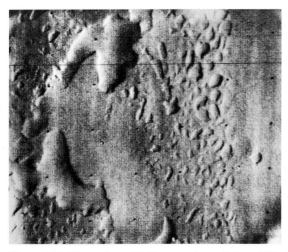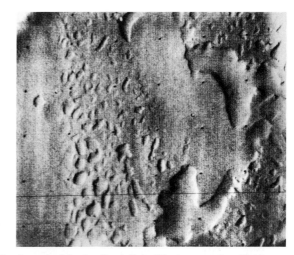

Figure 4-20. These pits and hollows are located about 500 miles from the Martian South Pole. The large enclosed basins are about 10 miles across; the smaller pits are 1 – 2 miles in diameter. The photograph was taken (c. 1975) from a distance of 2072 miles by Mariner 9's high-resolution TV camera. The photograph on the left is oriented correctly. (NASA Jet Propulsion Laboratory, California Institute of Technology, Pasadena)

bottom orientation is changed, shape perception is more affected than with a simple flip-flop from left to right—a mirror image (see figure 4-19).

The perception of symmetry has been found to occur spontaneously only when a shape is symmetrical about a vertical axis. This importance of the vertical axis in perception seems to be a biological adaptation. All land animals, humans included, have physiological systems that orient them to sky above, earth below. This orientation to sky/earth affects our perception of light and shadow: the default assumption is that light comes from above. Thus, hollows become bumps when a photograph is turned upside down (see figure 4-20), and faces look weird when light comes from below (see figure 4-21).

Drawing teachers sometimes ask students to copy upside-down drawings. When viewed upside-down, a drawing looks unfamiliar and is more easily seen as simply a pattern of lines and light/dark areas. Observations both in the laboratory and in art classrooms clearly indicate that people draw much more accurately when copying abstract or meaningless lines than when copying lines that they perceive as representing something. Teacher/writer Betty Edwards has incorporated upside-down approaches into a whole system for learning drawing and developing creative thinking. According to Edwards (1979, 1986), upside-down orientation stimulates right brain modalities of thinking and seeing. Some artists are in the habit of turning their

Figure 4-21. A portrait using lighting from below. (Carolyn M. Bloomer)

Figure 4-22. Oddities in visual realism: (Left) a two-legged horse, copied from a Greek vase. (Arnheim, 1974); (right) a three-legged cow. (Carolyn M. Bloomer)

drawings or paintings upside-down to check the composition. If the composition is balanced, it will appear equally (though differently) balanced when the image is inverted.

The role of learning in orientation constancy is unclear. Children under the age of six sometimes appear indifferent to orientation; they often read books upside-down. Five-year-olds may not be able to distinguish between a shape and its mirror image, even when the difference is pointed out to them. But when they are between five and seven years of age, children become increasingly sensitive to spatial orientation; the baseline appears in their drawings, and Western children are taught to read. Even at age eleven, however, children can still read a text turned at a 90-degree angle more easily than adults can.

Some cross-cultural observations suggest that image orientation is less important in some cultures that do not have a written language. Eskimo artists, for example, often carve figures without orienting them to the upright. It has also been reported that Eskimos can read as well upside-down as right-side-up. Reading requires habituation to the orientation of shapes relative to each other: the only means of distinguishing among some letters (such

as the letters *p*, *q*, *b*, and *d*) is by reference to their orientation. Letters and words must also be read in sequence in one direction: WARTS and STRAW are not interchangeable. Some symptoms of the reading disorder called *dyslexia* involve problems with form constancy and orientation of letters and words.

Form Constancy in Art

Some degree of form constancy is essential in all art imagery, because it gives viewers some basic information about what they are looking at. But form constancy can be handled in many different ways. Western tradition uses the projected shapes of objects, imitating their appearance to the eye as seen from a single fixed viewpoint in space. This view-centered approach (as the camera sees) requires distorting and correcting objects as experienced in the physical world. For example, the square sides of a cube must be distorted into trapezoids or parallelograms, and circular forms must be depicted as elliptical.

Showing only what the eye sees requires omitting parts of objects. When taken to an extreme, this approach can produce strange images such as the two-legged horse and the three-legged cow shown in figure 4-22. Even though this image follows the rules, it looks weird! Nonetheless, it suggests why people in other cultures might deem the Western style of realism to be strange. Even though two-legged horses are visually realistic, most Western artists shun them. Instead, artists normally manipulate their compositions in order to avoid such extremes.

More common in world art is a conceptual approach in which objects are represented by core characteristics felt by the culture to be essential to the identity of the object. For example, the tradition among Native Americans of the Northwest Coast is to depict a whole animal in a single image (see figure 4-23). The style is called *split representation*, because the image resembles an animal skin that has been split at the backbone and flattened out. Although different animal images depicted in this manner often look similar to outsiders, each one can be identified by a specific set of core features. Similar artistic styles have been found among peoples living in Siberia and New Zealand.

Ancient Egyptians anticipated that the images they carved and painted on the walls of the Pharaohs' tombs would come to life in the Pharaoh's afterlife (see figure 4-24). Every image, therefore, had to be complete and accurate. Thus Egyptian images—particularly of people—were drawn according to strict rules. Body proportions were specified, and every figure was equipped with two legs and two arms: it would not do for the Pharaoh to end up with a one-armed or one-legged servant. (One eye, however, was acceptable, since the hidden eye looked into the spirit world and therefore did not have to be shown.) The characteristic Egyptian formula for drawing the human figure is often referred to as a *canon of human representation*. The term *canon* implies a fixed, official character. Indeed, the Egyptian canon was followed there for 3,000 years. (During the brief reigns of Akhenaton and Tutankhamen, a more flexible naturalism in style was encouraged. After the death of these monotheistic pharaohs, however, Egyptian art and religion quickly returned to their ancient traditions.) The art of Aztec-Mixtec-Zapotec peoples of MesoAmerica similarly emphasized core features.

Each culture develops conventions to represent the aspects of reality that it most values. An artwork, then, can be seen as a visible cultural language in which certain visual signals transmit meanings related to whole sets of specific beliefs.

Figure 4-23. Anonymous (Tsimshian, British Columbia), *Bear,* 19th century. (Franz Boas, 1897)

In order to experience the intended closure, viewers need to do more than simply perceive the image; they must be able to read the symbolic language. Like spoken languages, though, visual languages are complex and multilayered, and they can vary significantly from culture to culture and from generation to generation.

Although many modern artists have been accused of not showing things as they are, works by artists such as Paul Cézanne, Henri Matisse (see figure 4-25), and the Cubists reflect a normal visual response to form constancy—one that psychologists have termed *regression to the real object*. In perception experiments, subjects were shown certain objects tilted in space and then asked to draw the shape they saw (that is, the shape projected onto the retina). Subjects tended to interpret the retinal shape as more closely resembling the physical shape of the object than it actually did. For example, a plate seen sideways would be drawn in a more rounded shape than was actually observed in the retinal image. These experiments show that,

Figure 4-24. Anonymous (Egyptian), *The Sculptor Apuy and His Wife Receiving Offerings From Their Children*, New Kingdom, (1320 – 1200 B.C.). Tempera copy of a wall painting. (The Metropolitan Museum of Art, New York)

even when we pay careful attention, our retinal patterns are experienced as being closer to our mental models of objects than they actually are. Thus, like size constancy, form constancy often makes it difficult for beginning or amateur painters to achieve a desired form of perspective.

Children's drawings show a high degree of form constancy. Children usually draw objects in their most recognizable orientation. Thus, people will be shown from the front, a car from the side, and a cup with a handle. In this way, children create forms that include the core features most essential to the identity of the object. This has been called *canonical representation*, and it is another aspect of the object-centered approach to drawing.

COLOR CONSTANCY

A blue wall looks blue in spite of a pattern of dappled sun and shadow. A lump of coal looks black and a piece of chalk white, regardless of whether they are seen in light or shadow. When you put on tinted glasses, you still see things as being their normal color. Such experiences demonstrate the existence of *color constancy*—stable perceptions of object colors, despite changes in the retinal image. Your perception of color is influenced to a great extent by context and by experience; in many cases, you effectively disregard retinal information.

Color constancy depends to some extent on familiarity with objects. When you try to ascertain the color of some object for which you have no memory or association—say, a piece of paper of unknown color—the perception of color results from the total contextual pattern of brightness, illumination, and shadow. When they view objects in a concealed context, where shadows cannot be seen, experimental subjects find color perception difficult and they are often fooled. For example, a greenish brown color was identified as green when presented in the shape of a leaf, and as brown when presented in the shape of a donkey. People sometimes perceive nonexistent colors when looking at familiar objects or images. Indeed, human perception takes the normal color of objects so much for granted that you may have been surprised to read in chapter 2 that the rods (used in night vision) do not register color at all. Unless some stronger illumination activates the cones, night vision exists only in shades of gray.

Color constancy appears to be highly dependent on whole-context information. A whole-context view gives information about illumination and about the relative reflectance of objects in the visual field. When laboratory subjects are shown color stimuli in isolation—that is, when they are denied perceptual information about illumination, surface slant, and object identity—they often make mistakes in identifying and matching colors. For example, subjects

Figure 4-25. Henri Matisse (French), *The Red Studio,* 1911. Oil on canvas, 71¼ × 86¼ inches. (The Museum of Modern Art, New York; Mrs. Simon Guggenheim Fund)

can correctly identify the walls of a room as being of the same color, even though the wall surfaces reflect varying amounts of light and shadow. When visual information about the structure of the room (where walls meet ceiling and floor) is removed, however, the walls are seen as equidistant colored planes that have profound differences in color.

Thus, color constancy depends on the viewer's being able to see both the object and its surroundings: on perceiving relationships within a total context. While the physically measurable color of an object may vary from situation to situation, it maintains a constant ratio of reflectance to other objects and surfaces within the scene. This is why you can adjust your perception so quickly to accommodate pink light bulbs, tinted glasses, or slides shown on a colored wall. The next time you encounter a display of color television sets, for example, pay attention to the differences in color from one set to another. Then choose one set to concentrate on. Notice how quickly the color seems to normalize. Paintings sometimes seem to have more fidelity to a scene than color photographs do. This is because artists are sensitive to the overall effect of the color rela-

tionships, whereas color film cannot make such human judgments.

Color Constancy in Art

In art, color constancy is often referred to as *object color*. Beginning art students tend to choose color on the basis of object color (use green for grass; use blue for water; add white for light; add black for shadow). The result is usually unconvincing and discordant, even though each choice by itself is not wrong. Color is like an orchestra: each instrument may be playing the right melody, but unless all the instruments are tuned to some common tone, the result will be dissonance. In order to ensure harmony, professional artists and "old masters" usually use a limited palette of six to eight colors and mix all intermediate hues.

It should come as no surprise that color constancy creates problems for art students. For most of them (as for most of us), object color has been continually reinforced through coloring books, school ditto sheets, and adult responses: "Color the tree green. Color the sky blue. Make the car red. Oh, no! Leaves aren't purple!" (see figure 4-

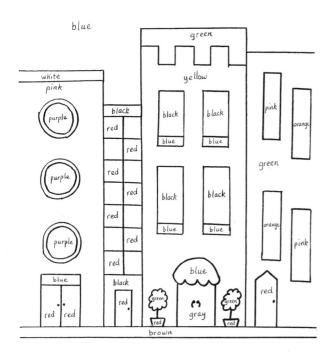

blue

green

white
pink

yellow

purple

black
red
red

black
red
red
red
red

blue

red red

black

black

black
blue

blue

black

red
red

blue

black
red

green
red

blue

gray
red

green
red

brown

pink

orange

green

orange

pink

red

gray

Figure 4-26. Color-in ditto sheet used in a New York City private school. (Courtesy of Nancy Cline)

26). While such strategies do teach children the culturally accepted object color, they discourage sensitivity to the rich color effects present in the environment, and they prevent the enjoyment of color as it registers on the retina.

You can experience more accurate color perception by looking at surfaces and shadows through a narrow tube or through a hole in the center of a blank card. This allows you to isolate colors from their surroundings and from the boundaries of objects. Artists who wish to paint the natural appearances of things must painstakingly train themselves to see colors in this way. The nineteenth-century Impressionist painters attempted to paint with just such an innocent eye—to render colors, shadows, and reflections as they register on the retina, rather than in obedience to traditional object color (see plate C-1). The studied effort of these artists to free themselves of color constancy resulted in brilliant images that are among the most popular artworks in today's museums.

OTHER CONSTANCIES

Perceptual constancy may be seen as the general process of extracting from your experience with the physical world the dimensions that are invariant or unchanging. Such constancies become a part of your preprogramming—your perceptual expectancies. Constancy operates, then, to normalize your immediate visual stimuli so as to make them consistent with your mental models. The mind persistently prefers closures that support the experience of consistency in the physical world. The phenomenon of constancy makes it possible for people to experience coherence and order in their environment, and it gives people a basis for trusting their sensory information. Seen in this way, size, form, and color represent only three of a number of possible constancies.

Object Constancy

Sometimes called *object permanence* or *existence constancy*, object constancy serves to assure people that physical objects have a relatively permanent existence. In accordance with this principle, you assume that objects still exist, even when you are not looking at them or for other reasons cannot see them. Researchers have been interested in whether object constancy is innate or learned. The child psychologist Jean Piaget conducted extensive observations of when infants would search for an object that he hid. He concluded that constancy was part of a biological timetable for cognitive growth, but that it could not develop unless the infant was permitted adequate opportunities for actively exploring his or her environment (see chapter 1).

Piaget's results, however, have been interpreted by some analysts as effects of attention and/or motivation. Later experiments by T.G.R. Bower (cited in Rock) have demonstrated some degree of object constancy in infants as young as 20 days old. Such infants evidenced surprise (as defined by accelerated heart rate) when a screen covered an object and the object was not there when the screen was moved away. Their attention span was limited, however: they did not show surprise when more than fifteen seconds had elapsed between covering and removal of the screen. Older infants (98 to 126 days old) were surprised by changes in the object's color or shape, as well as by its absence.

Whether or not object constancy obtains seems

to be determined by particular kinds of conditions. For example, if an object or image gradually disappears (as when something moves in front of it), the observer tends to infer that the object is still present behind the mask. If an object's image suddenly disappears, the viewer's impression is more likely to be that it has vanished and is no longer present. This response was found true for both infants and adults.

Constancies of Position and Direction

Another aspect of object constancy is constancy of position. When you move around in space, or when you move your eyes or head, the visual field moves across the retina (a phenomenon termed *image displacement*). Even so, the stationary things in your environment do not appear to move. This *position constancy* appears to result from a system of feedback in which body, eye, and head movements are taken into account in processing perceptual information. Likewise, you perceive where you are in relation to things (through direction constancy or egocentric localization) because the brain includes eye/head and body direction when interpreting the retinal image. Such constancies are essential for the survival of species that depend on movement.

Motion Constancy

When objects in your visual field move, their images move or displace across the retina. The images of moving objects that are farther from you displace more slowly than do the images of moving objects that are nearer to you. Yet (unless the movement takes place extremely far away), you can accurately perceive relative speed. This is called *constancy of perceived velocity*. Speed constancy appears to depend partly on size constancy and partly on the rate of image displacement relative to a frame of reference. These aspects of motion perception are further discussed in chapter 9.

Practically speaking, constancy is an efficient strategy that keeps us from having to pay attention to objects and situations as if we were seeing them for the first time. It allows us to keep some stimuli in the background so that we can concentrate on others. Observations of very young infants in various species suggest that the tendency toward constancy is a physiological aspect of the human nervous system. Learning and experience, however, are essential for the normal development of constancy.

By dealing automatically with recurring situations, constancies eliminate the need for constant evaluation and decision-making. They enable people to perceive the world as orderly and stable. At the same time, however, constancies require people to tune out some of the variety inherent in perceptual experience: they habituate people not to pay attention to some visual information. But notwithstanding its drawbacks, constancy allows human beings to operate with security and an optimistic confidence about the stability of things in a constantly changing visual world.

5
Color
It's All Relative

When you stop to think about it, the distinction between black-and-white and color is a very odd division in your visual experience. As you know from photographs, movies, and television, color can be completely absent from most images without affecting your perceptions of meaning. On the other hand, the market for black-and-white home-movie film or videotape is virtually nonexistent: for most people color is a profoundly important dimension of personal experience.

Our language patterns reveal an emotionally charged relationship to color:

My neighbor was green with envy.
The clerk turned red as a beet.
The child looked white as a sheet.
The sergeant suspected the new recruit was yellow.
After the breakup, I was really blue.

Color evokes moods, expresses feelings, and even affects your physical sense of well-being. Imagine cooking in a bright red kitchen on a sweltering summer day, sleeping and waking in a vivid orange room, or sitting in a classroom with black walls. Evidence has been found that human responses to color are to some extent physiological. Exposure to red, for instance, has been found to arouse a person's autonomic nervous system—to speed up heart, respiration, and eyeblink rates; to raise blood pressure; and to affect brainwaves. Blue, on the other hand, is soothing and helps reduce blood pressure and rates of breathing and eye-blinking.

Restaurants use red decors to stimulate patrons to be expansive and outgoing. In schools and libraries, soft warm wall colors (such as peach and tan) are said to encourage intellectual activity. Soft, cool colors (such as green and aqua) have been found to foster body movement in settings such as gymnasiums. For a long time, institutions such as factories, schools, hospitals, and public office buildings were decorated with conventional toned-down, bland wall colors—apparently in an effort to create a color-neutral environment that would not offend anyone. Studies found, however, that these institutional colors tended to depress people who spent long periods of time surrounded by them. Experiments have shown that more lively wall colors lift the morale of both workers and patients and reduce absenteeism.

While several colors appear to affect most people in generally consistent ways, some responses to color can be quite personal or can be socially influenced. Color has also been important in some theories of healing and metaphysics.

WHAT IS COLOR?

In physics and optics, colors are defined as component parts of light—the portion of the electromagnetic continuum to which our eyes are sensitive (see figure 2-1). We perceive differences in light frequencies just as we perceive differences in sound frequencies. Different frequencies of sound are experienced as differences in pitch, while different frequencies of light are experienced as differences in color. The color range that humans perceive extends from red (the longest visible wavelength, at about 350 billion to 400 billion cycles per second) to violet (the shortest visible wavelength, at about 770 billion cycles per second). The difference in wavelength between the longest and the shortest visible wavelengths is only 0.000012 inch. Writers do not agree on how many distinct hues human beings can identify within this range; estimates range from 200 to 1 million.

Color vision is due to specialized cone cells of the type possessed by birds, fish, and some mammals, including all the higher primates. Different species are sensitive to different light frequencies and thus inhabit different visual worlds. The color vision of bees, for example, includes short ultraviolet wavelengths that are invisible to people, but not the longer red wavelengths that people see. Deer do not see red either. Hence, the red or orange of a hunter's jacket has no special color for the local deer and bees, but will alert nearby birds, fish, apes, monkeys, and people. Particular flower colors appear to help plants survive: different flower colors attract different pollinators—for example, hummingbirds, moths, or bees.

Because of color vision, human beings see many more differences between things under a wider range of lighting conditions than would be possible if they saw only in shades of gray (a condition known as *monochromatic vision*). A dog, by contrast, can spot a rabbit only if it moves; lacking color vision, the dog is unable to differentiate certain figures (rabbits) from similarly textured and patterned grounds (grass). Hence, camouflage combined with a freeze reflex renders prey virtually invisible to color-blind predators.

In the evolution of diurnal (day-active) species, color vision conferred a survival advantage by sensitizing the organism to special information about the nature of objects and substances. For example, with color vision, certain ripe fruits and vegetables can be spotted from a distance. This may have been particularly important for the survival of human beings and other primates. Unlike almost all other species, human beings lack the ability to manufacture vitamin C within their own bodies; instead, it must be obtained from the diet. Human color vision is most sensitive to differences in midlength frequencies—the greens. This sensitivity to subtle differences in green colorations provided enhanced visual discrimination in the arboreal and savannah environments of our genetic predecessors.

The Spectrum

When a beam of light is spread out (or diffracted) as it passes through a prism, its various component frequencies are visible to the eye as a continuum of colors called the *spectrum*. After a rain, droplets of moisture suspended in the air act as diffractors, and through them you see a rainbow. The spectrum can be divided in various ways. In the fifteenth century, Leonardo da Vinci identified four primary colors: red, yellow, green, and blue, which are the spectral colors we see most easily in rainbows and prisms. These are sometimes called the *psychological primaries*, because their significance is based on how color is perceived rather than on the physical characteristics of light.

In 1666, Sir Isaac Newton named seven spectral zones: red, orange, yellow, green, blue, indigo, and violet, each having a different measurable wavelength. For Newton, these seven colors resonated with the seven musical notes of the diatonic scale (C was red, D orange, E yellow, and so on) and with the seven heavenly spheres (the known planets of Mercury through Saturn, plus the Sun and the Moon, but excluding Earth). Newton's color divisions are still taught to every Western schoolchild, although they do not represent the only way in which the spectrum can be analyzed.

Although the colors of the spectrum are all constituents of natural sunlight, the relative proportions of the colors in sunlight are quite variable. Standard white light exists only at midday, when colors are seen at their truest and shadows are black. In early morning and late afternoon, when the sun is low, blue frequencies are filtered out by the air, and the light is more reddish or yellowish—warm and glowing—while shadows are distinctly blue. At dawn and dusk, colors are muted and seem nearer to shades of gray, and objects do not cast shadows. In a forest, sunlight is noticeably green. Artists traditionally prefer to work in a studio that receives indirect northern light, in order to avoid the continual color variations that occur in direct sunlight throughout the day.

In everyday life, we are usually unaware (except momentarily) of these color differences in the surrounding (ambient) light. Color constancy corrects our perceptions so that you can disregard variations in light. If you responded to wavelengths themselves (instead of to their relationships to one another), you would perceive the same object as being a different color in every different lighting situation. Color vision would then become a source of constant confusion. The presence of color constancy tells you that color perception does not depend on wavelengths alone.

Because color film does not make the corrections of color constancy, differences in ambient light can cause colors to appear distorted in photographs. Since films respond to absolute frequencies of light, film types must be balanced for particular lighting conditions. Using daylight film under fluorescent light will produce images in which people appear to be a sickly green, and using it under incandescent light will bathe subjects in a golden Rembrandt glow. Both problems can be corrected by the use of appropriate filters. (For incandescent light and daylight film, the photographer should either use an 80A filter or use Tungsten film. (Tungsten film can be used in daylight with an 85B filter.) For fluorescent light, the photographer should either use an FL filter or use a combination of pale magenta and pale blue filters.) Since filters subtract part of the light, the resulting exposure time must be increased accordingly.

Light affects human biological functioning. Full-spectrum light entering the eyes affects the pituitary and pineal glands (and perhaps other parts of the midbrain as well). These glands govern body rhythms and some hormone production. The body's quantity of red blood cells decreases in darkness but increases in light. Three-month-long nights in latitudes above the Arctic Circle are associated with declines in fertility. Carefully scheduled doses of intense, full-spectrum light are used to reset the body clocks of travelers, so as to avoid the prolonged effects of jet lag.

Artificial Light. Because human beings evolved in an environment of full-spectrum sunlight, some people are concerned about the effects on people of prolonged exposure to reduced-spectrum, artificial light. The disruptive effects of artificial light on plant growth and fertility have been well-documented and are familiar to any plant hobbyist. Most forms of artificial light do not contain all the wavelengths found in natural sunlight; hence, they are termed *reduced-spectrum*. Incandescent lights have more orange, red, and infrared frequencies than does natural sunlight, but they are deficient in the violet end of the spectrum. Fluorescent lights, on the other hand, have more green frequencies than does sunlight. Consequently, colors seen under artificial forms of light (especially fluorescents) may at first appear noticeably different from how they look when seen in natural sunlight. Narrow-band fluorescent lighting has been linked to hyperactivity

and learning problems in children, and to problems of headache, eyestrain, fatigue, inability to concentrate, and skin eruptions in office workers. In response to such concerns, several companies now market "full-spectrum" fluorescent tubes.

In special situations, reduced-spectrum light may have beneficial effects. In jaundiced newborns (such as one who has an Rh-negative mother), exposure to artificial blue light for eight-hour periods over several days can help correct the condition and eliminate the need for blood transfusions. Short exposures of human skin to ultraviolet light promote calcium metabolism, but overexposure (as for tanning) can lead to skin cancer. Evidence of the idea that limited-spectrum (colored) light affects the body can be found from cultures as remote as that of ancient Egypt, which established temples of healing light; and it appears in writings from classical Greece at the time of Pythagoras (about 500 B.C.). The potential healing properties of colored light still interest both medical professionals and laypeople.

Reflected Color

Most objects are not sources of light; instead, they reflect light. Pigment molecules in their surfaces capture some photons from the light waves and cause the others to rebound back into space; that is, the surface absorbs (subtracts out) some wavelengths from the total light and reflects the unabsorbed wavelengths (see figure 5-1). For example, green leaves reflect the green portion of the light wave. When this reflected light enters the eyes, it is experienced as the color of an object.

This principle of *selective absorption* has some interesting consequences. If an object or surface is illuminated by light that lacks the frequencies it would ordinarily reflect (as in the case of a green leaf lit with red light), no light will be reflected, and the object will appear gray or black. Hence, changing the color of an illuminating light changes the color of the object seen. This being the case, imagine a picture or some stage scenery painted in such a way that entirely different compositions or color schemes are seen when the spotlight color changes. The same effects can be produced by viewing the picture or scenery through variously colored cellophane spectacles (although the effect may diminish as the mind adapts).

Pigment molecules absorb more frequencies from the light wave than they reflect; hence, object color always reduces the amount of reflected light that can reach the eyes. In the reflected color of opaque pictures (such as paintings and photographs), the reflectance of the brightest color (white) is usually about ten times the reflectance of the dimmest area (black)—thus producing a dynamic range of 10:1. By contrast, when colors are transmitted directly by light (as through stained-glass windows, slide transparencies, or video screens) only a small fraction of the light wave is subtracted out to create the color, and a much greater proportion of the total light from the light source reaches the eyes. Here the dynamic range is well over 100:1. Hence, opaque colors, by their very nature, can never achieve the vibrancy of color transmitted through light. In their continuing efforts to increase the reflectance of opaque painted color, artists have adopted a number of strategies such as underpainting techniques, glazing, and the use of light-reflecting vehicles (including oil and polymers).

In dim light, fewer light rays are present, so again an object has less color. At the other extreme, strong light may carry more rays than the pigment molecules can absorb. The unabsorbed light then reflects off the surface, creating full-spectrum (white) highlights. For this reason, colors may appear washed out in very strong light. To portray highlights in his landscapes, the English artist John Constable used patches of white paint; people called them ''Constable's snow.'' Unabsorbed light reflects as heat. Hence, white clothing reflects away heat from sunlight, while dark clothing absorbs it.

In reality, however, the situation is not quite as neat as the foregoing discussion suggests. In most cases, the light reflected by an object includes not only its main color, but some rays of adjacent hues as well (since substances that reflect only a single wavelength are rare). Hence, most colors are actually mixtures of wavelengths. Furthermore, available light rarely comes directly from a single source; instead, the ambient light is composed of rays that are reflected, deflected, and diffused. When the light rays from objects and shadows reach the eyes, they include unabsorbed light reflected from the surrounding surfaces.

Because they think of shadows as being produced by an uncomplicated absence of light, beginning art students often color them black or gray. But shadow color is created by complex interac-

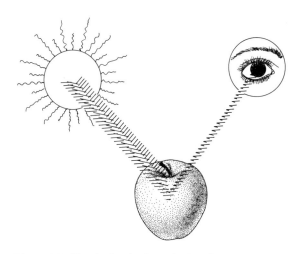

Figure 5-1. Absorbed and reflected color. (Eleanor Holland)

tions among the predominant and complementary colors of the illumination, the light reflected by the object's pigment, and subtle reflections of color from nearby objects. As was noted in chapter 4 (in the context of color constancy), looking at surfaces and shadows through a narrow tube or through a hole in the center of a blank card enables the viewer to isolate a colored area from its surroundings and from the boundaries of objects. Impressionist paintings often make use of the resulting appreciation of the complexity and uniqueness of light and shadow (see plate C-1).

Subtractive Color

As is the case with objects, paint color is determined by the wavelengths of the portion of the light ray that remains after the rest has been subtracted out. Hence, pigment mixing (as in the case of paints or dyes), is referred to as a *subtractive* process—color being the remainder. Magenta, yellow, and cyan (a turquoise blue) are subtractive primaries—colors that cannot be produced by mixing other colors. In grade school, students are (somewhat inaccurately) taught these as red, yellow, and blue. Pairs of primaries are used to mix the secondary colors: orange, green, and violet.

A balanced mixture of all three primaries (theoretically) produces black, since the resulting mix of pigment molecules should absorb (or subtract out) all the frequencies of visible light, leaving none to be reflected (see figure 5-2a). In this system, black,

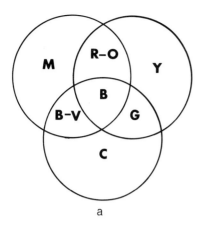 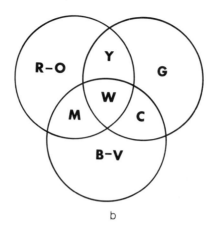

Figure 5-2. Primary and secondary colors: (a) pigments (subtractive process); (b) light (additive process).

white, and gray are called *achromatic* or *neutral colors* because their appearance results from the amount of light that is reflected, rather than from its wavelength. Theoretically, white should reflect 100 percent of the light falling on it, and black should absorb 100 percent. The actual reflectance figures, however, are about 80 percent and 4 percent, respectively, with grays lying in-between.

For several reasons, actual paint mixing often does not live up to theory. First, like objects, paint pigments do not reflect single wavelengths. Instead, they reflect a wider portion of the spectrum, with peaks at particular frequencies. Hence, any paint color is actually a mixture of colors. Second, the same identified color may vary greatly from manufacturer to manufacturer. The color theories we have discussed so far are based on the physics of light, which, for the artist, remains in the realm of theory. Artists work empirically, with impure materials; actual experience soon becomes a more reliable teacher than academic color theory.

Almost all color printing uses inks of the subtractive primaries plus black to produce a full range of color in the printed picture. The original image is photographed in black-and-white through four color filters. One filter records black-and-white values representing the total distribution of light across the scene. Each of the other three filters produces a black-and-white record of a different portion of the spectral range of color. Then four different negatives (or *color separations*) are produced (see plate C-2), and each is made into a printing plate. Each plate is coated with its particular color of transparent ink (magenta, cyan, yellow, or black), and the four images are printed on top of one another. All

the color reproductions in this (and most other) books are produced in this way. If you look at them with a magnifying glass, you can see the small dots of separate colors that make up the printed image.

Until recently, color separations and corrections were done by highly paid commercial artists. But now most large printing companies and design studios have what are called *electronic analog to digital scanning machines*, which produce them quickly, accurately, and relatively inexpensively.

A three-color process is also possible; in theory, any colors will work, as long as their combination includes wavelengths representing the entire spectrum.

Modern color photography (since the 1930s) depends on subtractive processes that use dyes in a way that resembles the color printing process. Like printers, early color photographers combined separate images that were made from separate exposures or with a multiple-lens camera. With modern color film, however, a single exposure creates separate but simultaneous images in three layers of silver-compound emulsions; each layer responds to only one-third of the light spectrum (red-orange, green, or blue-violet). The exposed film is developed into a multilayered black-and-white negative. When chemical couplers are combined with an oxidizing developer, a dye is produced in each layer. The resulting color negative is formed by three layers of color, with dark and light values represented by different densities of dye.

In the printing process, white light is passed through the negative: the dye layers absorb the original colors and transmit their complements (magenta, yellow, or cyan) to a paper-backed three-layer emulsion, which produces the positive color print. With color transparencies (slides), a reversal process creates positives from the film instead of from negatives. With Polaroid color pictures, nine layers of emulsions, developer-dyes, and other chemicals are included within a space about half as thick as a human hair (0.002 inch).

Additive Color

When all the various wavelengths of light are present (in combination) at one time, they produce a colorless or white light in which colors are not visible as separate entities. For this reason, light colors are called *additive*: the primary colors contain all the wavelengths necessary to add up to white light—namely, red-orange, green, and blue-violet (RGB). Paired combinations of these primaries produce secondary colors: yellow (red + green), cyan (green + blue), and magenta (red + blue) (see figure 5-2b). The primary and secondary colors of light and of pigment are the opposites (or reciprocals) of each other, because they are actually two dimensions (additive and subtractive) of the same phenomenon: visible light.

Early experiments with color photography (dating from about 1867) began with additive mixtures of colored light. The Victorian physicist James Clerk Maxwell demonstrated a full-color image by superimposing on a screen three projected transparent lantern slides. Each black-and-white slide was made by photographing the subject (a multicolored ribbon) through a red, blue, or green filter, and then projecting the transparent positive through a filter of the same color. (In 1935, Eastman Kodak revived the popular Victorian magic lantern shows by developing positive-transparency 35mm film: the modern 2″ × 2″ color slide.) Nearly a hundred years after Maxwell's demonstration, his experiments with color were further explored in a series of important demonstrations by Edwin Land, inventor of the Polaroid Land camera. (These demonstrations are discussed later in this chapter.)

Additive color theory applies to theatrical lighting and to computer or video images. The screen of a color TV or computer monitor is made up of tiny dots of light (called *phosphors*) grouped in RGB sets (known as *picture elements* or *pixels*). The phosphors emit light when excited by electrons; the amount of light emitted by a phosphor depends on the number of electrons striking it. When all three RGB phosphors in a set are illuminated, a white pixel results; when none is illuminated, a black pixel results. A full range of colors can be produced by varying the red, green, and blue combinations of phosphor excitement within the pixels. You can see pixels on a screen by looking at it through a strong magnifying glass.

Polarized Color

Ordinary light waves vibrate in an infinite number of directions perpendicular to the direction in which the light wave is traveling. When light passes through certain substances, some of these multidirectional vibrations are absorbed, and the vibrations of the emerging light are limited to a single plane. In such a case, the light is said to have been *polarized*. Familiar instances of partial polarization include reflections from glass or water, and road glare. Road glare is produced by light polarized in a horizontal plane. Polarized sunglasses (which contain a great many microscopic vertical slits) admit only vertical vibrations, and thus they block (or filter out) the horizontally vibrating light that creates the glare. If you look through two polarized sunglass lenses placed one on top of the other, and rotate one of them, you will see changes in the amount of light transmitted by the lenses. When the two sets of slits are at right angles to one another, all the light is blocked and the lenses appear black. Photographers use polarizing filters in this way to reduce reflections and to make the sky appear darker in color photographs (sky light is partially polarized).

Certain seemingly colorless and transparent materials are composed of crystalline structures (such as the minerals mica and tourmaline) or of stretched molecules (for example, cellophanes and some transparent plastics used in windows and windshields). If these birefringent materials are placed between two polarizing filters, sets of colors become visible. (Polarized colors are sometimes observable in these materials through polarizing sunglasses, through which they may appear as somewhat iridescent patterns.) When one filter is rotated, the sets of colors change (see figure 5-3). Because the stretching of molecules in birefringent material (and hence its refractive characteristics) is a consequence of stress, structural and mechanical engineers can build scaled-down transparent plastic models (for example, of bridges, buildings, or spacecraft), and then view or photograph the models through polarizers. When mechanical stress

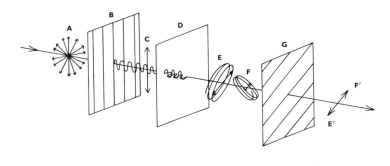

Figure 5-3. A: This line follows one ray of full-spectrum light. (In real life, many light rays would strike the polarizer from all angles and directions.) B: A vertical-axis polarizer. C: Only those light rays whose vibrations match the polarizer (B) are transmitted; the others are absorbed. D: The birefringent material divides the light between two paths: one faster, one slower. E and F: because the divided wave lengths travel at different speeds, their recombined form is distorted into an eliptical path, reshaping the light ray into an irregular 'corkscrew.' G: The second polarizer transmits only the portion of the 'corkscrew' that can pass through its diagonal axis, and absorbs the remainder. E' and F': The viewer sees only the few wavelengths of light transmitted by the second polarizer.

is applied to the model, the varying degrees of strain are manifested (through the polarizing filter) as varying colors. If the tests suggest that it is necessary to do so, the structure can be redesigned so as to disperse stress throughout the structure and thus avoid concentrations of stress that might result in collapse. This process, called *photoelastic stress analysis*, is also used by automotive engineers to ensure that car parts will withstand hard use: the parts are sprayed with plastic, subjected to testing, and then photographed in polarized light.

Although a theoretical explanation of polarized color is complex, birefringent materials can be empirically explored by artists. An image constructed of certain transparent (colorless) materials, when transilluminated by polarized light and viewed through a rotating polarizer, will possess constantly changing combinations of color. Not only can a single image be seen through the polarizer as embodying various color phases, but the entire composition can be radically changed, depending on the specific position of the polarizer, if the transparent materials that compose the different images have been cut at slightly different angles (see plate C-7).

COLOR SYSTEMS

Terminology

Color is traditionally said to have three dimensions: hue, value, and intensity. *Hue* refers to the basic name of the color (blue, turquoise, magenta, yellow, or the like). *Value* (also called *brightness* or *luminosity*) is the lightness or darkness of the color, as it corresponds to a scale of grays from black to white. Value can be thought of as the gray that the color would appear to be if it were photographed in black-and-white. *Intensity* (also termed *chroma*) refers to the purity, brilliance, or saturation of the color. A high-intensity green, for example, is the purest, most brilliant green imaginable. Color intensity is reduced by adding black, white, or the complementary color.

Not all hues have the same range of values. Yellow, for instance, is light in value and loses its identity when darkened beyond a certain point; consequently, a really dark value of yellow is the color of mud. Red, blue, and purple have dark values. On the other hand, when red is significantly lightened, it loses its basic redness and turns into pink. Blue and violet are not so subject to this kind of change. Lighter than normal values of colors (such as pink, baby blue, and aqua) are called *tints*. Darker than normal values (such as deep purple and forest green) are called *shades*. Hues modified by the presence of both black and white are called *tones*.

A pictorial image consisting mostly of values lighter than middle gray is called *high-key* (see, for example figures 2-12, 3-13, 7-4, and 7-5). High-key compositions often seem luminous, because the lighter but contrasting hues increase overall reflectance. When the majority of values in a composition are darker than middle gray, it is called *low-key* (see, for example figures 4-25, 6-17, 7-8, and 9-16). More detail can be portrayed in low-key compositions, because a broader range of values can be appropriated for highlighting, thus providing more numerous contrasts.

Where paint is concerned, a mixed color is always less intense than its component colors. A pigment that reflects almost nothing but green frequencies will seem more vibrant than a color mixed from blue- and yellow-reflecting pigments. This is because each additional pigment subtracts out (absorbs) additional wavelengths of reflected light. Therefore, very intense paint colors must be bought ready-made. Because of this subtractive effect, intense colors can be toned down without becoming muddy if another color (not black) is mixed in; one way to do this is to add a touch of the complementary color (for example, using green to modify red). A color can also be toned down by adding a little of each of the colors that are adjacent to it on the color wheel (described in the next subsection). Each adjacent color has a component of complementary color in it (so that, for example, orange and violet can be used to tone down red); tones produced by this method can be quite dynamic. Beginning artists sometimes try to tone down a color by adding black, only to be disappointed when the color becomes lifeless.

The Color Wheel. Art students traditionally learn to relate pigment colors by means of the color wheel (see figure 5-4). In the color wheel, colors are arranged in spectral order, with the high and low ends (red and violet) adjacent to one another. The primary colors are placed equidistantly apart. The secondary colors are placed between the primaries from which they are mixed. Tertiary colors are mixed from adjacent primary and secondary colors (or from two primaries). Colors next to each other are termed *analogous*, while *complementary* colors are exactly opposite one another. Any two complementaries always contain, between them, all three primary colors; thus, (theoretically) they will produce black when mixed together.

Color Schemes. Monochromatic schemes use one hue with variations in value and/or intensity. Analogous schemes use three to five hues that are adjacent to one another on the color wheel and that contain a hue in common—for example, yellow-green, yellow, and yellow-orange. The effects of analogous color schemes are usually restful and harmonious. Complementary schemes use adjacent hues, together with their respective comple-

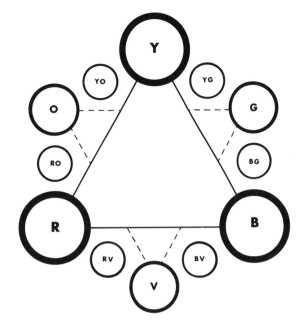

Figure 5-4. Color wheel. The primary colors are connected by a solid line, while the secondary colors are connected by a dashed line.

ments—for example, blue and blue-green with orange and red-orange. Complementary schemes usually seem energetic and intense. Split-complementary schemes are based on one hue and the two colors on either side of its complement—for example, blue with yellow-orange and red-orange. Triad schemes involve any three hues that are equidistant from one another on the color wheel.

The color wheel is useful for articulating order and relationships among colors. In the past, color-wheel recipes provided a standard method of color selection in fields such as interior decoration, textile design, and fashion. Every art student learns the color wheel, but few artists give it more than cursory attention, preferring instead to trust their own experience. Too much reliance on color-wheel formulas tends to dull sensitivity to the artist's perceptions. Newer methods of teaching about color, influenced by the artist/teacher Josef Albers, emphasize solving perceptual problems through systematic experimentation rather than by applying ready-made formulas.

Color Standardization

Certain people (including printers, designers, and paint, dye, and film manufacturers) need precise

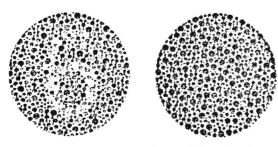

Figure 5-5. Testing for color blindness. The subject is shown patterns like this in which simple figures (such as the number 6 on the left in this example) can be differentiated only because of their color contrast with the background. People with normal color vision can see the figures. Different color combinations are used in order to diagnose the nature of the color perception problem. People with color blindness would see the figure on the right. (Eleanor Holland)

and unambiguous ways of identifying and reproducing colors. In the United States, colors—like weights and measures—have been standardized by the National Bureau of Standards (NBS). The Intersociety Color Council (ISCC) of the NBS has defined and named 267 standard colors designated by a universal notation system called *Centroid Colors*, which is correlated with other conventional color systems. (To obtain information on this system, write the National Bureau of Standards or Superintendent of Documents, U.S. Government Printing Office, Washington, D.C. 20402. Request *The ISCC-NDS Method of Designating Colors and a Dictionary of Color Names*, and *ISCC-NBS Centroid Color Chart*, NBS Standard Sample Number 2106, SD Catalog NOC 13.10:440.)

The dye industry uses the *Colour Index Name and Number Systems* and *Standard Color Card of America*, which identify 100 dye colors by chemical composition. The International Commission of Illumination (or CIE, for *Commission Internationale de l'Éclairage*) describes color samples in mathematical terms representing wavelength and purity.

One of the most widely used color systems was developed in 1898: the *Munsell Color Notation System*. The Munsell color tree is three-dimensional and in shape resembles a sphere. A ten-hue color wheel lies in the central horizontal plane, with the purest hues in the center, graying as they lie outward from the center. The color wheel is pierced by a ten-step, vertical, black-to-white axis in which lighter-than-normal colors (tints) occupy higher

positions and darker-than-normal colors (shades) lie in the lower positions. Colors can then be numbered according to their position relative to three axes: hue, value, and saturation (for example, 3Y 8.0/14.3).

The *Ostwald Color System* is similar in form to the Munsell system, but it emphasizes wavelength, purity, and luminance. Each color can be identified in terms of the percentage of color, white, and black needed to match the sample (for example, C = 40, W = 42, B = 18; total = 100). The Ostwald system is often preferred by artists. It is similar to a system prepared by bird-expert Robert Ridgeway that has been used for over seventy years by biologists. The Ridgeway color dictionary shows over 1,100 colors, identified by color, tint, and shade.

COLOR PERCEPTION

Thus far in this chapter, we have considered traditional explanations of color as understood in the contexts of physics and optics. Unfortunately, however, such theories do not explain color vision! As a result of color constancy, the human brain interprets colors in ways that seem to disregard the physical characteristics of wavelength.

The Retina

Because only the cones have color-sensitive pigments, and because cones are concentrated in the center of the retina, color is most clearly perceived in foveal and macular vision. (Rods have but a single visual pigment, rhodopsin, which responds only to brightness; hence, objects seen in peripheral vision appear relatively colorless.)

A normal cone cell contains three (RGB) types of light-sensitive visual pigments (see figure 2-7). When exposed to light, each pigment captures (absorbs) photons, causing its molecules to change structure, bleaching the pigment. At a certain threshold, these molecular changes activate electrochemical responses in the photoreceptor. Each type of visual pigment absorbs all wavelengths to some degree, but each absorbs more photons of a particular range of wavelengths than of others. How these pigments are distributed within a given cone determines whether the cone's peak sensitivity is to red, to green, or to blue portions of the spectrum. (Sensitivity to black and white appears to depend on the amount rather than on the frequency of light.) Whether or not a given cone reaches a threshold for firing depends on the number of photons it absorbs, which is only partly a function of wavelength. Wavelength is a factor in initiating visual pigment activity, but once pigments have absorbed the photons, color perception is stimulated by patterns of electrochemical activity—and wavelength is no longer of importance.

The actual firing of a cone cell is also affected by activity in its neighboring photoreceptors. Hence, color sensations depend on combinations of activity among (as well as within) the cones. This principle of lateral inhibition works to maximize the perception of contrasts (see chapter 2). With color vision, this means that differences in color enhance border contrast.

Color Blindness

Some people distinguish fewer colors than normal. Between 6 and 8 percent of human males and about 1 percent of females suffer various degrees of abnormal color vision. About three-quarters of these people are simply poor at matching colors (a condition known as *anomalous trichromatism*). The other 25 percent can match all the colors mixed from two primaries but not colors that involve the third primary (a condition known as *dichromatism*). The most common dichromatic deficiency is red-green blindness: various shades of these colors appear grayish and cannot be differentiated from one another. Rarer is blue-yellow color blindness. Rarest of all (affecting about 1 person in 30,000, and occurring in males and females equally) is a condition known as *monochromatism*. Affected people must depend entirely on low-resolution rod vision and can distinguish only difference in brightness; they are unable to see any colors at all. Because they lack cone vision, such people have poor visual acuity.

Color-blind individuals often become aware of their problem only when they are formally tested, perhaps in a routine eye or driving examination (see figure 5-5). This is because the handicap is not actually one of seeing colors (as the term suggests), but one of differentiating within a rather limited range of impure colors. So-called color-blind people usually recognize red and green (or blue and yellow) as different colors when the hues are bright and relatively pure. Their discrimination becomes faulty when the colors approach more neutral and mixed hues. Most color-blind people succeed per-

fectly well in typical art classes; when unusually subtle discriminations are called for, feedback from classmates is helpful. A recent treatment for color blindness involves wearing a pink contact lens on one eye only.

Because of normal genetic diversity in the human population, individual variations in color sensitivity are to be expected. True color blindness, however, is a recessive, sex-linked hereditary condition involving the X chromosome. Nonhereditary factors also affect color vision. Normal aging produces a lowered sensitivity to blues; thus, older people see objects as being more yellowish than do younger people. Nearsighted people are more sensitive to the red end of the spectrum, and farsighted people to the blue end. Moreover, the color of the iris can influence how many short and long wavelengths enter the eye. Give this some thought the next time you engage in an argument about whether something is gray-green or blue-green: it may really depend on who is seeing it!

Are there cultural as well as individual differences in color vision? The languages of some societies do not include names for certain colors; does this mean that individuals in these societies do not perceive them? Recent anthropological studies do not confirm the existence of significant variations in human color vision. Instead, differences in color vocabularies are associated with the presence or absence of Western-type schooling, which encourages the linguistic abstraction of certain qualities (including colors) from their natural contexts. Societies without Western-type schools usually have rich vocabularies for colors as fixed (nonabstracted) properties of the objects in which they occur—clearly showing that such peoples do indeed see and differentiate colors that they may have no reasons to name out of context.

Perceptual Color

Just how far color vision strays from a simple correspondence with wavelength is demonstrated by a number of perceptual phenomena.

Successive Contrast. Intense exposure to one color or value leads to the sensation of its complement when the color is withdrawn; this effect is called *negative afterimage* (see figure 2-14). (Following exposure to very intense colored light, a positive afterimage may occur briefly before the negative one appears.) The phenomenon is also termed *successive contrast*, because the experience of the complement follows perception of the stimulus color. Successive contrast is thought to result from fatigue in the cones or in their neural synapses (see chapter 2).

An artist who works too long at one sitting with a single color may find that the color seems to lose its brightness as it becomes contaminated by the subtle, filmy color of negative afterimages. A related effect occurs in white-walled factories, when workers are required to focus constantly on brightly colored objects. The continual reappearance of misty afterimage color on the white walls frequently causes workers to feel nauseated. The rationale for green walls and clothing in operating rooms is that green is restful to the eyes of medical personnel who must focus intently on red blood and body tissues.

Simultaneous Contrast. Complementary color contrasts occur not only after viewing but during viewing (simultaneously). For example, a gray circle on a green background will appear slightly pinkish. The presence of violet will enhance the yellow qualities of red. Conversely, red brings out the greenish qualities of blue. In this way, contrast between adjacent colors can be perceptually maximized.

A color's appearance always tends toward the complementary hue (and contrasting value) of the color surrounding it. Bright, intense colors are usually less affected by their surroundings than are tints, shades, tones, and other mixtures. Small areas of color are more subject to perceptual change than are large areas. Not only can one color be made to look like two (or more), as in figure 5-6, but two (or more) colors can be made to look like one.

You have probably experienced this chameleonlike quality of color. A chair, rug, or paint color selected in the environment of a store may appear surprisingly different in the color context of your own home. A scarf, belt, or necklace may seem garish and harsh with some color combinations but harmonious with others. Artists and designers in the fields of fashion, textiles, interior design, and advertising are constantly confronted with such delicate balances in color relationships.

Simultaneous contrast is easily produced, even with sheets of ordinary construction paper. With a hole punch you can quickly make many small identical-size circles of color. Lay circles of one color against several different background colors, and search out combinations that evoke the most striking differences. If a single swatch of color can seem brighter, duller, lighter, darker, or changed in hue—just by changing the visual context—think how complex the painting of a picture becomes! Nearly a century ago, John Ruskin issued the following warning to beginning painters (quoted in Arnheim 1954, p. 354):

> Every hue throughout your work is altered by every touch that you add in other places; so what was warm a minute ago, becomes cold when you have put a hotter color in another place, and what was in harmony when you left it, becomes discordant as you set other colors beside it.

Virtually the same thing had been said over 300 years earlier by Giorgio Vasari, an Italian architect, painter, and art historian (quoted in Birren 1965, p. 234):

> A sallow color makes another which is placed beside it appear more lively, and melancholy and pallid colors make those near them very cheerful and almost of a flaming beauty.

Simultaneous contrast achieves its most extreme effects in situations involving complementary colors. Such combinations may seem uncomfortably bold (as when red and green or blue and orange are juxtaposed); they are usually reserved for short exposure situations (for example, in posters, advertisements, and holiday settings), rather than for interior design or clothing. The artist Richard Anuskiewicz often uses this effect. In *Splendor of Red* (see plate C-3), only one color of red is present. The seemingly different shades of red in the painting result entirely from simultaneous contrast caused by differences in the thickness and in the colors (blue and green) of the radiating lines.

Border Contrast. The two parts of plate C-11 are composed of identically colored hexagons: only their arrangement is changed (with the exception of the central and four outlying hexagons, which maintain the same positions in both compositions). Here you can clearly see the importance of edges and boundaries (or contour enhancement, discussed in chapter 2) in color perception. As you continue to gaze at the left-hand figure of plate C-11, you will gradually come to see hexagonal edges that, at first glance, were all but invisible. Your visual system persists in searching for contrast and in maximizing it over time. These subtle effects were extensively used by the color-field painter Ad Reinhardt (see plate C-4). At first, Reinhardt's canvases appear to be painted a single uniform color. As the viewer continues to look at them, however, initially invisible differences become perceptible and eventually quite intense. (Of course, looking at a color reproduction of this kind of painting is an extremely poor substitute for the perceptual experience of viewing the actual painting.)

In the left-hand figure of plate C-6, each band of color seems lighter on the side of its dark neighbor, and darker on the side of its light neighbor. The longer you look, the greater the effect becomes. The same effect can be caused by differences in hue (as well as in value). In the figure on the right in plate C-6, the central bands seem to glow on each edge as a consequence of their neighbors on each side. Here, both simultaneous contrast and border contrast work to maximize color differences. Border contrast effects were often used by traditional quilters (see plate C-8) and have been enlisted by Josef Albers and other modern artists (see plate C-9).

Vibration. Bright colors of equal intensity sometimes produce a shimmering effect, in which the edges of shapes appear to move. Vibration occurs with intense colors that are (nearly) complementary in hue and are of approximately the same value. The zone of optical activity is along edges or contours, so vibration effects are enhanced by patterns that contain many edges (see figure 2-21). Vibration is related to the dynamics of paired complementary colors, to the effects of simultaneous and border contrast, and possibly to rapid tremors of the eye. Because color vibration is an intense, aggressive effect, it is often exploited in commercial advertising and psychedelic posters. When produced by a skilled optical artist (as in place C-3), the effects can be so intense that they may cause the viewer to squint—as if in the presence of a too-bright light!

Color in Black-and-White. If you spin a cardboard disk marked with a black-and-white pattern,

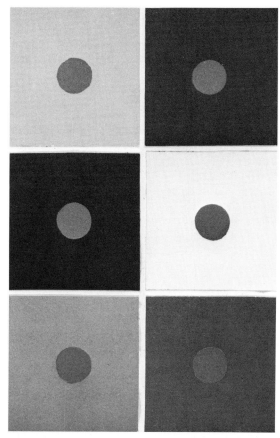

Figure 5-6. Simultaneous contrast: the gray circles are all of identical value.

you will see colors while the disk is in motion! Any pattern that contains roughly equal amounts of black and white will do. Blacks vary in their effectiveness (compare, for instance, Magic marker, ink, paint, and black paper), and the effect is apt to be more pronounced under fluorescent light. This phenomenon is sometimes generated by black-and-white television (especially with static "snow"), which may lead to perceptions of pale shades of pink or blue.

Optical Mixture. From a distance, the edges of small shapes are harder to see clearly (see figures 6-13 and 6-14). Similarly, from a distance, small areas of color lose their identities and are perceived as a blend of color rather than as separate hues. This effect is called *optical mixture*. Color printing processes take advantage of optical mixture by using tiny dots of magenta, yellow, cyan, and black ink. A color television screen or computer monitor applies optical mixture with pixels of red, green, and blue (RGB).

Optical mixture is the basis for the painting technique variously known as *Pointillism, divisionism,* and *neo-Impressionism.* European Pointillists of the late nineteenth century disdained what they considered the disorder and intuitive nature of Impressionist brushwork. Attracted by scientific theories and experiments with light and color, the Pointillists preferred precise and systematic applications of dotlike strokes of unmixed color. They theorized that optical mixture would create more luminous and intense effects than could be achieved with traditional mixed paint colors. Viewed from close up, these canvases look like confetti; but at various viewing distances, the colors lose their individuality and forms emerge.

Exemplifying nineteenth-century scientism, Georges Seurat sought to reconcile art and science, applying theories of contrast and complementarity. He limited his palette to four fundamental colors (red, yellow, green, and blue) and their intermediate tones, giving himself a twelve-step color wheel to work with. Seurat allowed himself to mix any of these twelve colors with white, but he never mixed one color with another. Pointillism was a slow, methodical process, and its lack of spontaneity and narrow emphasis on impersonal mathematical theories did not appeal to everyone. Several painters (including Vincent van Gogh and Camille Pissarro) seriously explored the technique, but they soon abandoned it. Seurat, Paul Signac, and Alfred Sisely, however, persisted and today remain the best known of the Pointillists.

Transparency. The perception of transparency occurs when both a shape or object and the surfaces or edges behind it are visible. When two apparently overlapping colored shapes are represented, and when the color of their common area is a mixture of the two colors, a perception of transparency will occur. You will find it virtually impossible to perceive a pattern such as the one shown in plate C-5 as merely two green squares, two yellow squares, and one yellow-green square. By varying color mixtures, artists can create illusions of varying depth: one surface can be made to appear to pass through, over the top of, or below the other.

This perception of transparency in two-dimensional opaque shapes arises from the human tendency to group elements into complete and continuous forms whenever possible (see chapter 3).

The Brain

Wavelengths and retinal stimulation alone do not account for color perception, since both are tuned out and corrected by color constancy. Continuing experiments by Edwin Land since the 1950s have challenged conventional theories about color perception. In essence, Land produced images in which color was perceived despite the absence of the corresponding wavelengths.

Land first took two black-and-white photographs of a scene. One exposure was made through a red filter, while the other exposure was taken with no filter at all. The photographs were processed as black-and-white transparencies (slides). Then the transparencies were placed in separate projectors, and their images were superimposed to create a single black-and-white image on the screen. When a red filter was placed in front of the red-filter transparency, the image suddenly exhibited a full range of color! The effect was stronger when the image contained recognizable objects than when it consisted of an abstract pattern. But in either case, a range of colors could be clearly perceived. According to conventional color theories, the combination of red and white projector lights should have produced only pink (and this was the case with a blank screen or with the projection of only one transparency). What was happening?

Land used two images: the first, made with the red filter, produced a photographic record of the distribution of longer wavelengths over a scene; the second recorded the entire spectrum (both shorter and longer wavelengths). By itself, neither image stimulated the perception of color. But when the two were superimposed into a single image (with the long-wavelength image projected through a red or long-wavelength filter), a third (invisible) picture was created by the differences between the two pictures. The third configuration, perceived subliminally by the brain, consisted of the distribution of ratios between short and long wavelengths across the surface of the picture. Land's experiments clearly demonstrated that the relationship among wavelengths (rather than their frequencies per se) are responsible for stimulating the perception of color.

C-1. Claude Monet (French), *The Houses of Parliament, Sunset*, 1903. Oil on canvas, 32 × 36⅝ inches. (National Gallery of Art, Washington, D.C.; Chester Dale Collection)

C-2. How plate C-1 was printed, using the four-color process. The top sections show the four color-separation plates (called *printers*). From left to right: yellow printer (photographed through a blue filter); magenta printer (green filter); cyan printer (red filter); and black printer (modified filter). The bottom sections show the sequence of printing: yellow; yellow + magenta; yellow + magenta + cyan; yellow + magenta + cyan + black.

C-3. Richard Anuszkiewicz (American), *Splendor of Red*, 1965. Liquitex on canvas, 72 × 72 inches. (Yale University Art Gallery; Gift of Seymour H. Knox)

C-4. Ad Reinhardt (American), *No. 10*, 1959. Oil on canvas, 108 × 40 inches. (Photograph courtesy of The Pace Gallery, New York)

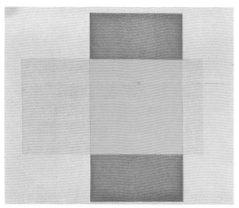

C-5. Illusion of transparency. (Photograph by Carolyn M. Bloomer)

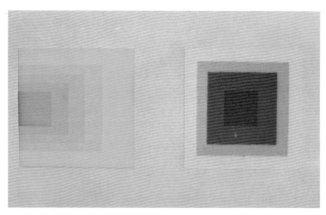

C-6. Border contrast or glowing stripe. (Photograph by Carolyn M. Bloomer)

C-7. Barbara Stewart McDonald (American). *Rosslyn and the River*, (four phases), 1986. Bicolor (birefringent materials and polarizing filters), 36 inches in diameter. These photographs represent four phases of a composition that changes smoothly and continuously as one polarizing filter is rotated. (Permission of the artist, Alexandria, Virginia)

C-8. Anonymous (American, Amish), *Diamond in the Square*, n. d. Cotton patchwork quilt. (Photograph by Myron Miller, New York, N.Y.)

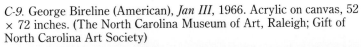

C-9. George Bireline (American), *Jan III*, 1966. Acrylic on canvas, 52 × 72 inches. (The North Carolina Museum of Art, Raleigh; Gift of North Carolina Art Society)

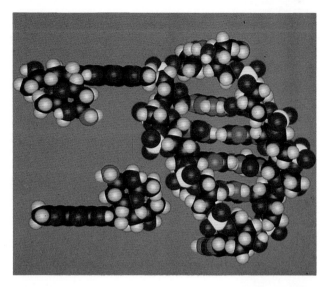

C-10. Computer-generated image of an antitumor drug showing two pharmaceutical molecules (left) adjacent to the DNA to which they are bound. The model is designed to depict a common, physical, plastic representation of molecules. (Michael Cory, Burroughs-Wellcome Company, Research Triangle Park, North Carolina)

C-11. Colored hexagons photographed from the screen of a computer. The same hexagonal colors appear in different arrangements in each image. Five hexagons (the central and four outlying ones) are the same color and appear in the same position in each image. (After Brou et al. 1986. L. Stauffer and C. Bloomer, Amiga 2000 with *DeluxePaint* and *DigiPaint* software.)

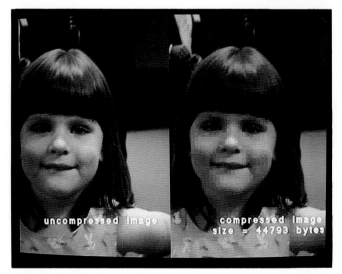

C-12. Image compression. Color video-processing boards capture, digitize, and compress images that can then be stored, transmitted by modem, or reproduced as hard copy. (Discrete TimeSystems, Inc., Arlington Heights, Illinois)

Color Constancy. Land's results provide a basis for understanding the phenomenon of color constancy. Even as lighting conditions change, the ratios of longer wavelengths to shorter wavelengths in a scene remain virtually unchanged. Hence, the relative stimulation of visual pigments in the cones stays essentially the same, since the pigments respond to a range of wavelengths (rather than to single frequencies). Land's experiments showed that the physical characteristics of a viewing situation can vary to a surprising extent without significantly affecting color perception. The brain extracts the constant (invariant) aspects of light and presents the viewer with a perceptual experience of constant color, independent of the effects of illumination and shadow (grass remains green, tree trunks brown, sidewalks gray, apples red, and so on). These color constants are referred to as *object color* or *local color*; they are a person's illusions of the real colors of things. For these reasons, people adapt very quickly to colored sunglasses, to changes in artificial and natural light, and to differences in color photographs and video images. Like other constancies, however, color constancy breaks down in unusual or extreme situations. When a significant range of spectral wavelengths is missing, colors may lack normal variation and/or intensity. But again, the critical variable is the constancy of wavelength relationships, not their absolute frequencies.

Because of color constancy, people have very poor color memory. Most people find it difficult to match from memory even colors that are quite familiar (such as Coca-Cola red); extreme errors are common. You have probably encountered the same problem in daily life when trying to match a paint sample or piece of clothing from memory. This is because your original perception of the color depended on relative wavelengths distributed over the entire visual field; hence, your subsequent memory of the color is embedded in your experience of an entire optical situation: it is context-bound. Trying to match absolute color (defined by wavelength) is next to impossible because you never perceived an absolute color in the first place! This context-bound quality of color led Josef Albers (1971, p. 23) to make the following observation:

No normal eye, not even the most trained one, is foolproof against color deception. [The person] who claims to see colors inde-

pendent of their illusionary changes fools only himself [or herself]. . . .

COLOR MEANINGS

Through time and across cultures, people have ascribed various meanings to color. Color invests ritual and custom with symbolic meaning, represents the identity of cosmological forces, and promotes desirable feelings and mind/body states. It is tempting to look for universals in color symbolism because of certain constants in human experience: the blue of sky and water; the red of blood, ripe fruit, and sunsets; the white of milk, semen, clouds, moon, and sun; the green of vegetation, foodstuffs, and copper ore; the black of blindness, night, organic decomposition, and iron; the yellow of pus, grain, and gold; the orange of fire; the browns of earth and tree bark; the rose and violet of dawn and dusk. But these experiences do not mean the same thing in every culture; they fit differently into different cultural world views.

Color and Culture

Color often plays a part in cosmologies or theories about the nature of the universe. Almost all cultures conceive of the world as being made up of several basic elements or forces (for example, $e = mc^2$). In the *Five Elements* (*wu xing*) theories of ancient China, each element was associated with a particular color and spatial direction: wood with green and east; fire with red and south; earth with yellow and center; metal with white and west; and water with black and north. As the essential pivot between earth and heaven, the Chinese emperor occupied the center position (hence, *Yellow Emperor*). Objects belonging to the imperial palace were identified by yellow, a color that others were forbidden to use. For some Native Americans of the Southwest (Hopi and Navajo), four cardinal directions also radiate from a center: east is white; west is yellow; north is black (a male color); and south is blue (a female color). In addition, red represents sunshine in these cultures. With the exception of black/north, however, the Native American color meanings do not agree at all with the Chinese schemes.

Such cultural differences are not the exception: they are the rule. In the American flag and in the West in general, white represents purity and innocence: it is the color for christening, first communion, and bridal gowns. But for many cultures, including the Chinese, Japanese, and many African peoples, white represents the absence of life and is therefore the color of death and ancestral spirits; for Buddhists, yellow is the color of death.

In the West, death, mourning, and the supernatural are associated with black. Black is the color of evil (black magic, black hats, and black hearts), but black is also the color worn by widows, graduating seniors, and Jewish and Christian clergy. (Buddhist monks wear brilliant saffron orange robes.) Black was the color of victory to the Native American Crow but a symbol of night to the Dakota Sioux. For ancient Egyptians, black represented the life-giving fertility of the soil deposited by the Nile.

In the West, red is associated with sin, sex, and danger signals ("scarlet letter," "red-light district," stop signs, and red-pencil corrections), but in the American flag, red symbolizes hardiness and valor. For the African Ndembu, sexual lust and adultery are symbolized by black, while red is ambiguous (Turner 1962). It can be positive if tinged with white (purified), as in maternal blood and huntsmanship, or dangerous if tinged with black, as in blood invaded by sorcery and disease. A healthy Ndembu is said to have white blood, whereas in the West a vigorous and energetic youth is deemed red-blooded, and a Western aristocrat is blue-blooded. Among Plains Native Americans, the symbolism of red varied; depending on the group, red might connote thunder, sunset, human being, blood, or earth. Around the world, red earth (ocher) has been commonly used in burial rituals. In China, red is worn by brides.

The symbolic meaning of a color is often closely associated with qualities or powers of objects and substances in the environment. A tree that secretes a milky sap, for instance, may ritually embody maternal milk and nourishment. A plant that promotes blood coagulation may be considered red, even though its physical color may not be red. In the Orient, the stronger (more *yang*) form of ginseng is called *red*, while the milder (more *yin*) form of ginseng is called *white*—even though both are beige in color. The rarity of certain gems, minerals, dyestuffs, or the like may also lend significance to certain colors. For example, purple symbolizes royalty in the West because only powerful and wealthy individuals could afford the time and resources required to extract a rare purple dye from a particu-

lar Mediterranean shellfish (*Murex*). In classical Rome, color was used to denote social status and political office. Today in graduation ceremonies, color is used to identify universities and academic degrees.

Color and Personality

In the late 1940s, a German physician, Max Luscher, related color preferences to personality characteristics. In the Short Luscher Test, the subject orders eight color cards in terms of preference. Dark blue, blue-green, orange-red, and bright yellow are termed *psychological primaries*. They represent, respectively, depth of feeling, elasticity of will, force of will, and spontaneity. Of the four *auxiliary colors*, black and neutral gray are considered achromatic, while brown and violet are characterized as relatively lifeless mixtures. The order in which a person ranks the colors is said to reveal his or her internal psychological organization of goals, anxieties, compensations, and conflicts.

According to Luscher's theory, the midbrain responds instinctively to colors contemplated independently of objects, and this response is neither conscious nor culturally learned. The significance of certain colors is seen as arising naturally from the biological environment of human evolution. This theoretical rationale, however, is based on a picture of early human life as involving continual bouts of attack/conquest (red) and self-defense (green) in a sabertooth-tiger-hunting life-style—a view of human evolution that anthropologists now agree is dubious. The course of hominid evolution is currently thought to have been dominated by gathering, foraging, and occasional scavenging—an opportunistic but significantly more placid life-style. Big-game hunting emerged only in the Ice Age, long after the species *Homo sapiens* had fully evolved (see chapter 1). An even more serious problem with Luscher's theory is that the midbrain evolved more than 60 million years before the appearance of the first hominids.

Norms for the Luscher Color Test were developed on a sample of 1,000 employed British males and females from a range of occupations in commerce and industry. As we have seen, Western responses to color are by no means consistent with those of other cultures. Some studies indicate that color preferences correlate with both culture and age. For example, Americans prefer blue over all other colors; Spaniards find white the most pleasing; French college students generally feel that purple is arousing, while green, yellow, and violet are calming; American third-graders consider blue a happy color, but college students find it sad; Czechoslovakian children prefer bright, highly saturated colors, but Czechoslavakian college students like pastels (Rivlin and Gravelle 1984). In light of all these factors, there is considerable room to doubt claims that the Luscher Color Test (or any similar test) can be universally applied to all humans.

Futhermore, colors are rarely seen by themselves, except in artificial laboratory-type situations. Consequently, human responses to color are responses to objects in specific circumstances. Consider, for instance, your differing reactions to a red apple and a red room, a green lawn and a green slice of bread, a violet evening gown and violet skin! The significance of color is complexly entangled with your experience in actual situations. Total context—and not color alone—triggers your reactions. How to evaluate responses to decontextualized color is not a simple problem. Even a pure color card in a test or experiment is perceived as meaningful only because of its situational context.

In spite of all these criticisms, however, the Luscher Color Test is interesting and often seems surprisingly accurate. But it may work for reasons that are not immediately apparent. Similarly, Tarot cards, astrology, *I Ching* (*yi jing*), and oracles, when used seriously, can be equally interesting and accurate. Such systems of meaning create new contexts within which we can redefine problems—a framework for visualizing new figure and ground relationships. Looking at a situation in a new way is often the first step in clarifying and resolving it. These meaning systems give people conceptual structures that stimulate them to exercise the creative flexibility of their minds.

COLOR AND ART

The artistic use of color has always been restricted by economic conditions, technical knowledge, and the meanings assigned by cultures to specific colors. The first pigments and dyes were made from things people found in their immediate environment: colored earth; minerals; and substances obtained from plants, animals, and burned materials. Prehistoric cave paintings were made with red and yellow earth (ocher) and soot mixed with an animal-fat binder. Ancient Pompeiian wall paintings were done with carbon (from burning wood), ocher (from mines), reds (from cinnabar, red ocher, and fritted white lead), and blues (from a baked mixture of sand and copper). With trade, artists secured pigments and dyes from other environments.

Until fairly recently, artists had to prepare their own paint by grinding dry pigments and mixing them with a liquid vehicle—a slow and painstaking procedure that spawned its share of guarded secrets and mysterious formulas. One of the most important problems was (and to some extent still is) permanence: some pigments fade quite noticeably with time and/or exposure to light (they exhibit what is called *fugitive color*). To modern artists who solve paint problems by visiting the local art store, the diversity of materials used in the past is astonishing. It includes such things as gum arabic, egg yolk, lime, wax, and a large number of variously treated oils and resins. The modern form of oil painting was developed in the fifteenth century, but the technique was not in common use until the seventeenth century.

Since the Renaissance, Western art traditions have emphasized object color as an aspect of the idea that retinal vision is the proper source of realism. Object color represents color constancy, and that is what viewers respond to when they say that an artist uses color ''realistically.'' The first Western artists since the Renaissance to perceive and use color in a different way were the Impressionists, who sought to portray light rather than objects—the sensation of light rather than the perception of things. They departed radically from the conventions of their time, which were defined in considerable detail by the French Academy of Fine Arts, a national school that specified the education of artists and sponsored and judged the major exhibitions. The Academy embraced a strict studio approach: art must be elevated from everyday life; figures must appear in classical or mythological settings; the composition must show careful arrangement by a rational intellect. The Academy art of that era exhibits such refinement in the modeling and illusionary painting of objects and bodies in space that, when they are reproduced, they resemble composed photographs (see figure 8-19). The Impressionists rejected all of these conventions. They painted everyday people in everyday settings; their compositions suggest the spontaneity and chance elements of candid snapshots; their brushstrokes are shockingly visible. At the same time, however, the Impressionists claimed to embrace a scientific, intellectual detachment from their subjects.

Although the Impressionists broke away from conventions of object color, they remained committed to the retinal image. Artists such as Gauguin and van Gogh found the role of detached observer to be too confining. They felt that color by itself was expressive, and they used color to express personally felt emotions rather than objective observations. This direction was carried forward by Matisse and other next-generation French painters who were stimulated by discoveries of non-Western art. Their compositions used simplified designs and brilliant colors, which so shocked the public that the artists were labeled *Fauves*—"wild and dangerous beasts."

The post-Impressionists and the Fauves liberated color from the retinal image and thrust it into the arena of feeling. They were followed by the Expressionists who expressed personal feelings toward external reality with powerful, energetic brushwork and color. Even with their so-called distortions of form and color, however, Fauvism and Expressionism were representational styles that portrayed identifiable things existing in the objective world. But by the 1930s and 1940s, the Abstract Expressionists (or Action Painters) appeared; rejecting the necessity of objective representation, they sought to use paint and color to express emotion uncontaminated by objective imagery. The major Abstract Expressionist painters (including Jackson Pollock, Franz Kline, and Willem de Kooning) were well-schooled in traditional, realistic drawing techniques. Thus their work does not reflect a lack of skill in the conventions of artmaking, but rather profound disenchantment with the expressive possibilities inherent in the representational approach. In the 1950s and 1960s, the Formal Abstractionists (optical artists and color-field painters) disengaged themselves from the raw emotional qualities of Expressionism and began to manipulate the pure perceptual properties of color in ways unrelated to feeling, emotional expression, or symbolic value.

Even from this cursory glance at the recent history of Western art, you can see that each point of liberation eventually became a fixed commitment that was found too confining by a new generation of artists. The growth of art is like that of the chambered nautilus, which periodically outgrows its shell and continually pushes outward, building new and progressively larger spaces in which to grow. The artists of the 1980s and 1990s are heirs to this tradition of exploration, and their various uses of color owe much to all that preceded them. In a broad sense, color has ceased to be a loaded issue. The philosophical problems that engage today's artists tend to be more focused on fundamental definitions of art itself and on art's place within a complex, technological society.

Space
The Daily Frontier

Have you ever walked along and—clunk!—stepped off a curb you failed to see? Or have you ever reached absent-mindedly to set a glass down on a table, only to find yourself disgustedly sweeping up the pieces a few moments later? Such experiences are surprisingly rare, considering how automatic and unconscious human movements generally are. This is because the entire human perceptual system is adapted to life in a three-dimensional world.

Infant studies suggest that spatial perception is an aspect of biological development. As early as six months after birth, a baby can distinguish between a nearby rattle and a rattle three times larger and three times farther away, even though the retinal images are the same size. The Swiss psychologist Jean Piaget observed and described systematic sequences of infant behavior, establishing how coherent perceptions of space emerge as the infant interacts with its environment.

In a series of now-classic experiments (Gibson and Walk 1960), babies of various species (including human) were placed on a sheet of heavy glass, beneath which checkerboard surfaces of varying heights were visible (see figure 6-1). The apparatus was called a *visual cliff*. The glass offered solid support, but underneath the glass were precipitous dropoffs. Even though the babies could touch and feel the glass (which made the apparatus safe to cross), all of them were reluctant—often terrified—to attempt to cross over the visually deep side, even when rewards awaited them on the other side. Such experiments demonstrated that the young of terrestrial species perceive space visually as soon as they are old enough to move about. For some species (such as chickens), this occurs within hours of birth.

The experiments also suggested that visual clues (including motion parallax and patterned gradients) influence behavior more than do other situational factors such as tactile evidence, reward, and maternal coaxing. This experiment can be interpreted in other ways, however. The cliff was not simply visual: underneath its glass top, it was also very real. In this sense, the term *visual cliff* is somewhat misleading, and *glass-topped cliff* would be more accurate. The babies were not victims of an illusion: their visual systems correctly perceived a cliff. At the same time, their sense of touch and bodily orientation correctly (but contradictorily) informed them of a solid, continuous surface.

Contradictory information from two or more senses is a signal that something is not quite right (see chapter 1). The reluctance of babies to cross the glass-topped cliff, then, may have been a response to dissonance in sensory perceptions, rather than a response to the visual information alone. Nonetheless, the experiments clearly showed that creeping infants perceive visual space both accurately and intensely. Such perceptions, however, require active interaction with the environment if they are to develop normally. For example, kittens who were carried through a maze (as compared with kittens who walked through it) failed to develop normal spatial perceptions (cited in Hall 1966, p. 62).

THE BODY

All living organisms orient themselves with respect to space in some way. Plants send their roots downward and their leaves upward. Simple one-celled animals can detect spaces, barriers, and changes in light outside themselves, and use these sensations

Figure 6-1. Visual cliff experiments: (Left) A mother coaxes her six-month-old infant to crawl to her across the glass-covered cliff. (Center) The infant seeks tactile information. (Right) A kitten contemplates the cliff through a sheet of heavy glass. The kitten's view will appear more dramatic if you close one eye and look at the picture directly above the kitten's head. (William Vandivert and *Scientific American*, 1960)

as the basis for approaching or avoiding something. Land animals require complex information about the space in which they live. Basic survival requires that they be able to avoid danger and to find food, shelter, and conditions favorable for reproduction. Just staying alive depends on gathering and assessing information about what is happening in the spaces within and beyond the boundaries of the individual's body. The mechanisms that convey this essential information to the organism are called the *sensory systems*.

The specific kinds of information and the specific ways in which the information must be understood by the organism depend on what is necessary for its survival, which in turn depends on the organism's environmental niche. In the complex web of life, no two environmental niches are identical; therefore, no two species' perceptual systems are exactly the same. Throughout the ongoing evolutionary process of biological adaptation, certain kinds of perceptions lead to survival (and reproduction); and certain changes in neurological organization of information about the spatial environment confer advantages upon the individuals that possess them. Because of their biological differences in perception, different organisms can truly be said to inhabit different perceptual worlds.

Land mammals are permanently oriented to the earth—to the pull of gravity and to surfaces of support. Because such mammals need to perceive their changeable orientations to objects (as well as their own movement through the environment), their sensing systems must supply information about three general kinds of events: things happening inside the body (conveyed by proprioceptive and kinesthetic senses); things happening at the edge of the body (conveyed by contact senses); and things happening at other locations in space (conveyed by distance senses). Sight, hearing, and smell are distance senses; touch and taste are contact senses. In addition, other body organs such as the inner ear orient the organism to its spatial environment.

The entire human perceptual system can be seen as being related to life in a spatial environment. It is in such an environment that human sensory capabilities become essential: the accurate perception of objects and spaces; the ability to know and adjust the orientation of one's own body in space; the ability to locate where things are happening and to identify what is happening; and the capacity to remember, recall, and communicate the locations of things. All of these abilities ultimately depend on the faculty of perceiving information about things both internal and external to the body.

The Bilateral Nervous System

The vertebrate body is *bilaterally symmetrical*; that is, relative to an axis (the spinal cord), each side of the body is a mirror image of the other. For the distance senses, this results in pairs of receptors—one for each side. Interestingly, these senses prompt the body to orient itself in a way that will balance inputs to the two receptors. For example, two-eared animals normally respond to sound by turning their heads (or outer ears) so as to equalize the sound intensities reaching each ear. Human infants, when only hours old, turn their heads to face a sound source. Animals also orient themselves to the source of an odor, by moving the body so as to face into the air stream that carries the smell to them. With mammal infants, when one side of the face is touched, the baby responds by centering its head so as to contact the touching object with its mouth (this reflex enables them to find a nipple). When looking, animals turn their heads to balance the images in both eyes. For creatures with front-facing eyes (such as human beings have), this centers the image symmetrically on the foveas of both eyes (an action known as *fixation*).

Hence, the symmetry of structure in the body and in the nervous system prompts organisms to create symmetry in incoming stimulation. This automatic response causes the organism to move into an optimum spatial and visual position in relation to the source of the stimulus. Thus, our senses not only inform us of the nature of a stimulus, they also inform us of its location in space, and they orient us bodily and visually to the source. Approaching a stimulus can then be accomplished simply by keeping the input symmetrically balanced while moving the body forward. The increasing intensity of a stimulus signals approach, while decreasing intensity signals increasing distance, change in course, or change in the stimulus location.

The Eyes

In regard to survival in a spatial environment, eyes have several functions: to detect the relative locations of objects and spaces, to detect changes occurring in the surrounding space, and to register and control equilibrium and movement in and through space. A sky/earth orientation habituates us to expect that stronger light comes from above and that weaker light comes from below (see chapter 4). Dark and light signal night and day. Differences in light reflectance inform us of the presence of objects. When we move toward something, its image in the visual field expands. Gradients of size, color, pattern, and texture orient us to relative distance. Transformations in light patterns convey messages of change and movement.

Convergence. Apart from the retinal image, the structure of the eyes provides subtle clues for judging distance. With primate binocular vision, the

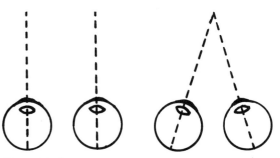

Figure 6-2. Convergence.

image must be in focus in both foveas in order for image fusion to occur (see chapters 3 and 7). Thus, the nearer an object is, the more the eyes must turn inward toward each other to see it (this is the phenomenon of *convergence*; see figure 6-2). Convergence creates tensions in the muscles holding and turning the eyeballs (see figure 2-19). The muscular tension is signaled to the brain and conveys some proprioceptive information about the distance of the object. Convergence is a weak cue for distance perception, but it is more significant for close objects than for distant ones. At a distance of about 3 feet, the experience of the three-dimensionality of viewed objects is optimal.

When the eye muscles become locked into converging and cannot relax enough to focus on distant objects, the problem is called *myopia*, or nearsightedness. Some ophthalmologists believe that myopia results from strain in the eye muscles from too much near-distance focusing (as with reading). According to one study, the typical high-school graduate has read 432 books over the preceding twelve years (averaging 36 per year), and an average college student reads 51 books each year. The rate of nearsightedness sometimes reaches 60 to 80 percent among undergraduate and graduate college students, in comparison to an estimated 25 percent among the general American population (cited in Kavner and Dusky 1978).

Specialists point out that myopia is rare (4 to 6 percent) among nonliterate societies and relatively unschooled populations (such as migrant workers). The incidence of myopia increases directly with the amount of time spent in Western-style schooling. For example, of nonliterate Eskimo children, only 2 percent were nearsighted, while among their peers who attended Western-style schools, the rate zoomed to nearly 65 percent. In Japan, when education was curtailed during World War II, the frequency of myopia among college-age Japanese dropped from 60 percent to 30 percent. In China, myopia decreased with regular eye exercises—ten minutes, twice a day. Myopia can be induced in monkeys and chimps by subjecting them to dim lighting and a limited visual field. Such observations weaken the traditional view that nearsightedness is mainly due to genetic inheritance.

The natural resting position of the human eyes is the same position that would gaze into the distance. This does not mean, however, that near vision was unimportant in the arboreal and savannah habitats of our evolutionary ancestors. By 2 million years ago, hominids used near vision to make tools, find and prepare food, groom each other, and so on. But such activities do not involve the unbroken and extended periods of near-vision concentration that are so common to modern schools and workplaces. Myopia, then, seems symptomatic of a mismatch between our biological adaptation to visual space and the demands of modern life.

Our culture requires and highly prizes skills that involve near vision. The current growth of computer technology can only increase the problem. People who spend long periods working with computer graphics (on two-dimensional terminal screens) often report an alarming disorientation and lack of depth perception for an hour or so afterward. This is particularly frightening to people who must drive home during the readjustment period. To protect vision when doing any kind of close work for extended periods of time, ophthalmologists advise looking across the room (10 to 15 feet) or out a window every twenty minutes or so, until small objects become clear, and moving around every hour or so. But when people work in small, windowless offices, such advice is easier to give than to take.

Binocular Vision. Each eye sees a slightly different image (this is the phenomenon of binocular disparity; see chapter 3). Hold your fist several inches from your face. Look at it first with one eye and then with the other. You will notice that one eye sees more of one side and the other eye sees more of the other side (this is called *binocular parallax*). With two eyes, then, you actually see a little way around an object. One-eyed people can accomplish this only with head movement.

With a little experimentation, you will find that the difference between the images in each eye is much greater for close objects than for distant ones. In fact, for distances greater than 20 feet, the difference is too subtle to be significant. Binocular disparity is important only for depth perception of relatively near objects. For our evolutionary ancestors, judging the depth of field beyond 20 feet apparently provided no great advantage to survival (otherwise, our eyes might have evolved to be farther apart than they are). By contrast, birds of prey such as hawks have such visual acuity that they can accurately judge depth and distance over an expanse of several miles!

MENTAL IMAGERY

People organize experience into mental images or cognitive maps. Some are highly conventionalized and shared by many people (for example, road maps, repair manuals, and seating charts), but others are peculiarly individual. Imagine that this morning you were in a hurry to leave home. When you arrived at school or work, you discovered that you had forgotten your list of things to do today. How would you set about recalling this list? Would you try to visualize the list itself and the location and appearance of various items written on the paper? Would you mentally try to experience the actions you need to carry out or the places you need to go? Would you attempt to form a logical reconstruction of the words to remind you? Are you likely to hear an internal voice advising you of your commitments? Do the people with whom you must interact come to mind first? Do the pressures of your own inner-felt needs give you the answers?

Each of these seven methods of remembering involves a different type of mental imagery: visual, kinesthetic, spatial, verbal, auditory, interpersonal, and intrapersonal. Except for the verbal mode, they all relate to spatial perceptions of either external or internal space—the way things in space look, sound, are located, or are experienced. These styles of memory are remarkably congruent with Howard Gardner's theory of multiple intelligences (see chapter 3). They suggest that the human brain is structured to learn, process, and remember information in a variety of ways. Further, individuals tend to vary in the modalities they favor; this is referred to as differences in *cognitive style*.

Unfortunately, in Western societies the verbal

mode is almost exclusively considered to be the correct mode. Until recently, many people believed that true thinking could take place only with words. Have you ever had someone tell you that "if you can't put it in words, then you obviously don't know it?" And yet this is clearly not the case! Do paintings and melodies exist in your mind as verbal descriptions or as visual and auditory images? How effectively could you communicate your knowledge of "Jingle Bells" using only words? Who knows how to draw a bicycle: the person who can only explain how to draw it, or the person who can actually draw it? Of course, they both know, but the ways in which they know (verbally, kinesthetically) are qualitatively different.

Even a great deal of our verbal vocabulary consists of metaphors of spatial experience. Reconsider such phrases as: behind schedule, ahead of time, out of time, under pressure, on top of things, over a disappointment, an upright citizen, room to consider, point of view, take a position, hear the other side, open up a new field, gather or dig up facts, orientation, upper class, upwardly mobile, a backward country, a deep subject, on the level, and in the mainstream. We have become so habituated to these terms that we overlook their underlying connotations.

Recent research shows that people use mental images in solving problems related to both reasoning and physical skills (Kosslyn 1980, 1985). Further, people manipulate mental images much as they might manipulate three-dimensional objects, and they examine their mental images to discover information. In one experiment, subjects were asked to solve spatial problems like the one illustrated in figure 6-3. The problem was to identify which two drawings represent the same object in different spatial orientations. The more rotation required to ascertain whether two drawings matched, the longer subjects took to arrive at the answer. In other experiments, when scanning their mental maps, subjects required more time to travel greater distances. When asked questions about evaporation processes, subjects spontaneously invoked various concrete models while reasoning out their answers (Collins and Gentner 1987).

The introspective observations of many artists, scientists, and writers further support the idea that thought need not be (and may usually not be) verbal. The cognitive style of one of the most brilliant minds of our century, Albert Einstein's, appears to

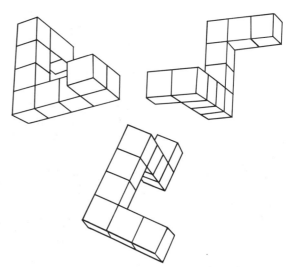

Figure 6-3. Orientation problem. Which two drawings represent the same object in two orientations?

have been visual-kinesthetic. In a letter to Jacques Hadamard, Einstein wrote (Ghiselin 1955, p. 43):

> The words of the language, as they are written or spoken, do not seem to play any role in my mechanism of thought. The physical entities which seem to serve as elements in thought are . . . of visual and some of muscular type. . . .

Since the time of the ancient Greeks, spatial imagery has been favored as a technique for remembering. The idea is that abstract ideas or items on a list can be more easily remembered if they are associated with some familiar place, such as a public building or one's own garden, house, or body. The Roman orator Cicero, for example, when preparing to give a speech, would place sections of his speech in different locations in his house and garden. Then he practiced each part at its location. Later, as he delivered his speech, he imagined himself walking through his home, picking up topics where he had placed them. Such techniques later came to be highly developed as an essential skill for rhetoric. This method is still a mainstay of modern self-help books on memory improvement.

The use of spatial memory skills is more highly valued in some cultures than in others. Australian aborigine children, for example, consistently score three years ahead of white Australian peers in their

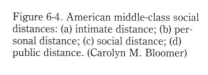

Figure 6-4. American middle-class social distances: (a) intimate distance; (b) personal distance; (c) social distance; (d) public distance. (Carolyn M. Bloomer)

ability to remember the positions of objects on a board, whether the objects are different or identical. According to Dr. Judy Kearins, aborigine superiority was consistent for all spatial tests and for all age groups between five and sixteen (cited in Restak 1984, pp. 202–3). Some analysts have speculated that aborigine life requires closer attention to subtleties in spatial position than does life in other parts of Australia, because their landscape—to outsiders—appears to be relatively featureless. Likewise, the high-status navigators of the Puluwat Atoll in the Pacific must learn and apply a range of spatial, temporal, visual, kinesthetic, and tactile memory skills. In general, emphasis on memory skills is greater among cultures that do not have a

written language. With writing, knowledge tends to get stored in books and records rather than in people.

That human thinking takes a variety of forms should not be too surprising. Most of our brain space is involved with processing spatial information of one sort or another: the frontal lobes deal with complex movement and planning (imaging the future); the parietal lobes with sensory (spatial) information; the right temporal lobe with visual-spatial integration; and the occipital lobe with visual information. The seat of language, the left temporal lobe, is only one element in this complex and interdependent cognitive system. The traditional emphasis in schools on verbal-mathematical intelligence clearly ignores a good deal of students' cognitive potential.

EXPERIENCING SPACE

You experience space with the motion of your body. When you move, you feel alive; you rejoice in space. When your freedom to move is restricted, you react—often violently. Even infants will rage at being penned in or pinned down, and so do adults: people do not volunteer for prisons and straitjackets. In military basic training, aggressive violation of trainees' personal space is used as a tool for developing obedience through fear and frustration.

Personal Space

Each individual carries around a personal-space bubble that is protected as an invisible, movable territory. You are not usually aware of this bubble until you feel that someone else has intruded into it. When people talk, they maintain a natural distance from each other. Occasionally, though, you may encounter someone whose personal space is different, and you feel uneasy: you think of such people as not keeping their distance, as too close for comfort, or as bearing down on you. As an experiment, try moving into another person's space bubble and see how he or she reacts (but choose your ''victim'' carefully!).

Different cultures have different norms for personal space. Some ethnic groups establish wide spaces among people and talk with expansive gestures that define and maintain the space. Other groups value proximity and place themselves close enough to touch or even to breathe on one another while talking. Anthropologist Edward T. Hall has studied the kinds of distance people in different cultures keep in relation to one another; he calls his findings *proxemic patterns*.

American middle-class adults, Hall found, use four kinds of distance (see figure 6-4). The closest is *intimate distance*—less than 18 inches. When this close to another person, you can feel warmth from the person's body, and smell his or her body and breath. The person's face (or only part of it) fills the field of vision and is so near that it is difficult to focus on. Details such as pores, eyelashes, and body hair are easily seen. The potential for touching is unlimited. Comforting, protecting, and lovemaking are done in intimate distance.

Personal distance is between 18 inches and 4 feet; it includes distances from just inside to just outside touching range—a space within which physical domination can take place. The other person's head and shoulders dominate the visual field, and can be seen in great detail and three-dimensionality. The gaze moves around the face, and convergent vision is noticeable. Close friends or relatives often converse at personal distance.

Social distance ranges from 4 to 12 feet. The field of vision takes in most or all of the other person's body, but the detail seen when at intimate or personal distance is lost. Social interaction is not essential, but if you fail to recognize another person approaching you at this distance, you may be called a snob. Polite company and formal working relationships usually take place at social distance.

Public distance is more than 12 feet. The eyes' lines of sight are nearly parallel; as convergence becomes less, the sense of three-dimensionality diminishes, and the other person's body appears more flat. Talking across public distance requires raising your voice, and subtleties of voice and expression are lost; public distance is too far for natural conversation.

Each type of distance sets parameters for a distinctly different type of social relationship, but the specifics differ from culture to culture. Arabs, for example, usually consider it impolite if you deny the other person the aroma of your breath, and body odors are felt to communicate important information about the other person's health and emotional state. Germans, on the other hand, may feel intruded upon by someone who is merely looking at them from outside an open door. When middle-class Americans travel to another culture, they may find themselves quite uncomfortable with spatial relationships that are natural to that culture.

These distances are portrayed in art imagery, although we are usually only subliminally aware of it. The sculptures of ancient Egyptian pharaohs, for example, represent the perception of someone seen from public distance (see figure 6-5). No matter how physically close we get to one of these sculptures, our perceptions are limited to those of public distance. One reason is the smooth surface: we cannot see more detail by moving closer. This perceptual distancing is enhanced by the pharaoh's posture of stable, alert repose and by his gaze, which seems to ignore us. The whole effect helps promote a realistic portrayal of the social, religious,

Figure 6-5. Anonymous (Egyptian), *Mycerinus* Old Kingdom, Fourth Dynasty (2599–2571 B.C.). Alabaster, 83 inches high (Museum of Fine Arts, Boston; Harvard/MFA Expedition)

Figure 6-6. Anonymous (Roman), *Augustus of Primaporta*, c. 20 B.C. Marble, 80 inches high. (Vatican Museum, Rome)

and political status of a pharaoh: half-god, set apart from ordinary mortals, untouched by time, existing in an impenetrable space.

Augustus of Primaporta, on the other hand, is a leader seen at social distance—quite a different image (see figure 6-6). Like the pharaoh, the Roman ruler is represented as a healthy and well-proportioned man. The small size of the cherub and the dolphin beside his right foot adds to the viewer's impression of his size, which is somewhat larger than life. As the viewer moves closer, the details of Augustus' clothing become clearer and clearer—as they would if he were a real person. Instead of seeming remote, Augustus appears to be moving forward in space, gesturing to someone outside his personal-space bubble, possibly greeting the viewer. Nonetheless, it is impossible to relate to him at personal distance because he stands on a pedestal: a person approaching him must look

up to him at a progressively sharper angle, and the shadow of his hand eventually falls over the viewer. The Roman ruler was an approachable man—not a god, yet governing under divine mandate—a military conqueror who moved about in real space with superior power, heroic strength, formal friendliness, and unquestioned authority.

With both of these sculptures, the viewer's relationship to the subject is directed and carefully controlled. Their perceptual qualities permit the viewer to relate to the subjects in some ways but not in others. In a similar light, it would be interesting to consider the use of perceptual distance in well-known sculptures such as the Lincoln Memorial, the Kamakura Buddha, the Statue of Liberty, and Michelangelo's *Pieta*.

It is also provocative to consider how photography and television have changed our perceptions of national leaders and other people in the public eye through the creation of perceptual distance. Before the use of photographs became customary, American statesmen maintained a public distance from their citizenry: they were seen only from this distance, in artists' depictions, or not at all. Now, television presents our leaders in the language of social or even personal distance—the visual equals of friends, relatives, and co-workers. Subtleties of voice, facial expression, and personal mannerism that could not be noticed across public distance have come to seem important and relevant. As the video camera dominates public communications, American election campaigns are increasingly involved with issues of personality and image. Expertly applied facial makeup and professional voice and body language coaching are now accepted realities of national political life. And in large part, they are an outcome of changing visual representations, which have led to corresponding changes in the electorate's perceptions.

An interesting use of personal space occurs with Duane Hanson's *Young Shopper* (see figure 6-7). I first encountered this sculpture in the lobby of a museum. As I passed hurriedly through the entrance, I vaguely noticed a large woman loaded with shopping bundles. I thought her oddly different from the usual museum-goer, but I quickly dismissed this prejudice and hurried on into the museum. Later, upon returning to the lobby, I saw the same woman standing just as I had left her earlier. Incredulously, I realized that this was not a woman but a shockingly lifelike sculpture. Approaching it, I felt uncomfortable, as if invading the personal space of a real person. I forced myself to study the details of her physiognomy at very close range; I became even more ill at ease. I felt guilty, as if I were about to be lectured for staring impolitely at the flaws and curiosities of a real stranger's body. It would have been easy to dismiss these feelings, but by lingering and exploring my discomfort, I experienced a profound complex of personal and cultural inhibitions about personal space. The *Young Shopper* was a minisession in sensitivity training.

Architectural Space

The way your surrounding space is structured—the way you can or cannot move within it in relation to your immediate needs—largely determines how you experience it. Small rooms can feel either cozy and comforting or crowded and closed-in. Large rooms

Figure 6-7. Duane Hanson (American), *Young Shopper*, 1973. Polychromed polyester resin and fiberglass, with clothes and other apparel; life-size. (Collection of Dr. Edmund Pillsbury, New Haven; photograph by Eric Pollitzer, courtesy of O. K. Harris Gallery, New York)

can seem spacious and expansive or empty and anonymous. Simply rearranging furniture in a room changes your relation to its space. Notice the furniture arrangements in homes you visit; they express a family's sense of interpersonal space and distance.

The placement and movability of furniture structures the relationships of the people who are in the room. Studies of hospitals and nursing homes have shown that the amount and kind of interaction patients have with each other is a direct consequence of furniture arrangements. In such institutional settings, chairs are usually arranged in straight lines for the convenience of workers who must sweep around them, but this arrangement dis-

Figure 6-8. Tokugawa Yori-fusa (Japanese), *Koishikawa Koraku-en,* begun in 1629. Edo (Tokyo) area. The garden was originally built as a setting for elaborate tea ceremonies; its name is derived from a Confucian text: "The wise ruler takes his ease only after the country prospers and the people are contented." (Mark Holborn)

courages face-to-face conversation. When chairs and tables are rearranged to encourage patient interaction, patients tend to talk to each other much more.

In schools and offices, space arrangements reflect social philosophy and status relationships. Modern offices have sometimes been referred to as "sensory reduction chambers." In the typical classroom, teachers have much more space available to them than do students, and they also have freedom to move about, which students do not. Student desks typically are aligned in straight rows facing forward so that students can have eye contact with the teacher but not with each other. Corridors are hard-surfaced and impersonal. During the years I supervised student teachers, I had occasion to visit a great many public schools. In a surprising number of instances, the front entrance was difficult to find. Once inside the building, I often encountered directions to the art room that were so complicated that a student escort was required. The corridors were like identical mazes, lacking windows that would have given a sense of direction or orientation with respect to the outside environment. On the other hand, as psychologist Robert Sommer (1969, p. 100) observed, the typical school building may provide "good training for an adult world of deadlines, rush hours, crowding, impersonality, and alienation from work."

The philosophy of an entire society is often expressed through its architectural treatment of space. In a medieval cathedral, the viewer feels awed and humbled within the lacy, complex, upward-reaching spaces. Modern glass-and-steel buildings emphasize simplicity, efficiency, and technological power. In each of its epochs, a culture reveals (as well as imposes) its philosophical concepts about humankind through its structuring of public and private space.

But cultural norms vary widely. Westerners tend to lay importance on linear space, whereas the Japanese emphasize points of convergence. As a consequence, Japanese cities traditionally name intersections but not streets. Moreover, houses are numbered in the order in which they were built, rather than according to their position on a street. In Japanese homes, furniture is placed in the center of the room rather than around the walls. Activities are not limited to single-purpose rooms: one room may be used at different times for eating, conversation, study, musical recitals, and sleeping. Actually, the single-activity room—bedroom, dining room, living room, and so on—is rather recent, even in the West, appearing in the eighteenth century. It is interesting to note modern countertendencies: the all-purpose room, the family room, and the great room.

Westerners learn to think of space as empty ground, whereas the Japanese assign meaning to space as intervals of space-time (*ma*). Japanese gardens manipulate spatial perception in a number of senses. By means of stepping stones, pathways,

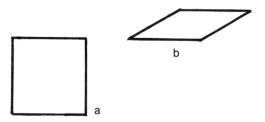
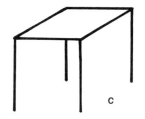
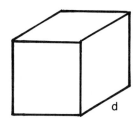

Figure 6-9. Examples of 2-D and 3-D perception.

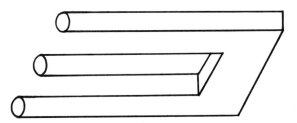

Figure 6-10. Ambiguous trident—a so-called irresolvable image. Test the effect of culture on your own seeing. After studying this figure, put the book down and try to draw the figure from memory.

and carefully planned views, the viewer is made to step, bend, look, and experience the garden from precisely planned positions and viewpoints (see figure 6-8). As the views change, so also may the temperature and humidity, the light and shade, and the smells.

Responsible architects, urban planners, and interior designers must take careful account of the human feelings that will be evoked by their engineering of space. Some sociological research suggests that hostility and aggression result when living conditions do not meet personal and ethnic space requirements. But generalizations can be misleading in this area. Western habits are by no means universal. Most human beings live peaceably in much smaller and more constricted living spaces than Westerners could tolerate.

PICTORIAL SPACE

Pictorial space is two-dimensional: pictures have height and width, but not depth. Western traditions of picture-making have accustomed people to assume that a picture represents a two-dimensional translation of three-dimensional space. Hence, your visual system has been taught to search automatically for ways in which a picture can be interpreted as an image of physical space. For example, you see figure 6-9a as being a square. Figure 6-9b is ambiguous: you can see it as being either a flat shape (a rhombus) or a square tilted in space. With four lines added to the rhombus, you no longer interpret the drawing as being a flat pattern, but as being a three-dimensional table (see figure 6-9c). One more line creates a three-dimensional cube (see figure 6-9d). It becomes almost impossible to see these last two figures as being flat—even though they are flat. The perception of least resistance seems to be that of seeing depth. Our culture believes so strongly that this is natural that children

who see flat test pictures as flat test pictures may be diagnosed as being unable to perceive depth!

Experimental evidence (reviewed in Cole and Scribner 1971) shows, however, that this type of pictorial depth perception is extensively conditioned by culture. For example, African villagers whose art did not include Western pictorial depth techniques did not interpret Western-style pictures (see figure 4-10) as being three-dimensional, although they could do so once the pictorial rules were explained to them. They also perceived drawings as being flat patterns rather than as being representations of three-dimensional objects. As a consequence, they found no ambiguity in a drawing similar to figure 6-10, and they were able to draw it from memory more easily than could Westernized subjects, who found it confusing.

Looking at flat pictures is not the same as looking at space: each involves quite different perceptual tasks. Tests of depth perception often use drawings that represent three-dimensional solids (such as figure 6-3); and children who fail to recognize the implied three-dimensionality of these representations are said to "lack depth perception" and may be labeled "perceptually handicapped" or "learning disabled." But two-dimensional drawings cannot possibly test actual depth perception. Instead, they can only establish whether or not the

Figure 6-11. David Hockney (English), *Christopher Isherwood Talking to Bob Holman, Santa Monica, March 14, 1983,* 1983. Photographic collage, 43½ × 64½ inches. Notice how points of special interest (such as faces and hands) are represented by several images, reflecting the fixation patterns of normal scan paths (see figure 2-20). (© David Hockney, 1983; permission of the artist)

child has learned to read the flat patterns in the culturally desired way.

The problem of seeing depth in flat pictures is complex. The art of most cultures does represent three-dimensional space in some manner. But the cultural rules for organizing pictorial space are quite varied. The Western fixed-viewpoint is but one of many ways in which pictures can mirror the perceptual experience of space.

Motion Parallax

Our perception of physical space is produced by a continuous succession of changing relationships in the visual field (this phenomenon is called *motion parallax*; see chapter 9). Even slight head movements enhance the experience of space. One of the most fundamental aspects of looking at a picture is that, when you move your head, the objects represented in the composition do not change their positions in relation to one another. Lack of motion parallax tells you that you are looking at a flat surface.

Holographic photography is an interesting exception to this rule: it produces uncanny two-dimensional photographs in which motion parallax can be experienced. A *hologram* is a recorded pattern of interference between reflected and projected portions of a split laser beam. Looking at a holographic plate is rather like looking into a box or at a diorama and being able to move your head around to inspect the objects—except that the box does not exist. In fact, you are looking at what appears to be a piece of flat, plastic film! Holograms are now common on credit cards because they cannot easily be counterfeited.

The Visual Field

Westerners tend to assume that traditional realistic paintings portray the visual field of the retina at a given instant of time, but this is not precisely the case. The visual field has three zones of clarity: foveal, macular, and peripheral (see figures 2-16 and 2-17). But Western paintings (and photographs) typically portray objects in planes of uniform clarity

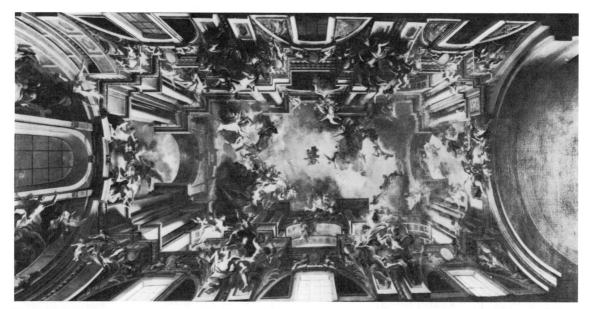

Figure 6-12. Fra Andrea Pozzo (Italian), *The Glorification of St. Ignatius,* 1691–94. Ceiling fresco in the nave of Sant' Ignazio, Rome.

across the surface of the canvas. When variations in focus occur, they almost always represent depth of field (see chapter 7), which is a different dimension from the one being considered here. In physical space, the perception of such consistent clarity can only result from a number of fixations over time. The nature of such a series of fixations is revealed in the photographic compositions of David Hockney (see figure 6-11). The modules in these compositions result from standing in one position and aiming the camera at different portions of the visual field.

Traditional realistic pictures represent an integrated mental image—a summed total of an infinite number of separate fixations, as made from a fixed viewpoint in space. You, in turn, view these pictures with a series of separate fixations, just as you might do if you were looking at the subject in physical space. Looking at a Western picture, then, resembles looking at a scene through a single stationary window. Chinese scroll paintings, by contrast, present continually changing viewpoints as the viewer's eye travels across a gradually revealed landscape.

At the same time, the frame of a Western picture is usually visible in peripheral vision, providing a constant reminder that you are looking at a flat work of art. If the painting is large enough, you can eliminate the boundaries of the painting from your visual field by moving closer; as a result you can feel yourself being drawn more strongly into the picture. When the picture is not framed, but instead is placed in a plausible three-dimensional context, the illusion of space is often astonishing. In Fra Andrea Pozzo's ceiling fresco, for example, the heavens seem to open above the heads of the worshipers as St. Ignatius ascends to meet Jesus (see figure 6-12).

An object's appearance in the visual field depends on your distance from it. When an object is nearby, you see it with great detail and clarity. As distance increases, however, the image becomes more generalized, and less detail is conveyed. For example, figure 6-13 is a block portrait of a well-known American. At reading distance, the details of the squares and their edges are quite distinct, and the picture does not even appear to represent a face. But if you squint, jiggle the picture, or view it from a distance of about 12 feet (or thirty to forty times the height of the picture), the contrasting edges of the squares become less apparent, and you will be able to see the subject instantly. The contemporary American artist Chuck Close used this same principle in a series of portraits composed entirely of his own thumbprints (see figure 6-14).

A number of such block portraits were made by scientists trying to determine the minimum amount of visual information people need in order to recog-

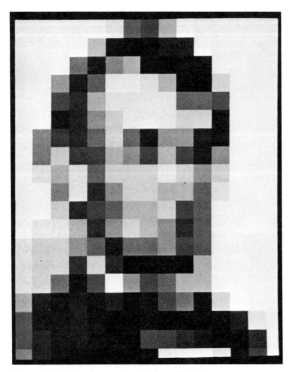

Figure 6-13. Block portrait of 16 × 19 (304) squares. (Leon Harmon and *Scientific American*)

Figure 6-14. Chuck Close (American), *Robert/Fingerprint*, 1978. Pencil and stamp-pad ink on paper, 29½ × 22¼ inches. (The Ackland Art Museum, The University of North Carolina at Chapel Hill; Ackland Fund)

nize individual faces (Harmon 1973). They found that recognition levels of up to 95 percent correctness could be achieved when a photograph of a face was reduced to a composition of 16 × 16 (256) squares, each consisting of one of eight or sixteen shades of gray. The same technique of blocking out the details of a picture is now often used with videotapes when it is desirable to protect an individual from being recognized. Squinting at such a picture, however, is often surprisingly revealing.

These pictures seem paradoxical: they appear to lose detail when viewed from close up, whereas at a distance they seem to possess more detail than they actually do. This strange phenomenon arises from the presence of misleading patterns or visual noise. At a closer distance, you really do see more detail, but much of that detail is irrelevant and distracting (for example, the edges of the squares, or the ridges of the fingerprints). From the proper distance, however, the irrelevant detail is less visible; then, as your visual system makes closure, your mind enhances the form by filling in details that are not actually present. Thus, the same object is per-

ceived as being a physically different object when seen from different distances. Because of object constancy, however, you only occasionally become aware of this phenomenon in everyday seeing, and usually only when faced with unfamiliar objects or unusual viewing conditions.

With movement in space, objects in the visual field change in character. Hence, the visual field (what registers on the retina) changes as the structure of the retina interacts with distance. Looking at pictures engages this phenomenon in two ways: first, with the distance from which the picture is viewed; and second, with the distance from the subject as represented in the picture. Andrew Wyeth's *Braids* capitalizes on both factors (see figure 6-15). When the original painting is seen from a distance of two or three feet, every stitch in Helga's sweater appears to have been painstakingly painted. Closer inspection, however, reveals the existence of relatively few sparsely rendered stitches. For the most part, the sweater consists of abstract brush-strokes that, when viewed from the appropriate distance, convey the illusion of sweater

Figure 6-15. Andrew Wyeth (American), *Braids,* 1979. Tempera, 16$^1/_2$ × 20$^1/_2$ inches. (© 1986 Leonard E. B. Andrews)

yarn (compare this with figure 2-17, Rembrandt's self-portrait).

Field and Frame

Both photographs in figure 6-16 show the same tree, yet one seems much closer than the other to the viewer. A powerful representation of space and distance is created by the relationship of the subject to the edges of the composition. This pictorial construction of the field of vision is called the *field-and-frame relationship.* The *field* is what is in the composition, and the *frame* is its border.

Pictorial field-and-frame relationships parallel normal visual experience. From a distance, many things register on the retinal field. Thus, a wide-angle, panoramic scene encourages the sense of viewing from far off and evokes a strong feeling of removal from the subject (see figures 2-12, 3-13, and 6-17). Conversely, when an object is large or very close, it fills the visual field and eliminates the surrounding context. Thus, a restricted view elicits a feeling of closeness to the subject (see figure 4-4). In this way, field-and-frame relationships correspond to particular perceptual distances from a subject.

Movie and television directors use field-and-frame relationships to control the emotional involvement of an audience, by representing specific perceptual distances (compare figure 6-4). Long shots are used to create the illusion of a public distance—an objective, overall, often impersonal perspective. Closeups imitate personal or intimate distance in order to generate gut-level involvement in scenes of violence or intense emotion. Frequent movie and television viewing—in which field and frame are easily controlled—have so habituated audiences to accepting preprogrammed involvement that many people feel a frustrating sense of distance from live theater performances: because actors are seen from public distance, focus and emotional involvement depend on the viewer's own (somewhat rusty) imagination and perceptual selection.

In his painting *Into the World There Came a Soul Called Ida* (see figure 6-18), Ivan Albright portrayed characteristics of close distance. Not just Ida herself, but all the objects are rendered with a wealth of detail. In real life, you would have to be quite near to Ida—in intimate distance, and perhaps even peering through a magnifying glass—to see

Figure 6-16. Field and frame. (Frank Mulvey, *Graphic Perception of Space.* Van Nostrand Reinhold, 1969)

Figure 6-17. Domenikos Theotokopoulos [El Greco] (Spanish; Cretan-born) *View of Toledo,* c. 1600. Oil on canvas, 47³/₄ × 42³/₄ inches. (The Metropolitan Museum of Art, New York; bequest of Mrs. H. O. Havemeyer, 1929; The H. O. Havemeyer Collection)

Figure 6-18. Ivan Albright (American), *Into the World The Came a Soul Called Ida,* 1928–29. Oil, 55 × 46 inches. (Iv Albright and The Art Institute of Chicago)

Figure 6-19. Winslow Homer (American), *Breezing Up*, 1876. Oil on canvas, 24^1/$_8$ × 38^1/$_8$ inches. (National Gallery of Art, Washington, D.C.; gift of the W. L. and May T. Mellon Foundation)

the details shown in this painting. At the same time, the field-and-frame relationship (a full-body view of Ida) is characteristic of public distance. Thus, Albright's painting is a perceptual paradox. We are placed at a polite public distance while at the same time we are overwhelmed by intimate, claustrophobic detail.

General Relativity

People perceive space and distance best when the visual field consists of familiar objects that are situated in familiar relationships and shown in familiar contexts (see chapter 4). By creating such a visual field, the artist can put to use the viewer's taken-for-granted assumptions about the nature of the objects in the picture. Traditional artworks tend to support rather than to challenge these tacit assumptions. A simple and direct use of such relativity is shown in figure 6-19. Cover and uncover the distant ship on the right of the composition; notice how its presence enhances your sense of space.

Now look at figure 6-20. Familiar and unfamiliar objects are juxtaposed in ways that are quite alien

Figure 6-20. Marc Chagall (French), *I and the Village*, 1911. Oil, 75^5/$_8$ × 59^5/$_8$ inches. (The Museum of Modern Art, New York; Mrs. Simon Guggenheim Fund)

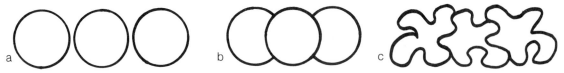

a   b   c

Figure 6-21. What is on top?

to everyday notions of how things are located in space. You can pick out normal spatial qualities in small areas of the painting, but the artist effectively and purposefully prevents you from applying everyday perceptual techniques to the painting as a whole. This painting denies objective space in favor of a subjective, highly personal mental map of relationships. It shows not outward but inward space.

Vertical Positioning

Human beings raise their eyes to see distant things and lower them to look at nearer objects. Pictures

Figure 6-22. Pablo Picasso (Spanish), *Accordionist (H arlequin)*, 1911. Oil on canvas, approximately $51^1/_4 \times 35^1/_4$ inches. (Solomon R. Guggenheim Museum, New York; photograph by David Heald)

reflect this when nearer objects are placed toward the bottom of a picture and more distant ones are placed higher up. Position on the picture plane is a reliable and universal indicator of relative distance (see figures 2-12, 3-13, 4-7, 4-11, 4-25, 6-17, and 7-5). Often a horizon line is used to represent an imaginary eye level. In this case, objects above the horizon descend as distance increases, while objects below the horizon line ascend as distance increases. With aerial views, object positions can radiate outward in any direction as they increase in distance from any given point.

Interposition

Interposition is the perception of an object positioned in-between the viewer and another object. The more completely seen object is perceived as being in front of the less completely seen object. Interposition is basic to everyday vision, since you can never see any three-dimensional object (except a fully transparent object) in its entirety at once: some part of the object is always masked—either by other objects or by intervening surfaces of the object itself. Motion parallax is the experience of changing interpositions in combination with object constancy and the tendency to complete forms that are incompletely seen. Some researchers feel that the perception of interposition is the strongest cue people have for perceiving depth.

In pictures, interposition is represented when the shapes of nearer objects are complete and the shapes of objects behind are incompletely shown. In drawing, the technique is often called *overlapping*. In figure 4-17c, you perceive the left-hand square as being situated between yourself and the square on the right. In figure 6-21a, the three circles appear to be equally distant from you: they are all complete. In figure 6-21b, however, the center circle alone maintains completeness and therefore is seen as being on top of the others. This principle holds only for normal shapes, however. The third grouping of irregular shapes is ambiguous (see figure 6-21c): you cannot tell which one is on top. Indeed, with a little concentration, you can make yourself see a number of different overlap combina-

Figure 6-23. Thomas Cole (American), *The Pic-Nic,* 1846. Oil on canvas, 44⁷/₈ × 71⁷/₈ inches. Skillful combinations of depth cues give an illusion of space in this painting. The field-and-frame relationship promotes a sense of distance both from and within the scene. The landscape ascends toward the horizon with distance, while the clouds descend. Among the trees, people, and hills, every interposition acts as a depth indicator, creating a series of perceptual closures. The canvas is nearly 4 by 6 feet in size; hence, the great number of fixations a viewer makes in looking at it adds to the perception of deep space. (The Brooklyn Museum; A. Augustus Healy Fund)

Figure 6-24:. Michelangelo Buonarroti (Italian), *The Deluge.* Detail from the ceiling fresco of the Sistine Chapel, 1508 – 12. Because Michelangelo was a sculptor, his two-dimensional works reflect a special awareness of space. (The Vatican, Rome)

tions. This effect of ambiguous spatial readings was used by the Analytic Cubists to despatialize pictorial images (see figure 6-22).

Pictures representing any degree of interposition always appear to Western viewers to have more depth than compositions that lack interposition altogether. The drawings of children and untrained artists often lack overlapping and seem flat. Painters and photographers use interposition to great advantage when they employ such devices as overhanging branches or foreground areas of rocks, bushes, or blades of grass to interrupt a more distant scene (see figure 6-23). The pictorial representation of complex interpositions of parts of the body is called *foreshortening*. Foreshortening produces powerful illusions of depth and volume; it is a device characteristic of post-Renaissance Western drawings and paintings (see figure 6-24).

are pictorially represented as transparent, the picture is often called an *X-ray drawing*. The X-ray style is characteristic of the bark paintings of Australian aborigines (see figure 6-25), where the skeleton and internal organs of animals are shown. Christian art does something like this when it depicts the heart of Jesus.

CULTURE AND PICTORIAL DEPTH

Looking at pictures is a process of interpretation. People do not automatically see depth in pictures. Instead, people learn cultural rules for interpreting pictures. Western pictorial perception has been profoundly shaped by the images and world views that linear perspective represents. So complete has been this conditioning that Westerners usually suppose that seeing illusions of depth in pictures is something that the human visual system does naturally and automatically. If it is natural to see depth in flat patterns, then visual realism gives the illusion of being a natural art style—something discovered by Western artists, rather than something invented by them.

Because of this belief that pictorial depth perception is natural, Westerners tend to judge art in particular ways—for example, interpreting the lack of linear perspective in another culture as evidence that the culture has not yet discovered it. They are seen as not being developed or evolved enough (that is, as being primitive), or as following the wrong path (that is, as being naive and unsophisticated). The underlying assumption is that the natural course of human artistic development will inevitably move in the direction of Western realism.

Besides being ethnocentric, such views betray an ignorance of facts. Linear perspective has been known to many cultures, including the ancient Romans and the Chinese. But they have chosen not to apply it to serious artmaking. In the case of China, this was because the emphasis on visual appearances was taken to be too vulgar a concern for serious artists. Only in the West has pictorial tradition concentrated on the visual field of a single retina located at a fixed point in time-space. How and why Western tradition developed along these lines is the subject of the next chapter.

Figure 6-25. Anonymous (Native Australian, Northern Territory), *Two Kangaroos,* n.d. Painting on bark, 40³/4 × 25 inches. (The Metropolitan Museum of Art, New York; The Michael C. Rockefeller Memorial Collection, Bequest of Nelson A. Rockefeller, 1979)

With transparent objects, you can see interposition and the total form at the same time. Consequently, drawings that feature simultaneous overlapping and complete form represent the experience of transparency and produce a perception of depth (see figure 6-25 and plate C-5). Some drawings of this type are ambiguous, since the viewer has no way of telling which surface is supposed to be nearer. Because they can be perceived in alternate ways, these drawings are often called *reversible illusions* (see figure 3-22). When opaque objects

7

Depth and Distance
The I as a Camera

As you sit reading this book, look up and glance around the room. Notice how things change in appearance as they are farther away from you: parallel lines in the floor seem to move closer together; horizontal edges appear to slant; textures compress; details become harder to see. These gradual changes in the appearance of things because of increasing distance from the viewer are called *perceptual* or *distance gradients*. Gradients are a different type of distance cue from those discussed in chapter 6. Interposition, position, and motion parallax give you information that you can verify directly. That is, you can walk around in space, examine the objects in question, and evaluate the correctness of your perceptions.

But gradients do not exist in physical space. As you approach objects, the gradients disappear. For example, railroad tracks appear to converge at a point on the horizon, but if you walked to that point, you would find the tracks to be the same distance apart as they were where you started. Similarly, houses are not smaller because they are farther away, nor do objects acquire more detail as you approach. Thus, although these gradual patterns of change register on the retina, they do not characterize things in the physical world. Gradients are, instead, an attribute of the visual field; they are retinal patterns that tell you where you are located in relation to objects in the space around you.

People tend to think of the visual field as a copy or mirror of the physical world. But the visual field is radically different from the external world. The physical world is continuous; it is everywhere around you. But the visual field is normally shaped like an oval that extends in front of you approximately 180 degrees horizontally and 150 degrees vertically (see chapter 2). And whereas the physical world has no focus, the visual field has different degrees of clarity. Things appear sharp and clear only in the center (due to foveal vision), and they become increasingly vague toward the periphery (see figure 2-17). Objects in the physical world are separate and distinct, yet in the visual field they appear doubled except when focused in central vision.

In perception, the physical world is characterized by constancy (see chapter 4). People think of the external world as there, existing independently of them, and remaining the same regardless of who perceives it. It is stable; it does not continually recompose itself every time a person moves. The visual field, on the other hand, changes constantly with every shift (however slight) of eye, head, or body position; its composition is internal and specific to an individual's temporary location in time and space. Because of these continual changes in the visual field, you are able to perceive spatial relationships between yourself and your surroundings.

PATTERN GRADIENTS

In figure 7-1, patterns of gradual compression lead to an illusion of space and distance, because of gradients in density, interval, or shape. As the patterns progress upward from the bottom to the middle of the frames, they become progressively denser, and the spaces between the elements become increasingly smaller. The effect is of single, continuous surfaces extending into space to meet a horizon. When the regularity of a gradient is interrupted—suddenly or gradually—the viewer imagines a change in plane: an edge or a contour (see figure 7-1d).

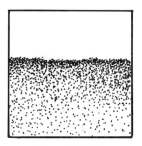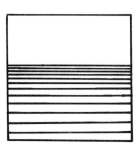

Figure 7-1. Distance gradients: (a) density gradient; (b) interval gradient; (c) shape gradient; (d) interrupted gradient.

Pattern gradients are important cues for depth perception. The visual cliff discussed in chapter 6 was dramatized by a simple geometric pattern: the checkerboard. If you look at figure 6-1c from the kitten's-eye view, you will notice that the rate of change in the checkerboard pattern signals whether you are looking at the surface face-on or at an angle. Likewise, in art images, geometric gradients often present more dramatic illusions of space than do the less regular patterns of more natural scenes (see figure 7-2). Geometric patterns can be precisely varied, but in natural scenes, depth and distance gradients may be more variable and less rigidly patterned (see figure 6-23, for example). Gradients are apparent in photographs, as well.

GRADIENTS OF DETAIL

The farther away objects are, the less detail is apparent in the visual field. Within limits, simply focusing on an object seems to bring it nearer. Focusing causes the image of the object to fall on the fovea (the area of clearest vision). The sensation of increased detail results in a perception of nearer distance. Leonardo da Vinci termed this gradient the *perspective of disappearance*. He defined it as the extent to which objects in a picture "ought to be less finished in proportion as they are remote." An ancient Chinese treatise states the same principle as "Distant men have no eyes. Distant trees have no branches."

With increased distance, visual information becomes more generalized. As a consequence, when identifying distant objects, you must rely more heavily on logic and on past experience. In familiar environments, you tend to make few errors, because you see what you expect to see. In unfamiliar territory, your experience may be quite different. In a strange neighborhood, for example, you need to be closer to a street sign in order to read it. Likewise, you can identify a good friend from two blocks away, but someone whom you have seen only once or twice may have to come within 10 feet before you can be certain who it is. And the syndrome of general irritability during vacation trips is often fueled by errors and time lost in locating unfamiliar signs and landmarks soon enough to stop or make the right turn.

As you saw with *Mycerinus* (figure 6-5), *Augustus* (figure 6-6) and *Ida* (figure 6-18), the amount of detail portrayed affects your perceived distance (as opposed to your physical distance) from the subject. In a traditional painting such as Thomas Cole's *The Pic-Nic* (see figure 6-23), the artist only needs to depict distant hills, trees, and mountains in a general way. The viewer identifies them instantly and is not confused by the omission of detail. But the use of detail gradients is effective only when the subject is at least somewhat familiar. Yves Tanguy's *The Furniture of Time* (see figure 4-7), for example, shows the viewer unfamiliar objects. Their surfaces suggest either that they are very smooth, or that the observer is viewing them from some distance. But which is the case? Here, the perspective of disappearance is not enlightening.

GRADIENTS OF SHARPNESS

As objects are seen progressively farther from you, their edges seem less distinct and more blurred: things seem to merge into one another. Determining where one object ends and the next one begins becomes more difficult. Texture is most susceptible to blurring. The patterns of highly textured surfaces (such as a plowed field) appear increasingly compressed with distance. By the time a texture

Figure 7-2. Victor Vasarely (French), *Sreech,* 1983. Acrylic on canvas, 48 × 48 inches. (© ARS N.Y./S.P.A.D.E.M., 1989)

Figure 7-3. Tracks. (Bruce Thompson)

reaches the horizon line, it seems to have disappeared completely (see figure 7-3).

This effect occurs because of grain in the retinal image (see figures 2-4, 2-16, and 2-17). With a near object, the image is distributed across a greater number of photoreceptors, giving a finer grain to the image transmitted to the brain. Furthermore, small areas of the object can be closely examined with high-resolution foveal fixations. For both reasons, near objects have more apparent detail. With distance, the opposite is true. The object's image covers a smaller area of the retina and is thus grainier; therefore, the sensation of detail relayed to the brain is reduced. Similar effects occur in photographs, because film emulsions register gradients in much the same way as does the retina. With film, the amount of apparent detail (or blur) varies with differences in the size of the photosensitive particles (silver bromide crystals), and with the number of particles that compose an object's image (see chapter 8).

Your visual system almost magically correlates blur with viewing distance (this is known as the *image-distance ratio*). In the block portrait of Lincoln (see figure 6-13), and in Chuck Close's thumbprint portrait (see figure 6-14), visual information remains constant. As you move nearer or farther,

what varies is the relationship of the portrait to the number and location of the retinal photoreceptors that it stimulates. At the distance at which the amount of detail in the face matches the amount of detail that seems natural for a face seen from that distance, the image appears to resolve with startling clarity.

In chapter 2, we discussed the perceptual effects of varying viewing distances, in relation to paintings by Rembrandt; these effects are also quite noticeable in Impressionist and Pointillist works (see plate C-1), and they are present to some degree in all pictures. The dynamics of perceptual differences in the near-, middle-, and far-distance viewing of pictures can be quite exciting to explore. Viewers miss a great deal when they look at a painting or drawing from a single distance instead of experimenting by moving nearer and farther from it. This interactive dimension is virtually

Figure 7-4. Attributed to Wu Chen (Chinese, 1280 – 1354), *Bamboo in the Wind*, Yuan Dynasty. Hanging scroll, 29⁵/₈ × 21³/₈ inches. (Museum of Fine Arts, Boston; Chinese and Japanese Special Fund)

absent from reproductions in books, where sharpness gradients are determined not by the human eye (for which the works were intended), but by the arbitrary technical limitations of film grain and printing processes.

GRADIENTS OF COLOR

Color gradients are especially observable in landscapes. With increasing distance, colors appear paler, less intense, and more grayish or bluish, because distance diffuses the amount of reflected light. Because of color constancy (see chapters 4 and 5), color gradients are difficult to separate out from the effects of light and shadow over short distances. When the air is clear, color gradients are usually noticeable only across great expanses of space. In the presence of fog or the haze of air pollution, however, such effects become obvious over much shorter distances. People ecstatically exclaim "What a clear day!" when distant objects are visible with unusual brilliance and clarity. Perhaps because of their experience with such atmospheric conditions, people tend to perceive brightly colored objects as being nearer to them than less bright objects.

Color gradients can evoke illusions of space on a flat surface, as in *Bamboo in the Wind* (see figure 7-

Figure 7-5. Vincent Van Gogh (Dutch), *The Crau from Montmajour*, 1888. Pen, reed pen, and black chalk, 19 × 24 inches. (Reproduced by courtesy of the Trustees of the British Museum, London)

4), where other depth and distance clues (size, vertical positioning, and sharpness of edges) remain uniform. Wu Chen's painting is representative of the way Chinese and Japanese artists traditionally used gradients of black ink to create spatial qualities (see figures 2-12 and 3-18).

Aerial Perspective

In Western art, the three distance gradients of detail, sharpness, and color are commonly grouped together and called *aerial perspective*, because their gradations are a function of the volume of air through which observed objects are seen. Leonardo da Vinci is often given credit for first describing aerial perspective and explaining its use in painting. Since the Renaissance, aerial perspective has been favored by Western artists as a technique for enhancing illusions of space and distance. In his pen drawing *The Crau from Montmajour* (see figure 7-5), Vincent van Gogh combined size gradients with gradients of detail, sharpness, and color (value). Aerial perspective is also obvious in *The Pic-Nic* (see figure 6-23) and in Monet's *The Houses of Parliament, Sunset* (see figure 2-23 and plate C-1).

GRADIENTS OF LIGHT

People see objects because their surfaces reflect light (see chapter 5), but the amount of light reflected depends on how the surface is oriented in relation to the light source. The same surface reflects light differently depending on whether it is facing toward, away from, or at an angle to the light rays hitting its surface. Differences in light reflectivity are also caused by material composition, color, and texture. These differences in reflectivity convey visual information about the form and nature of an object. Without these variations, your eyes would register no differences, and you could see nothing. Thus your perceptions of objects and of their contexts in space depend entirely on variations in light entering your eye.

Gradual transitions from light to shadow lead to the perception of a curved surface. Abrupt changes from light to dark are seen as a change in planes, such as occurs with an edge or a corner. When a surface faces a light source, it reflects light back, and the viewer calls it *bright*. A surface that faces away from the light source reflects very little light

Figure 7-6. Egg and cube. (Bruce Thompson)

MENTAL IMAGE

Figure 7-7. Shadow letters.

and is said to have an *attached shadow*. (An attached shadow is part of the perceived surface of the object, in contrast to a *cast shadow*, which falls onto a surface outside the object.) All of these effects can be seen in the photograph of the cube and egg shown in figure 7-6. Sensitivity to these variations in light reflectivity enables you to perceive surface, edge, texture, solidity, form, and distance between objects. Indeed, you can read images when given only the deepest shadows as in figure 7-7 and in high-contrast photography (see figure 3-15).

As the sources and intensities of illumination continually vary, shadows change in intensity and color. Even though gradients of light (that is, shadows) are crucial for your identification of objects and substances, you normally discount shadows in conscious perception. Tuning out the variability of light enables you to maintain object and color constancy (see chapters 4 and 5). Otherwise, you would see the same object as a different object with every change in light conditions.

Something that shows no variation in light reflectivity is perceived as featureless. In a featureless visual field, you can perceive neither objects nor depth and distance. Indeed, in relatively featureless landscapes such as those of the Arctic, a desert, or a dead calm sea (the doldrums), people sometimes become disoriented, anxious, or even psychotic. In the Arctic, under certain weather conditions, the horizon disappears. In the undifferentiated light and snow-covered terrain, nothing can be seen. This alarming situation is called *whiteout*.

Figure 7-8. Michelangelo Merisi da Caravaggio (Italian), *Supper at Emmaus,* 1598 – 1601. Oil on canvas, 56 × 77½ inches. (National Gallery, London)

People who live in such locations, however, are sensitive to features that are all but invisible to strangers. It is well-known, for instance, that Eskimos have twenty-six different words for differentiating snow and twelve different terms for winds. This suggests that human perceptions of depth and distance, as well as of environmental features, are to some degree learned, and that accurate perception is specific to particular cultures and environments.

Chiaroscuro

On a two-dimensional surface, such as a painting, drawing, or photograph, gradients of light and dark can produce illusions of depth. Dark areas appear to recede from the viewer, while light areas appear to project toward the viewer. The manipulation of light-to-dark gradients is one of the first techniques traditionally taught to Western drawing students. This play of light and dark in the composition of an artwork is called *chiaroscuro*. The term comes from two Italian words, meaning ''light'' and ''dark,'' respectively. During the Renaissance, the use of chiaroscuro became widespread in Western painting and drawing.

Chiaroscuro is the most prominent feature of the painting *Supper at Emmaus* by Michelangelo Merisi da Caravaggio (see figure 7-8), where the use of light and shadow conveys both factual and symbolic information. From the angles of the short shadows cast by the bread and the dishes and from the patterns of light and shadow on the men's heads and faces, we can conjecture that an unseen light source exists above, slightly to the left, and somewhat forward of the standing man on the left of the painting (the innkeeper). An odd shadow appears on the wall behind the man facing us. Such a shadow would have to have been cast by a light source near his left elbow, but the picture gives no other indication of such a light. Art historians state that this negative halo is the shadow cast by the innkeeper; it falls on the wall, but not on the man's face! The painting has some other unnatural aspects, too. The bowl of out-of-season fruit seems to project beyond the edge of the table. The extended hands of the man on the right are both the same size, even though one is represented as being much nearer to the viewer than the other. The painting appears visually realistic, but these subtle inconsistencies create an element of strangeness.

The title reveals that the subject of the painting is an event related only in the Gospel of Luke: the moment on Resurrection Sunday when Jesus revealed himself to two of his disciples (Cleopas on the left, and either Peter or James the Great on the right). The grapes, bread, wine, and water symbolize the Eucharist; the apples, the Fall of Man; the bursting pomegranate, the crown of thorns; the

Figure 7-9. Kung Hsien (Chinese), *Landscape,* 1688 (Qing Dynasty). Album leaf, ink on paper, 8³/₄ × 17¹/₅ inches. (The Metropolitan Museum of Art, New York; Sackler Collection, 1960)

seashell worn by Peter/James, a pilgrimage. Not recognizing the holy presence, the innkeeper has not removed his hat. A sacred event is portrayed as an ordinary, everyday scene involving real people. Many of Caravaggio's contemporaries were offended by his rustic depictions of religious scenes and persons. His paintings were said to lack decorum.

Caravaggio used chiaroscuro to create dramatic illusions of depth and realism, but at the same time he also employed light and shadow as powerful symbols. The fact that the innkeeper's shadow does not darken Jesus' face is a literal image used to symbolize supernatural power. In the late sixteenth century, the principle of organizing a composition around a dramatic and direct light source was a new idea. Caravaggio was excited by it; he is reported to have said repeatedly that "all things are revealed by light."

Caravaggio's method was to create a light side and a dark side of the painted objects. This technique is called *tenebrism,* meaning "dark manner." The compositions of Caravaggio's followers (called the *Caravaggists*) were characterized by the dramatic lighting effects of tenebrism. The drama and symbolism of light is found, of course, in the work of many other artists, including Rembrandt, Goya, Kollwitz, and Picasso.

Shadows in Art

With regard to shadow, artists have three alternatives in depicting objects: (1) using no shading (that is, using line or shape alone); (2) using shading that enhances three-dimensional form (this is termed *modeling*); and (3) using shading that represents shadows made by specific light sources. Western tradition, of course, favors the third alternative. For this reason, the absence of depicted shadows in art from other cultures often makes the image seem flat to Westerners. The term *flat* has been used to describe a number of art styles, including Japanese prints, Egyptian tomb paintings (see figure 4-24), pre-Renaissance European art (see figure 4-11), and works by modern artists who use unmodulated areas of color, including Manet, Gauguin, Matisse (see figure 4-25), Miro, and Modigliani.

Kung Hsien's *Landscape* (see figure 7-9) is an example of art from a tradition in which shading is used to model form, without indicating a primary light source. The artist, a Chinese contemporary of Caravaggio, used patterns of light and shade to accent the roundness of forms in the landscape. The overall light obviously comes from above, but not clearly from the right or left. Since no cast shadows are shown, the location of the sun cannot be determined, and the time of day cannot be identified. One Western viewer suggested that this

Figure 7-10. Shahm (Persian), *Gulistan of Sa'di: The Old Wrestler Defeating a Young Opponent,* 1567 – 68. 10¹/₂ × 6 inches. An old wrestler knew 360 tricks, but taught only 359 to his arrogant pupil. In a bout in front of the king, the pupil attempted to show his superiority, but the old man defeated him with the secret hold. (Reproduced by courtesy of the Trustees of the British Museum, London)

Why are shadows so important in Western art traditions but not in the art traditions of other cultures? To explore this question we must ask ourselves, what do shadows represent? and why should this element be significant to us? Shadows are but one aspect of momentary appearance; because of object constancy, shadows rarely play any important part in how we conceive of an object or in how we remember it. Hence, shadows do not indicate the essence of an object, but they do reveal information about time and place. For this reason, drawings or paintings that lack shadows do not fix the subject in time and space in the same way as traditional Western works do; they are apt to have a more timeless quality.

The artistic imagery of any society is generated from the culture's world view and its epistemology (the way the culture defines reality and human knowledge). This being the case, other cultures evidently have been less interested in how things look from precisely imagined viewpoints in time and space. By the same token, the representation of things as seen by a hypothetical viewer at a particular point in time/space must be somehow important to Western definitions of reality and knowledge. Hence, chiaroscuro (like linear perspective) is an expression of broader Western preoccupations with time and space.

SIZE GRADIENT

In the visual field of the eye, a gradient of decreasing size presents information about distance. As an object is located at a greater distance, it stimulates a smaller and smaller portion of the retina. Across the time and space of human history, few artists have portrayed distance with a gradient of gradually decreasing size (that is, with a *distance continuum*). Such perspective is not normally present in the art of ancient civilizations, of pre-Renaissance Europe, of so-called ''naive'' or ''folk'' artists, of small-scale societies, or of non-Western civilizations. Traditional Oriental landscape painting, for instance, makes use of three discontinuous distances: near, middle, and far. With each distance, objects show uniformity in size and detail (see, for example, figure 2-12). Something similar happens in Kitty Good's painting entitled *Choppin' Cotton—1908* (see figure 7-11).

About such works people often assert that the

indeterminancy of the sun's location in Chinese landscape paintings always reminded her of a cloudy day. On a cloudy day, sunlight is diffused and shadows are paler and less clearly defined. The Persian miniature shown in figure 7-10 exemplifies art from a tradition that uses line, shape, and pattern, but no shading. These small artworks were commissioned by rulers who wanted to record significant events that occurred during their reigns.

Figure 7-11. Kitty Good (American), *Choppin' Cotton—1908,* 1972. Oil on canvas 24 × 30 inches. (Permission of the artist. Collection of Dr. and Mrs. Michael Durfee, Raleigh, N. C.; photo by W. H. Huffines)

artists did not use perspective. But if by *perspective* they mean the representation of distance, their assertion is quite wrong. In *Choppin' Cotton*, for instance, distance is represented by (1) position on the picture plane; (2) decreased size; (3) decreased detail; (4) decreased sharpness; (5) paler color; (6) interposition; and (7) the field-and-frame relationship. The same can be said for Limbourg's late medieval work (see figure 4-11), and for traditional Oriental landscapes (see figure 2-12). What is missing to the Western eye is not perspective per se, but a particular type of perspective: a representation of the scene as the Western viewer thinks it would appear in the visual field of a single retina observing from a fixed point in time and space. This type of perspective is called *vanishing-point, linear, central,* or *Renaissance perspective.*

Linear Perspective

Linear perspective is a mathematically based system for representing size gradients as they would occur in a single retina fixed upon a particular location in space at a particular instant in time (see figure 4-8). It provides a camera's-eye view, but it antedated the camera by at least four centuries! The principle of linear perspective is most familiarly illustrated with the example of railroad tracks (see

Figure 7-12. Railroad tracks at South Windham, Connecticut. (Carolyn M. Bloomer)

Figure 7-13. Albrecht Dürer (German), *Draftsman Drawing a Portrait*, c. 1525. Woodcut, 5 × 6 inches. (Staatliche Museen, PreuBischer Kulturbesitz, Kupfer-stichkabinett, Berlin)

figure 7-12). Seen from a fixed position in space, rails that remain consistently parallel appear to converge or vanish at some point on the horizon. This point, appropriately enough, is called the *vanishing point*. Leonardo da Vinci, (quoted in Instituto Geographico de Agostini 1956, p. 436) explained how to draw using this type of perspective:

Of a mode of drawing a place accurately: Have a piece of glass as large as a half-sheet of royal folio paper, and set this firmly in front of your eyes, that is, between your eye and the thing you want to draw; then place yourself at a distance of two thirds of an ell [that is, 16 to 20 inches] from the glass, *fixing your head with a mechanism in such a way that you cannot move it at all. Then shut or cover one eye,* and with a brush or drawing chalk draw upon the glass that which you see beyond it; then trace it on paper from the glass; afterward transfer it onto good paper, and paint it if you like . . . (emphasis added).

Figure 7-13, Albrecht Durer's *Draftsman Drawing a Portrait*, shows a drawing mechanism based on this principle. But what an unnatural way to look at the world—with a fixed, immovable head, and a

single eye! With this type of perspective, the image is not of the world the artist knows: shapes or elements that form the conceptual image of an object are not used. Instead, the object is drawn as a projection constructed by light rays focused on a single hypothetical point (this is called an *optical array*). The outline of a projected object can be thought of as a silhouette (see the discussion of form constancy in chapter 4). Even though visually accurate, projected views can be strange, as in the case of the two-legged horse and three-legged cow shown in figure 4-22. Photographs are projected images.

This tradition of projected imagery is what Westerners have in mind when they use the term *artistic realism*. Yet projected images mirror neither perceptual nor cognitive experience. First of all, most people see the world with two eyes—eyes that are in constant motion, set into a head that normally moves, atop a body that is absolutely still only in death. Indeed, in the absence of motion our photoreceptors cease to function (see chapter 2). Linear perspective, however, represents a momentary view from a fixed point in space. This freezing of a visual instant also contradicts our experience of time as a phenomenon that never halts, but instead marches inexorably onward. The contradiction presented by the perspective picture, then, enables the viewer to do symbolically what he or she cannot do actually (except in memory or photographs): stop time.

Cezanne and the post-Impressionists broke with this tradition in the nineteenth century (see chapter 5) when they focused on ideas, feelings, and experiences with objects, rather than on the impersonal appearances characteristic of a single, fixed viewing point. This revolution was scorned by most contemporary artists, by critics, and by the general public. The post-Impressionists, however, are revolutionary only within the historical context of Western art. In the art styles of other cultures (including Western pre-Renaissance art), the construction of images is based on what is known, felt, or valued about objects, and not on their outward appearance as seen from a single viewing point.

Indeed, many cultural traditions reject imitations of outward appearance as shallow and superficial. They do not regard the retinal image as a source of essence, spirit, or inner truth. Hence, the absence of linear perspective results not from ignorance but from alternative pursuits of meaning. In traditional China, for example, central perspective was

Figure 7-14. Two examples of central perspective:
(a) Chinese peep-show picture. (Fritz van Briessen and J. P. Dubosc)
(b) Pier Leone Ghezzi (Italian), *The Lateran Council of 1725,* 1725. Oil on canvas, 95⅞ × 122½ inches. (North Carolina Museum of Art, Raleigh)

a

b

reserved for peep shows designed to amuse children (see figure 7-14a). Linear perspective, the Chinese asserted, derived from unrefined sense experience, and therefore was not appropriate for serious art, which dedicated itself to sophisticated metaphysical expressions. In the West, however, precisely this technique was applied to serious religious subjects (see figure 7-14b).

It would be a mistake, however, to think that Western artists intended to represent only appearances! The masterpieces of the Western realist tradition are considered to be great precisely because

Figure 7-16. East wall of Bedroom M, Villa of P. Fannius Synistor at Boscoreale (near Pompei), c. first century B.C. Fresco. (The Metropolitan Museum of Art, New York, Rogers Fund, 1903)

they seem to transcend mere imitation of the visual field. But why, then, are ideas of timeless truth and essence embodied in images of appearance and fixity?

Discussions of linear perspective usually emphasize its objectivity: supposedly it provides a pure vision, uncontaminated by thought or feeling, showing only what the eye can see. The illusion lies in the idea that the artist is depicting exactly what could have been seen by anyone—by any retina that happened to be at the same precise imagined point in space-time—and therefore that the painting is the product of an anonymous eye through which every viewer must see the picture. Linear perspective is thus seen as a method for representing raw data, preconceptual imagery, the sensation of a visual field. The artist's explicit viewpoint, like that of a scientist or journalist, is made to seem impersonal. The scene appears to have been documented rather than created (see figure 7-15).

On the other hand, Western culture has long viewed artists as possessing passionate personalities and as being driven by the need to express their unique and personal visions. Appreciators of art value the artists' individuality and their persistent struggles in the face of opposition. Yet these individual, personal visions have been expressed through a methodology of science and mathematics. Consequently, subjectivity must be conveyed in the form of an objectivity that appears to deny self. At the same time, however, an observing self (the

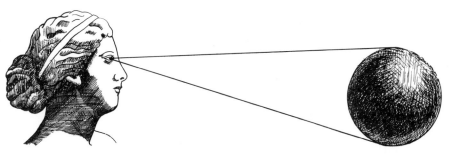

Figure 7-17. The visual cone.
(Eleanor Holland)

artist, the viewer) is central to the pictured world: the pictorial image radiates outward (in accordance with the characteristics of the visual cone) from the single point in space-time occupied by the anonymous, invisible, and observing retina. An objective image obviously requires an observing self in order to exist. Paradoxically, then, the selves of both artist and viewer are simultaneously affirmed and denied by linear perspective.

Medieval Optics. The paradoxes and contradictions of linear perspective become more understandable when we look at them in the context of cultural history. Linear perspective and the ideas that underlie it have embodied different meanings for different people at different times in Western history. Although people usually assume that this method of picture construction was an invention of the Italian Renaissance, its essential elements can be traced directly to ancient Greece, to Arabian science, and to historical developments in European religion, philosophy, and mathematics. Linear perspective represents a synthesis of concepts and methods drawn from geometry, optics, cartography (mapmaking), and theology.

In the ancient worlds of Greece and Rome (from approximately 500 B.C. to A.D. 500), artists used vanishing-point drawing systems to make backdrops for stage plays. The interior walls of Roman houses were often decorated with paintings of architectural columns and moldings that appeared to frame views of landscapes, villas, or distant cities. A number of such classical paintings show an awareness of vanishing points (see figure 7-16). These artists clearly intended to produce illusions of deep space.

But the most important contribution of the ancients was not technical but conceptual. Central to the later development of linear perspective was the Greek concept of the *visual cone*. The geometer Euclid (fourth century B.C.), as well as the Stoics and Pythagoreans, believed that the eye emitted

visual rays (this is known as the *extromission theory*). In traveling toward objects, these rays left the eye in the shape of a cone—the apex being at the eyes, and the base at the object seen (see figure 7-17). In the second century A.D., Ptolemy, a Greco-Egyptian, asserted that the clearest and most precise impressions of objects were conveyed by the shorter rays near the center of the visual cone. (This would have accounted for the phenomenon of foveal vision.) The shortest ray of all was the center ray, which was truly perpendicular to the object, and which embodied the axis of the visual cone. This ray was called the *centric ray* or the *axis visualis* (and during the Renaissance, the *prince of rays*).

By the eleventh century, Arab scholars had established that visual rays came from objects and not from the eye. According to Samuel Y. Edgerton, Jr. (1975), the three outstanding contributors to this theoretical development were Alkindi (ninth century), Avicenna (early eleventh century), and Alhazen (early eleventh century). Using empirical observations, the third of these men developed an optical theory of vision. Like Ptolemy, he had observed that the greatest visual acuity existed in the center of the visual field. Because of this, Alhazen's model perpetuated the idea of the specialness of the centric ray.

By the thirteenth century, religious scholars in Europe had seized upon Alhazen's optics as a model for how God's grace spread throughout the world. Medieval Christian thinkers thought of light (created by God on the First Day) as constituting the divine energy activating the universe, and they viewed geometry as proof of divine harmony. Optics—an integration of geometry, light, and vision—became a tool for both studying the physical world and grasping the spiritual order underlying it; it became a way to understand the nature of God. For Christian opticians, the centric visual ray and the moral power of God were intertwined.

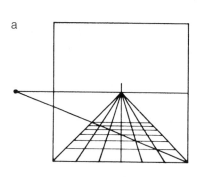
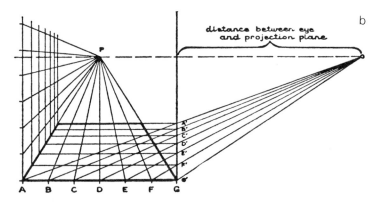

Figure 7-18. Antecedents of linear perspective theory: (a) Empirical or geometric perspective. (Panofsky 1955); (b) abbreviated perspective. (Panofsky 1955)

These religious scholars not only read and wrote about optics, they also manufactured optical mechanisms such as telescopes. Around 1265, an English Franciscan, John Pecham, wrote a book called *Perspectiva communis* that launched Alhazen's optical ideas in Europe, where they persisted in Western thought until the seventeenth century.

Like the ancient Greek philosophers, however, these medieval scholars were concerned with diagramming human vision; they were not interested in the composition of drawings and paintings. Indeed, in the Middle Ages, artists were viewed as skilled craft workers or mechanical artists, who were simply instruments for transmitting ideas that originated in God. Medieval treatises on art were not based on theory; they were essentially how-to instructions for what to do, accompanied by examples of how to do it.

Medieval artists composed the material surface of a picture—its lines, colors, and so on—as an array of symbols, not as a depiction of visual appearances. Thus, in representing three-dimensional space on a two-dimensional surface, they were not guided by standards of *verisimilitude* (of making the picture visually realistic), but rather by a desire to arrange symbols effectively. Since books were rare and most people could not read, the symbolic arrays in medieval religious pictures were among other things a means of communicating religious concepts to common people. This is not to say that pre-Renaissance artists ignored processes of observation, but that imitating the visual field was not their standard for correctness in composition.

Renaissance Perspective. Applying theories of vision to the composition of pictures was not widespread until the Renaissance. And then it seemed all the more natural because of certain techniques that had already been incorporated into artistic practice. For example, toward the end of the Middle Ages, the idea of looking through a picture-plane—as if the painted objects existed behind the surface—gained popularity. Gradients of size and detail were depicted; floors, ceilings, and landscapes receded illusionistically into the picture. Lines representing edges perpendicular to the picture plane (called *orthogonals*) tended to converge. By the middle of the fourteenth century such drawing methods (*prospectiva naturalis*) resembled the style and precision of linear perspective. Art historians usually refer to these methods as *protoperspective* (that is "primitive perspective"), because they were based on tradition and observation rather than on theoretical principles.

One such method involved drawing a diagonal from a distance point across the converging orthogonals (see figure 7-18a). When horizontal lines (or transversals) are drawn across the intersections, a size gradient is generated. Here, the distance points are the result of geometrical or empirical determination (in what is called true linear perspective, the distance point is transformed into a theoretically determined vanishing point). Medieval architects practiced another method: horizontal and vertical diagrams of an object were combined to compose a perspective drawing. This process was called *parallel projection* or *costruzione legittima* ("legitimate construction"). It was a tedious and

Figure 7-19. Tommaso de Ser Giovanni di Mano [Masaccio] (Italian), *The Tribute Money,* c. 1427. Fresco in the Brancacci Chapel, Santa Maria del Carmine, Florence. (Soprintendenza alle Gallerie, Florence)

cumbersome way of doing things. Italian painters later developed a simpler system known as *abbreviated perspective* (see figure 7-18b). All of these techniques were invented by artists and draftsmen applying observation and practice—without the use of mathematical or optical theories.

Sometime during the first quarter of the fifteenth century (historians' dates for the event range from 1401 to 1425), the first demonstration of theoretical perspective (*prospectiva artificialis*) was made by the Italian artist and architect, Filippo Brunelleschi. After 1425, another perspective phenomenon also appeared: the heads of figures portrayed as standing on the same level as the viewer are always aligned on a common horizon line (this feature has been termed *horizon line isocephaly* by Edgerton; see figure 7-19).

By 1436, another Italian, Leone Battista Alberti, had produced an influential treatise on painting, *Della pittura* (the Latin version was called *De pictura*). Alberti was perhaps the first Western writer to treat painting as being more than a skilled craft. He intended to raise artistic standards by instructing artists in how to paint "as the eye sees." He advised the artist to look through a network of colored string placed in front of the scene to be painted (quoted in Edgerton 1975, pp. 68–69):

. . . a veil loosely woven of fine thread, dyed whatever color you please, divided . . . into as

many parallel square sections as you like, and stretched on a frame. I set this up between the eye and the object to be represented, so that the visual pyramid passes through the loose weave of the veil.

This arrangement came to be known as *Alberti's veil* (*velo* or *reticulato*). The network of string organized the scene within a grid, and also provided a means for accurately transferring the scene to a proportionately gridded surface (see figure 7-20). Alberti's veil translated what was seen—the visible world—into a geometric composition. In the Renaissance, such mathematical methods were taken to be harmonious with natural law, and therefore to have the power to dispel error and to guarantee correctness and pleasing proportions.

Alberti further advised the following (quoted in Edgerton 1975, p. 118):

First of all, on the surface on which I am going to paint, I draw a rectangle of whatever size I want, which I regard as an open window through which the subject to be painted is seen. . . .

Here Alberti affirms the idea of a painting as a window on the world: something the viewer is to look through, rather than at. The viewer is thus supposed to relate to a painting in somewhat the same

Figure 7-20. Abraham Bosse. *Un dessinateur faisant au carreau le portrait d'un seigneur,* from *Divers manières de dessiner et de peindre,* c. 1667. Etching. (The Metropolitan Museum of Art, New York; Harris Brisbane Dick Fund, 1946)

way as to a mirror—that is, to perceive the image without perceiving the surface on which the image is located. This tradition of an illusionary surface is part of the reason why smooth-surfaced paintings are customarily admired with comments such as "You can't even see the brush strokes." Brush strokes would remind us that the painted surface is in fact opaque, and not a window at all.

Alberti's veil and window both presuppose the idea that a picture can be constituted by a plane intersecting the cone of vision—a plane that is inserted between the object and the observer (see figure 7-21). The picture plane was thus incorporated into a model that, up to this time, had been strictly a metaphysical, geometric, and optical paradigm for vision (and not for art). As a consequence, artistic composition suddenly acquired a theoretical basis, grounded in centuries of theological and philosophical scholarship. Art and geometry joined in a completely new relationship. Founded in divine order, linear perspective offered Renaissance art-

ists a means of producing morally responsible works that harmonized with universal, God-given principles. It was now possible for artists to be respected for using their creative minds to manipulate ideas and not simply materials. This new synthesis of art, mathematics, and metaphysics led Leonardo da Vinci and others to claim a place among the liberal arts for painting as a "divine science."

Even today, Western art forms that seem to lack a strong theoretical basis are not classed as high or fine art. This includes stained glass, calligraphy, ceramics, metalwork, all of the fiber arts, and the work of self-taught artists. Among art historians, these are labeled *applied, minor, primitive, naive, decorative,* or *folk arts,* or *crafts.* Although much has happened over the past few decades to break down these arbitrary categories, they still dominate art history textbooks, university slide collections, art museums and galleries, art publications, and the writings of art reviewers and art critics.

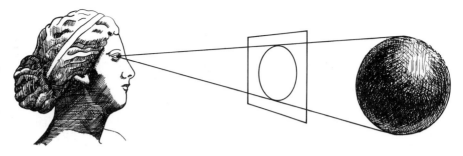

Figure 7-21. The picture plane intersects the cone of vision and stands between the object and its observer. (Eleanor Holland)

Linear perspective was only one expression of a broader Renaissance craving for precision, correctness, harmony, predictability, and verisimilitude. An insatiable fascination for mathematical applications extended to theories of esthetic perfection, to canons of human proportions, and even to the construction of letters (see figure 7-22). Of special concern was an esthetic principle from the classical philosophers, which Renaissance theorists embraced: that Beauty arises from harmony of the parts in relation to each other and to the whole. Alberti's emphasis on the centric point (a central vanishing point) introduced a means of constructing whole pictures in which each part could be related to each other part (and to the whole) with mathematical (divine!) precision.

The central viewpoint also created a feeling of monumentality and moral authority by locating and emphasizing the narrative focus of a painting. If the centric point (center of projection) was placed above the viewer's physical eye level, the viewer's mind's eye could be felt as floating above the body's eye. In addition, some central perspective pictures generate an illusion of following: as the observer moves, the whole scene seems to turn or rotate behind a centrally placed element. Some writers have argued that these effects were intentionally manipulated to create transcendent spiritual feelings. Thus, linear perspective offered a number of effective ways to encode meaning and significance into pictorial construction (see figure 7-23).

Clearly, Renaissance artists were not using linear perspective to generate visual realism for its own sake. They went to great lengths to avoid two-legged horses (see figure 4-22). Alberti, da Vinci, Durer, and others, despite the mechanical aspects of their perspective drawing instructions, all cautioned the artist against extremes. For this reason, perspective pictures usually represent only a part of the visual field—namely, the portion that extends

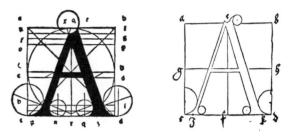

Figure 7-22. Renaissance typography.

approximately 37 degrees horizontally and 28 degrees vertically. (You will recall from chapter 2 that the whole visual field extends approximately 180 degrees horizontally and 150 degrees vertically.) In the linear perspective system, objects lying outside this limited field appear to be exaggerated or distorted (see figure 7-24).

Thus, normal perspective ignores peripheral vision and approximates macular vision. In practice, artists have favored empirical standards of perception over the purity of theory. The idea that linear perspective is a system for detailing the optical array in a fixed retina is simply a myth. Perspective pictures appeared lifelike, not because they were objectively observed, but because they were carefully composed.

Linear Perspective as Science. Alberti's veil and window, as well as the larger system of linear perspective, are early instances of a more general and profound epistemological stance that made possible the beginnings of modern science in the seventeenth century and began a 500-year tradition of visual realism in art. The relationship of the picture plane and the cone of vision (see figure 7-21) constituted a powerful image for philosophical categories that came to dominate Western thought.

In the optical paradigm of linear perspective, the seer is separated from the seen. A single reality is

Figure 7-23. Raffaello Sanzio [Raphael] (Italian), *The School of Athens,* 1510–11. Fresco. In this completely fanciful scene, ancient Greek philosophers gather around Plato and Aristotle, each with a pose and gesture symbolizing his doctrine. Pythagoras, Diogenes, Euclid, and Herakleitos are among those portrayed. Raphael's "Greek" faces include portraits of himself and Michelangelo, as well as of other contemporaries. (Stanza della Segnatura, Vatican Palace, Rome)

assumed to be out there, existing independently of the people who see it. Observer is divided from observed, mind from matter, and subject from object. Furthermore, an interposed element (the picture plane) is invoked to organize, clarify, and systematize that reality for the viewer. If we substitute a lens for the picture plane, this metaphor of the philosophical relation of human beings to their world becomes more familiar. These divisions are often attributed to the seventeenth-century thinker Rene Descartes and referred to as *Cartesian dualism,* but they were anticipated 200 years earlier in the perspective theories of fifteenth-century artists.

The theory and practice of objectivity are based on the assumption that observer and observed are essentially independent of one another. Objective understanding of the external world aims to eliminate personal or subjective relationships to the object of study (observer bias). In the ideal scientific (or positivist) observation, the observer's individuality is irrelevant: the world can be described without any mention of the human observer. As with linear perspective, the gaze of the scientific observer constitutes the picture, but at the same time is not visibly present in the picture. Method becomes the standard for correctness: not who observes, but rather how the observation is made. With scientific method, anyone (theoretically) can find truth by following correct procedures. Knowledge is thus assumed to be independent of the individual knower: it is democratized.

If only one reality exists, then inevitably it will be found over and over again by everyone who follows proper procedures. Indeed, the so-called truths of objective observation are tautologically defined by their continuous reconstitution as discovery. Observations are deemed valid when separate investigators follow standardized procedures and obtain identical results. This scientific standard of replication is precisely what Alberti, Durer, and others hoped to teach: a method of picture construction that allowed anyone trained in its basic principles to make a truthful picture.

The concept of replication is also fundamental to the illusionary qualities of linear perspective. The impression is that anyone's (or everyone's) retina would have registered the same scene in the same way, had it been present at that precise point in time and space. What Westerners think of as the lifelike aspect of linear-perspective pictures derives from the detached and uninvolved quality of a fixed gaze directed toward precisely located and locatable objects and events (data). Linear perspective, then, is a model of scientific methodology.

This idea of the existence of an external reality somehow independent of human beings frees individuals from having to feel responsible for it. People can see themselves as examining and representing (but never as creating) the world. The belief that Western scientific methodology is the only valid method for finding *the* truth can lead believers to treat other cultural traditions in illegitimate ways. Westerners often act as if theirs is the only standard of real value. Other world views are often labeled as mistaken: superstitious, naive, primitive, and so on. From such a position, other cultural beliefs are not simply different, but less valid. This ethnocentric attitude often lies at the core of Western criticisms of artworks that do not embody retinal imagery.

Renaissance Humanism. How did a method that began as a religious celebration of divine harmony come to be considered scientific? First, bear in mind that the roots of modern science itself arose in the Middle Ages, when the physical world was observed and intensely studied as God's handiwork. As the idea of an earth-centered (or geocentric) universe became less and less plausible, the starring role of human beings in the drama of a divine universe also came into question. Changing views of the nature of the world gained momentum in the sixteenth century with Copernicus, and in the seventeenth century with the theories and

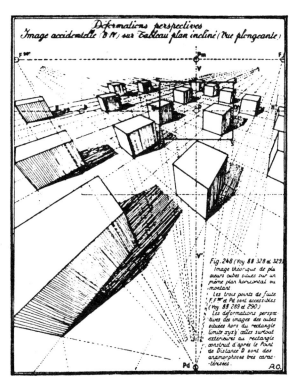

Figure 7-24. The distorted cubes on the left and lower margins lie outside the 37° × 28° field. (P. Olmer; permission New York University Press)

observations of Galileo. Eventually, the idea of an impersonal and sun-centered (or heliocentric) universe became accepted.

As the specialness of humankind began to erode in the macrocosmic view, Renaissance humanism restored people to center stage. Literature, science, history, language, and philosophy became increasingly secularized—that is, independent of religious authority. These subjects began to be studied for their own sake, not as divinely given, but as humanly generated. Thus, true knowledge no longer depended on divine revelation. Likewise in the new perspective system, the human eye became central and indispensable to the whole picture. Linear perspective pictures are virtually created by a hypothetical retina; human vision plays the double role of both observer and creator of knowledge.

Even past history was viewed as consisting of separate periods of time, each characterized by human achievements. (Western historians still conceive of history this way, as when they refer to the

Age of Belief, the Age of Reason, the Age of Technology, the Enlightenment, the Agricultural Revolution, the Industrial Revolution, or the Dark Ages). According to some historians, the Renaissance was the first period in history to give itself a name (''the rebirth''). This new Renaissance consciousness of historical distance is echoed in the perspective distance between the observing viewpoint and the observed scene.

Modern Relativity. Nineteenth-century French Impressionists (see chapter 5) were probably the last group of Western artists to continue the tradition of picturing retinal images at fixed viewpoints in time and space. While the Impressionists are usually described as revolutionary in the context of their own time, they can also be thought of as the final act in the drama of retinal realism that emerged in the fifteenth century. This is not to say that visual realism ended with the Impressionists. But it is to say that retinal realism in the twentieth century plays a different role in a different historical drama.

The final break from the observer/observed paradigm began in the late nineteenth century, when Cezanne and the post-Impressionists rejected the idea that art should be the direct representation of objects or the faithful translation of sensory impressions. The normal goal of art, they said, should be ideas. For human beings, of course, ideas are at least as real as (and perhaps more real than) the transient and impermanent sensations of retinal vision. (Linear perspective, in fact, is an idea.) Rather than imagining themselves as separate from their subjects, the post-Impressionists saw themselves as actively creating the very objects they represented. This concept paved the way for the exploration of radically new options for painting in the early twentieth-century, including Fauvism, Cubism, Constructivism, Futurism, and Abstract Expressionism. By 1950, *nonobjective art* had become a household term.

For scientists, the new paradigm surfaced in the early twentieth century with Einstein's theories of relativity and the new physics. Einstein's theories reject the idea that space and time are absolute entities (as posited by Descartes and Newton). According to this view, the characteristics of space and time can only be described in relation to moving frames of reference: they have no existence independent of things. Similarly, Heisenberg's uncertainty principle in physics has brought into question (at least at the subatomic level) the assumption that the observer can be separated from the observed, asserting to the contrary that the nature of an observation is determined in part by the position of the observer. In other words, scientifically derived facts can be absolute only in relation to a frame of reference: they are relative to context. If Renaissance and Enlightment observers gazed from a fixed viewpoint, twentieth-century observers see from a moving vehicle. The ramifications of theories of relativity are just now surfacing; they are markedly disquieting to many people.

This brief review of cultural history suggests an intriguing pattern. Developments in artistic practices seem consistently to have anticipated changes and reconstructions in dominant Western world views. In this historical view, Western visual realism is neither God-given nor natural (in the sense of something universally latent in all peoples). Its 500-year persistence in Western art is best understood in light of its positioning in a broad cultural and historical landscape of changing ideas about the nature of reality and knowledge. Even in the West, linear perspective has never consisted of a single static idea. Enmeshed within an ecosystem of complex cultural beliefs, its meaning, its applications, and its significance have all changed and varied with time.

Like all artworks, those of the Western tradition are not so much representations of worldly objects as they are structures for materializing cultural meanings. By looking at art in this way, you can open yourself up to discover greater richness and complexity in the traditions of both your own and other cultures.

8

Photography
The Camera as an I

Try, for a moment, to imagine life without photographs. So much would depend on memory: the images of friends, family members, and classmates at various times in their (and your) lives; the look of the places where you have lived over the years; the sights you have seen in traveling; the changes in yourself over the course of a lifetime. You would also be much more dependent on artists for your images of public persons, news events, advertising, wanted criminals, and certain medical and dental records. Some things, such as movies and television, would not exist at all.

But in addition, people in the West tend to consider photographs as more truthful, more objective, more real than memories or the drawings of artists. Memory and hand-made pictures are subject to inaccuracies, distortions, interpretations, wishful thinking. The same person or the same event is recalled quite differently by different people—as studies of eyewitness testimony clearly show. Even one person's memory of something or someone changes over time. But photographs seem to resolve such inconsistencies by presenting unassailable evidence of the way things really were, regardless of differing human opinions.

This attitude toward photographs is not simply the inevitable result of technological invention. Rather, both photography and Western attitudes toward it are expressions of broad and complex Western ideas about knowledge and reality that emerged after the Renaissance. As the world came to be defined more and more in terms of what could be seen, visible facts and visual appearances began to play a much larger part in Western perceptions of reality. The development of photography, then, involves more than the history of a modern technol-ogy; it is the chronicle of dramatic transformations in Western perception, from the Renaissance to the present.

BEFORE PHOTOGRAPHY: CHANGES IN PICTORIAL VISION

Although linear perspective flowered during the Renaissance, it was not practiced then in the same way as it is now. Renaissance artists did not use perspective methods to document retinal vision. Rather, they applied the concepts of Alberti's veil and the cone of vision as compositional devices—systems for organizing picture space in an orderly and rational way.

Such perspective compositions emphasized symmetry about a central point, and they incorporated all elements necessary to depict an entire subject, even when such a composition presented an optical impossibility (as in figures 7-14b, 7-19, and 7-23). Perspective geometry created a pictorial stage upon which all the necessary parts of a composition could be positioned mathematically and hierarchically. The central axis of the picture's subject was typically aligned with the line of sight, giving Renaissance paintings their striking qualities of centeredness and direct gaze. Renaissance artworks did not imitate natural human vision; they artificialized and idealized it. In fact, Renaissance artists called their perspective *prospectiva artificialis* to differentiate it from nontheoretical and naturalistic perspectives that were based solely on observations of the visual world or on empirical geometry (see chapter 7). This theoretical and intellectual aspect of picture-making prompted

Figure 8-1. Emanuel de Witte (Dutch), *Protestant Gothic Church,* 1669. Oil on panel, 44.5 × 33.5 cm. (Rijksmuseum, Amsterdam)

Leonardo da Vinci and others to claim that painting was a science and to advocate its being accorded a place among the liberal arts.

The logic of Renaissance perspective compositions is beyond the capabilities of photography. A photograph is a selective description; painting is a logical composition. The photographer takes, shoots, or captures a subject; the painter creates or composes a picture. Had photography been available to Renaissance artists, they would likely have used it to document details, much as they used preliminary on-the-spot sketches. Renaissance attitudes might have reflected that of the twentieth-century American artist, Edward Hopper (quoted in O'Doherty 1964): ''I once got a little camera to use for details of architecture and so forth, but the photo was always so different from the perspective the eye gives, I gave it up.''

Interestingly enough, in the centuries preceding the invention of photography, changes began to occur in the composition of paintings—changes characteristic of photographic images—even though

photography had not yet been invented! One such development is the appearance of pictures in which the axis of the subject no longer coincides with the line of sight. For example, in Emanuel de Witte's seventeenth-century *Protestant Gothic Church* (see figure 8-1), the axes of the church architecture (indicated by the two foreground columns and the wall in the upper left background) run at an oblique angle to the line of vision (which is perpendicular to the picture plane). The difference in effect is striking when compared to the image of Raphael's sixteenth-century *The School of Athens* (see figure 7-23), where the line of sight forms a unity with the axis of the receding architecture.

Another difference between these two paintings lies in the use of symmetry. In Raphael's painting, variations in figures and statuary are secondary to the predominant structure of symmetry. De Witte's church, on the other hand, juxtaposes quite varied elements; compositional balance derives from visual weight rather than from symmetrical correspondence.

Yet a third significant difference lies in the unabridged quality of *The School of Athens*. Raphael presents the viewer with a whole subject. Everything of importance to the scene is included within the frame of the picture: the viewer looks at an entire microcosm conceived by the artist. This quality of completeness is strengthened by the overarching curve of the vault, which reinforces the boundedness of the scene and keeps the viewer's gaze centered in the picture. In de Witte's painting, by contrast, the viewer sees only a portion of the church, and the larger whole is left to the imagination. Architectural elements are cut off by the boundaries of the picture; hence, the church structure is perceived as extending beyond the picture frame. De Witte's image is that of photographic vision—an arbitrarily framed fragment selected from a larger context of space-time. Raphael's picture is an intellectual construction, formally arranged to conform to the systematic and abstract rules of symmetrical perspective composition.

From the Renaissance onward, artists recorded their more spontaneous visual experiences in their sketches. Publicly displayed works continued to be composed by the rational mind, but the sketches show more relaxed explorations of the visual world, closer in spirit to characteristics now associated with photography. Details are extracted from larger contexts; compositions are spontaneous and un-

conventional, their forms unique and unexpected; momentary accidents of light and shadow are recorded (see figure 8-2). Public paintings were created by the intellect, but these private sketches were inspired by the eye.

The sketches of Renaissance artists were usually monochromatic, rendered in pencil or ink. In the seventeenth century, artists began to use oil paints for out-of-door sketching; the very use of oil paint suggested an elevation in artistic importance. By the early nineteenth century, oil sketching was common. Because the informal sketches were not meant to be viewed publicly, they offered a kind of loophole in the conventions of artistic style—a segment of artistic life in which artists felt free to explore their individual, immediate perceptions. This is demonstrated by substantial differences between the oil sketches and the finished, officially exhibited works. The contemporary art historian Peter Galassi (1981, p. 24) suggests that this gap was fertile ground for a critical transformation in artistic vision:

> It announces the impending struggle between an inherited rhetorical art and an art devoted to individual perceptions of the world. . . . [T]he innovations of the landscape sketch in oil were possible because they did not challenge the authority of public art.

Toward the end of the nineteenth century, the Impressionists collapsed this gap by elevating spontaneous out-of-door oil sketching to the level of serious public art. They redefined painting as a visual pursuit, rather than as an intellectual, academic, and studio-bound project. Impressionist pictorial sensibilities were precisely those of photography: the capturing of momentary visual experience through the faithful and objective documentation of light. Impressionism and photography embody the same perceptual consciousness, a mind-set in which vision becomes the primary sense through which people comprehend and express their relation to the world.

INVENTING PHOTOGRAPHY

Although people think of photography as a modern technology, the optical and chemical knowledge

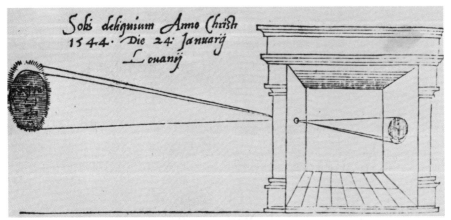

Figure 8-3. Gemma Frissuis (Dutch), *Camera obscura*, 1544. This earliest known published drawing of a *camera obscura* shows how to use a darkened room to view a solar eclipse. (Gernsheim Collection, Humanities Research Center, University of Texas at Austin)

Figure 8-4. Jan Vermeer (Dutch), *The Girl With the Red Hat,* c. 1665. Oil on wood panel, 9¹/₈ × 7¹/₈ inches. (National Gallery of Art, Washington, D.C.; Andrew W. Mellon Collection)

necessary for its design accumulated over centuries. The actual invention of photography, however, depended on the emergence of a particular relationship between the seer and the seen: a cultural ethos in which pictures created by the camera could be interpreted as being meaningful in and of themselves. Like linear perspective, the camera image needed a larger social and philosophical context to inspire the attention, energy, and passion necessary for its development. This context was provided by the ascendancy of the scientific attitude, but also by world views associated with industrialization and market economies, the rise of Western middle-class (bourgeois) life, and democratic political philosophies.

The Camera Obscura

At least 2,500 years ago, people knew that, if they made a small hole on the outside wall of a dark room, they could cause an inverted and reversed image to be projected onto the opposite wall. Ancient Greeks and Egyptians used such darkened chambers to observe solar eclipses indirectly, in order to protect their eyes from being damaged by looking directly at the sun. (You, too, can safely watch a solar eclipse by applying this principle. Punch a small hole in one side of a cardboard box, and aim the hole at the sun. Watch the progress of the eclipse on the side of the box opposite the hole. You may be surprised that such a simple device can produce an image of such dramatic clarity.) Alhazen, the tenth-century Arabian scholar of optics, wrote in detail about the phenomenon, as did his medieval European followers (see chapter 7). The first known published drawing, however, only appeared late in the Renaissance (see figure 8-3). The phenomenon was given the Latin name *camera obscura*—literally, ''dark chamber.'' Our word *camera* is simply an abbreviation of *camera obscura*.

Optical similarities between the *camera obscura* and the human eye did not go unnoticed: the *camera* precisely embodied the cone of vision and the

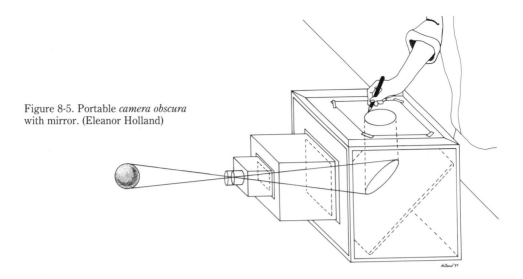

Figure 8-5. Portable *camera obscura* with mirror. (Eleanor Holland)

principles of Alberti's veil and window. Hence, Renaissance artists and draftsmen found the *camera obscura* a useful resource for making perspective calculations. By the sixteenth century, Giovanni Battista della Porta was recommending the *camera* as a substitute for drawing skill (quoted in Upton and Upton 1976, p.2): "If you cannot paint, you can by this arrangement draw [the outline of the image] with a pencil. You will have then only to lay on the colours." During the next three centuries, the *camera obscura* was used and refined by artists, scientists, and amateur painters.

When a double-convex spectacle lens was inserted into the peephole of a room-size *camera obscura* (or *camera immobilis*), the image was startlingly brilliant. Owing to its outward curve, the surface area of the lens gathered a greater number of light rays, which reconverged to form the image as a result of the outward curve on the opposite side of the lens. A piece of paper could be moved backward and forward until the image was precisely focused on it; and the whole perspective could then be traced with a pen. Traveling *cameras* (the *camera portabilis*) were fabricated from tents, sedan chairs, and carriages. Smaller boxlike *cameras* (*cubicula*) were mounted on tripods or placed on windowsills; the viewer would then cover his or her head with a black cloth to create the darkness required to see the image.

In the seventeenth and eighteenth centuries, these drawing machines became standard equipment for artists, although their role in artistic production is conspicuously neglected by conventional art histories. Paintings by the Dutch artist Jan Vermeer contain a photographic perspective and dots of paint that resemble optical *disks of confusion*—a phenomenon not normally seen by the naked eye (see figure 8-4). These and other qualities have convinced most scholars that Vermeer made use of a *camera obscura*. The *camera obscura* is also associated with Vermeer's contemporary Jan van der Heyden, and with the eighteenth-century Venetian artists Francesco Guardi and Antonio Canaletto (see figure 7-15), who may have used it for preliminary drawings.

By the eighteenth century, a 2-foot portable box model had been developed that had a lens at one end and a pane of ground or frosted glass at the other. A mirror was placed at a 45-degree angle inside, so as to right the upside-down image (see figure 8-5). When a piece of paper was placed on the glass, the image could easily be traced. This optical construction is strikingly similar to that of the modern reflex camera, lacking only the film.

Other Drawing Aids. By the late eighteenth century, the rising middle class was demanding unprecedented numbers of pictures that previously only the rich had been able to afford. Hundreds of thousands of oil paintings blanketed Europe. Portrait painters did thriving business. Optical-mechanical devices held the promise that anyone could draw quickly, without the necessity of long and arduous training. A popular mechanism was the *camera lucida* (see figure 8-6a), which literally (but rather inaccurately) means "light chamber." A glass

a

b

Figure 8-6. The *camera lucida:* (a) nine-teenth – century version, using a glass prism; (b) late twentieth – century version, using a piece of Lucite. The latter is marketed as *Phantom – Line;* the package entices, ''Become a Freehand Expert.'' (Phantom – Line Graphics, Providence, Utah)

prism attached to a rod was suspended at eye level. When the viewer looked through a peephole centered over the edge of the prism, the image appeared to lie on the paper. The user could then trace the illusionary image with a pencil.

Although patented in England in 1806 – 7 by W. H. Wollaston, the *camera lucida* had been described nearly 200 years earlier by the seventeenth-century scientist, Johannes Kepler. Its nineteenth-century reinventor called it ''The Royal Road to Drawing.'' The *camera lucida* became extremely popular with travelers, since it could easily be carried about and did not require the viewer to be in darkness in order to view the image. The device persisted and until recently could be found offered for sale in tiny ''you can learn to draw'' advertisements in the backs of popular magazines. Modern versions use a piece of lucite instead of a prism (see figure 8-6b).

The *cameras obscura* and *lucida* were only two of the tools with which amateurs might attempt to produce pictures and portraits. With the *physniotrace,* invented in 1786, the artist traced a sitter's profile using a stylus connected to an engraving tool, and this tool, in turn, engraved a scaled-down profile onto a copper plate from which hundreds of

prints could be made. The simple black cut-paper silhouette, made by tracing the shadow of a person's profile, enjoyed great popularity. Wood engraving was revived and lithography was invented; as a result, unlimited quantities of pictures could be printed and published. But of all these devices, the *camera obscura* was particularly tantalizing—so nearly did it seem to present an exact copy of nature. If only the image could be permanently recorded!

The Nineteenth Century

Since antiquity, light had been observed to cause changes in particular substances (including chlorophyll and dyes). In the seventeenth and eighteenth centuries, European scientists had known that certain silver compounds darkened on exposure to sunlight. In 1802, short-lived ''sun prints'' were made with silver nitrate on paper and leather. With bitumen on pewter, an eight-hour exposure produced a faint *heliograph* (''sun picture'').

Finally, in 1837, Louis Jacques Mande Daguerre, a French theatrical scene designer, made a photograph of the corner of his studio. His process was complicated. Copper plated with silver was rubbed with pumice and oil, washed with dilute nitric acid, heated, washed again, and coated with fumes of silver iodide. The plate was then exposed in a *camera* for a period of five to forty minutes and afterward

Figure 8-7. Louis Jacques Mandé Daguerre (French), *A Parisian Boulevard*, 1839. Daguerrotype. When this picture was taken, the street was bustling with pedestrians and vehicles, but only two people remained in one place long enough for their images to be recorded. These are the man in the lower left who stopped to have his shoes shined, and the shoeshiner. (Bayerische Nationalmuseum, Munich)

developed in hot mercury vapor. A New York *Star* correspondent attended a special demonstration of Daguerre's process in Paris and reported that "the picture thus literally executed by the sun, was handed about. I never saw anything more perfect . . . ." (quoted in Newhall 1978, p. 19).

Daguerre called his invention the *daguerreotype*. The French government purchased it. Within five months more than thirty editions, translations, and summaries of Daguerre's instructions and technical specifications had been published in more than a dozen European cities and in New York. Daguerreotype studios opened to offer the public "Sun Drawn Miniatures." We can guess at the mass excitement from the report of an observer, M. A. Gaudin (quoted in Newhall 1978, p. 18):

Opticians' shops were crowded with amateurs panting for daguerreotype apparatus, and everywhere cameras were trained on buildings. Everyone wanted to record the view from his window, and he was lucky who at first trial got a silhouette of rooftops against the sky. He went into ecstasies over chimneys, counted over and over roof tiles and chimney bricks, was astonished to see the very mortar between the bricks—in a word, the technique was so new that even the poorest proof gave him indescribable joy.

Daguerreotypes had some disadvantages. Long exposure times were required, so moving subjects did not appear in the photograph, because they did not stay in one place long enough to be recorded (see figure 8-7). Hence, busy city streets appeared in daguerreotypes to be depressingly vacant; some called them "cities of the dead." To create a more pleasant image, artists would sometimes draw in people and vehicles by hand. Another disadvantage was that a daguerreotype was one-of-a-kind. It could be duplicated only by copying the finished plate with a camera or by hand. Nonetheless, many daguerreotypes were slavishly traced and transferred to copper aquatint plates for publication. By this means, daguerreotype pictures made by travelers and journalists in foreign lands brought to Americans and Europeans the endless fascinations of armchair travel.

In portraiture, the daguerreotype left much to be desired. Because of the long exposure times, the subjects' eye-blinks produced eyeless portraits, and the sitters usually assumed stony, unflattering facial expressions. Within a few years, however, improved lenses and more sensitive photographic plates shortened the required exposure time to less than a minute. The surface of the daguerreotype was rendered less fragile by being washed with a solution containing gold; the image thereby acquired the soft, dark purplish brown tones that

Figure 8-8. Lewis W. Hine (American), *Carolina Cotton Mill*, 1908. (International Museum of Photography at George Eastman House, Rochester, N.Y.)

are now associated with this early technique. Nonetheless, the metallic glare made daguerreotypes difficult to look at, and the plate was still sufficiently fragile that it had to be kept in a case under glass.

In the meantime, experimenters continued to search for a process that could fix the image on paper. In 1840, an Englishman, William Henry Fox Talbot, announced his success with a negative-to-positive process (still used today) by which any number of paper photographs could be contact-printed from a single negative. Talbot called his invention the *calotype*, from the Greek words *kalos* ("beautiful") and *tupos* ("impression"). But like many others, Talbot (quoted in Newhall 1978) continued to describe photography as a substitute for artistic skill and training:

There is, assuredly, a royal road to *Drawing* . . . . Already sundry amateurs have laid down the pencil and armed themselves with chemical solutions and with *camerae obscurae*. These amateurs . . . find the rules of *perspective* difficult to learn and to apply—and . . . moreover have the misfortune to be lazy— [they] prefer to use a method which dispenses with all trouble.

By 1851, the collodion "wet plate" process was being used to produce sharp and reproducible images, combining the best qualities of the da-

guerreotype and the calotype. Furthermore, exposure times could be reduced to five seconds. The "wet plate" became almost universal among photographers for the next thirty years. But convenience was not one of its virtues. The glass plate, spread with a photosensitive emulsion, had to be exposed and developed before the emulsion dried. This meant that a darkroom had to be available virtually at the photographer's elbow. Adequate equipment and supplies for wet-plate photography weighed more than 100 pounds and so were not easily portable.

Popular Portraiture. In the mid-1800s, fascination with the new image-making process seemed boundless. When a process for retouching negatives was invented, people became less apprehensive about having their pictures taken. In 1854, Adolphe-Eugene Disderi patented the *carte-de-visite*—eight to twelve poses taken on a single wet-plate negative, with the resulting print cut up to make separate calling-card-size pictures. By 1860, in response to the popularity of these pictures (called, at the time, *cardomania*) elaborate photo albums were manufactured to hold standard-size *carte-de-visite* portraits of family members, friends, and famous people.

Photographers competed to take portraits of public figures; since 1840, virtually every well-known person who has lived has been photographed. In 1859, Napoleon III halted his troops on their way to Italy while he had his portrait taken at Disderi's Paris studio. In England, during the week of Prince Albert's death in 1861, 70,000 portraits of him were sold. In one year, 3 million pictures were cranked out by 10,000 American daguerreotypists. Photos of popular Civil War heroes sold in America at the rate of 1,000 prints per day. Actors and actresses wanted publicity photographs, and as a result theatrical photography became a specialty. Photographs were used on tombstones and on political campaign buttons. Portrait painters were driven very nearly to the brink of extinction; many gave up painting to make more profitable livings as photographers.

Photography as Entertainment. In response to the public thirst for more and more realistic and sensational illusions, stereoscopic pictures were made by means of twin lenses placed 2½ inches apart (approximately the distance between two human pupils). When viewed through a stereoscope (see figure 3-7), the pair of photographs would appear to form a single three-dimensional image. During the second half of the nineteenth century, millions of stereographs were produced. Earlier attempts to produce this effect by hand drawing had failed because calculating the correct perspective proved to be too complicated.

Glass lantern slides (transparent positives) were used to produce illustrated lectures and entertaining picture shows; they were sometimes projected in sequences to produce a primitive animation effect. Photographs taken in series from a single location could be fastened at the sides to create panoramas up to 8 feet long. Sometimes these made a complete circle that could be viewed from within. In the 1880s, the halftone process for reproducing images was invented (see figure 2-4); for the first time, type and photographs could be printed together on the same page (before this time, separately printed pictures had to be tipped in by hand).

Photojournalism. Events and places became the subjects of endless documentation. The Englishman Roger Fenton took a photographic van into the battlefield of the Crimean War in 1855 – 56. In 1858, Francis Frith, another Englishman, photographed the pyramids of ancient Egypt for the first time, developing his wet plates in a mobile wicker carriage. Two French photographers accompanied Napoleon III's 1859 expedition to the Alps. In the early 1860s, portraitist Mathew Brady photographed the devastation and carnage of the American Civil War. Government expeditions were sent out to photograph the Grand Canyon, Niagara Falls, the building of the transcontinental railroad, the Old West, and countless other things.

This journalistic use of photography expressed an important element of nineteenth-century intellectual life: a passionate desire to see things as they are—in real life, as lived by real people. This desire for so-called natural imagery was also reflected in the objective and scientific emphasis of novelists such as Emile Zola and Marcel Proust, who wrote journalistically of the details of ordinary life and of the roles of environment and heredity in forming character. Jean Francois Millet, Jean Baptiste Camille Corot, and other artists of the Barbizon School moved to country villages to paint peasant life and rural landscapes, while the Impressionists

worked to record bourgeois life with innocent eyes. In this intellectual milieu, seeing became a new kind of project—one that permeated artistic, scientific, intellectual, and social circles.

Photography fit perfectly with this passion for naturalistic visual truth. The comforts of nineteenth-century middle-class life had been made possible by industrialization, which simultaneously forced masses of poor people to live and labor under conditions that by modern Western standards would be considered inhumane. In some inner cities of Europe, the life expectancy of a newborn infant was only seventeen years. In London, more than 600 charities worked to counteract the myriad social problems spawned by poverty: drunkenness, prostitution, child neglect, crime, disease. Only a few visual artists (such as Honore Daumier and Kathe Kollwitz) portrayed the plight of the poor, who were totally ignored by the Impressionists.

Photography, on the other hand, seemed ideally suited to provide vivid, incontrovertible evidence of how the other half lived. Sentimentalized images of London street urchins elicited upper- and middle-class sympathy for the urban poor. Typically, however, these pictures of ragged children were carefully contrived in the photographer's studio. In other instances, photography became a powerful and persuasive instrument for social and legislative reform. For example, the documentary photographs of Lewis W. Hine, made for the U.S. Child Labor Committee, led to the establishment of child-labor laws (see figure 8-8). Photographs also persuaded the U.S. Congress to create Yellowstone National Park; the photographs convinced legislators that the natural wonders of Yellowstone were genuine, whereas previous reports from travelers had been discounted as mere tall tales.

Scientific Interests. As exposure times became briefer and briefer, the camera revealed aspects of motion that the human eye is incapable of seeing. Some people had more than a passing interest in frozen movement. Oliver Wendell Holmes, an American physician (and father of the Supreme Court justice of the same name), was engaged in designing artificial limbs for soldiers maimed in the Civil War. For this purpose, he undertook studies of how people walk; photographs of street scenes were invaluable to Holmes because they showed people engaged in all phases of natural walking.

Photographing motion held great appeal for sci-

Figure 8-9. Eadweard Muybridge, *Horse Galloping: Daisy with Rider,* 1878. Reproduced from Muybridge's *Animals in Motion* (New York: Dover Publications, 1957).

entific minds. For example, the question of whether or not all four hooves of a galloping horse are ever off the ground at the same time had been argued since the days of ancient Egypt. Artistic convention portrayed galloping horses with their legs in the air, front legs stretched forward and hind legs stretched backward, like those of a hobby horse. In the late 1800s, Eadweard Muybridge set up a series of timed cameras. The resulting photographs (see, for example, figure 8-9) clearly revealed that when the horse's four hooves were all off the ground, they were bunched together under the horse's belly! Compared to the prevailing standards of illustration, the photographs seemed unreal and artistically incorrect.

Muybridge's photographs were published in magazines and journals, including *Scientific American.* He went on to conduct more extensive studies of motion, using from ten to forty cameras at a time, some equipped with multiple lenses designed to be triggered by an electromagnetic shutter of his own invention, which could be set to operate over predetermined intervals of time. Muybridge's goal was to create a visual dictionary for artists. Eventually he produced more than 100,000 photographic plates of humans and animals in motion. Muybridge's images continued to remain at odds with longstanding artistic formulas, however, and as a consequence, his photographs were sometimes perceived as distortions, despite the unquestionable evidence produced by the camera. One observer (quoted in Newhall 1978, p. 83) remarked, "No artist would have dared to draw a walking figure in attitudes like some of these."

Muybridge's photographs now seem quaint. But, although fashions in clothing and gestures change, the mechanics of the human body remain the same. For this reason, Muybridge's volumes remain a standard reference for phases of motion, and they continue to be used today as a source of data on kinetics by many artists and illustrators.

Cameras for the Masses. For the first forty years after its invention, photography was almost exclusively the province of professionals and serious (and wealthy) amateurs. The technical skill required and the cumbersome equipment involved limited most people to the role of consumer. Then a Rochester, New York, bank clerk, George Eastman, invented a way to mass produce roll film. In 1888, Eastman offered for sale a box camera that he christened *Kodak*—a word he himself had made up to be short, distinctive, easily remembered, and easily pronounced. His advertising slogan was, "You press the button, we do the rest" (see figure 8-10). The Kodak camera cost $25 and came loaded with enough film for 100 negatives. After exposure, the entire camera was returned to the factory for processing. Prints, negatives, and the camera were then returned to the owner; for an additional $10, the camera came back loaded with a fresh roll of film. Photography was now within the reach of all moderately affluent people.

The Twentieth Century

In spite of modern refinements, such as built-in light meters, zoom lenses, and automatic winding, cameras themselves have changed remarkably little

Figure 8-10. Fred Church (American), *A Kodak Camera with Its Inventor, George Eastman,* 1890. (International Museum of Photography at George Eastman House, Rochester, N.Y.)

Figure 8-11. Dorothea Lange (American), *Migrant Mother, Nipomo, California,* 1936. (Library of Congress, Washington, D.C.). Lange's field notes read as follows: "Camped on the edge of a pea field where the crop had failed in a freeze. The tires had just been sold from the car to buy food. She was 32 years old with seven children." (Quoted in Newhall 1978, p. 143)

over the last 150 years. Modern cameras are more convenient to use, but their basic principles of construction and operation remain the same as those of their early predecessor, the portable *camera obscura* (see figure 8-5). Light, gathered and focused by a lens, enters a dark chamber, but instead of falling on a piece of frosted glass, it exposes photosensitive chemicals. Within ten years of Daguerre's ground-breaking invention, surprisingly successful color photographs were being made, but not until the 1930s and 1940s did a color process become practical enough for large-scale popular use (see chapter 5). Today, while most professional photographers still prefer to work in black-and-white, nearly all of the pictures taken by nonprofessionals make use of color film.

Early in the twentieth century, Alfred Stieglitz (Georgia O'Keeffe's husband) fought to have photography recognized as an art equal in status to painting and sculpture. An advocate of avant-garde arts, Stieglitz edited magazines (*Camera Notes* and *Camera Work*), ran galleries, arranged exhibitions, and aided struggling artists. Between the two world wars, photographers turned away from sentimentality and imitations of painting, in favor of what they

called "pure photography." This trend took divergent forms ranging from a search for straightforward realism (as in the work of Edward Steichen, Edward Weston, Dorothea Lange, and Walker Evans) to artistic images highlighting and extending the blatant artifice of photographic techniques (as in the works of Surrealists Man Ray and Laszlo Moholy-Nagy).

In the 1930s, with the establishment of the Farm Security Administration (FSA), photography was institutionalized as an instrument for educating the public about social and economic conditions in the United States. During the Great Depression, the FSA employed over a dozen artists and photographers (including Dorothea Lange, Walker Evans, and Ben Shahn) to record all aspects of American rural life. These documentary photographs led to soil conservation laws and legislation designed to improve the quality of life for rural Americans. Thousands of FSA photographs are now archived in the Library of Congress, and many of these are now considered classics (see figure 8-11).

By the 1940s and 1950s, various branches of photography were affecting one another. Photojournalism influenced portrait photographers to make narrative use of background and setting. The imagery of the Surrealist experimenters inspired photojournalists and portraitists alike to become more imaginative. Photography became a medium for expressing more personal sensibilities: the decisive moment (Henri Cartier-Bresson); the strangeness of the familiar (Bill Brandt); pristine precision (Ansel Adams); dreamy lyricism (Harry Callahan); color in motion (Ernst Haas). This was also the era of *Life* magazine and of the *Family of Man* exhibition organized by Edward Steichen.

In the 150 or so years since its invention, photography has developed many variations and found many applications, including moving pictures, stop-action photography, stereoscopy, microphotography, holography, and telescopic and space photography. Fixed images like those in photographs are also generated by means of forms of energy other than light: shortwave radiation (X rays), heat (infrared photography and thermography), and sound (sonograms and radar).

HOW PHOTOGRAPHY WORKS

In ambient light, rays from every point on the surface of an object are ordinarily reflected in all directions. Such reflected light ordinarily bounces around, striking surfaces in a random jumble. A small pinhole opening, however, changes the effect. Only a few rays can pass through the tiny hole—namely those that travel in a straight line from the object (see figure 8-12). When these few rays strike a surface opposite the pinhole, they form an image. When this happens in the eye (where the pupil corresponds to the pinhole), the effect is termed the *optical array*. If the surface opposite the pinhole is in a darkened chamber (that is, if all other light is excluded), the image will be visible to the eye. If the surface is composed of light-sensitive chemicals (as with film), the chemical responses to the varying light intensities will create a latent image that can later be developed and printed by means of further chemical processes.

Exposures: Aperture and Shutter

When you take a picture with a modern camera, the shutter moves to expose the film to light for a fraction of a second. A larger opening will let in more light, a smaller opening less (as in the pupil of the eye). In early cameras, the size of the opening (or aperture) was controlled by separate metal stop plates. In modern cameras, a diaphragm is positioned between the lens and the shutter. Usually constructed of overlapping metal leaves, the diaphragm can produce a range of aperture sizes. Aperture size is identified by an f/stop number. Larger numbers (such as *f/16* or *f/22*) designate smaller openings; smaller numbers (such as *f/4* or *f/2.8*) refer to larger openings.

Aperture creates *depth of field*, a term that applies to the particular slice of deep space in front of the camera that will appear in focus. Depth of field extends in front of and behind the point of focus; objects outside this slice of space will be less clear. With smaller apertures (such as *f/16* or *f/22*), everything remains in focus from nearby to the farthest distance (infinity). This is why, given sufficient light, a pinhole camera can take sharp pictures, even without a lens. As the aperture becomes larger, the focused slice becomes shallower and shallower. Depth of field is crucial in determining the mood and style of a photograph.

Shutter speed refers to the length of time the shutter remains open. Like aperture size, shutter speed provides a means of controlling the amount of light that reaches the film. Shutter speed is indicated by a dial on the camera with the numbers *30, 60, 125, 250, 500, 1000*, and so on. Each number represents the denominator of the fraction of a second during which the shutter is open; for example, a setting of 60 means that the shutter will be open for 1/60 second. If the subject is moving, a shutter that is fast enough can stop the action and prevent blur.

For a given subject in a given lighting situation, a number of different combinations of aperture and shutter speed can be used to expose the film to the correct amount of light. But not all combinations create the same effect in the final photograph. A combination of fast shutter and big aperture stops action but also reduces depth of field and blurs the background and foreground. A combination of slow shutter and small aperture gives greater depth of field, but slight movements of the subject or the camera may cause blurring. Fully automatic cameras make arbitrary shutter speed and aperture size judgments for the user, based on the kinds of pictures the manufacturers assume most people want, regardless of the subject. A semiautomatic,

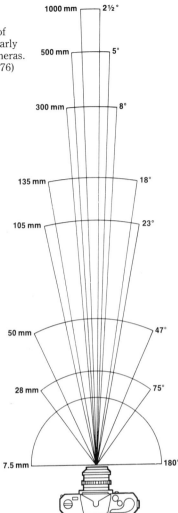

Figure 8-13. Angles of view for lenses popularly used with 35-mm cameras. (Upton and Upton 1976)

aperture-preferred camera allows the user to set the f/stop and thereby control depth of field.

Lenses and Filters

The purpose of a lens is to gather and focus the light entering the camera. Because its surface area is increased by a convexly curving surface, a lens conveys more light rays to the film than does a simple hole. The *length* of a lens is the distance between the lens and the film. The closer the lens is to the film, the wider is the resulting field of vision. The farther the lens is from the film (that is, the longer it is), the narrower the field of vision becomes (see figure 8-13). The effect is rather as if you looked through a hole in an index card or through a circle made by your thumb and forefinger.

When the opening is close to your eye, you see more because your angle of vision is wider; when it is farther from your eye, the angle of vision is narrower and a relatively small section of the scene fills the opening. A wide-angle (for example, 28-mm) lens produces the effect of seeing through a wide cone; a telephoto (for example, 200-mm) lens produces the effect of seeing through a narrow tube. A zoom lens moves easily from one focal length to another.

A 50-mm lens is called a *normal* lens; its angle of vision is 47 degrees. This is comparable to the visual field represented in normal perspective (see chapter 7) and accounts for only about one-fourth of the whole 180-degree field taken in by our eyes. A 180-degree (7.5-mm) camera lens is called a *fish-eye* lens and produces photographs that appear wildly distorted. A telephoto lens also produces distortions, by giving the impression of compressed space—as if objects or people were piled up against one another.

A filter is a disk of colored glass that screws onto the camera lens. Filters change the composition and amount of light entering the lens by absorbing certain wavelengths of light, thereby preventing them from reaching the film. With black-and-white film, filters can create value differences in the final print. For example, a yellow filter absorbs blue light and thus increases the contrast between sky and clouds by making the sky darker. Filters are also used to reduce glare (as with a polarizing filter) and to correct for color in lighting situations that do not match the film specifications (see chapter 5).

Film

The image on a film is created by a reaction between light and an emulsion of photosensitive crystals (silver and bromine) on the film surface. The emulsions on slow films (such as ASA 25 and ASA 64) are fine-grained: they are made up of smaller crystals, but because there is a greater number of them, longer exposure times are needed to produce the chemical changes necessary to create an image. Fast film emulsions (such as ASA 500 and ASA 1000) have larger crystals, but fewer of them, and so need shorter exposures. Larger crystals make a print grainy because less detail can be registered. The problem is essentially one of dot size (discussed in chapters 2 and 10). With fast color film, the color is also thinner.

A general rule is that you should use the slowest film appropriate for the lighting situation. An exception is black-and-white Polaroid Land film, which is virtually grain-free even when it is high-speed (ASA 3000). Color films have three layers of color-sensitive emulsion; each layer resembles the single layer used in black-and-white film, except that it responds to only one color of the light spectrum (red-orange, green, or blue-violet; see chapter 5).

Developing and Printing

In the process of developing, silver bromide crystals in the film emulsion react with chemicals to form an image. Leftover crystals are dissolved with a fixer (or hypo) and washed away. When it is to be printed, the negative is placed in an enlarger, which projects light through the negative. The negative acts as a filter, causing the light to fall onto photosensitive paper in varying densities. While being projected by the enlarger, the image can be enlarged or cropped. Lightness, darkness, and contrast in the final photograph are controlled by varying exposure times. The image can be manipulated by increasing (*burning*) or decreasing (*dodging*) the amount of light that reaches the paper from particular parts of the negative. Like films, different photographic papers have different sensitivities, and these affect the character of the final print.

As anyone who has worked in a darkroom knows, printing a negative is a process of constant decision-making, in which the consequences of various options must continually be evaluated. In the darkroom, the negative is not merely printed, it is selectively interpreted. Far from being an objective product of the pencil of nature, a photograph is a tightly controlled human creation. A single negative can be used to create many different images (see figure 8-14). This is why automatic processing (as with Polaroid cameras or commercial photo labs) is no substitute for darkroom skills.

PHOTOGRAPHY AND PERCEPTION

The invention of photography is often referred to as a "revolution." People usually take this to mean a revolution in technology and communications. Like other technologies, photography is often thought of as being neutral, as embodying no particular system of philosophical values. So ubiquitous in a Westerner's everyday existence are photographic

Figure 8-14. *Estranged Vista/Asheville.* Four different photographs produced from a single negative. (© Artie Dixon, 1989)

images that they seem natural and inevitable. People do not generally give much thought to how—or even whether—photography has affected their perception of reality. They take it for granted that photographs provide objective records of the way things actually were. Although to some extent people know that photographs constitute manipulated images, they still feel that overall the process of photography itself is inherently truthful, realistic, and unbiased.

But the camera, like other technologies, is a cause as well as an effect of cultural values. The real revolution initiated by photography is not technological but perceptual. Photography has transformed the world you live in. Not only does it help shape the way you see things, it profoundly contrib-

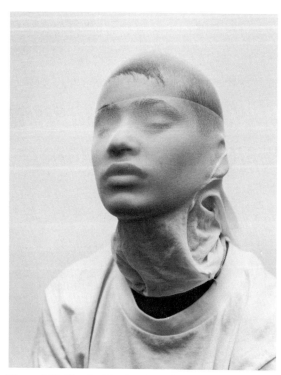

Figure 8-15. For the identity of this photograph, see page 165.

utes to the way you think about the world. It forms a part of the seamless web of your culturally learned perceptions.

Photography and Context

The subject of a photograph always exists in a double context. First is the original context in which the photograph was taken—the time and space of the living subject. Second is the context within which the photograph is viewed: its perceptual context. Take, for example, a photograph of a masked boy (figure 8-15). Seeing it in a family album as a Halloween snapshot might bring back memories of startling disguises. Viewing it in an exhibition of photographic art, you might wonder at its drama as an artistic statement. Observing it as a newspaper photo while drinking your breakfast coffee, you might pass over it as just another anonymous item in a mosaic of morning news. Watching it as a still shot in a televised evening news story about urban crime, you might find it terrifying. The perceptual context determines how you attribute meaning to the photograph.

Photography as Fiction. The original context in which a photograph was taken and the perceptual context in which it is viewed are discontinuous— separate events unconnected and unrelated in time and place. Furthermore, the original context has been erased by the photographic act itself. The field-and-frame relationship and the angle of vision created by the camera lens (together with any cropping of the image during printing) have eliminated the surrounding visual field, and placed the viewer at a predetermined perceptual distance from the subject (see chapters 6 and 10). The camera's position defines some objects as foreground and others as background. The lens and aperture settings bring some things into focus while blurring other things.

Thus framed and composed, a photograph presents a visual center and a hierarchy of importance that did not previously exist but that have been imposed on the original context. The photographer has created the subject. Film, camera, developing, and printing determine other qualities in the final image, such as whether the image will be harsh or soft, detailed or vague, and warm or cool. These visual dimensions of a photograph embody predefined perceptual characteristics that cause us to perceive elements of the picture as having intrinsic relationships to each other and varying degrees of importance. These transformations of the original context resemble the perceptual decisions a person makes in real life while actively processing information from the visual field. Thus, photography appears to mimic vision. But the perception elicited by the photograph is not the viewer's own; it is someone else's determination. Photographs give the viewer neither raw visual data nor objective recordings.

Projection. Because the original context has been supplanted by the photographic process, a photograph always presents you with some degree of mystery. You must infer an original context; and you do this in a number of ways—from knowledge and associations you have in relation to the subject and the situation that you assume you are looking at, and from the information (or lack of it) that accompanies the photograph. Ultimately, your own personal experience, gut feelings, and leaps of imagination tell you what the photograph means. As with other perceptual closures, the meaning you find is merely a best guess derived from your individual experience with similar images. What you see in a photograph is your own projected meaning, and in an odd way, a reflection of yourself. Figure 8-16 offers a simple example of how vigilant you must be to restrain and qualify automatic, uninformed projections. Photographs do not and cannot speak for themselves.

The Camera's Presence. The original context of any photograph has been affected by another factor: the presence of the camera and the photographer. The camera does not show itself taking a picture, and yet it was undeniably there. The fact of its presence lends photographs their sense of truth. But when people in a photograph seem to be looking out at you, how often do you remember that they were actually responding to a camera? What was the relationship between the photographer and the subject? How did the presence of the photographer change—or even create—the original context? Can you see in your imagination a larger scene that includes the photographer taking the picture? How does this scene account for what you see in the image? You must ask such questions about any photograph. As long as you cannot visualize, in your mind's eye, the photographer and camera as part of the original context, you remain vulnerable to the incomplete and often intentionally misleading expressions of reality offered in photographs. You are not in charge of your own seeing.

Photography and Objectivity

The camera's only reality is light; the camera can record only visible, material appearances. Thus, the reality of photography is the objective or sensory world. Like science, the camera is engaged with empirical realities—visible facts and material evidence—rather than with realities that are felt or experienced. Photography resonates with scientific empiricism, whose investigative realism is limited to phenomena that can be observed and measured. When you look at a photograph, you assume the role of an observer looking into an image of reality from which you are utterly separated. Toward the subject of the photograph, you feel both present and absent, because the photograph gives apparent reality to what you are not experiencing. The objectifying separation of observer from observed is doubly embodied: in the relation of the viewer to the photograph, and in the relation of the camera to the subject.

Figure 8-16. Look at this photograph and consider its possible meanings. After you have crystallized your own perceptions of this image, look at page 165 for information about the original context of the photograph.

Photography as Equalizer

In the world created by photographs, anything visible can be made important: a barn door, a green pepper, a passing cloud, an uncleared dinner table, a street beggar, the corner grocer, a crying child, a row of garbage cans, a drop of milk. To the indifferent lens of the camera, great and small are equal. Thus, photography influences your ideas about what is worth looking at, as well as about what you are entitled to look at. Your attention is attracted to otherwise unexceptional items; private worlds are made into public objects; viewers become voyeurs. Photography is a powerful means of shaping the way you relate to people, objects, and events, and of altering the values you assign to them. Advertisers know this well; so do politicians, journalists, and advocates of social and legal reform. Paradoxically, the power of photographs to affect people's perceptions and behavior is strongly asserted by some segments of our society (such as advertisers and educators), but is just as strongly denied by other sectors (such as producers of violent or pornographic films and videos).

Interestingly, the equalization of objects that is made possible by photography parallels democratic social philosophies that emerged in the eighteenth century; the French and American revolutions emphasized equality under the law. It also echoes the interchangeability of commodities, consumers, and workers in industrialized, money-based market economies. Because photography marches to the same drummer, you painlessly assimilate its technology into your cultural perceptions.

Photography and Truth

Photographs seem truthful because they present images that you imagine you would have seen if you yourself had been there. But the photograph is a perceptual *fait accompli*. By itself it provides no way for you to know in what other manner you might have understood the subject, had you been in a position to engage your own perceptual sensibilities. The power of a photograph is to convince you to see reality in a single way: the myriad alternative meanings that might have been derived from the original context have been collapsed into this single one. By preprogramming your seeing, the photograph encourages you to mistake it for your own perceptions. But your perceptions of a photograph have been done to you, not by you.

In this sense, photographs preempt the normally complex process of human seeing. Of course, other visual artworks act similarly. But the difference is that other art forms raise no questions about their nature as a product of human skill and imagination. But because photographs begin with light waves that physically existed in some instant of space-time, people tend to accept them as direct records, as minimally mediated physical evidence. They forget that photographs, like other human-made images, are created by people.

This discussion is not meant to deny the value of photography in enlarging human awareness and enriching human lives. But it is intended to warn you against mistaking the source of photography's power—which lies not in its objective truth, but rather in the ability of the human photographer (like other human artists) to generate images of meaning and value from materials and ideas at hand. Photographs are not privileged recordings of life; they are images born of human sensibilities.

Photoanalysis

A good exercise in raising your consciousness about the way you look at pictures is called *photoanalysis*: the examination of body language, touching, distance, positioning, facial expression, and so on, as represented in photographs. The term was coined by New York psychiatrist Robert U. Akeret, who found that patients who had been briefly oriented to photoanalysis were often able to see how their troubled family relationships were visibly embodied in the images of family snapshots. Akeret (1973) offered an example of how this type of analysis works by scrutinizing a well-known portrait of the Kennedy family taken in 1934. He noted that the sons were clustered around their parents, while the daughters were on the periphery. The parents were spatially separate from one another, relating more to their children than to each other. Especially close relationships were suggested by Robert's having his arm around his mother, and Edward's snuggling between his father's legs.

Akeret asserts that such formal portraits enact conscious decisions about the image that the family desires to project publicly: how its members want to be seen (which may be significantly different from how they usually are). Candid family photos, on the other hand, usually catch people in spontaneous actions. Portraits may also reflect the influence of the photographer. For example, wedding photographers, often unaware of the true relationships between people, may take candid shots based on visual esthetics or human interest. A married couple may later find wonderful pictures of little-known or disliked guests, while more positively valued individuals are conspicuously absent. Formal and spontaneous photos give different but equally provocative kinds of information.

Photoanalysis appeals to the desire many people have to find a magic key, an instant explanation. But photographs are not magic keys. Photoanalysis was productive for Akeret's patients because they were privy to important aspects of the original context of the snapshots, and they usually had a body of many snapshots to look at. Hence, their perceptual contexts were not at all the same as a stranger's would have been. As viewers know less about the original context of a photograph, their perceptions are necessarily forced into being more projective and speculative (as with figures 8-15 and 8-16).

Ultimately, photography is a sampling process: a record of the constantly changing light rays that

Figure 8-17. Photograph as source for painting: Sescau was one of Toulouse-Lautrec's closest friends: (Left) Paul Sescau (French), *A la Mie,* 1890. (The University of Chicago Press); (right) Henri Raymond de Toulouse-Lautrec-Monfa (French, 1864–1901), *At the Cafe La Mie,* n.d. Watercolor and gouache on paper mounted on millboard mounted on panel, 20⁷/₈ × 26³/₄ inches. (Museum of Fine Arts, Boston; S. A. Denio Collection, and General Income)

existed at a single point of space-time. In some cases, the sample may constitute what you consider to be a representative condition, but in other instances the sample may represent a momentary and novel conjunction of events and actions—accidents of light and circumstance that are not at all typical. Photographs portray possibilities of appearance; but your perceptions of them represent probabilities of meaning.

PHOTOGRAPHY AND ART

Nineteenth- and twentieth-century Western culture has perpetuated certain Romantic ideas about what an artist is. Early on, Western students are taught to think of an artist as someone who draws freehand. Indeed, the standard denial of artistic skill is "I can't draw a straight line without a ruler" (as if artists can draw straight lines without rulers). Integral to this concept of an artist is the idea of talent or genius: an artist is thought to have mysterious inborn and irrepressible abilities that are independent of the practical world, and that especially have

no need of artificial aids. Artistic production is a higher calling, set apart from ordinary life. These notions create an aura of magic about art and artists—a mystique that denies artists the right to be (like other people) exceedingly practical about achieving their goals.

In this view, the use of mechanical devices contaminates the purity of art, bringing it dangerously close to what ordinary people could accomplish. (Renaissance artists are forgiven for their fascination with mechanical drawing aids, because their distance in historical time lends them a sort of quaint innocence.) Artists themselves, however, seem not to have found the use of mechanical devices problematic. Throughout history, artists have persisted in enlisting whatever technical aids were at hand, and they continue to do so. The normal relationship between art and technology appears to be one of collaboration rather than mutual exclusion.

Until the late 1800s, art and the camera peacefully coexisted. In its various forms during the centuries following the Renaissance, the *camera obscura* had been widely used and advocated, not

Figure 8-18. Henry Peach Robinson (English), *Fading Away*, 1858. This image was created from a combination of five different negatives. (The Royal Photographic Society, London)

only by lesser artists, but by such well-known masters as Jan Vermeer (figure 8-4), Antonio Canaletto (figure 7-15), Benjamin West (figure 9-14), Gilbert Stuart, and Sir Joshua Reynolds. The invention of permanent images in the form of photographs did not at first change this practice. Photography was used or advocated as an artistic aid by such nineteenth-century artists as Jean-Auguste Dominique Ingres, Eugene Delacroix, Honore Daumier, Gustave Courbet, Edouard Manet, Edgar Degas, Henri Rousseau, Paul Gauguin, and Henri de Toulouse-Lautrec (see figure 8-17).

As photography developed a momentum of its own, independent of artistic and scientific applications, photographers moved to establish their medium as an autonomous art—equal to but completely independent of painting. The mechanical aspects of photography, however, raised logical difficulties. Since the photographic image was made by a mechanical device, then theoretically, anyone could trip the shutter and produce it. Where was the art in such a process?

The response of one group of early photographers, the Pictorialists, was to create photographs that resembled paintings. To accomplish this, they often manipulated photographic images by retouching negatives, painting over the print, or combining several negatives to produce a finished print (this last was called *combination printing*; see figure 8-18). The Pictorialists studied the academic conventions of artistic composition, applied them as

standards for competitive exhibitions of art photography, and included artists and art critics on their juries. When viewers occasionally mistook a pictorial photograph for the reproduction of a painting, the photographers were delighted. Photography was officially recognized as an art in 1896, when, for the first time, an American museum (the United States National Museum in Washington, D.C.) bought photographs for its permanent collection.

At this time, European academic painters were producing classical, mythological, historical, and romanticized images rendered with smooth, invisible brushwork that echoed the illusionistic realism of photography (see figure 8-19). These conventional paintings, like those of the Renaissance, were carefully composed in artists' studios. A strong countermovement, however, emerged among other painters. Forerunners of the Impressionists and post-Impressionists—artists such as Corot, Millet, Gustave Courbet, and others—maintained that beauty based on nature was superior to the artifice of academic convention. In an astonishing statement that could just as forcefully have dealt with photography, Courbet (quoted in Lowe 1982) argued that painting is

> essentially *concrete* art [and] can consist only of the representation of *real and existing* objects. It is a completely physical language that has as words all visible objects. . . . Imagination in art consists in knowing how to

Figure 8-19. Guillaume-Adolphe Bouguereau (French), *The Birth of Venus,* (detail) c. 1879. (Caisse Nationale des Monuments Historiques et des Sites/S.P.A.D.E.M.)

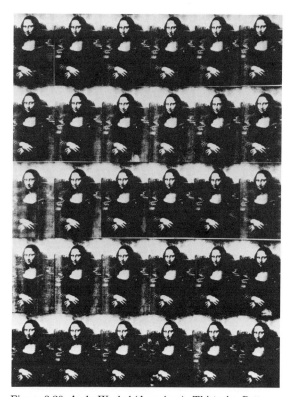

Figure 8-20. Andy Warhol (American), *Thirty Are Better Than One,* 1963. Silkscreen on canvas, 110 × 94½ inches. (Mr. & Mrs. Peter M. Brant, Greenwich, Conn.)

find complete expression of an existing object, but never in imagining or creating the object itself (emphasis in original).

Courbet's manifesto clearly articulated the passion of nineteenth-century aspirations for naturalism, whether in art, photography, literature, or science. It was entirely consistent with the vital pulse of Western consciousness for more than three centuries, from Francis Bacon to Dorothea Lange, who had tacked on her darkroom door Bacon's words, "The contemplation of things as they are/Without error or confusion/Without substitution or imposture/Is in itself a nobler thing/Than a whole harvest of invention" (Elliot 1966, p. 6).

With the coming of the twentieth century and the disillusionments of World War I, the commitment of artists to Courbet's type of representationalism dissolved in the face of Fauvism, Futurism, Constructivism, Dadaism, Cubism, Surrealism, Expressionism, and eventually Abstract Expressionism. As artists pursued greater abstraction and subjectivity, the mutually supportive association between art and photography became increasingly

Figure 8-15. John Rosenthal (American), *John Keats, Mask,* 1985. The subject is the photographer's son. (Courtesy of the artist)

Figure 8-16. Dorothea Lange (American), *One Nation, Indivisible, San Francisco, 1942.* The picture shows Japanese-American children saluting the American flag during World War II, shortly before Japanese-Americans were rounded up by the American government and "relocated" in detention camps on grounds of national security. While younger viewers tend to see this photograph as a heartwarming statement about the American melting pot, older people who remember this government action are more apt to discern irony and utter poignancy in this image. (Courtesy of the Dorothea Lange Collection, (© The City of Oakland, The Oakland Museum)

irrelevant, and photographers continued to explore their own ideas of realism, surrealism, and personal expression.

But artists' use of mechanical assistance remained a bothersome issue for conventional art historians and the general public. Controversy has again and again attended art movements in which mechanical or random (seemingly irrational) techniques appeared to supplant creative processes: the use of found objects (as by Marcel Duchamp and Pablo Picasso); the use of random or unconscious processes as by the Surrealists, Dadaists, and Abstract Expressionists (such as Jean Arp, Jackson Pollock, Morris Louis, and Helen Frankenthaler); and even the Minimalist use of masking tape, compasses, and protractors (as by Kenneth Noland and Frank Stella). Pop artists and Photorealists openly used photographic reproduction processes (see figure 8-20) or directly copied photographs or parts of photographs. The techniques look like something that—at least theoretically—anyone could do. And if anyone could do it, how could it be real art?

By now, the once scandalous Pop and Photorealist art have receded into the mists of art history, and artists of the 1980s are moving eagerly into video and computer technology. Painters are once again free to use the camera as an artistic aid or as a final medium. The divisions between art and photography are fluid. At the same time, photography has emerged as an autonomous medium that includes practices of photojournalism and documentary recording, as well as the artistry of personal expression.

Earlier controversies surrounding art and photography have been laid to rest, but new questions have taken their place. How does endless photographic reproduction affect the value of an art object? Traditionally, art objects have been seen as one-of-a-kind items. Is the art, then, in the object or in the image? And if art is in the image, then why are reproductions of the image not also art? What does it mean to see the *Mona Lisa* on bath towels and corn-chip packages? Is the value of an image degraded when it becomes as commonplace as corporate trademarks, as compared to when it could be seen only by privileged eyes? What is lost when the experience of seeing a reproduction substitutes for gazing at original art? Who is the artist when an artwork is a painted copy of an image made by someone else? Is it art when a photograph is merely copied with paint onto canvas? Is it art when the art image itself consists of reproductions of reproductions (as in figure 8-20) or of photocopies or of color Xeroxes? To what extent are such questions even important? These are some of the issues that follow the artist into the last decade of the twentieth century.

9

Motion
The Moving Picture

Is a lizard alive? Yes.
A nail? No.
A tree? No.
Is the sun alive? Yes. Why? Because it moves
when it has to.
Are the clouds alive? Yes, because they move and
then they hit. What do they hit? They make the
thunder when it rains.
Is the moon alive? Yes, because it moves.
The fire? Yes, because it crackles.
Is the wind alive? Yes, because on a windy day it's
cold, it's always going faster.
A mountain? No, because it's always in the same
place.
A motor? Yes, because it moves.
You know what it is to be alive? Yes, to move.
(Collected by Piaget 1969.)

For children, motion is magical, life-giving. A child's world is a field of movement, activity, and spontaneous forces. Things of the world are classified according to whether they do or do not move.

Many dictionary definitions of the word *free* are expressed in terms of motion: able to move in any direction; not held, as in chains, etc.; not kept from motion, loose; not held or confined; unhindered, unhampered; not restricted by anything except its own limitations or nature. Freedom, Western society's most cherished value, amounts to the state or quality of being *free*. And those who would control others—whether for good or for ill—begin by controlling their motion:

"Stay close to Mommy, now."
"Sit in your seat. Raise your hand if you need to leave the room. And sit still!"
"Atten-hut! Forward march! Left, right, left, right. . .''

"No running. No fishing. No hunting. No skating. No swimming. Do not walk on the grass."
"Stop!"

Consider, too, such terms as *emotion, demotion, promotion, commotion,* and *locomotion.*

Motion attracts attention: it is a visible sign that something is happening that you might need to respond to. Both human beings and animals react strongly and automatically to motion, because it signals change. Change is of supreme importance to survival, being intimately related to both food and danger. The ability to detect change in the environment is so basic that it appears to be innate and unlearned.

The perception of motion can be most simply defined as the perception of a particular rate of change. Like light and sound, motion represents only a tiny, perceivable segment of a much larger continuum. Some motion is too slow to be seen, such as the movement of the hour hand on a watch or the opening of a flower. Some motion is too rapid to be seen, such as the change in frames on a motion picture screen, or the flicker of an incandescent light bulb. Because of past survival needs, human sensitivity to motion has evolved to apprehend specific and particular speeds of change. As Rudolf Arnheim (1954, p. 371) noted, it is important for human beings to "see people and animals move from one place to the other; but we do not need to see the grass grow."

THE BODY

The human body is designed for a lifetime of movement. Your joints and muscles exist for one purpose: to allow you to move. A basic neurological pattern for walking is present in infants before birth. Newborns, even before they can focus, track moving objects with their eyes. Motion is reassuring to infants; they calm down when rocked or carried.

Your body requires movement to sustain life. Without exercise, your health declines and your metabolism becomes sluggish. Muscles atrophy. Just sitting too long in one position leads to cramped muscles, stiff joints, and poor circulation. Complex neurological feedback systems monitor your movements through space. Special structures in the inner ear respond to changes in your orientation to the earth. Without changing stimulation, your vision ceases to function. Motion activates your body, gives you knowledge of yourself and tells you that you exist. Most people fear paralysis, the loss of motion, as a kind of death.

Body Awareness

Proprioception, *kinesthesia* and *somaesthesis* are terms used to refer to an organism's awareness of itself: its posture and equilibrium, its movements, and its internal body states. Many parts of the body participate in these processes of body consciousness: muscles, joints, skin and body tissue, the viscera, and the vestibule of the inner ear. In proprioceptive awareness, the brain/body distinguishes between stimuli coming from inside the body and stimuli coming from outside the body; it differentiates internal events from external stimulation. Without such a distinction, for example, every time the eyes moved, the brain would respond as if the world was moving. By taking into account motions of the body itself, these self-referential systems make possible your experience of the constancies of object permanence, size, color, form, motion, and direction in the world around you (see chapter 4). Disturbances such as hallucinations involve a failure in these feedback systems.

Body awareness derives from autostimulation or feedback: activity in one system feeds information into another system; the second system in turn relays information back to the first system, which responds by refining the behavior. The cycle repeats until the activity is completed. An example of such a feedback process is eye-hand coordination, as in drawing or handwriting. What the eye sees is used to direct the muscular movements of writing, which in turn feed back to the visual system. Such activities engage a good deal of the

brain: the cortex, the cerebellum, the brainstem, and all their interconnecting structures (see chapter 3).

Continuous cycling of information among perceptual and body systems enables you to maintain posture, equilibrium, coordination, and orientation, and allows you to carry out all manner of simple and complex behaviors: walking, eating, picking things up and setting them down, drawing, typing, playing badminton, peeling potatoes, driving a car, playing a musical instrument—all actions that involve posture, manipulation, or locomotion. You are usually conscious of these complex feedback cycles only when learning a new skill (such as swimming, driving a car, or dancing). With habitual actions, whole sequences become automatic and preprogrammed motor programs.

Neuroscientists have found that the brain cells of the motor cortex (between the frontal and parietal lobes) become active before movement actually takes place; the intent to move triggers preliminary neuronal activity (called *readiness potential*). Hence, mentally rehearsing physical movement can cause the brain to organize readiness potentials. Such mental rehearsal has been shown to improve later performance. In one study (cited in Kosslyn 1985), subjects spent five minutes each day for six days imagining themselves doing certain physical activities with which they had little real experience, such as performing gymnastic exercises and shooting basketballs. On the seventh day, their actual performance was better than that of control subjects who had not mentally practiced. While mental practice was not as effective as physical practice, it was clearly better than nothing. The mental practitioners had given their brains a head start in organizing a motor program. This kind of kinesthetic visualization is commonly used by athletes, dancers, actors, and traditional Chinese and Japanese brush painters.

The Inner Ear

A powerful source of proprioceptive information about posture, orientation, and movement is located in the vestibule or nonauditory labyrinth of the inner ear (see figure 9-1). The function of the inner ear is independent of vision; organisms maintain a sense of direction even when blind or in darkness. We have no direct sensation of this area, because it is not connected to the higher centers of the brain. However, the labyrinth transmits feed-

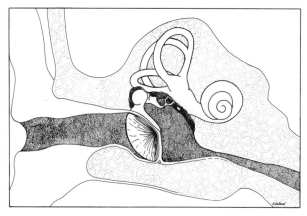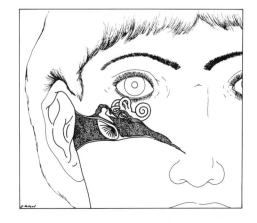

Figure 9-1. The inner ear. (Eleanor Holland)

back signals through lower brain levels, which cause the body to adjust its posture automatically and maintain equilibrium. This kind of vestibular system is evolutionarily older than vision and is present in comparable forms in all vertebrates from fish to human beings. It may have evolved from a simple gravity detector (called an *otolith*), which later developed two specializations: an auditory sensitivity to mechanical sound waves, and an orienting sensitivity to motion.

Within the labyrinth of each ear are the three semicircular canals, which are positioned at right angles to one another. Together they can define any movement relative to three axes: up/down, side/side, and front/back. The semicircular canals are filled with a fluid that reacts to motion in somewhat the same way as water in a jar does. If you speed up, slow down, or change the direction the jar is moving in, the water will slosh against the sides of the jar until it reestablishes inertia. But if the motion remains constant, the water soon catches up with it, and the sloshing subsides. For example, you can swing a bucket of water over your head in a full circle without spilling it, if you maintain constant speed; the problem comes when you stop. Much the same thing happens with the liquid in the semicircular canals. As a child you probably tried twirling around and around, and then stopping: the world seemed to keep moving. This experience of dizziness and disequilibrium is caused by the continued motion of the fluid in the semicircular canals, which gradually subsides until inertia is recovered.

The semicircular canals are an adaptation for detecting transitions in movement (that is, for starting and stopping), rather than for detecting the motion of constant velocity. Trains, planes, and cars played no role in the evolution of human perception. Consequently, human beings are biologically adapted to moving through space at less than five miles per hour! For example, after the initial start up of a modern vehicle, the fluid in the canals quiets down, and your proprioceptive sensations become indistinguishable from those signifying a state of rest. At this point, the experience of moving is primarily visual. When the trip ends, you again make a transition—one that is especially noticeable after a boat trip or carnival ride, when the earth seems to undulate beneath your feet.

Some individuals are especially sensitive to subtle motion in the fluid of their semicircular canals, and may be affected to the point of nausea; this is termed *motion sickness*. Motion sickness is more common among people who suffer from chronic ear or sinus infections. But habituation to modern travel is a countervailing factor. Fifty years ago, even in industrialized countries, motion sickness was not unusual. Today, however, in countries where most of the population has been exposed to such travel while still in the womb, motion sickness is rare. In countries where modern air and ground transportation is an out-of-the-ordinary experience, motion sickness continues to be frequent. Sea sickness, on the other hand, seems to be common among land-dwellers everywhere. The drug dimenhydrinate (Dramamine) reduces sensitivity to inner ear activity, but its precise mode of action is not known. Some antihistamines (such as Bonine) are also helpful in relieving symptoms of motion sickness.

Certain people (dancers, sailors, aircraft pilots,

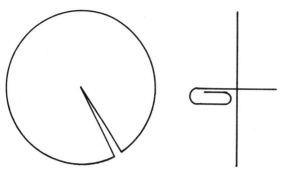

Figure 9-2. Faraday disk. Cut a very narrow slit in a lightweight cardboard circle. Spin it on a shaft made from a bent paper clip. While the disk is in motion, you can see everything behind it.

Figure 9-3. Front and back of a thaumatrope disk. (British Crown Copyright, Science Museum, London)

and astronauts, for example) have to suppress normal reactions to forces of rotation and gravity. They appear to train themselves to substitute visual, tactual, and kinesthetic signals for signals from the labyrinth. But even these professionals are sometimes subject to vestibular illusions. Pilots flying in the zero visibility of clouds or fog have occasionally been startled to find their instruments indicating that the plane had turned completely upside-down without their noticing it!

Apparently, some people are naturally more trusting of the visual field, and let it override proprioceptive information. Psychologist Herman Witkin devised a series of now-classic experiments in which subjects sat in a tilting chair and were asked to orient themselves or a luminous rod vertically to the earth. To confound the situation, the subjects were situated in a small room that could itself be tilted by the experimenters. Some subjects tended to use visual cues and lined themselves up with the room. Others disregarded the visual environment and oriented themselves according to their bodily sensations. Witkin (1949) called these styles of responding *field-dependent* and *field-independent*, respectively.

Witkin found that individuals applied these strategies consistently over a number of different experiments, and that the choice of strategy correlated with some perception and personality test results for traits such as passivity/activity, dependence/independence, and shyness/self-confidence. Cross-cultural studies, however, have not produced consistent correlations between the tilting-chair responses and other perception tests. Instead, it appears that cultures teach, encourage, and value the development of visual and proprioceptive strategies in different ways. Workers from southern Nigeria, for example, more often made responses based on proprioceptive cues, while Americans more often decided on the basis of visual cues (Wober 1967).

The Visual System

Your visual system is organized for a world of motion. Your eyes face to the front so that you can avoid colliding with things as you move forward. Muscles move your eyes smoothly and rapidly up and down and side to side. Your head pivots nearly 180 degrees. These structures enable you to track moving objects over a 360-degree field by moving only your head and eyes (these are known as *pursuit movements*). The retina itself actually requires change in order to function. If you fixate on a single unmoving object, within a few seconds the image fades, reappears, and fades again (see chapter 2). The continuous clarity of image that you normally experience is due at least in part to rapid tremors or oscillations of the eye, which continually shift the image onto fresh photoreceptors. Your body is definitely not structured for a static world!

Because rods and cones are concentrated in different areas of the retina, you have both visual acuity and motion sensitivity. While you fixate on details in the center of the visual field, the outer fringes of your vision (where the rods predominate) maintain a radarlike sensitivity to motion. Thus you perceive motion out of the corner of your eye even before you know what is moving (see the peripheral vision experiment in chapter 2). In addition, motion registering in the retinal periphery triggers a reflex that causes you to turn your head or eyes automatically toward the source of the motion. You are prompted to react much faster than you would if you had to rely on conscious decisions; at the same time, your eyes, ears, and nose are oriented to receive maximum information about the source of movement (see chapter 6).

The brain, too, may contain cells specialized for motion detection. Experiments with implanted electrodes (pioneered by David H. Hubel and Thorsten N. Wiesel) have monitored single brain cells in animals such as cats and frogs. Some brain neurons were found to be so specialized that they reacted only to movement—and then only to movement in a single direction! These specialized cells were called *motion detectors*. Whether human brain neurons function in the same extremely limited and selective way is still a subject of debate. A motion-detector hypothesis, in any case, does not fully account for the complexity of human motion perception.

Persistence of Vision. When seen in rapid succession, separate but similar images seem to merge into one another, and the experience becomes that of perceiving a single image. This happens because retinal nerve fibers continue to generate signals for a fraction of a second beyond time of the actual exposure to the stimulus (this is called *retinal lag*; see chapter 2). Around 1825, this phenomenon was dramatically demonstrated by the English scientist Michael Faraday. In front of a pattern, he rotated an opaque cardboard disk containing a single narrow slit. While the disk was in motion, the entire pattern behind the disk could be seen (see figure 9-2). The same effect occurs with an electric fan: you see through the blades as long as they are moving. You may also have noticed that when driving past a slat fence you can see what is behind it.

Persistence of vision was observed as early as the first century B.C. and was mentioned by Ptolemy and Leonardo da Vinci. In the early 1800s, a number of toys and entertainments based on this phenomenon appeared in Europe. One of the simplest, the *thaumatrope*, consists of a disk with a picture printed on each side and two strings for twirling the disk between thumb and forefinger. While the disk is spinning, the two pictures merge into one (see figure 9-3).

Another popular toy was the *zoetrope* (also known as the *daedalum* and the *wheel of life*). A paper strip depicting phases of movement (for

Figure 9-4. Toys based on persistence of vision: (a) zoetrope. (British Crown Copyright, Science Museum, London); (b) phenakistoscope or stroboscope. (Jane Filer)

example, a juggler juggling or a seagull skimming the water) is inserted into a revolving metal drum pierced with thin slots (see figure 9-4a). The viewer looks through the slots, while the drum is rotated. A similar device is the *phenakistoscope* or *stroboscope* (see figure 9-4b). A series of sequential images are drawn radically around a disk, and a slot is cut into the edge of the disk above each image. The viewer faces the pictures toward a mirror; then, when the disk is spun, the reflected illusion of

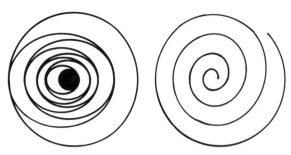

Figure 9-5. Motion illusions. Copy these or similar patterns onto cardboard disks, and spin the disks slowly on a turntable or on a shaft made from a bent paperclip.

a moving picture is seen through the slots. In both cases, the slots act as momentarily opening shutters, and the view is blocked between exposures. Similar toys are occasionally reproduced by modern manufacturers or are displayed in science museums.

Critical Fusion Frequency. Because of retinal lag (or persistence of vision), people perceive a flashing light as a steady one when the flashes occur more frequently than 30 to 50 times per second, depending on the brightness of the light (see chapter 2). This rate is too rapid for the eye to be able to separate the flashes. If your eyes were perfectly accurate, retinal stimulation would correspond exactly to the time length of the stimulus, and you would see the light going on and off.

American electricity uses alternating current (AC), which phases at 60 cycles per second—above the critical fusion frequency. Hence, an incandescent light bulb appears to give off a steady light. In fluorescent lights, however, capacitors slow the current down to about 45 to 50 cycles per second; and with television screens, the picture frame is scanned by an electron beam 30 times per second. Because these frequencies are so near the critical fusion frequency, you may sometimes experience flicker in your peripheral (rod) vision from fluorescent lights, TV sets, and computer monitors. When you look directly at the light or screen, using macular (cone) vision, the flicker disappears.

Critical fusion frequency is important in motion pictures. When a motion picture is projected, the light is on only while a frame is actually being projected onto the screen; between frames, the light is off. In early movie projectors, the on-off cycle was slow enough for viewers to be well aware of it;

hence, film shows became known as "the flicks." Flicker still exists in movie projection, but now it takes place at a rate of 72 flashes per second (twenty-four frames, each projected three times). This rate is well above the critical fusion frequency, so the image appears to be steady. Critical fusion frequency demonstrates once again the limitations on your ability to perceive reality.

Aftereffects of Seen Motion

Have you ever absent-mindedly watched the credits roll upward at the end of a TV show, and afterward felt as though the television set was drifting downward, even though you could see that it was not moving? The same thing can happen when you gaze at flowing water (such as a river) and then look at a fixed object (such as the river bank): the bank seems to drift in a direction opposite to that of the moving water. For similar reasons, standing on a dock can give you the sensation that you are slowly drifting away. This illusion, documented as far back as Aristotle, is known as the *waterfall effect*, the *spiral aftereffect* or the *aftereffect of seen movement*. (When a spiral pattern is rotated in one direction and then stopped, it will appear to rotate in the opposite direction.)

Like afterimage (see chapter 2), these illusions appear to arise from the fatiguing of certain stimulated cells. Some theories suggest that they result from an overloading of the specialized cell circuits in the brain that respond to motion. Other theories assert that adaptation processes in the retina are at least partly responsible. The reasons why such effects occur may not be clear, but they depend on the presence of a moving pattern displacing across the retina. The aftereffect appears only in the part of the visual field that corresponds to the portion of the retina that was stimulated by the moving pattern. If you track the moving pattern (such as by actually following the TV show credits upward), aftereffects are much less likely.

Possibly related responses occur when various types of patterned disks are slowly rotated (at about 33 rpm). Spirals seem to expand and contract. Eccentric circles or rings appear to rotate independently of both one another and the disk itself. Shapes extending beyond the edges of the disk may look three-dimensional. Several such patterns are shown in figure 9-5. If you interrupt the cycle of retinal lag by rapidly blinking your eyes, you can stop the movement stroboscopically. In 1935,

Figure 9-6. Motion parallax. (Carolyn M. Bloomer)

the artist Marcel Duchamp designed similar patterns—an early form of kinetic art that he called *Roto-Reliefs*.

THE VISUAL FIELD

Whatever is present in your vision at any given time-place constitutes your visual field (see chapter 2). A visual field is specific to an individual, a moment in time, and a location in space. The visual field has many qualities that are unique and not characteristic of objects in the physical world: limited field, zones of clarity, depth and distance gradients (see chapter 7). Changes in these aspects of the visual field give information about movement in space.

Flow Perspective

Whenever you move, the composition of the visual field changes. With continuous forward motion, objects and textures in the visual field stream or flow by. Gradients of size, detail, pattern, sharpness, and color undergo continuous transformation. Flowing or streaming of the whole visual field indicates that you yourself are moving. When only a part of the visual field moves (*figural motion*), you perceive the movement of an object in the environment. These transformations in the visual field (or in flow perspective) subliminally inform you about yourself (in terms of location and movement) and also about the topography and layout of the physical environment outside. Movement through space is necessary in order for you to form a mental map of

a territory. Like other perceptual gradients, flow perspective is an artifact of the visual field, and therefore it produces visual data that can arise only from an observer's unique location in space and time.

Motion Parallax

You have only to shift the position of your head slightly to alter the relationships among objects in your visual field (see figure 9-6). The change in object relationships produced by motion of the head or body is called *motion parallax*. People are very aware of motion parallax when riding in a car or train. In travel through wooded areas, motion parallax among the trees is a dizzying flickering experience: the world seems to be whirling by. In travel through open, spacious landscapes, it is easy to imagine that you are traveling on the outermost rim of a gigantic disk: near objects stream by so rapidly that they register as blurs, while more distant objects move less. Objects in outer space are so far

Figure 9-7. Greek, *The Wrestlers*, third to first century B.C.. Plaster cast from the original in the Uffizzi Gallery, Florence. (Slater Memorial Museum, Norwich, Conn. Photograph by Bruce Thompson)

away that no distance or speed you can travel is sufficient to generate motion parallax. The moon, for example, appears to maintain a constant distance from you, and thus appears to follow you.

Movie directors must be concerned with motion parallax. A flat backdrop behind the actors does not give a realistic illusion of depth, even when it moves, because motion parallax is missing. Motion parallax is also an important aspect of viewing sculpture. Because sculptors create forms in space, they are deeply involved with how motion parallax affects the way the sculpture appears from various viewing locations. Unlike the painter, whose work can only be viewed frontally, the sculp-

tor must create an image that is satisfying from many viewpoints (see figure 9-7).

MOTION PERCEPTION

You experience many—perhaps most—objects in your environment as relatively unchanging (this is the phenomenon of object permanence; see chapter 4). These inanimate objects change over long periods of time, or move on a molecular level imperceptible to your senses. But these changes are not generally considered motion, because they are not visible: they do not register in people's eyes as something happening. In general, perception of motion is an either-or experience: things are perceived as either moving or stationary.

Motion perception occurs when you see visible changes in the shapes or forms of objects, in spatial relationships among objects (parallax), or in spatial relationships between yourself and your environment. These changes create displacements in the visual field: as one thing changes position in the visual field, another takes its place. The rate of displacement on the retina determines whether you perceive movement. These direct perceptions of motion can involve either real or apparent (illusionary) motion: either something (object or self) is actually moving, or it appears to be moving when it is not (for example, motion pictures).

Some displacements in the visual field are too fast to be experienced, as in the case of a frog's tongue capturing an insect, or of a bullet shattering an apple (see figure 9-8). The human nervous system cannot match the speed of the action; it is over before eye and brain can register and process it. A similar limitation in film creates what is called the *wagon-wheel effect* in motion pictures. The spoked wheel is in continuous motion, but the movie camera records it only every ¼24 second. When the series of frames is projected, the sequence of separate images (through serial transformation) may convey backward rather than forward movement (see figure 9-9).

Some displacements (such as the movement of the hour hand on a watch) occur too slowly to be experienced as change. These displacements are perceived as a sequence of stable conditions, rather than as activity. In both instances—movement that is too rapid and movement that is too slow—our perception of motion depends on experience, memory, and logic, rather than on any direct perception of change. This constitutes indirect or inferred perception of motion.

Time is motion. You gauge time through your sense of how long it takes to do certain things, and by observing events taking place. Thus, perceptions of time come from memories and experiences of motion and change. Measures of time can be highly personal and unrelated to clock time. When you are deeply engrossed in what you are doing, hours seem to fly by like minutes. Clocks measure time intervals objectively, independently of the significance of events.

Sleep studies show that motion experienced in

Figure 9-8. Harold E. Edgerton (American), *Shooting the Apple*, 1964. Single-flash stroboscopic photograph. Moments after being pierced by a .30-caliber bullet traveling 1,900 miles per hour, the apple completely disintegrated. Such photographs require an exposure of approximately 1/1,000,000 second. (An ordinary electronic flash gives an exposure of approximately ¹/₈₀₀ second.) Because the top speed of a camera shutter is about 1/2,000 second, the shutter remains open in stroboscopic photography; exposure time is determined by the duration of the flash, which can be accurately controlled. (Harold E. Edgerton)

dreams actually takes place within seconds, although to the dreamer it seems to last much longer. During a sudden trauma, the same phenomenon sometimes occurs. An automobile accident may be experienced with a sensation of slow motion—each detail perceived with crystal clarity—even though the whole disaster takes place in the twinkling of an eye. This experience has commonly come to be portrayed in film and video through the use of slow-motion or stop-action techniques.

Frame of Reference

You usually see a moving object against a background: a person walks across a room, for example, or an automobile moves along a highway. As the object moves, you see it change location (displace) in relation to its surroundings. The background forms a frame of reference against which you measure the object's displacement. You operate on the general assumption that figures move and backgrounds stand still.

Figure 9-9. Wagon-wheel effect.

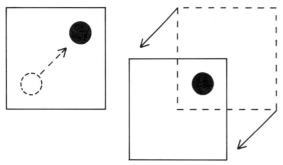

Figure 9-10. Figures are assumed to move: dotted lines represent starting positions.

In the absence of other visual information, laboratory subjects perceive a dot as moving when the frame around it is moved (see figure 9-10). Similarly, when clouds scud across the face of the moon, the moon appears to move because the observer normally perceives the moon as a figure. Both examples also demonstrate that the perception of motion does not depend on figural displacement on the retina; in each case, motion perception can occur while the eyes are fixated on the seemingly moving figure.

Modern travel can cause you to confuse frames of reference. When a train on an adjoining track begins to move, it sometimes seems for a moment that your train has started up. The same illusion can occur in a stopped automobile when a nearby car begins to move (causing you to hit your brakes). The confusions occur because you perceptually define the scene outside the window as ground. When something in the ground changes, you automatically assume that you are moving. Witkin's tilting-room experiments played with this assumption by moving the subject's entire environment while at the same time withholding the additional visual information that would normally be available in a real-life situation (for example, in the subway). For some subjects, the illusion was so strong that they felt as if they were falling off the chair!

Perception of Velocity. The perception of velocity appears to depend on the perceived size of the frame of reference through which an object travels. When two objects appear to move the same distance in the same period of time, they are perceived as moving at the same speed. Hence, perception of velocity depends on how an object's position changes relative to its surroundings—in other words, how it changes with respect to its frame of reference.

A small object in a large field seems to move much more slowly than does a large object in a small field. Watching airplanes flying at high altitudes, an observer often has difficulty comprehending the extreme speed at which they are moving. The size of a plane's image in relation to the huge expanse of sky makes its velocity appear to be very slow. The same effect can occur on land, too. In the Southwestern desert or on the Great Plains, sky and land take up so much of the visual field that an automobile's displacement seems to occur very slowly. Travelers who are not familiar with this phenomenon usually feel as if they are going about 40 miles per hour, even when the speedometer registers 80!

An object moving across a uniform background appears to move more slowly than does an object moving across a variegated background. A background with variety provides many stable reference points, and therefore presents continuous reminders that motion is taking place. Hence airplanes appear to travel faster among clouds than across a clear sky.

Autokinetic Movement. This is a case of the wandering spot. Station yourself at one end of a completely dark room, and at the other end place a small point of light (such as a flashlight in a light-proof box that has been pierced with a small nail hole). After a few seconds, the light will appear to drift. If you introduce more points of light, they will stabilize in relation to one another (grouping), but the whole group may seem to move about. This

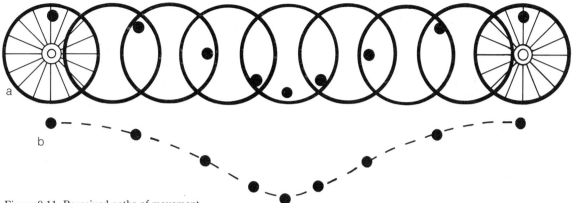

Figure 9-11. Perceived paths of movement.

phenomenon is called *autokinetic movement*. Theories vary as to the exact cause of this peculiar perception, but it provides additional evidence for the importance of reference points in the visual field. The illusion disappears as soon as the observer is able to perceive his or her position in relation to the light.

Hierarchy of Dependence. Some objects in the visual field are automatically established as a dominant framework to which the perceptions of other objects are subordinated. This hierarchy of dependence is an especially convenient concept to use in discussing motion; motion perception can be easily conceived in relation to constant or fixed (dominant) frameworks (see, for example, figure 9-10). Theoretically, the hierarchy-of-dependence model can accurately predict what will be perceived as moving and what will be perceived as stationary.

Such general principles have practical applications to animation (film, video, or computerized), light shows, visual training, and experiments in perception. In all these instances, the amount of visual information available to the viewer can be carefully controlled. All other factors being equal, then, the following rules obtain:

1. When displacement occurs, a figure tends to be seen as moving, and its framework or ground tends to be seen as stationary.
2. A fixated object assumes the character of a figure and thus tends to be seen as moving; a nonfixated or blurred portion of the visual field assumes the role of stationary ground.
3. Variable objects (objects that change size or shape) tend to be seen as moving in relation to unchanging objects.
4. When two objects of different size are close to each other and one is displaced, the smaller object will be seen as moving.
5. Where objects differ in brightness, when displacement occurs, the dimmer object appears to move.

Although these principles seem simple and straightforward, their real-life effects are often startling. For example, consider a wheel to which a single light has been affixed. When the wheel moves forward in a situation where only the light can be seen, the light appears to follow a curvilinear path (see figure 9-11b). This is the way a moving bicycle wheel's reflector looks at night. By contrast, when the whole wheel can be seen, the hierarchy of relationships changes, and the perception is greatly different: the light is perceived as rotating while moving forward (see figure 9-11a).

Apparent Motion

When you look at flip books, motion pictures, and television, you see apparent (or illusionary) movement: movement where none exists. The perception of apparent movement has been investigated in many laboratory experiments. In one such experiment, for example, subjects are placed in a dark room and shown two lights: one goes on when the other goes off. If the lights are fairly close together and the on-off interval is short enough, observers perceive a single light moving from one location to the other. This phenomenon of apparent movement

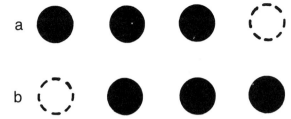

Figure 9-12. Apparent movement: (a) three dots; (b) three dots move to the right.

is often used in commercial signs and marquees: single lights flash on and off in succession, but the viewer perceives a moving image such as an arrow. Apparent movement is also called *stroboscopic movement, beta movement*, and the *phi phenomenon.*

Apparent movement derives from the perceptual tendency to group separate elements together to form a single figure (see chapter 3). For example, experimental subjects are shown three lights (see figure 9-12a); then a fourth light appears at the same time that the first light goes off (see figure 9-12b). Subjects perceive an entire group of three dots moving to the right. (Notice the difference between this phenomenon and autokinetic movement.) Because the mind prefers to perceive whole figures, it keeps elements grouped together as a unit, even when they are displaced. Hence, the perception is that the same figure was first in one place, and then in another. If the successive elements are different in shape or color, one will appear to turn into the other. Apparent movement is strengthened by persistence of vision, which encourages the fusion of successive images. The perception of apparent movement is evident even in newborn animals, insects, fish, and humans.

Serial Transformation. A familiar example of apparent motion is the flip book, where the eye is exposed to a rapid series of pictures. Slight differences between successive pictures represent changes in an object's position or location (a process called *animation* or *serial transformation*). As you flip the pages, the illusion of motion can be quite compelling. Animation is effective for the same reason that other instances of apparent motion are: the images are similar and close together in location (and hence, grouped), and persistence of vision causes them to run into each other perceptually. The separate frames of motion picture film exemplify serial transformation.

Serial transformation is used to make animated films. An action is broken down into a series of similar images, which are then projected in succession. The greater the number of slightly varying images shown over a given time interval, the smoother the motion appears. Animation in early Walt Disney films is often judged superior to that used in many modern productions because of the greater number of drawings per second of film running time. This is all the more admirable because they were drawn by hand. Today, much of the work of film animation can be done by computers.

The use of serial transformation to produce popular entertainments, however, preceded Disney by at least fifty years. In the mid-1890s, Alexander Black, a New Yorker, produced very successful picture plays, using lantern slides. About 250 glass-mounted photographs were successively projected on a screen while dialogue was read aloud. Black (quoted in Newhall 1978, p. 91) described his technique in this way: "By carefully registering the backgrounds of the successive pictures in a scene, the figures alone are made to appear to move. . . ."

Eadweard Muybridge's motion studies (circa 1878) are also serial transformations (see chapter 8). Muybridge experimented with putting his own photo sequences in a zoetrope and produced a convincing illusion of a solid miniature horse trotting and galloping. (You, too, can use Muybridge's photos for this effect. Simply photocopy figure 8-9; cut and tape it into one continuous strip; and then construct your own version of a zoetrope (see figure 9-4), sizing the cylinder to fit the photostrip.) In 1888, Muybridge consulted with Thomas Edison about the possibility of using his version of the zoetrope in conjunction with Edison's phonograph, so as to reproduce action and words simultaneously. But the scheme was temporarily abandoned.

Motion Pictures. By 1895, the French brothers Louis and Auguste Lumiere had invented the *Cinématographe,* which used flexible transparent roll film and continuous photography. Within a year, films were being regularly shown in European and American cities. In 1898, Muybridge (*Animals in Motion* p. 16) made the following speculative remarks:

. . . there can [be] but little doubt that in the—perhaps not distant—future, instruments will be constructed that will not only reproduce visible actions simultaneously with audible words, but an entire opera, with the gestures, facial expressions, and songs of the performers, with all the accompanying music, will be recorded and reproduced . . . for the instruction or entertainment of an audience . . . and if the photographs should have been made stereoscopically, and projections from each series be independently and synchronously projected on a screen, a perfectly realistic imitation of the original performance will be seen . . . by the use of properly constructed binocular glasses.

Muybridge anticipated talking movies by thirty years and 3-D movies by nearly sixty years! His conception of 3-D movies is not as surprising as it might first appear. At the time when Muybridge wrote, stereoscopic photography had been popular for more than thirty years.

Early motion-picture cameras were slower than modern movie cameras; they photographed fewer frames per second. Thus, fewer successive images were used to portray a particular movement, and the transitions from frame to frame were less smooth. With very rapid movements, some parts of an action occurred in-between frames and consequently failed to be recorded on film at all! Under these conditions, the projected image appears speeded up, jerky, and awkward—effects that contribute to the comic qualities of early silent films. The opposite effect, slow motion, is produced by exposing more frames per second than normal, and then projecting the frames at normal speed. The transitions between frames are extremely smooth, and the effect is one of great ease and fluidity.

In time-lapse photography, brief exposures are made at regular timed intervals of minutes, hours, or even days. The time-lapse technique is often used with natural subjects such as the movement of clouds and the development of flowers or fruit. When these exposure sequences are projected at normal speed, the action appears to be speeded up: a plant grows, flowers, and dies in a minute or two; days pass in seconds as the sun rises and sets and clouds gather and dissipate in short surrealistic cycles. Time-lapse photography creates the illusion of movement in objects in which changes normally occur at too slow a speed to be perceived as moving. As a consequence, time-lapse photography sometimes reveals patterns of change that otherwise would go unnoticed; this is of particular interest to scientists such as biologists and meteorologists.

A variation of time-lapse photography is sometimes used to produce animation. The movie or video camera is placed on a tripod (to avoid inadvertent changes in the field/frame relationship). A few frames are exposed. Then the animator makes slight changes in the scene and shoots a few more frames. Then more slight changes, and a few more frames. The cycle continues until the action is completed. This technique can be used for animation with drawings, or with actual objects (such as ''Gumby and Pokey''). When the film or video is projected at normal speed, the effect of movement seems to magically appear.

ART AND THE PERCEPTION OF MOTION

From the cradle to the grave, people entertain themselves with motion: jointed dolls, jack-in-the-boxes, spinning tops, limber jacks, gyroscopes, kaleidoscopes, slot cars, pecking chickens on a paddle, tropical fish, wind-up toys, carnival rides, computer games, kites, spitballs, push toys, pull toys, sports cars, dangly earrings, ant farms, home videos, porch swings, and rocking chairs. Perhaps human beings never totally lose the childhood sensibility that equates motion with life.

Folk Art

Motion has long been used in folk art. Often the wind is harnessed as a natural energy source for such objects as weather vanes and the famous Japanese kites. The whimsical whirligig, which apparently originated in Europe, has been around for hundreds of years. The word *whirligig* appears in the English language as far back as the early fifteenth century; it derives from the Middle English *whirlen* (rotating movement) and *gigg* (to turn), and it has been applied to items as various as spinning tops, revolving cages for criminals, merry-go-rounds, swivel chairs, and water beetles.

Although folk art is often created anonymously, it usually involves generations of custom and traditions of craftsmanship. Cultures in the Near and Far East have centuries-old traditions of shadow puppets, elegant in decoration and highly sophisticated in movement and story-telling. Europe also has a

Figure 9-13. Peter Paul Rubens (Dutch), *Descent from the Cross,* 1612. Oil on panel, 156 × 121 inches. (Notre-Dame Cathedral, Antwerp)

rich heritage of puppets and marionettes; Punch and Judy are only two of many classic characters. Older Americans remember Charlie McCarthy; younger ones may recall Howdy Doody, Lamb Chop, and a host of Muppets from Sesame Street.

Motion and Painting

An art object that does not move cannot stimulate a direct perception of motion. Nonetheless, artists can structure two-dimensional images in a number of ways, so as to incorporate aspects of movement.

Optical Movement. Many optical artworks seem to shimmer, vibrate, or dance in front of the viewer's eyes (see, for example, figures 2-15 and 2-21, and plate C-3). These illusions of motion are caused by physiological characteristics of the human visual system. Optical art is almost always abstract, since other dimensions of meaning tend to distract from the perception of pure sensation. Hence, optical art is characterized by geometric and otherwise non-representational compositions.

The Pregnant Moment. When a motion is depicted at an unstable point a few moments before its climax, the viewer's imagination can then fill in the remainder of the action. This has been called the *pregnant moment* or *directed tension.* Consistent with the Gestalt principle that the mind will com-

Figure 9-14. Benjamin West (American), *The Death of Wolfe,* 1770. Oil on canvas, 153.7 × 213.4 centimeters. James Wolfe, a popular (and young) British general, was mortally wounded during the 1759 Battle of Quebec, which secured Canada for the British Empire. According to factual reports, only three men were near him when he died. (National Gallery of Canada, Ottawa)

plete a form in order to make it meaningful (see chapter 3), the pregnant moment stimulates the viewer to anticipate the next phase of the action. Anticipation requires perceptual energy, causing closure to be dynamic and self-reinforcing. Thus, pregnant moments are more perceptually engaging than are actions portrayed in resting or stable states.

Peter Paul Rubens's deposition painting *Descent from the Cross* (see figure 9-13) is a classic pregnant moment. Later artists used the same technique (even similar postures) to stimulate patriotic or semireligious feelings. In these secular and historical compositions, a dying hero is shown surrounded by friends and aides, just as in religious pictures Jesus is attended by saints and disciples; a flag appears in place of the cross (see figure 9-14).

Serial Imagery. In his *Pieta* (see figure 9-15), the medieval painter Giotto portrayed various phases of motion in a series that moves from figure to figure. If you look at each human figure in turn, you will see that the transitions from one to another resemble a serial transformation. The group forms a unit

Figure 9-15. Giotto di Bondone (Italian), *Pieta,* 1305. (Cappela Degli Scrovegni, Padua)

Figure 9-16. Henri Matisse (French), *Dance (First Version),* 1909. Oil on canvas, 102¹/₂ × 153¹/₂ inches. (The Museum of Modern Art, New York; gift of Nelson A. Rockefeller in honor of Alfred H. Barr, Jr.)

Figure 9-17. Paul Cézanne (French), *The Basket of Apples*, 1890–94. Oil on canvas, 25¾ × 32 inches. As a consequence of multiple fixations, the front and back edges of the table do not line up. (© 1988 The Art Institute of Chicago; Helen Birch Bartlett Memorial Collection, all rights reserved)

Figure 9-18. Giacomo Balla (Italian), *Dynamism of Dog on a Leash,* 1912. Oil on canvas, 25 × 42½ inches. (Albright-Knox Art Gallery, Buffalo, N.Y.; bequest of A. Conger Goodyear and gift of George F. Goodyear, 1964)

because the figures exhibit an integrated and logical series of postures and gestures that are kinesthetically related to one another by virtue of carefully graded differences. By contrast, the angels are not serially related to one another and hence convey an impression of frenzy, agitation, and disunity. The effects of motion in such pictures are, for the most part, subliminal, suggesting an aura of mystery. More modern artists, such as Henri Matisse, have also used serial transformations (see figure 9-16).

Another type of serial imagery is the comic-strip format, in which a narrative action sequence is portrayed by successive pictures. We tend to associate this technique with pure entertainment, but it has been used in other societies as a serious means of portraying historical events or cultural narratives. Serial images are common, for example, in Australian aborigine bark paintings, in Egyptian tomb paintings, and in the 1,000-year-old Chinese tradition of serial pictures (*lian huan hua*).

Multiple Viewpoints. Another method of acknowledging movement is to incorporate several different viewpoints within a single composition. This approach is often associated with the Cubists as a technique for showing time (the fourth dimension) as a series of simultaneous fixations (simultaneity of vision). However, both Pablo Picasso and Georges Braque are said to have denied that multiple view-

points were a basis for Cubism. Cubism is perhaps more productively examined as an intellectual method of deconstructing and reconstructing pictorial space (see chapter 7).

The composite image in a work incorporating multiple viewpoints represents a whole perception constructed from separate fixations that reflect changes in eye, head, or body position, approximating the way we normally look at the world. It is incompatible with compositional systems of linear perspective, however, since lines need not zoom arrow-straight to vanishing points. The paintings of Paul Cézanne reflect this multiple-fixation form of picture construction (see figure 9-17)—in its time a revolutionary break from the conventions of Renaissance perspective. The contemporary English artist, David Hockney, has extensively explored multiple fixations (see figure 6-11). Multiple viewpoints are also implied in panoramic pictures and in Chinese scroll paintings that invite the viewer to travel mentally across a landscape.

Multiple Imagery. Objects may be portrayed ambiguously, such that several phases of motion can be perceived in a single image. One way of doing this is to blur the edge of an object being represented as moving. This illusion works because, when you perceive a moving object, its edge is constantly displacing across the retina and so cannot be

182

Figure 9-19. Marcel Duchamp (French), *Nude Descending a Staircase, No. 2,* 1912. Oil on canvas, 58 × 35 inches. (Philadelphia Museum of Art; The Louise and Walter Arensberg Collection)

Figure 9-20. Harold E. Edgerton (American), *Gussie Moran,* 1949. Stroboscopic photograph. While the shutter is open, the electronic flash fires in rapid succession. (Harold E. Edgerton)

clearly seen. In a picture, when the edges of a fast-moving object appear clear and sharp (as in high-speed or stop-action photographs), the object appears frozen rather than caught in motion (see figure 9-8). Once film became fast enough to record a moving subject (such as rolling wagon wheels) clearly, the resulting photographs were sometimes touched up with blurry edges to make them seem more realistic.

By the early part of the twentieth century, photographers had developed techniques for making stroboscopic and multiple-exposure high-speed photographs. This was but one manifestation of a much broader Western fascination with the move-ment and speeded-up quality of urban industrial life and with scientifically factual evidence. Another response was the Futurist movement in painting, which sought to explore the destruction of form by motion. In 1910, the Futurist Umberto Boccioni (quoted in de la Croix and Tansey 1975, p. 733) wrote about motion as follows:

> Everything moves, everything runs, everything runs swiftly. The figure in front of us is never still, but ceaselessly appears and disappears. Owing to the persistence of images on the retina, objects in motion are multiplied and distorted, following one another like waves through space. Thus, a galloping horse has not four legs, it has twenty, and their movements are triangular.

Giacomo Balla's *Dog on Leash* (see figure 9-18) was inspired by early stroboscopic photography. Indeed, Balla had a multiple-exposure picture taken of himself beside the painting; in the photograph, his own image appears in the same Futurist style as

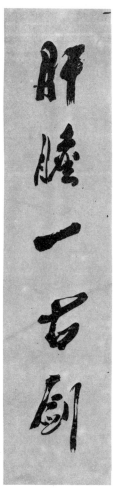

Figure 9-21. Lin Yanxin (Chinese, Fujian Province), *Gan-dan yi gu-jian; feng-xue wan mei-hua,* c. 1980. Ink on paper. In this traditional Chinese ten-syllable poem, the first phrase (on the right) implies that one individual's courage has the strength of an ancient sword; the brushwork is vigorous and angular—like sword strokes. The second phrase (on the left) alludes to the stirring up of 10,000 plum blossoms by the wind and snow; the brushstrokes are attenuated and swirling.

his artwork. In the same year (1912), Marcel Duchamp, also fascinated by the scientific analysis of motion, painted his *Nude Descending a Staircase* (see figure 9-19). By the mid-twentieth century, Harold C. Edgerton had taken stroboscopic photography to new heights (see figure 9-20).

Visible Process. Another way of involving motion in painting is to create an image that displays the pro-

cess of creating the work. Brushwork is emphasized in the traditional ink painting and calligraphy of China (*guohua* and *shufa*) and in Zen (or Chan) Buddhism (see figure 3-18). Brushstrokes convey visual information that reveals to the viewer how fully the brush was loaded, in what direction it was moved, in what sequence the strokes were laid down, how much pressure was applied, how fast the brush moved across the paper, and how absorbent, resistant, or textured the paper was. The character of the brushstroke can also suggest special energies associated with the subject of the painting. The viewer then vicariously reconstructs the movements that the artist made in creating the artwork, in effect imagining the process of making the painting. Ink and brush act as a tell-tale record of motion, a trail of footprints left by the energetic choreography of the artist's hand and mind (see figure 9-21). Such paintings not only stimulate a visual experience, but engage kinesthetic imagination (compare the idea of readiness potentials) as well. The preliminary sketches and drawings of Western artists often show this same kind of kinesthetic energy; through them, it sometimes seems possible to feel the artist's thought processes (see figure 9-22). This system of esthetic values contrasts sharply with the traditional Western view that brushstrokes should remain invisible, so as to produce an illusion of visual reality, rather than a frankly painted image.

The action painters and Abstract Expressionists of the 1930s and 1940s can be compared to the Zen/Chan painters in their rejection of illusionism and in their intention to have the finished artwork reveal the process and movements involved in the act of painting (see figure 9-23). But when the works of Jackson Pollock, Franz Kline, and Willem de Kooning were first shown, public reaction was extremely negative. Seeing visible, aggressive brushstrokes on a canvas, when you are used to thinking of brushwork as invisible, can be quite shocking. The artists became objects of ridicule. Pollock, in fact, was dubbed "Jack the Dripper."

Imagined Process. Conceptual artists of the 1970s also involved viewers in the process of artmaking. Like Oriental brushwork and Abstract Expressionism, Conceptual art calls upon intellectual and kinesthetic imagination. A piece of Conceptual art is often a minimal object, accompanied by a description of the steps by which the piece was made or

Figure 9-22. Dennis Zaborowski (American), *Nocturnal Tryst,* 1987. Charcoal and colored chalk on paper, 50 × 76 inches. (Permission of the artist)

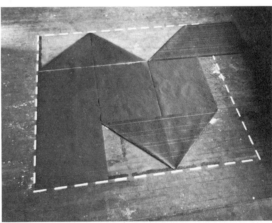

Figure 9-24. Peter McLean (American), *Arrangement: 100 Square Feet Tar Paper to 100 Square Feet Floor,* 1973. Floor space: 10 × 10 feet; tar paper: 3 × 33⅓ feet. (Permission of the artist)

Figure 9-23. Hans Namuth (German), *Jackson Pollock,* 1950. (Permission of the artist)

a

b

Figure 9-25. (a) Montague Dawson (English, 1895–1973), *Decks Awash,* n.d. Oil on canvas, 40 × 50 inches. (The Warner Collection of Gulf States Paper Corporation, Tuscaloosa, Ala.); (b) James Montgomery Flagg (American), *I Want You For U.S. Army,* 1917. Poster. (Permission Trustees of the Imperial War Museum, London)

the nature of its materials (see figure 9-24). In the extreme, a Conceptual artwork is simply a set of instructions specifying how viewers themselves can independently construct the piece.

Conceptual artists argued against traditional Western definitions of art as unique objects. Instead they focused on the artist's idea or concept as the true locus of art. When the idea is seen as the art,

the art object becomes secondary: from a single idea, any number of objects can be made independently and still be authentic art. Like earthworks (see figure 2-22), Conceptual art challenges the definition of art as a commodity to be bought and sold, as well as the conventional art-establishment structures devoted to marketing, exhibiting, and possessing works of art. The dematerialization of

Figure 9-26. (a) AGAM [Yaacov Agam] (Israeli), *Double Metamorphosis II,* 1964. Oil on aluminum, 106 × 158¼ inches. (The Museum of Modern Art, New York. Gift of Mr. and Mrs. George M. Jaffin); (b) James Searight (American), *Mirror VIII,* 1985. Angled glass mirrors, on fiberglass-reinforced cement, 26 × 26 inches. The viewer becomes subject matter as a reflection in the mirrored surfaces. (Permission of the artist)

a
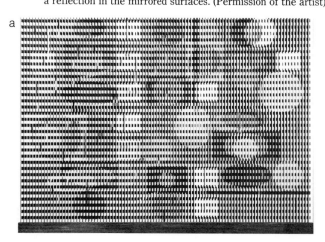

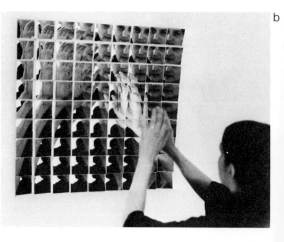
b

Figure 9-27. Patrick Dougherty (American), *Woodwinds,* 1988. Interior environmental sculpture of maple saplings. (Permission of the artist)

Figure 9-28. Peter Vogel (German), *Art-Environment,* 1980. Dance improvisation with Christine Brodbeck. The works move and make sounds when a shadow falls on the piece. (Peter Vogel and Arras Gallery)

art is likewise a factor in Performance art or happenings, where the conventional separations between art, life, and theater no longer apply.

The Moving Viewer

European Ice Age artists (15,000 – 10,000 B.C.) used the natural contours of cave walls to enhance the illusion of three-dimensionality in painted animals. As viewers looked at these painted images from various locations, slight motion parallax added a quality of realism. Located within the deep, dark recesses of caves, these paintings could be seen

only with the aid of hand-held oil lamps, whose flickering light lent an additional quality of dramatic kinetic movement. Anthropological evidence now suggests that viewing these cave paintings was an element in initiation rituals for young adolescents.

Some traditional paintings generate a peculiar illusion of following the viewer. This may happen with the eyes of a portrait, or it may occur with a picture that has a dominant object in the central foreground. In the latter situation, as the viewer walks past the painting and fixates on the central object, a strong sensation of motion parallax can be

Figure 9-29. Alexander Calder (American), *Sumac,* 1961. Steelwire and painted sheet metal, 49³/₄ × 94 inches. (Mr. & Mrs. David Lloyd Kreeger, Washington, D.C.; photography by Perls Gallery, New York)

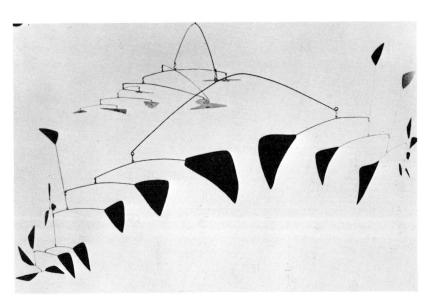

Figure 9-30. Caroleigh Robinson (American), *Pond Take, One String,* 1986. Wood, aluminum rod, polychrome, monofilament, hardware, anchors, 36 × 75 inches. (Permission of the artist)

felt: the background seems to rotate around the central object (as with the ship's mast in figure 9-25a and the pointing finger of Uncle Sam in figure 9-25b). The fixated object is perceived as a stationary figure. When the viewer moves, the background displaces in the visual field and is perceived as motion parallax. With portraits, the face displaces and seems to rotate around the gaze line, which is perceived as constant.

Viewer movement has always been of paramount importance to sculptors, because sculptures exist in three-dimensional space and, unlike paintings, are not subject to being viewed from a single location. Rather, the perception of a sculpture involves successive views experienced over time (see figure 9-7). The totality of a sculpture is like that of a piece of music: no single note reveals the whole: the parts must be experienced through sequence in time. Beginning in the 1960s, Optical artists introduced a variety of relief constructions that incorporated elements such as multiple planes, modular units, and transparent layers (see figures 9-26a and 9-26b). What viewers see depends on their location in space: the artwork springs to life with each movement they make.

The Interactive Viewer. Since the 1970s, environments and earthworks (see figures 2-22) and 9-27) have required more active participation from their observers. Viewers actually enter large-scale constructions and move through sequences of carefully orchestrated perceptual situations; this esthetic can be compared to that of traditional Japanese gardens (see figure 6-8). The creators of most such environments intend for viewers to have intensely personal and varied perceptual experiences of them. These artists challenge the artificial distance between observer and observed that has been so much a part of the traditional Western world view (see figure 9-28).

The Moving Artwork

In 1913, contemporaneously with the Cubists and the Futurists, the French artist Marcel Duchamp began experimenting with movement in art. In the 1930s, he produced his Roto-Reliefs (compare figure 9-5). About the same time, another artist captured the public imagination with mobiles: Alexander Calder began producing sculptures of abstract metal shapes, delicately balanced and hinged to move gracefully in chain reactions in response to slight air movement (see figure 9-29). Roto-Reliefs and mobiles are types of kinetic (moving) sculpture.

The idea that an artwork can move and change through time and space is no longer unusual. Contemporary artists work with modern technology to produce computerized movement, electromagnetic fields, sound-activated structures, and many other effects. Some work with nature to create carefully orchestrated and continually varying relationships of line, form, and color that change with time of day, weather, and observer location (see figure 9-30).

Motion is basic to human life. Even as art has been conceived as consisting of unchanging, timeless objects, the problem of incorporating aspects of motion into artworks has continually fascinated artists—and is certain to continue to do so.

10

Electronic Visions
Mind and Media

Have you ever spent untold hours trying to straighten out a problem caused by computer errors in billing or school grades? or thanked the gods for being able to get Saturday night cash from your bank's automatic teller? Our increasingly high-tech world provokes ambivalent feelings, ranging from sci-fi excitement to profound uneasiness and foreboding. On the one hand, people delight in the convenience of VCRs, itemized grocery receipts, and typewriters that correct embarrassing mistakes in spelling and grammar. On the other hand, they feel uncomfortable about the potential for snooping and for inaccurate records that is made possible by the extensive databases of personal information now routinely maintained by banks, utilities, hospitals, insurance companies, credit bureaus, marketing researchers, and government agencies such as the Census Bureau, IRS, Social Security Administration, FBI, CIA, Civil Service Commission, Justice Department, and the military. Back in the 1960s, the Johnson administration dropped plans to develop a National Data Center (which would have centralized all this statistical information) because of public opposition.

The current Information Age seems to lock people into an oscillating friend/foe relationship with their own mechanical contrivances. One reason why technology engenders suspicion is that most people have little if any first-hand experience with the way it works: they are passive recipients and observers of conveniences and developments that they have played no part in creating, have received little education about, and exert practically no control over. How many people can explain, for example, exactly how a telephone, radio, television, refrigerator, heat pump, computer, or FAX machine works—let alone build one! Industrialized and tech-

nological societies employ specialists to grow food, manufacture clothing, dispose of waste, build homes, repair cars, pipes, furnaces, air-conditioners, electronic typewriters, and boom boxes. As a consequence, individuals depend on specialists, and in their working lives tend to become specialists themselves.

MEDIATION

You depend on other people not only for your material goods but also for information about the world you live in. If you lived in a self-sufficient village, you would participate in (or at least be able to observe directly) all the activities that went into creating the fabric of your life. But this is not so in a complex technological society: no one person can be in direct contact with all the activities needed to keep the society going. Consequently, much of the information in your head must come from second-hand sources; it is mediated information.

A medium (plural *media*) is an inter*media*te link, a go-between, a connector, an interface. In the context of communication, a medium (such as a newspaper, book, or video) conveys information; it acts as an interface—normally a simplifying one—between your personal perceptions (which may be, for example, that Mikhail Gorbachev is a contemporary hero) and an actual person, object, or event (here, Mikhail Gorbachev in all his complex and sometimes contradictory human qualities and entanglements in historical and political time and space).

Mediated information is indirectly acquired: it is perceived from the medium rather than from sensory contact with the real-life event. In our original

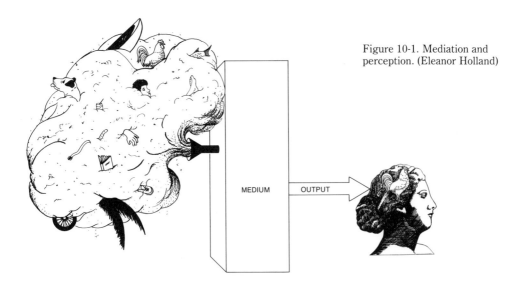

Figure 10-1. Mediation and perception. (Eleanor Holland)

MEDIUM   OUTPUT

information-processing model, we located processing within the person (see figure 1-13). With mediated experience, the picture is slightly different. The medium conveys preprocessed information, which is then processed again by the individual. In this larger picture, an individual's sense experience, which we have heretofore considered as input, actually consists of media output: the person is a receiver rather than a primary processor of information (see figure 10-1).

Mediation is not, however, exclusively a phenomenon of a technological society. The human experience of meaning has always involved mediation. The interface of cultural world views (embodied in languaging, custom, ritual, and belief) gives order, meaning, and coherence to individual experience, and enables people to make sense of their world. In small-scale societies, or in the absence of modern mass-communications media, perceptions of information and meaning are mediated (or preprocessed) by words, by art images, and by cultural programs of behavior. In a small-scale society, however, people are the active channels for conveying mediated information (see figure 10-2a). Maintaining a complex, technological society, on the other hand, depends on disseminating information to huge numbers of people who are often dispersed across distance; mediated information is a necessary substitute for direct experience, and depersonalizing the channels of communication is both practical and efficient (see figure 10-2b).

When your information comes directly from people, you are privy to aspects of its mediation: you can ask questions of the people involved, and you can take into account an individual's character, reputation, and insightfulness as you know them from personal experience. Facial expressions, eye movements, voice tonalities, gestures, and body language all convey something of what a speaker is thinking. Even when looking at art objects, you are aware that they were made by human beings, and you can usually surmise something about how they were made. But with impersonal media (such as newspapers, radio, and TV), it is virtually impossible to know the full process by which the information was organized. You were neither present when the story was constructed, nor privy to the techniques by which it was fabricated. Creating a single 30-second TV news story, for example, involves scores of people: writers, directors, producers, assistants, floor managers, make-up artists, graphic designers, video operators, lighting technicians, sound engineers, photographers, reporters, editors, anchor people, executives, and so on. Each of these individuals makes decisions that contribute something to the final form of the broadcast information. Imagine how many people you would need to interview in order to evaluate a television network's coverage of the latest airplane disaster. And even if you could track down the making of one news story, how could you possibly do the same for the hundreds of other real-life happenings that are eventually deemed newsworthy? It is infinitely easier to assume that the news-processors make the same judgments you would make—and that means trusting them.

Perceptual Transparency

A medium engages perception in particular ways. To begin with, you do not normally attend to sensations as sensations (see chapter 1). Instead, your perceptual systems tune out a medium's sensory characteristics in order to pick up on its information value. For this reason, the medium's physical qualities tend to be perceptually invisible or transparent: you learn not to see them. For example, when people in nontechnological societies first see photographs, they do not recognize the images contained therein because they perceive a photograph as a photograph—that is, as a piece of paper covered with blotches of color. When they learn to recognize images in photographs, Westerners commonly say that they have learned to ''see'' them; but what has really happened is that they have learned to perceive the images as information. Similarly, the artistic convention of the picture plane as a transparent window asks viewers to perceive by looking ''through'' the surface (see chapter 7). The same thing happens with written words. Reading is a visual activity, but just try to look at the words on this page as purely abstract patterns! Or try to hear your own spoken language as you would hear a foreign language—namely, as mere sounds. This is no problem when you have no information value for the sensory stimulus: a person with no knowledge of written Chinese can easily appreciate 美 as an abstract pattern; a Chinese reader, however, inevitably perceives the meaning *beautiful*.

Because mediated information is derived from sense experience with the medium rather than from direct sensory contact with the real-world source, it is perceived vicariously through an out-of-body experience that gives you knowledge of things that you have not actually experienced. Although direct perception is normally multi-sensory, mediated information is sense-reduced: the medium can stimulate only one or two senses (usually vision and/or hearing). As a result, your cognitive schemata—your mental images—of mediated information cannot be validated through being cross-referenced with information from your other senses. The potential value of sensory redundancy and dissonance is lost (see chapter 1). Your sense of truth then depends on more generalized cognitive processes, such as logical or rational coherence, or on gut-level feelings.

Because your perceptual systems are attuned to

Figure 10-2. Personal and impersonal mediation: (a) *Botswana Storyteller*. (N. R. Farbman, LIFE magazine, © TIME Inc.); (b) *Watching TV*. (Carolyn M. Bloomer)

extracting meaning, your perception of information itself does not depend on the nature of the stimulus. Both direct and mediated stimuli provoke experiences of meaning and closure, and both enter your head via sensory channels that you are biologically adapted to trust. Thus, indirectly acquired (mediated) information and directly acquired (real-life) information have a certain equivalence in your perception (if not at higher cognitive levels). This perceptual equivalence sometimes causes people to confuse indirect and direct forms of experience, as in the following incident:

An enthusiastic video salesperson joined a group of teachers in their lunchroom. Looking for a way to pitch his product, he quizzed the art teacher.

"Do you teach your students about mixing colors?" he asked brightly.

"Of course."

"Well, that's great. Did you know that you could use the video system to demonstrate color mixing?"

"I don't quite see the reason. My students learn about color by experimenting with paint."

"But you don't understand. I mean, you could *really* show them how with a videotape," he countered enthusiastically.

"You don't understand. My students mix real colors in real life with real paint!" The teacher was beginning to get indigestion.

"But they could *really* see it on video," the salesperson insisted, his voice pursuing the teacher as she grabbed her tray and stalked out.

This salesperson was confused about the difference between real-life (direct) experience and mediated (indirect) experience, as well as about their relative merits for teaching art. For him, the mediated (that is, videotaped) image was somehow larger than life! But in everyday speech, people are guilty of the same confounding: "It was as pretty as a picture," or "Being in my family is as good as watching the soaps," or "It would have made a great movie." Mass media have established new standards against which people measure real-life experience, rather than vice versa.

TELEVISION

Dealing with television is something new in human perception. Of the 2,500 generations of *Homo sapiens sapiens* who have walked the earth, only 2 (that is, 0.08 percent!) watched TV. In 1950, about 10 percent of American households had a television set; by 1960, only about 10 percent were without one. More than half of all American families have changed their sleeping patterns and mealtimes because of television, and in some cities, planners have had to redesign municipal sewer systems to accommodate floods from collective toilet flushes during the commercial breaks of popular programs. In more than three-quarters of all American homes with children, TV is used as an electronic babysitter, and more than half of all elementary school children watch TV while eating dinner and doing homework. In 1984, the average TV set was on for a little more than 7 hours per day—nearly half of an adult's daily waking life. Average American preschoolers view TV nearly 4 hours daily, and the typical American eighteen-year-old has spent more time watching television than doing any other single activity, except sleeping—including attending school.

Besides raising the question of what people did with their time before the advent of TV, statistics such as these raise serious questions about whether and to what extent television affects people's minds—their thought processes, perceptions, and attitudes. Some research indicates that TV negatively affects creativity because it displaces time that would otherwise be spent in problem-solving and life-experience, and because it discourages information-processing skills such as the elaboration of ideas and personal reflection. And although other factors are also involved, data indicate that poor readers and low scholastic achievers spend proportionately more time than do high achievers watching television (Williams 1986).

A New World

Without question TV affects how people perceive the world they live in. Like photography, TV defines what is important. It selects and organizes a limited number of subjects from the infinite variety of real-life events. TV creates a neatly pigeon-holed world: everything is assigned an entertainment category, a place, an allotment of time, and a value (prime time, daytime, or late-night). Information is formatted to accommodate commercial breaks, organized to resolve problems within thirty or sixty minutes, and edited to reduce the demands for mental effort on the part of viewers.

Because this mediated world is presented as normal and standard and more-or-less coincident with the real world, it can alter people's perceptions of what they can reasonably expect from their own lives. For example, several studies have shown that heavy TV viewers perceive the real world as being more violent than it is perceived to be by less avid viewers—and more violent than crime statistics suggest is the case. In addition, many people experience frustration in response to the perceptual dissonance that exists between their own lives and life as portrayed on TV.

Communities of Strangers. As radio did earlier, television promotes common perceptions and a shared world-view among millions of people who will never know or meet each other. Such shared perceptions encourage people to feel a closer connection with each other and a stronger identification with the collective body of their nation, especially in times of crisis. At the same time, such collective perceptions can be used to marshall public opinion, create mass enthusiasms and popular heroes, increase product sales, and promote political candidates.

Television has put many new neighbors into viewers' heads—mediated people who keep viewers company in their living-rooms, bedrooms, and kitchens. Manipulations of camera position and field-and-frame relationships present televised people as if they were within social or even intimate distance (see chapter 6). Because of the nearer distance conveyed by TV, you may feel personally acquainted with scores of politicians, talk-show hosts, newscasters, disaster victims, and fictional characters, even though you have never talked or interacted with any of them. In fact, actors in TV series often complain that their fans refuse to believe that they are not the characters they portray. In a non-TV world, such perceptions would be associated almost entirely with real people in your immediate environment: family and neighbors.

Social Scripts. Human beings learn how to act by mirroring other people (see chapter 1). On TV (and in movies) you see people doing things you would never see in real life—often things you could never in your wildest dreams imagine doing. On TV, behaviors otherwise quite alien to your thinking are made to seem normal, glamorous, or cool. Like real human beings, TV people provide role models and offer vicarious resolutions to viewers' own life situations. A psychologist working with troubled adolescents noticed one result of this phenomenon: some of his teenage clients would consciously assume the personas of one well-known TV character after another, appropriating various media scripts as ways of solving problems in their own lives. Numerous studies have shown that children mirror both the antisocial and prosocial behaviors depicted in cartoons, commercials, and dramas.

The controversy over exactly how powerful mediated images are is riddled with contradictory assumptions. On the one hand, media violence is often dismissed as harmless ("it's only TV") on the grounds that people naturally know the difference between reality and fiction. On the other hand, advertisers invest billions of dollars in commercials because market researchers and sales statistics provide them with clear evidence that what people see on TV powerfully influences their buying behavior. U.S. Olympic diver Greg Louganis's attitude is revealing: in 1988, he refused to watch videotapes showing a dive in which he injured his head on the diving board; he feared that having that image "in his head" would harm his ability to execute subsequent dives successfully.

TV as a Medium

Is television fundamentally different from other mediated images? There is good reason to think so. When you read or listen to radio talk, the medium is limited to words, and you must create meaningful mental images from perceptions that are already in your head. Television (and movie) images resemble your own mental imagery, but they are not of your own making and they are not grounded in your direct sense experience.

Electronic Imaging. Despite television's ubiquity, most people remain blissfully ignorant of how it works. Here is a brief outline of what happens. At the TV station, scanners in the TV camera convert light and color from the original scene into corresponding video signals that are then transmitted over wires or broadcast through space as waves. At the receiving end, scanners in the TV set reconvert the broadcast waves into amplified electronic picture signals and beam them at the screen. The standard color television screen is a piece of glass coated with RGB phosphors, which momentarily glow with various degrees of brightness in response to fluctuating intensities of voltage (the picture signal) fired at it by three (RBG) electron-scanning guns in the back of the vacuum tube.

Every $\frac{1}{60}$ second (to match the alternating 60-cycle electrical current, or AC), the guns scan $262\frac{1}{2}$ horizontal lines alternately (a procedure called *interlacing*); this is perceptually equivalent to refreshing the entire video fame (525×380 pixels) thirty times each second. The glowing appears more or less constant because of persistence of vision and the critical fusion frequency, and also because the images have few high-contrast edges and are constantly changing. However, as with fluo-

a

b

c

Figure 10-3. Effects of television image grain on information content: (a) Long shot limits information to whole body language and general context; (b) Medium shot presents an intermediate level of visual information; (c) Close-up eliminates context in order to convey information about facial expression. (Carolyn M. Bloomer)

rescent lights, the glow and fade cycle is near enough to the critical fusion threshold that, in your peripheral vision, you can sometimes see flicker. A TV set is also known as a *cathode-ray tube* or *CRT*.

Fuzzy Image. Television may seem to resemble photography, but the two media are quite different. With conventional photographs, light is used to initiate chemical reactions that create patterns on chemically treated paper. The television image, on the other hand, involves a whole series of transformations in energy forms (or *transductions*). Light from the original scene is first separated into various frequencies by a beam splitter, then sent through separate RGB filters and camera tubes, then converted into video signals, and finally separated by a coder matrix into broadcast signals of luminance (brightness) and chrominance (hue). In your receiver, a decoder matrix converts the broadcast signals into video signals and feeds them to their respective RGB electron scanners, which

beam the picture signal to the RGB phosphor groups that make up the video frame. Thus, the television image is repeatedly and profoundly mediated: between the original event and your perceived image of it, many fundamental transformations intervene; but to your senses only the final image is perceptually real.

As with photographs, the size of the basic picture elements (the grain, as discussed in chapter 2) determines the clarity or resolution of the image. When stimulated by grainy images, your visual system has to work harder to clarify the image. In comparison to that of photographs, the grain of video images is quite gross. The fewer picture elements yield less visual information, and the mind has to fill in more blanks. One writer described staring at the TV picture as "like looking at the world through a tea strainer" (Mander 1978, p.267). Large screens do not improve the situation: they simply spread the same limited visual information out over a larger area, actually worsening the image when it is viewed from close up. The main advantage of large TV screens is that they can be viewed from a greater distance (which is in fact necessary if the viewer is to experience a level of clarity comparable to that found on smaller screens). With the introduction in 1965 of the portable video recorder (camcorder), videotapes have rapidly replaced home movies. Although they lack the resolution of traditional photography and motion picture film, they are easy to use, readily available, and convenient because the image does not have to be sent away for developing.

In communications terminology, the intended image is called the *signal*; background and blanks from which the signal must be differentiated are called *noise*. This is similar to our perceptual terms *figure* and *ground*. A perceptually salient stimulus is one with a high signal-to-noise ratio (SNR or S/N). Video images have an inherently low signal-to-noise ratio. To compensate for this, television programming tends to involve pictorial content characterized by a high signal-to-noise ratio. Perceptual salience is promoted by techniques such as making the subject of the image large (that is, by filling the frame) rather than small, generalized rather than detailed, simple rather than complex, obvious rather than subtle, and moving rather than still (see figure 10-3). This technical factor is one reason why television programming so often depicts uncomplicated themes involving action, aggression, violence, and emotions that can be clearly communicated by whole-body language, by intense or exaggerated facial expressions, and by dramatic sound tracks. Conversely, subtle or low-key content (as in friendship, love, tranquillity, warmth, and environmental ambience) is the exception rather than the rule.

Television pictures will exhibit much greater clarity and resolution as HDTV (high-definition television), with its higher signal-to-noise ratio, becomes standard. Hence, representations of more sensitive and subtle subject matter will be more feasible; how (or whether) this will stimulate change in the content of commercial network programming remains to be seen. But the success of public television's programming shows the possibility, even with pre-HDTV technology, of handling more sophisticated subjects effectively.

Perceptual Mode. Watching television engages your perceptual system in a peculiar way. It requires you to keep your body relatively quiet, often in a semidarkened room, and to maintain a fixated gaze on a glowing screen animated by relatively indistinct and marginally flickering images (see figure 10-2b). Because your sensory systems require change and variation in order to function, TV watching represents precisely the kind of perceptually monotonous activity that turns your mind off and encourages drowsiness, daydreaming, and mental fatigue (see chapter 1).

Some research suggests that watching TV changes brain-wave activity. The faster beta waves diminish, while the slower alpha and delta waves increase and become progressively slower the longer the person watches. Alpha waves are characteristic of hypnotic and meditative states; they normally disappear when you open your eyes or begin to pay attention to an external stimulus, while delta waves are associated with sleep. The hypnotic qualities of television are one reason why people sometimes feel compelled to watch the screen when they say they do not want to, and even as they grumble "What a waste of time!" An artwork constructed simply of four television sets elicited a similar response: museum-goers gazed at it in fascination—as if they had never before seen TV.

Because of television's sensory qualities, TV directors have to be concerned with keeping viewers conscious and alert. One way to do this is to create constant change by means of what are called *technical events*: shifts in imagery, action, camera position, or sound. The more abrupt and intense such changes are, the more they are apt to jar the viewer into attention. Action, pain, and crisis accomplish this more easily than do subtlety, serenity, and normalcy. Content requiring reflective, even meditative responses (such as realistic portrayals of nature and environmental subjects) tend to become perceptually monotonous. Consequently, when these subjects are addressed on television, they are inevitably overlaid with dramatic or humorous musical sound-tracks, and phases deemed less interesting are preemptorily edited out. The resulting information about the world has not only been mediated, it has been significantly falsified.

TV as Perceptual Training. In American television, the typical interval between technical events is only 1 to 3 seconds! If you find this figure hard to believe, switch on any commercial network and

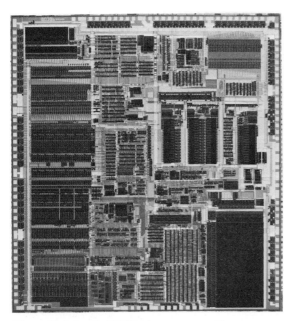

Figure 10-4. Intel's i386™ microprocessor. (Courtesy Intel Corporation)

count the intervals for yourself, using the traditional "one chimpanzee, two chimpanzee, three chimpanzee. . ." method. For a telling comparison, try the same thing with reruns of television shows from the 1950s or with old movies; here the average interval between technical events is much longer: between 10 and 70 seconds. Clearly, as American TV viewers have become habituated to the medium over the past 40 years, the pace of sensory stimulation has steadily increased. In newly modernizing nations, such as the People's Republic of China, the interval between technical events often can be measured in minutes, not seconds.

When TV viewing replaces a significant amount of a person's life experience, it acts as a perceptual training program. The perceptual rhythm of TV then establishes a perceptual expectancy for real life. When a typical American child enters school, he or she has been subjected to about 30 hours per week of such training over a period of 4 or 5 years. Habituation to experiencing perceptual shifts every few seconds encourages a short attention span, and standardized TV show length creates an expectation that 30 to 60 minutes is long enough to resolve important problems. The drudgery of school learning—or even of life itself—may be experienced as dull, anticlimactic, and boring. The perceptual

rhythm of television is vastly different from that of books, photographs, and art, where you go at your own pace. In spite of these problems, however, the involvement of human beings with television shows no sign of abating.

Sensory Discontinuity and Perceptual Switching. TV images (for example, of a far-away war, a local teachers' strike, a dramatized murder) generate perceptions of places you are not in and of people whom you are not seeing. Criminals, celebrities, wild animals, and violent actions enter your home and your mind. You receive an unending bombardment of audio-visual messages about food that is not in your cupboard, soap that you would never use, appliances that you cannot afford, and life-styles that you disapprove of; and yet this out-of-body information enters your brain right along with your here-and-now life experience. The content of TV and the content of real life are separate and discontinuous, so you must engage in continual perceptual switching back and forth among what is real here and now, what is real someplace else (according to news items and documentaries), what is purportedly real in the future (if you buy certain products), and what is purely imaginary (fictional drama). That your mind can perform these acrobatic feats is astonishing.

Coping satisfactorily with discontinuous sense experience is partly natural and partly learned. Being human has always involved a complex interrelating of reality and imagination, as well as an interrelating of perceptions of both direct and mediated information. But the perceptual switching demanded by modern life—arising from continual sense bombardment from mediated information—is something new. Learning what to accept and what to reject as real can be especially confusing (and dangerous) for children, because of their natural propensity to reality-test the behaviors they see. It is not unusual to read of children causing injury to themselves or others by imitating what they have seen on TV.

In summary, TV seems to affect behavior in at least three ways: by providing specific instructions about how to carry out behaviors; by increasing the perceptual salience of certain behaviors (disinhibition); and by presenting certain behaviors as appropriate and acceptable (value-shaping). These effects are intensified by perceptual transparency, which causes viewers to perceive the information

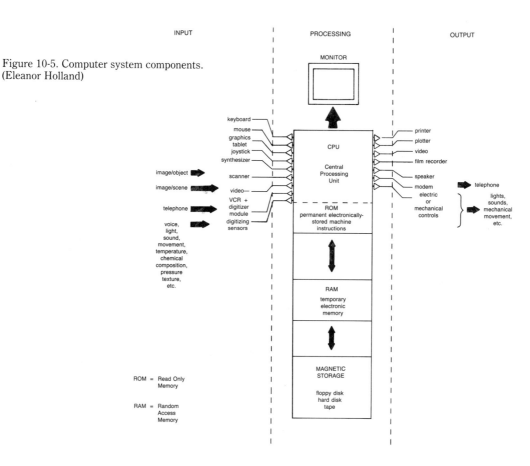

INPUT   PROCESSING   OUTPUT

Figure 10-5. Computer system components. (Eleanor Holland)

value of images rather than the methods that created them. It is the mediated product, and not the mediating process, that people perceive.

COMPUTERS

Like television, computers are powerful instruments for mediating information. Modern computer systems are made possible by electronics, a science that deals with electrons that have been liberated from the outer orbits of metal atoms by means of heat, light, and electrical fields. In computers, electrically charged atoms follow circuits controlled by transistor switches (called *gates*) that may either allow or prevent electron passage. The gates and circuitry are designed by specialists in computer logic and computer science.

Since 1940, computer technology has developed at breakneck speed. Electronic data entry and programming eliminated the old IBM punch cards. Tiny semiconductors now accomplish the switching

formerly done by thousands of vacuum tubes. Extensive electrical wiring (as much as 500 miles of it in a single computer) has been replaced by printed circuit boards, with some circuitry being contained on individual silicon chips (see figure 10-4). Miniaturization has not only made computers more compact and less expensive, it has made them faster as well. Today, computers may perform 100 million or more calculations per second, a breathtaking increase over rates of 6 per second in 1940 and 5,000 per second in 1946. One writer calculated that, if automobile efficiency had improved at an equal rate between 1945 and 1975, the 1975 Rolls Royce would have sold for $2.75, would have possessed enough power to push the ocean liner *Queen Elizabeth II* across the Atlantic Ocean, and would have run for 3 million miles on 1 gallon of gasoline (Evans, quoted in Burnham 1983).

Computer Systems

A computer system deals with three major operations: data input, data processing, and data output

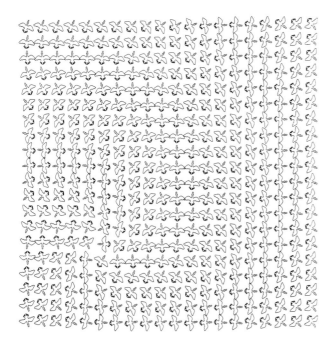

Figure 10-6. William Kolomyjec (American), *Birds,* 1980. Ink on paper, plotter drawing, 12 × 12 inches. This image was created by iteration (an image is repeated, with slight variations—in this case, variations in orientation). (William J. Kolomyjec; © Kolomputer Design)

(see figure 10-5). Common input devices include the typewriter-style keyboard, the mouse, the graphics tablet, and the piano-style keyboard synthesizer. Typical output devices include printers, sound speakers, and servo motors (robots). Input and output devices are sometimes called *peripherals.*

The input device converts the original form of the data (for example, light, sound, or keyboard fingering) into electronic signals (digital binary pulses) that stream through circuitry in the central processing unit (CPU), following pathways determined by a set of electronic instructions (called *software* or the *program*). CPU activities can be monitored by means of a cathode-ray tube similar to a television set. The output device converts the CPU's electronic signals into some form that can be perceived by people or used by other machines. In addition to (or instead of) being outputted, the data can be placed in magnetic storage (memory) and retrieved into the CPU at a later time. The most common

storage devices are magnetic tapes, floppy disks (diskettes), and hard disks (installed in the computer). In the work-place, computers are often interconnected so that they can communicate with one another (this is termed *networking*). Messages between computers in different locations can be both sent and received over telephone lines by means of a device called a *modem* (short for *modulator-demodulator*).

The mediating processes of computers fall into several general categories. With database applications, items of information (records) are stored, sorted, combined, analyzed, and retrieved in various combinations. With word processing, text can be entered, edited, formatted, indexed, saved in and retrieved from memory, and checked for spelling, grammar, style, readability, and length. Computer graphics and image-processing programs make possible the production and manipulation of visual images. With desk-top publishing programs, graphics, text, typography, typesetting, and print output can be combined to produce complete, professional publications. Music programs are used to compose and manipulate sound patterns. Computer Assisted Instruction (CAI), simulations, and games involve interactive programs especially designed for education, skill learning, and recreation. The potential for computerized mediation of words, numbers, images, and sounds appears to be virtually limitless.

Computer Graphics and Image Processing

As with color television, visual information in the typical color computer-monitor image (there are also monochromatic monitors) is conveyed by RGB phosphor groups (pixels) made to glow as a result of bombardment by an electron beam scanner. On home computers, screen resolution ranges from 320 × 200 pixels (*low-res*, about 1,000 per square inch) to 640 × 400 (about 4,000 per square inch). Resolution in scientific, medical, and commercial graphics may reach 2,048 × 2,048 pixel displays. (A typical video frame, in contrast, contains 528 × 380 pixels and uses about as much computer memory as would be required to store 100,000 words—about as many words as are in this entire book.) Because computers work with fixed amounts of memory, increases in color information (hue and intensity) will correspondingly decrease the number of pixels that can be individually manipulated, and vice versa. In low-res mode, the fewer pixels allow more hues and intensities, but image edges appear jagged (a feature known as *aliasing*), giving a computer look to the image. High-res images look smoother, but fewer hues and intensities can be used. Thus, unless memory is increased or other graphics-related hardware is provided, pixels and resolution must be traded off. For this reason, a good deal of research is now being directed toward finding ways to represent pictures with greater electronic efficiency. Image compression and fractal analysis are two current approaches.

Grain in computer imaging is often even more problematic than it is in television pictures. Because a TV image is constantly changing, aliasing is less noticeable. But the image on a computer monitor is often stationary, so jagged edges are much more prominent, even when the screen's resolution is technically equivalent to that of a television. In comparison with the resolution of photographic film, the resolution of both television and computer images is quite coarse. As a consequence, computer games, for instance, typically depend on relatively simple shapes, a few bright colors, and rapid animation.

Mediating the Drawing and Painting Process. With "paint" and "draw" software, the user creates images with a mouse (which rolls across a pad) or with a graphics tablet (a stylus on a touch-sensitive pad). In either case, the person's finger, hand, and arm movements are converted into electronic pulses (digitized) for processing by the CPU. By interacting with the image as displayed on the monitor, the user can create and edit images with lines of different sizes and types, use grid coordinates, select and change colors, fill areas, smear, blend, shade, overlay, stencil, "cut and paste," resize, repeat, stretch and compress, rotate and flip, change colors of individual pixels or pixel groups, define and redefine perspective, merge images, and so on (see figure 10-6). As a visualizing tool, the computer enables an artist to perform rapid exploration and evaluation of design, composition, and color possibilities.

In spite of the familiar terminology, however, computer drawing and painting differ in important ways from conventional drawing and painting. First and most obviously, the eye-hand feedback process is mediated by the computer: the mark does not appear on the surface that the hand interacts with (see figure 10-7). Instead, it appears on a

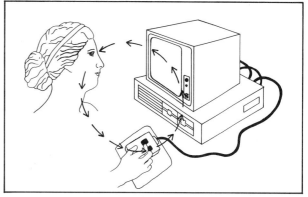

Figure 10-7. Traditional drawing (above) and computer drawing (below). (Eleanor Holland)

screen, so you must keep your eyes trained where your hand is not.

Second, with conventional drawing and painting, the various qualities of line and surface texture are directly produced by changes in the movement and pressure of your hand, arm, and body. But all the characteristics of a computer image (except in the case of some expensive graphics pads) are produced by only three manual actions: keyboard activity, mouse-button clicks, and directional hand movement within a small area (the standard mouse pad is 8 × 9 inches). Hence, you must repeat identical motor behaviors in order to produce vastly different effects.

Third, computer drawing and painting skills are not transferable to other areas of life: the ability to click buttons or slide a mouse around is not of much help in handling real pencils and real paint. By contrast, skills with traditional art materials are readily transferable from one form to another because materials in the physical world share general prop-

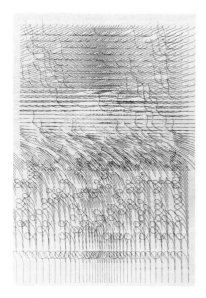

Figure 10-8. Colette and Charles Bangert (American): (Left) *Large Landscape: Ochre and Black,* 1970. Computer-plotter, inks on paper, 33 × 23 inches; (right) *Circe's View: Greening the Brown,* 1986. Computer plotter, colored inks on paper, 8¹⁄₂ × 11 inches. (Permission of the artists)

erties (such as flexibility, brittleness, creaminess, stickiness, absorbency, and so forth).

Fourth, conventional artmaking usually involves your whole body: you use large muscle groups (arms, shoulders, torso) in a variety of different ways, as well as walk back and forth to view the emerging image from various distances, look back and forth from the model to the picture, and so forth. Computer imaging, by comparison, is physically restricting: you are constrained to stay in one place, maintain a single focal distance, and move only one arm—primarily from the elbow down—in a limited repertoire of actions.

Thus, working with computer imaging and working with conventional art media engage your perceptual systems (including proprioception) in vastly different ways. Computer imaging involves an unnatural correspondence between kinesthetic activity and external results, but at the same time it can enact your thought processes more rapidly. For the latter reason, computer imaging is often said to be more efficient than conventional drawing and painting. However, this is true only if you consider ordinary expenditures of time and physical energy to make no significant contribution to artistic production. Many artists, though, adamantly insist that their physical interaction (or dialogue) with a medium is essential to their creative perception.

Insofar as physical interaction with the unique properties of materials stimulates image-making, computer graphics cannot replace pencil, paper, paint, and brush.

On the other hand, computer efficiency may be desirable and appropriate in situations where image production requirements are purely technical, or where technicians without art training must be employed. This is clearly the case for some problems in graphic design (for example, visualizing different ways a logo can be treated), in structural engineering (for example, creating mathematically precise schematics), and in animation (for example, drawing hundreds of similar images). Hence, the issue is not simply one of time-and-motion efficiency; it is one of the more complex and difficult problems of precisely assessing qualitative gains and losses that are inevitably tied to specific goals and situations.

Although computers are sometimes said to provide the artist with greater control over the image-making process, this assertion, too, is subject to considerations of context. Graphics programs give you an overwhelming number of imaging options, but these can be accessed only within set limits determined by the program. You can overcome software limitations in only one way—by writing or rewriting the program—and this job is best left to professional programmers, whose cognitive styles often differ from those of artists. In comparison, the possibilities offered to an individual working artist by conventional art media are virtually inexhaustible; for tens of thousands of years, artists have improvised new techniques and methods from the same old materials (paint, for example).

The problem of dependence on technical knowledge has been resolved in an unusual way by the husband-and-wife team of Colette and Charles Bangert—one an artist, and the other a computer scientist. Inspired by elements of the Kansas landscape, the Bangerts combine their mathematical and esthetic sensibilities to produce originally programmed computer drawings (see figure 10-8). But interestingly, the computer drawings are often inspired by qualities in Colette's handmade drawings, and vice versa.

Imported Images. Images that originate outside the computer can be converted into electronic form by means of a video device or optical scanner and fed into a computer. You can then manipulate and reconstruct these digitized images in various ways so as to make them more attractive and easier to perceive. For example, you can enhance edges, textures, and other features by increasing contrast between neighboring pixels, by increasing pixel number, or by using mathematical filters. You can statistically analyze contrasts in pixel value and color to discover new patterns (called *feature extraction*), and you can mathematically recompute them to improve image readability. You can compress an image by extracting data (thereby decreasing redundancy; see plate C-12), and so reduce the amount of memory needed to store or display it. You can mathematically average multiple images to produce a representative composite image. You can juxtapose various types of digitized images to make a seamless electronic collage. Such image-processing techniques are used extensively in space photography, in military reconnaissance, in medicine, and in advertising.

Outputting the Image. When you create a traditional artwork, it is finished when you are finished with it. Computer images, however, normally undergo an additional transformation after the image itself has been completed; they are converted from a screen display into some other form. For example, you can output the image to a printer

Figure 10-9. James Searight (American), *House Plants I,* 1984. Metal, plastic, electronic parts, including digital computer, 60 × 28 inches. A small, three-legged computer runs the "flowers," which then open and close, blink and respond to the sun or the viewer, depending on time of day and availability of the sun. (Permission of the artist; photograph by Ralph Gabriner)

or plotter and, if you wish, enhance it with paint, pastel, or collage. You can record the image directly onto film with a film-recorder, or you can photograph the screen to produce a color print or slide. (In the case of color prints, color vibrancy will be lost because the monitor image is created by additive light color, while hard-copy prints rely on subtractive pigment color; see chapter 5.) You can simply translate the image into a conventional drawing or painting, or you can project a slide of it and hand-paint the projection. You can interface computer images with live (or *grabbed*) video pictures to create special effects such as collaging, colorizing, restructuring, or 3-D imagery. Contemporary artists who have explored some of these approaches to computer-assisted art include David Hockney, Andy Warhol, Philip Pearlstein, Kenneth Noland, and Peter Max.

Kinetic sculptors can program computers to operate light or sound equipment, activate motors, open and close valves, track events by sensors, or respond interactively with viewers (see figure 10-9). Dancers use computer modeling of human body motion to explore choreography. In performance settings, computerized lighting systems, live and video-processed images, and electronic music can all be synchronized and integrated to produce special effects.

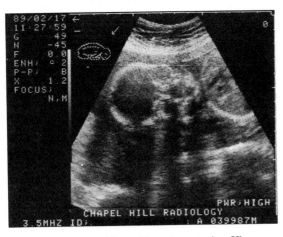

Figure 10-10. Normal fetus, 21-weeks gestation. Ultrasound. Special training is needed to perceive the information given in an ultrasound image. (Chapel Hill Radiology, Chapel Hill, N.C.)

Modeling Space and Light. With 3-D or modeling programs, the computer generates a representation of the three-dimensional object and can create projection drawings of the object from different viewpoints. This is Alberti's veil (see chapter 7) brought to mechanical and mathematical perfection. You define the primary features of an object, and the computer calculates all of the intervening edges and surfaces. Texture can be simulated by means of *bump mapping.* You can produce stereo imagery by having the computer calculate a different image for each eye. Software can also incorporate optics, as with *ray tracing*, a technique originally developed to research nuclear radiation shielding: you specify the position and intensity of light sources in the imaged scene, the various reflectancies of object surfaces (for example, shiny metal, velvety fabric, rough stone, or still water) and the location of a hypothetical observer; then, by calculating the incidence and diffusion of light beams and reflectance, the computer produces a mathematically accurate representation of light-generated effects such as highlights, shadows, reflections, refractions, texture, translucence, and transparency.

Available 3-D programs enable architects, engineers, and sculptors to visualize (and if necessary, to modify) the appearance of a structure as seen from various viewpoints before any money need be invested in the actual construction. Modeling programs are especially valuable for artists who work on a large scale, or who design art for specific sites; the artist may also use the computer to calculate costs and materials, to make templates and cut out pieces for scale models, and even to control the machinery used in the actual sculpting process.

Animation. Animation programs enable computers to produce illusions of movement. With in-betweening, for example, the artist composes key frames, and the computer generates a series of transitional (or in-between) frames. Architects and engineers use animation to simulate tours of a proposed building; if ray tracing is also introduced, even variable effects of sunlight at different times of day can be represented. Animation can be combined with video to show, for example, how a person will age; Nancy Burson, an artist, employs this technique so effectively that the FBI has been able to use her reconstructions to locate missing children.

Because computers can calculate at such high speeds, they are used to make animated films that otherwise would be too difficult or too expensive to produce. Even at a cost of $200 to $2,000 per minute, computer-generated special effects are still only half as expensive as hand-animation! Now-classic computer sequences in movies include the "Genesis Effect" scene in *Star Trek II*, "Glassman" in *Young Sherlock Holmes*, and a 37-second sequence in *Return of the Jedi* that took 4 months to produce. The corporate development of such commercially profitable effects for television and motion pictures is responsible for many of the advanced processes now in use.

Extrasensory Imaging. Earlier efforts to extend the scope of information available to people about the surrounding world tended to focus on amplifying low levels of the types of sense-data people can normally perceive (such as light, sound, and pressure). The resulting inventions include magnifying lenses, spectacles, telescopes, microscopes, stethoscopes, and devices for measuring blood pressure. Modern science, however, has tapped into extrasensory energy—that is, energy forms for which we have no direct sense receptors (see chapters 1 and 2). Such extrasensory energies include broadcast frequencies, X-rays, ultrasound, infrared, electrical discharges, radioactive isotopes, magnetic fields, and polarized light. In order to be humanly perceived, these energies must first be

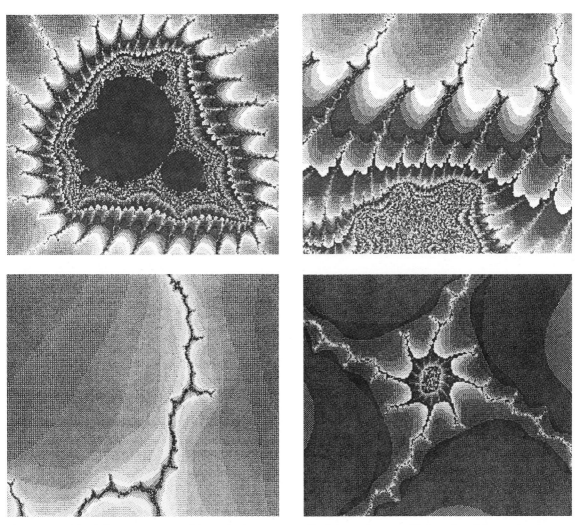

Figure 10-11. Mandelbrot sets generated by an Amiga computer. Each image is a magnified portion of the previous image. (Don Nelson)

sensed by nonhuman means, and then converted (that is *transduced*) into a corresponding pattern in an energy form that is available to the human senses, such as sound or light. Extrasensory imaging is applied in many areas of science, such as medicine, structural engineering, satellite communications, space exploration, transportation, air-traffic control, and military reconnaissance.

In medicine, extrasensory imaging allows medical personnel to observe and measure body processes that previously could be explored only in experimental animals, in cadavers, or during surgery. With digital radiography, a high-performance video camera digitizes output from X-ray beams passing through a patient or traces pathways and concentrations of injected radioactive isotopes in various parts of the body. Unlike conventional X-ray films, these digitized images can be analyzed, combined, and enhanced as in other computerized image-processing systems. Digitized cross-sections of the body can be created by means of photoelectronic devices, as with computerized axial tomography (or CAT scans) and positron emission tomography (or PET scans). When planning operations, physicians can refer to 3-D databases of digitized images of tissue slices (reproduced in natural

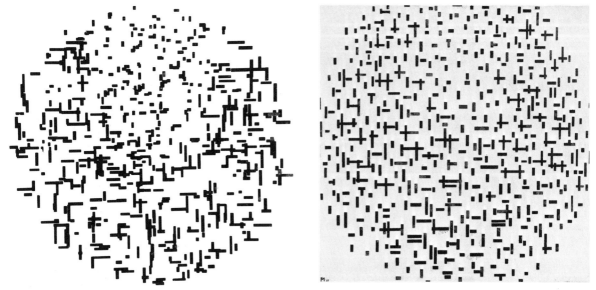

Figure 10-12. Can you tell which is which? (For the answer, turn to page 206.) One composition is: Piet Mondrian (Dutch), *Composition with Lines,* 1917. Oil on canvas, 42⅝ × 52⅝ inches. (Kröller-Müller State Museum, Otterlo); the other is: A. Michael Noll (American), *Computer Composition with Lines,* 1964. Digital computer and microfilm plotter, 11 × 8½ inches. (© A. Michael Noll 1965)

color) so detailed that they reveal individual bundles of muscle fibers.

The transduction process of extrasensory mediation is typified by ultrasound (or sonograms), which is used to detect tumors or other organ abnormalities as small as 1 or 2 centimeters in size. Ultra-high-frequency sound waves (ranging from 1 to 10 MHz, or 1,000 to 10,000 cycles per second) are directed toward an organ (such as the uterus, gallbladder, or thyroid) by a small hand-held device (transducer) about the size of a computer mouse. Sound in the body, like light, propagates, refracts, reflects, and scatters; as these echoes return to the transducer, they are digitized into video signals and imaged in a small black-and-white video monitor. The image can be photographed at any time, or stored on disk in either 64 or 128 shades of gray. Fetal ultrasound (see figure 10-10) is often advised in pregnancies where family genetic history, the woman's age, or other factors indicate potential problems. By 14-16 weeks' gestation, such things as cleft palate, spina bifida, and urinary-tract problems in the fetus can be detected.

Even higher resolution is provided by nuclear magnetic resonance (NMR), or magnetic resonance imaging (MRI). The patient is placed in a magnetic field; then, when a radio frequency pulse is applied parallel to the magnetic field, electronic signals are derived from the action of excited water molecules in body tissues as they return to their resting state. With thermography (or infrared thermal imaging) fraction-of-a-degree temperature differences can be represented as varying colors on a video display.

Technological mediation changes your perceptions of the world in powerful ways by changing the mental models that you carry around in your head. You may visualize your teeth as a series of X-ray images, your brain as a colorful thermograph, the planet Earth as a satellite picture, a bridge as a rainbow of stress lines, the air around you as a space filled with innumerable waves of electromagnetic radiation.

Computers and Creativity

In the Computer Age, as in the Renaissance, art and science tend to merge. Indeed, the first computer images were produced by mathematicians and engineers working with powerful mainframe computers. For example, the first graphic images to be electronically generated (rather than just copied) by a computer were made in 1950 by a mathematician; they consisted of abstract electron patterns beamed onto an oscilloscope and then photo-

204

graphed. The first computer-generated animation was made in 1963 to study satellite positions in space. Fractal geometry, now used in computer imaging, was developed by IBM mathematician Benoit Mandelbrot as a way to model infinite structural nesting, in which every large form is composed of smaller, virtually identical units (see figure 10-11). Natural-world phenomena with fractal properties include blood vessels, tree branches, clouds, and coastlines. Not only is fractal geometry a way to conceive of infinity in structure, but its mathematical principles can be applied to problems of digital-image generation and storage, and to HDTV transmission.

Because of the ease and speed with which computer-generated elements can be cut, sized, moved, changed, canceled, stored, and reproduced without image degradation, computers encourage exploration and improvisation in virtually any field. Drug researchers, for example, use molecular-modeling programs to explore the bonding (''lock and key'') potential of chemical compounds (see color plate C-10). Computers recognize patterns and detect movement in data relayed by remote sensors (as with satellite photography). Computers model and simulate environmental and climatological phenomena in order to predict problems or suggest remedies—for example, the greenhouse effect on vegetation distribution, or thermal convection in nuclear power-plant cooling water.

Computers and Art

Relations between proponents of computers and the rest of the art world are reminiscent of the earlier tensions between proponents of photography and painting: in general, the artists themselves seem less concerned with the debate than are historians, critics, and the general public. Artists have always been quick to appropriate technological improvements: easels in the twelfth century, oil-base paint in the fourteenth century, lithography in the eighteenth century, ready-made tube paints and photography in the nineteenth century, and acrylic paint and plastic resins after World War II. Eventually, of course, each technological improvement became so thoroughly integrated into artistic practice that people today have difficulty conceiving of them as ever having been novel or controversial. Just how and when this will happen with computers invites speculation.

The first exhibitions of computer-generated vis-

Figure 10-13. Lillian Schwartz (American), *Mona-Leo,* 1989. Juxtaposed halves of *Mona Lisa* and reversed *Self-Portrait* by Leonardo da Vinci. Image filmed by 35mm camera. (© 1989 by Computer Creations Corporation, all rights reserved)

ual art and digital graphics were held in 1965. At that time, computer art was typically made by computer-coordinated plotter-pens that produced one-color drawings. Art critics called it cold and soulless. But interestingly, an experiment at Bell Telephone Laboratories found that 72 out of 100 people could not correctly identify a computer-generated composition when it was paired with a similar image composed by the famous twentieth-century artist Piet Mondrian (see figure 10-12). And more: 59 percent preferred the computer's composition, which had been generated by a digital computer and a microfilm plotter using pseudo-random numbers. Apparently people associated mathematical randomness with artistic creativity, because Mondrian's composition was described as ''machine-like'' (Noll 1966).

Computers and Art History. Computer technology has many implications for visual research. Digitized X-ray images can be used to analyze a painting's various layers without physically changing or harming it. Although the use of X-rays is not new in museums, digital computer systems offer the advantages of image processing, manipulation, stor-

Figure 10-14. Nancy Burson (American), *Warhead I,* © 1982. Computer-processed image is a composite of faces of five world leaders in percentage proportionate to the number of warheads in each country. They include: Reagan (U.S.), Brezhnev (U.S.S.R.), Mitterand (France), Thatcher (England), and Deng (China). (Copyright Nancy Burson, Richard Carling, and David Kramlich).

age, and replay. Statistical image analysis (similar to voice prints) can define a particular artist's personal hand. By revealing characteristics of the artist's style and working methods, such techniques provide empirical evidence for classifying and authenticating art works.

Art-historical images can be digitized, overlaid, juxtaposed, resized, and combined to discover new relationships. For example, when artist Lillian Schwartz was juxtaposing digitized art images on a computer screen, her accidental discovery (shown in figure 10-13) led her to assert a new and controversial theory about the identity of the Mona Lisa.

Computers and Education

CAI, or computer-assisted instruction, holds great promise for certain kinds of learning. Self-paced typing and foreign language tutorials, for example, respond immediately and accurately to a student's mistakes and successes, selecting individualized practice material. Simulation programs teach theory and practice in fields such as space exploration, natural history, geography, and anthropological fieldwork.

For reasons discussed earlier, the role of com-

Figure 10-12. The image on the left is by A. Michael Noll. The image on the right is by Piet Mondrian.

puters in art education is hotly debated. On the one hand, computers do not teach the traditional art media skills customarily taught in school art classes. On the other hand, however, computers encourage creative exploration and cognitive understanding of formal art elements (that is, line, shape, color, and texture), as well as of pictorial systems (such as linear perspective, 3-D projections, and chiaroscuro). The time-and-effort efficiency of computer-assisted instruction simply cannot be achieved any other way within the limited timeframes of school art classes. At the high-school and college level, classroom experience with computer graphics can help prepare commercial art students to solve graphic design problems by the methods used in real-life work situations. A great many options for studying art-historical works are possible with digitized images, but because of as yet unsurmounted memory and resolution limitations, computer-displayed images remain extremely poor substitutes for traditional slides or printed reproductions.

In 1985, according to a U.S. Department of Education Survey, 90 percent of all American school children attended a school that possessed at least one computer, but only about 25 percent of all teachers used computers regularly with students. Only one in three high-school students used computers in school; those who did averaged slightly less than 2 hours per week on them, and their use was related primarily to programming and secondarily to word-processing. In the lower grades, computers were used mainly for arithmetic, reading, and spelling. Less than 2 percent of computer use involved the arts. Although computers (and video) are commonplace in many aspects of our everyday life, schools have a way to go. So long as high-tech mediation is allowed to remain unfamiliar and mysterious, students will have no clear basis for evaluating the differences between real-life experience and mediated information. Knowledge puts people in control; ignorance dooms them to be controlled.

Questions About Computer Safety

Computer monitors are usually cathode-ray tubes (CRTs). Like TV sets, such monitors generate and emit nonionizing electromagnetic radiation—that is, weak pulsed magnetic fields and radio waves, including infrared radiation, radio frequencies (RF), and radio waves of very low frequency (VLF, 15 to 20 kHz) and extremely low frequency (ELF, 30 to

60 cycles per second, the same as a typical household appliance). In addition, electron and phosphor activity on the screen generates ionizing radiation (ultraviolet wavelengths and X-rays). The long-term effects from such exposure are not yet clear, and they remain controversial. Related concerns have been raised in regard to color television sets, but computer operators must sit closer to their screens than the 4-to-6-foot distance recommended for safe television viewing.

In 1990, 70 million North Americans, including 40 to 50 percent of the workforce, will be using CRT monitors or VDTs (video display terminals) on a daily basis. Ergonomics (the study of people in their physical environment) has established that improper chairs, posture, and lighting conditions lead to aches, pains, and fatigue among computer operators. Adverse effects of VDTs on vision are well documented. People who spend more than about 6 hours per day at a monitor screen frequently suffer from temporary eye fatigue, eye pain, eye muscle spasms, reductions in visual acuity, difficulty in changing focus (lens accommodation; see chapter 2), and problems with depth perception (see chapter 7). Ophthalmologists and optometrists recommend that computer workers exercise lens flexibility by gazing into the distance at least once an hour until distant objects can be clearly seen. Clusters of radiation-induced lens opaqueness (a type of cataract) have also been reported among VDT operators. Since 1980, a number of clusters of adverse pregnancy outcomes (pregnancies involving miscarriage, stillbirth, birth defects, or health problems in newborns) have been confirmed among women who worked at VDTs more than 20 hours a week (DeMatteo 1988, 1989). For these reasons, some legislators and employee unions advocate the establishment of mandatory requirements for companies employing VDT workers to provide appropriate furniture and lighting, annual eye care, and short periods of alternate tasks every few hours.

For ordinary users of TV, VDTs, and home computers, information and options regarding personal exposure are difficult to come by. Not all monitors emit nonionizing radiation; brands differ, but so do models within brands. Emissions levels are higher from the top and sides of a CRT than at the screen; thus, nonusers at distances closer than 3 feet can be exposed. (If you place an AM radio near your CRT, emissions will register on the radio as static.)

Monochrome monitors appear less problematic, since they do not employ the high voltages required for color displays. The extremely high costs involved prevent most ordinary users from buying measuring and shielding equipment or a nonradiating Tempest-rated monitor (developed by the U.S. military to prevent VDT spying). Exposure to electrical (but not to magnetic) emissions from the CRT screen can be significantly reduced by installing a conductive micromesh shield grounded to the set or to the building's electrical wiring system. The situation surrounding VDT safety is likely to remain muddled until consumer advocacy, industry standards, and governmental regulations become more clearly formulated.

LOOKING AHEAD

The mediation of information by television and computer technology is becoming increasingly complex. With two-way interactive television, which combines both technologies, viewers are able to send their own signals back to the broadcast source or to some other destination by touching a keyboard. Researchers can instantly poll viewers for their votes on products and public issues or for their responses to panel discussions—a system that was given a pilot trial during the 1988 U.S. presidential debates. In some American cities, interactive systems have already been established whereby subscribers order goods and services and perform banking transactions by home computer terminal.

Interactive television will make possible more sophisticated educational programming (such as medical courses). Continuing research into voice recognition systems will soon produce computers that can respond to your voice. Electronic newspapers have already reached the experimental stage: individual subscribers use a computer terminal to select articles that they wish to have transmitted. By the year 2000, census data may be collected via two-way interactive cable TV, home computers, or computer-assisted telephone systems. Farther in the future, you may have the power to choose your own viewing position for a football or basketball game, or enter a movie disk by modem and participate in the drama as you wish. You may be able to watch video movies starring computer-synthesized images of actors who are no longer living. The era of the totally mediated image is fast upon us.

As surely as the Industrial Revolution changed the way you use your muscles, the Information Age is changing the way you use your mind and the way you perceive the world around you. As second-hand perceptions substitute for more and more real-life experience, your relationship to mediated information will not become simpler. In the absence of direct, multisensory experience, for example, mass media forces you to rely primarily on appearances: does it *look* real? does he *appear* sincere? is it a convincing *image*? As your mind increasingly comes to depend on second-hand images, themselves mediated information, assessing reality becomes difficult, even arbitrary. Consider figure 10-14: if you were to watch such a totally synthesized face attached to a totally synthesized body giving a synthesized "live" TV press conference, how could you judge whether or not it was real?

11

Art, Perception, and Creativity
Meaning Revisited

Some people imagine that, if they simply gaze at a painting, its meaning will automatically be revealed to them. But meaning does not reside in objects: meaning exists in people's minds. We can experience objects as meaningful only because of the information-processing systems that are already in our minds (see chapter 3). Because each person's mind is unique, the same object cannot stimulate precisely the same meaning for everyone who sees it.

LOOKING AT ART

Seriously looking at art is not easy. Of course, you can simply go to an exhibition and wait to become awed; and you may find things of extraordinary interest or beauty this way—especially when looking at traditional Western art, where the conventions and historical settings are already part of your mind's preprogramming. But contemporary art or the art of other cultures, which often does not conform with these familiar systems for processing visual data, may seem bewildering or frustrating. You may ask yourself questions such as these: Why is this considered to be art? What am I supposed to see? What makes this a masterpiece? Why is this work special when it looks like something anyone could do?

The Viewing Context

The way in which art objects are normally displayed in museums and galleries only increases their mystery. Little information is given to help you perceive meaning in the works. Labels tend to be minimal, noting only the artist's name, the title of the work, the medium, and the year it was made. Art objects can be explored only from a discrete distance; touching is almost never allowed, and sometimes physical barriers are used to prevent viewers from getting up close. The works are displayed as separate objects, isolated from one another in frames, on pedestals, and inside locked display cases. Clues to the original conditions under which the work was produced (for example, the appearance of the artist's studio, and details about the artist's society) have been eliminated. Although exhibition catalogs are frequently available, most people view an exhibit first and read the catalog afterward.

For these reasons, viewing art sometimes feels like a guessing game in which you are given a few subtle clues and then expected to ferret out the intended meaning: a test of your worthiness and sensitivity as a viewer. The underlying message is that art objects speak for themselves, that they have an inherent power to communicate to you—if you will only contemplate the object. And as a corollary, if you fail to experience meaning, the fault is yours. Hence the defensive protest "I may not know anything about art, but I know what I like!" But must the process of perceiving art really be made so mysterious?

Context is the most powerful external influence on the perception of meaning. When an object is displayed in a museum or gallery setting, your mind automatically interprets this as a signal that the object is to be contemplated for esthetic meaning, rather than to be perceived as serving some material purpose, and that certain experts in the field have judged it worthy for this purpose. Hence, the contextual framework of viewing art triggers an expectancy for perceiving particular kinds of meaning. Even profoundly mundane objects, if framed by the context of an art exhibition, can be perceived as having esthetic meaning. For example, you would perceive Picasso's *Bull* (a bicycle seat and handlebars) or Duchamp's *Fountain* (a urinal) quite differently if you were to see them in their original settings. Therefore, *art*, as such, cannot be inherent in the objects themselves; rather, it represents a particular way of perceiving: a process of projecting esthetic meaning onto objects (see chapter 1). If you are to go beyond superficial perceptions of artworks ("I don't know anything about art . . ."), you must expand the information-processing system in your mind. There is no easy way to do this; it requires work.

Beyond the Viewing Context

Like photographs, artworks have both an original context (the conditions under which they were produced) and a viewing context (the conditions under which they are seen). You can expand your understanding of an artwork by studying the original context, pursuing such questions as these: When and where was this work made? Why was it made? What purpose did it serve for the artist? What meanings did the work have in the cultural and historical context of its time? What esthetic conventions and controversies existed then? How does this work compare with other art produced in the same period? How does it compare with works that preceded and succeeded it? Who was the artist, and what circumstances of the artist's life and personality are relevant to the work? Who and what influenced the artist? What influences did this artist have on other artists? Who owned the work, and what purpose did it serve? Have opinions about this artist changed over time? How is the original context of the work different from that of your own time and culture?

These are not easy questions; answering any one of them could fill a book. Furthermore, the opinions of scholars, historians, and critics sometimes differ radically. Nevertheless, each new bit of knowledge will enrich your perceptions of meaning in the work, and will add to your self-confidence as a viewer. A single fact can sometimes have surprising power. For example, museum-goers will silently gaze for long periods at van Gogh's simple composition of a wheat-field from which crows are rising into the blue sky. This was his last painting; shortly after completing it, he committed suicide. One of the continuing attractions of the *Mona Lisa* is that the identity of the sitter remains an unsolved mystery. More recently, tens of thousands of viewers were intrigued by the fact that Andrew Wyeth's "Helga" paintings had been a well-kept secret for decades (see figure 6-15).

Appreciating versus Liking. Because knowledge leads to enriched perceptions, a work you thought dull or meaningless at first can come to seem quite interesting; occasionally you find yourself becoming utterly delighted and fascinated by a particular work, style, or artist. But you need not like an artwork to respect its value or to understand why other people may find it meaningful.

To like a piece of art without appreciating it is to enjoy a state of blissful ignorance. To appreciate it without liking it brings intellectual satisfaction. But to like and to appreciate an artwork simultaneously is the best of two worlds.

Looking at Non-Western Art. The art of other cultures also has a double context: the living context in which the object was made and used, and the vastly different context in which you view it. Most small-scale societies do not share the Western concept of art as items created by a talented few, displayed for the contemplation and appreciation by a cultural elite, and owned by collectors and museums.

Nonetheless, objects from these societies are collected, displayed, and analyzed in accordance with Western ideas and artistic standards. Like the found objects of artists such as Picasso and Duchamp, these objects from small-scale societies become art because expert Western opinion classifies them as such and because they are displayed as art in museums and galleries. Again, the culturally constructed viewing context, rather than the original nature of the object itself, leads people to perceive it as art.

As with exhibitions of Western art, the label that accompanies a work usually communicates little information about the object's original context. As when viewing Western art, you can only achieve a substantive appreciation of the work by expanding your knowledge of the original context. Where was the object made, and why was it made? What meaning did it embody in the society it came from? How does the object fit into this society's traditions and belief systems? How was it used? How does it compare in pattern, iconography, and craftsmanship with others from the same or similar cultures?

What—if anything—is known about the person who made it? Who collected it, and under what circumstances?

Art objects from small-scale societies that do not possess a written language are often used to record information (for example, genealogies), to transmit beliefs (such as in religion), or to decorate objects used in daily life (textiles, pottery, tools, and so forth). Non-Western civilizations with written languages (for example, China, India, and Japan), like their Western counterparts, have long and complex artistic traditions, explicit criteria for judging artistic value, and a large body of scholarly writings on art, art criticism, history, and esthetics. To respond intelligently to the art of either small-scale or complex non-Western societies, you must acquire at least some rudimentary knowledge of these things. Otherwise, you perceive the objects only in terms of Western values, which are very likely to lead you to false conclusions about the nature and meaning of the works.

Formal Elements

Art objects are often analyzed in terms of visual elements such as line, shape, form, color, balance, proportion, pattern, rhythm, and texture. These qualities (called *formal elements*) are visual aspects of an object's physical form; *formal analysis* is the process of using these elements as the basis for esthetic understanding. Formal analysis asks such questions as these: How are figure and ground compositionally arranged? What qualities of line, shape, and color are present? How are design elements varied and repeated? What stylistic characteristics are consistently present in work from this artist, culture, or historical period? How are these similar or different from the styles of other artists, cultures, or historical periods? What esthetic qualities are embodied in this style? Based on these elements, how can we judge the esthetic merit of this work?

In formal analysis, these questions about form are considered independently of other aspects of the object, which are referred to as *content*; content includes the subject of the work, as well as what we usually think of as meaning. Form and content are usually seen as separate—either oppositional or complementary. By setting content aside, formal analysis concentrates on visual characteristics that are present in all visual art, regardless of where, when, or by whom it was made. Thus, formal analysis is a method of investigating art objects without considering specific contexts of meaning and culture. Proponents of formal analysis often argue that true esthetic perception requires pure contemplation of the formal elements themselves, without regard to other meanings. Some formalists also assert that certain visual patterns have universal meanings (for example, that horizontal lines convey stability while diagonal lines convey dynamism), and therefore that certain esthetic perceptions are rooted in biological experience or in the nature of the human mind.

Formal analysis is particularly useful for describing and comparing the design characteristics of various styles, historical periods, and cultures. Thus, Baroque art, for example, can be characterized by the compounded repetition of sensuous curves (see figure 6-12). Renaissance perspective by central symmetry (see figure 7-23). Eskimo art by the use of split representations (see figure 4-23), and so forth. Specific artworks can also be discussed in these terms—without ever addressing such questions as why nineteenth century artists and viewers would concern themselves with stark naked women with winged babies fluttering about their heads (see figure 8-19)!

Formal analysis permeates art history courses, and can be carried to complex levels of sophistication in scholarly studies of art history, esthetics, and comparative (or cross-cultural) art. In addition, the basic vocabulary used in most art classes (the terms *line*, *shape*, *color*, and so forth) is derived from formal analysis. But when used by itself to explain artistic styles or esthetic qualities, formal analysis is problematic. While line, shape, and color are undeniably present in almost all visual art, they are aspects of sense experience that tend to become perceptually transparent for artists and viewers alike; that is, their information value (or meaning) takes precedence over their sensory qualities (see chapter 10). Hence, artistic uses of formal elements are always subordinated to the artist's intent to convey and perceive meaning—and meaning cannot be effectively separated from the social, historical, and cultural contexts that frame its perception.

In its simplest terms, saying that all art consists fundamentally of line, shape, and color is like saying that all food is made up of protein, carbohydrates, and fats. The statement is undeniably true, yet it hardly explains the myriad different values people accord to things in specific social and cultural contexts. Thus, formal analysis provides no satisfactory basis for answering the more perplexing questions of difference and change in art forms and styles. As we have seen throughout this book, identical arrangements of line, shape, and color are often perceived differently by different individuals, and they convey different esthetic qualities in different cultural contexts. In spite of these criticisms, however, formal analysis remains a useful tool when its descriptive vocabulary is applied to discussing objects within a larger context of meaning.

Perceptual Analysis

Throughout this book, art has been analyzed from the vantage point of perception, which has been defined as *a process of attributing meaning to sense experience*. Perceptual analysis is generated by such questions as these: What representational systems and conventions are employed to depict the subject? How does this system embody or challenge the world view of the artist's time and culture? How does the object structure sensory data? What are the perceptual qualities of space and distance, composition, color, motion, figure and ground, texture, and so forth? How are these made meaningful in the context that was originally meant to frame the object's perception? How are these similar to or different from traditional Western representations? By what standards, and by whom, was this artwork originally judged? Was the object originally intended to be perceived as an art object in the Western sense?

Although perceptual meanings clearly exhibit various degrees of cultural and historical relativity, some characteristics of perception are taken to be universal—for example, perceptual constancy and the perceptions of figure and ground, color, space, and motion. But as in the case of formal analysis, the universal presence of such elements does not explain the endlessly fascinating, compelling, and mysterious differences in perception. As a way of looking at art, perceptual analysis can be both enlightening and difficult: enlightening because it shows you new ways of seeing; difficult because it requires some knowledge of original context.

ART AND CREATIVITY

The Western stereotype of artists is of people who are naturally intuitive, nonrational, and "right-brained." Artists spontaneously generate novel ideas, are self-centered, seem slightly crazy, and are doomed to be misunderstood by those around them. Art depends on inspiration and talent rather than on perspiration and education. Talent constitutes a kind of magic that some people have and others do not—a seed whose irrepressible drive to sprout is nourished by adverse circumstances (such as poverty). Books and movies about artists romanticize these qualities. When asked to identify a prototypical artist, most people recall Pablo Picasso's passion for life, Salvador Dali's theatrical behavior, Paul Gauguin's wanderlust, or Vincent van Gogh's insanity—rather than the relatively quiet and stable lives of Claude Monet, Auguste Renoir, Henri Matisse, and Andrew Wyeth.

As most practicing artists will confirm, however, this cultural stereotype is largely mythical. Producing art is hard, perplexing, stressful, and only occasionally romantic work. The lives of artists, like the lives of other people, are filled with humdrum activities of day-to-day life that are edited out of their biographies. Even so, artists in Western society do seem to be different from other people.

Creative Personalities

Studies show that creative people, regardless of profession, tend to have certain personality traits in common. Such people tend to prefer certain kinds of complexity and novelty, and to enjoy constructing order from stimuli or situations that other people perceive as chaotic or disordered (see chapter 1). Whereas other people are likely to discount or reject their intuition and their unconscious mind as reliable sources of ideas, creative individuals tend to trust and act on their hunches, sudden insights, and dreams. With respect to issues in their professional fields, people with creative personalities place a high value on truth and intellectual honesty and are remarkably tenacious in their pursuit of accurate and meaningful answers to the particular questions that bother them. In addition, they have more confidence in their own judgment than in the judgment of other people. As youngsters, creative individuals do not always perform well in school because these personality traits often lead to friction in their relationships with teachers and peers.

Creative people can perceive the world as other people do, but also in ways that others do not. The perceptual and cognitive styles of the creative personality are unusually sensitive to the relation of parts to a whole. Consequently, creative people are quick to recognize weak links or missing elements and are eager to generate possibilities for alternative meanings. Details tend to have more perceptual salience for creative people than they do for other people: creative individuals notice more.

The Creative Process

For centuries, the mysteries of creative thought have intrigued people everywhere. A number of Western writers have divided the creative process into separate stages, which can be called *preparation, incubation, illumination*, and *verification*.

Preparation. In the initial stage of the creative process, a problem is defined and relevant information is collected (but not subjected to any final evaluation). The collection process must be extensive enough to push beyond the usual and the predictable, into a freewheeling mode of thought. The process is also called *brainstorming* or *conceptual blockbusting*. The preparation stage calls for fluency and flexibility in generating ideas, as well as the ability to withhold judgment or closure. Delaying closure is important because ideas that at first seem irrelevant may later prove to have unexpected value.

Brainstorming is productive for groups as well as for individuals. Members of the group are encouraged to call out any thoughts that pop into their heads, regardless of how silly or how irrelevant they may seem. The ideas are listed for all to see, in the order in which they are presented, without being rejected or evaluated. The process continues until all ideas are exhausted—at least for the present. Brainstorming can be used for all kinds of group problem-solving. For example: What rules should we have for our classroom? How should we spend the money in our club's treasury? How can we increase factory production? Brainstorming is a means of promoting divergent (or creative) thought processes, so it is appropriate for open-ended problems—problems that have no single solution. Closed-ended problems, which have a single correct answer (for example, how much money is in our club's treasury?), are usually more suited to convergent thought processes—that is, to linear or logical analysis.

For an artist, the preparation stage typically begins with the problem of having a definite yet unformed idea for an artwork. The artist then proceeds to explore many conceivable ideas for forming the work. These may involve various activities: making numerous sketches; experimenting playfully with materials, tools, colors, textures, compositions, and images; engaging in freewheeling mental visualization; perusing past notes, sketches, or relevant art historical works or writings; making field trips for first-hand study of a subject. The preparation stage may last for hours, months, or even years, and it comes to an end only when the exploratory activities no longer produce new ideas.

Incubation. When preparation activities have been exhausted, the next step is simply to stop thinking about the problem and to distract the mind with other things. During this stage, the preparatory material is being worked over by unconscious portions of the mind. Incubation periods may be short (for example, the time required to go out to a movie, get a good night's sleep, or clear the mind through meditation) or long (lasting months or even years). The incubation process is commonly referred to as *putting it on the back burner*, *sleeping* (or *sitting*) *on it*, or simply *taking a break*.

Illumination. Illumination, the third stage of the creative process, characteristically occurs suddenly and unexpectedly: in a flash of sudden and exhilarating insight the problem appears to resolve itself, and the solution is revealed in great clarity. Illumination is sometimes called the *aha!* or *eureka!* experience. For the artist, this is the instant when the form of the artwork is seen clearly in the mind's eye. Anecdotes abound about ways in which this phenomenon has been experienced by famous people. The scientist Friedrich Kukelé for example, had been working on the problem of the molecular structure of benzene; the answer appeared to him as a dream image of a snake with its tail in its mouth. According to folklore, the concept of gravity was revealed to Sir Isaac Newton in the instant that an apple fell on his head. Zen Buddhist masters may step on their pupils' toes, pinch their pupils' noses, or present them with puzzling stories (*koans*) in order to distract the pupils' minds and provoke sudden flashes of philosophical understanding.

The irrational quality of the illumination experience has resulted in many colorful explanations for creative insight, including the temperamental Muse responsible for artistic inspiration, and picturesque images of artistic madness. Creativity is made to seem mystical and unpredictable—the capricious gift of some supernatural power, given to some lucky individuals and denied to others. But illumina-

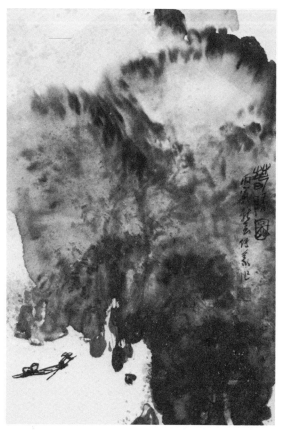

Figure 11-1. Wei Chuanyi (Chinese), untitled, c. 1985. Ink on paper, approximately 17 × 26 inches. (Permission of the artist)

tion is actually a familiar and common phenomenon. If, for example, you have forgotten someone's name, you may first run through your mental files, try out various letters of the alphabet to see if they will trigger the name, try to recall being introduced to the person, or attempt to visualize the person's business card. And then, shortly after you give up on the problem, the name suddenly and mysteriously pops into your head. This illumination is actually a closure prompted by the awareness of a specific problem and a preparation process (the mental efforts to remember), followed by an incubation stage (giving up and turning your attention to other things). In order to dispose of this old business, your unconscious mind strives to construct an answer. Like a dog with a meaty bone, your mind will continue to gnaw away at the problem until it

can be finished and buried. For this reason, during the preparation stage, it is essential to refrain from closure-prompting evaluations and to gather a broad range of information, in order to seduce the unconscious mind into continuing to work on the problem.

Verification. The final step in the creative process is to reality-test the illumination (or closure) by actualizing it. For the person who has forgotten a name, verification consists of confirming the name as finally remembered with another person. For Kukelé, it meant applying mathematical calculations to the hexagonal ring idea of the benzene molecule in order to verify its correctness. For an artist, verification means actually making the artwork. Sometimes the verification step will reveal that the illumination was a false alarm; in this case, the preparation and/or incubation steps must be repeated, as in the expressions *back to square one!* or *back to the drawing board!*

Using the Creative Process. By looking at creativity in terms of these four stages, you can understand where the process sometimes gets derailed. If too few ideas are generated during the preparation phase, or if they are too tightly evaluated, the unconscious mind will not be made sufficiently uncomfortable about the problem to continue to explore it. Many people, especially students, skip the incubation step, particularly when facing an impending deadline; they feel guilty if they are not giving the problem their undivided and constant attention. But without incubation, the unconscious mind lacks sufficient leisure time to resolve the problem.

Sometimes, too, people will disregard an illumination experience that appears to lack a rational basis—if, for example, it occurs in a dream or takes the form of an intuitive hunch or feeling. Creative personalities are less apt to disregard an insight for such reasons. Finally, some people stop at the illumination step, failing, for one reason or another, to reality-test or verify their insights. Their ideas may then be referred to as *half-baked, untested,* or, on a more complex level, *still in a theoretical stage.*

The four steps (preparation, incubation, illumination, and verification) can be applied to any open-ended problem: writing a paper or speech, studying for an exam, planning a menu or vacation, deciding on a career, and so forth. These steps are also useful for getting past so-called creative *blocks.* If, for example, you feel stuck while working on an artwork or writing a paper, simply carry out preparations for the next step; then relax and incubate. You will return to the problem with fresh ideas. After you have consciously applied these steps to a few of your own problems, you will find the process habit-forming.

Creative Perception

These understandings about creative thinking and creative personalities can be specifically applied to learning to see more creatively. Illumination (or closure) is preceded by preparation and incubation; illumination represents the mind's desperate attempt to construct closure and thereby rid itself of the problem. Hence, the key to creativity—whether in thought or in vision—is to delay closure as long as possible. But because our perceptual systems are geared to reach closure quickly and parsimoniously, putting off closure usually requires some conscious mental effort. Thus, while simple in principle, delaying closure is often neither easy nor comfortable to carry out in practice.

To postpone closure, you must coax your mind into seeing a stimulus as ambiguous, unfamiliar, or empty of meaning. One way to accomplish this is to clear the mind and simply contemplate the object until it no longer seems familiar. This is what happens when you write a word over and over again or stare at an image for a long time. In the case of ambiguous objects such as rocks, clouds, or ink-blots, you must mentally set aside your first closure and continue contemplating the object. As you persist, your mind will continue to offer new closures for your approval, and sudden and surprising perceptions will take place. As long as you keep setting aside these closures as they occur, your mind will keep looking for a conclusive meaning, and you will become aware of more and more possible meanings.

Artists have long been aware of this phenomenon. Leonardo da Vinci, for example, advised exercising the imagination by contemplating stains on a wall. Traditional Chinese painters of the "splashed" or "splattered" ink style (*po-mo*) used a similar technique, sometimes delaying for months before brushing in the few final strokes that transformed an ink-blotch into an identifiable form (see figure 11-1). Similarly, Song Di, an ancient Chinese scholar offered the following advice (Bush and Shih 1985, p. 122):

First look for a damaged wall, and then stretch plain silk against it. Gaze at it day and night. When you have looked for a sufficient length of time, you will see through the silk the high and low parts, or curves and angles, on the surface of the wall, which will take on the appearance of landscape. . . . As your spirit leads and your imagination constructs, you will see indistinctly the images of human beings, birds, grasses, and trees, flying or moving about. Once they are complete in your eyes, then follow your imagination to command your brush.

Another approach to creative perception involves brainstorming about ambiguities in the relations of parts to wholes—especially in searching for weak or missing elements whose deficiencies are not at first apparent. Here, you might explore questions such as the following: What would be the effect of removing or changing this part, or of arranging the parts differently? What if the whole configuration were slightly different: how would this affect each part? Which elements are essential to the whole, and which could be eliminated without affecting meaning? In what ways do details affect the perception of the whole or of the parts? How could two or more seemingly unrelated things be combined to make a larger whole? What if one was inside the other, or if their size relationships were different? These are precisely the kinds of questions that artists (and scientists) continually ask themselves in the process of creative problem-solving, and they are also the kinds of questions that viewers should ask themselves when looking at artworks.

Another characteristic of creative seeing is the perception of details often overlooked by other people. Because the purpose of perception is to find meaning, your mind is normally aware of only as much detail as is necessary to achieve closure. Ordinary seeing tunes out many details, while lack of closure prompts attention to detail. Hence, creative disregard of closure through persistent looking will cause ordinarily unnoticed details to take on more and more perceptual salience. What is at first perceived as an ordinary leaf, for example, can become a highly specific and intricate pattern of colors, lines, and textures that signal information about species, season, weather, local pests, soil conditions, and so forth.

A good deal of creative seeing thus resembles

the kind of thinking often called *daydreaming, reverie, wool-gathering,* or, more respectably, *contemplation.* In today's fast-paced society, taking time for this kind of thinking (which usually promises no immediately visible results) is often thought of as wasting time. In addition, modern life rarely presents many natural opportunities for quiet contemplation. But creative thinking requires this kind of time. In order to perceive art and the world around you more creatively, you must make time in your life to do so. There are no shortcuts.

Originality

People think creatively a good deal of the time, although they do not usually label it *creative thinking.* Even such mundane activities as constructing sentences in a conversation or planning a wardrobe represent unique solutions to open-ended problems. Nonetheless, society clearly values some types of creative thinking more than it does others. Michelangelo's paintings on the Sistine Chapel ceiling, or Einstein's theory of relativity, for example, are not thought of as equivalent to conversational sentences or coordinated clothing. Not only do artworks and scientific theories address issues different from those of day-to-day living, they also embody qualities of uniqueness and original expression that can be assigned value in the context of culturally defined traditions. Thus, while creative thinking can be said to be a universal characteristic of individual human behavior, originality can be viewed as a value judgment that takes place in a sociocultural context.

For this reason, some behaviors can be creative in an individual context, and at the same time lack originality in a social context. Children's drawings exemplify this difference. From about 2 to 5 years of age, the developmental progress of any individual child's drawing behavior is a highly creative and imaginative process—as every parent and preschool teacher knows. At the same time, however, young children pass through apparently universal stages of image-making (just as they do when learning to walk and talk). Thus, although a child's drawings are unique and creative in the context of his or her individual cognitive experience, they cannot be considered original in a broader sociocultural context because they conform to familiar and predictable patterns. Moreover, significant deviation from this pattern (that is, originality), although occasionally indicative of artistic talent, is more often symptomatic of brain damage, mental retardation, or emotional disturbance.

Students are often perplexed by the double standards of creativity and originality. For example, a student may produce a painting (or a poem, an essay, or a scientific model) that required significant creative effort. The teacher, however, may criticize it on the grounds that it is "clichéd" or "lacks originality." Hence, although the project is both creative and original in the context of the student's experience, it is not original in the context of the teacher's experience with a wide range of student works; the student perceived new-found meaning, but the teacher did not. Further, what is clearly original in the context of a particular classroom may not be so among a broader range of classrooms. Hence, teachers may submit student works to a regional or national competition, only to have them rejected as lacking in originality. Part of the educational process consists of learning to distinguish between individual creativity and culturally defined originality. Therefore, when you hear something called "original," you must always ask "original in what context?"

As cultural and historical circumstances change, so do definitions of originality. For example, Freud's psychoanalytic theory or Jackson Pollock's action painting style are considered to be original for their time. If proposed today, they would hardly create a stir; if proposed much earlier in history, they would have been deemed merely eccentric or irrelevant, and subsequently lost. For this reason, you often hear the phrase "an idea whose time has come."

Independent Discovery. The assimilation of a new idea—whether by an individual or by a society—depends on a certain readiness to accept it (see chapter 3). This readiness, in turn, requires a suitable climate of related ideas and unresolved problems. In any historical or cultural milieu, many people share similar configurations of knowledge, so the information needed for creative solutions resides in a number of different persons. Thus, in terms of the creative process, the preparation stage has been similar for various different individuals. As a consequence, two (or more) persons, unbeknownst to each other, may experience the same illumination and apply similar processes of verification. By the same token, the value of the new idea can be recognized by a number of other people.

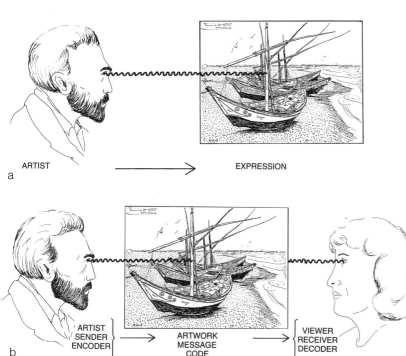

ARTIST   →   EXPRESSION

a

ARTIST
SENDER   →   ARTWORK   →   VIEWER
ENCODER   MESSAGE   RECEIVER
                                CODE   DECODER

b

Figure 11-2. Expression and communication: (a) art as personal expression; (b) art as communication. (Eleanor Holland; interior art: Vincent van Gogh, *Fishing Boats at Saintes-Maries-de-la-Mer* (Kunstarchiv Arntz, Haas, Oberbayen))

This phenomenon, called *independent* or *simultaneous discovery*, is well-known in both science and the arts.

The idea of innate genius cloaks the creative process in mystery and adversely affects the way people think about themselves, especially in regard to art. Since talent is taken to be innate—like Type A blood, you either have it or you don't—most people, by about the age of 10 or 12, have become thoroughly convinced that they do not and never can have artistic ability. Because of this notion of talent, the arts are relegated to the periphery of American education: why spend valuable resources on something only a few students can be successful at? And yet it is not asked, why invest in teaching mathematics to everyone when only a select few will become mathematicians? The question is a serious one, because the evidence for multiple intelligences (see chapters 3 and 6) strongly suggests that every normal person has functional capacities for each of the various cognitive modes. While such capacities are normally distributed in varying combinations and degrees among the population (as are all other inherited capacities and acquired abilities), they are present to some degree

in all individuals and ought not to be neglected in the educational process.

ART AS COMMUNICATION

Over the last century or so, Westerners have usually thought of art as original and creative self-expression—a process that is complete as soon as the artist is finished with it (see figure 11-2a). By the same token, the viewer is considered incidental to the art-making process, and artists do not usually feel responsible for viewers' perceptions. Because of the high value accorded to originality and innovation in Western art, new artistic movements tend to present viewers with new forms constructed according to new and unfamiliar rules. Hence, a time-lag normally appears between the appearance and acceptance of new art styles by artists and critics, and their acceptance by the general public. For this reason, Western artists are often seen as misunderstood during their lifetimes, only to be appreciated many years later, usually after they have died.

But art can be seen as a communication process

involving a sender (the artist), a medium (the artwork), and a receiver (the viewer) (see figure 11-2b). If the communication process succeeds, the medium prompts a meaningful closure (a message) in the mind of the receiver that is in accord with the intended meaning (the message) of the sender. Hence, the receiver's perception of meaning is required to complete the process. Judgments of art objects in non-Western societies tend to emphasize communication value. Ritual objects, for example, are judged on the basis of their effectiveness in communicating cultural beliefs; originality and personalized expression may be considered incidental or even counterproductive to this purpose.

In China, the process of artistic production was traditionally considered incomplete without a sensitive receiver. A Chinese legend tells of a musician who had found only a single listener capable of fully appreciating his music. When this listener unexpectedly died, the musician put away his instrument and never played another note. Likewise, traditional Chinese esthetic theories and practices emphasize the representation of essences that will resonate with a viewer's cultivated perceptions of nature and social life. Consistent with this, innovation and stylistic changes tended to build on (rather than to reject) past artistic achievements.

Whether Western artists like it or not, they too depend on other people's perceptions and judgments. No artist works in a vacuum; the serious artist who does not seek to have his or her work exhibited in some context is rare indeed. But viewers are commonly expected to appreciate an artwork simply by gazing at it. Because seeing is usually assumed to be a natural and more or less physiological process, schools rarely systematically teach about principles of visual perception. Art students are taught methods of producing and looking at images (that is, techniques for manipulating perception), but little attention is given to more fundamental questions such as: What happens when someone looks at something? What processes of eye, brain, and culture lead a person to perceive meaning in a particular way? And why is the meaning not the same for everyone? How might understanding these things affect the way people make and look at images?

These are questions without final answers. Visual perception is far from being an objective, unlearned, physiological recording process. Rather, it involves the ever-compelling questions of how individuals and cultures create meaning from visual experience with the world. In the end, meaning does not reside in the external world of objects; it is something constructed by human minds. As an aspect of the human condition, visual perception remains an inexhaustible and continually revealing subject of inquiry.

Studio Activities

The following projects and experiments are designed to suggest ways in which you can further explore some of the principles and concepts of each chapter. These activities can be carried out either individually or in a classroom setting; many require no special background in art. Within chapter groupings, the activities are arranged in a general sequence from simple to complicated.

* = With appropriate software and graphics capabilities, a personal computer can be used to perform the activity.

\# = The activity can be done as a problem in photography.

CHAPTER 1

*#1. SYNCHRONIZATION: Blend sight and sound.
Experiment with your mind's automatic response to integrate sight and sound into a single perceptual experience. Watch a TV program or videotape with the sound turned off. At the same time, turn on different kinds of music: classical, rock, folk, jazz, and so forth. Cartoons, sports, or slapstick comedy will be particularly effective. You can use the same approach with filmed or computerized animation sequences.
Materials: TV; tape deck or record player. Optional: Animated film; VCR and videotapes; computer-animation display.

2. YOUR MEMORY: How accurate is it?
Take a piece of paper about 12″ × 18″ and fold it into thirds. Then try to recall all the objects in your purse, desk drawer, medicine cabinet, or other place unavailable to your immediate vision. Use one third of the paper to list the names of objects, and another third to make memory drawings of each object you recall. When you can remember no more objects, check to see what you have forgotten. On the last third of the paper, make observation drawings of five or six objects that are also represented by memory drawings.

How accurate was your memory? What techniques did you use to recall the objects (for example, usage, shape, spatial location, name, and so forth)? How do your observation drawings compare with the memory drawings in size, shape, and detail? What does this tell you about perceptual salience in memory?
Materials: Pencil, paper (12″ × 18″ or larger).

3. DESIGN BY ACCIDENT: Capitalize on ambiguity.
Create ambiguous patterns using one of several techniques. For example, drop diluted oil paints onto the surface of water in a dishpan or tray, and transfer the resulting patterns to a piece of paper (marbleizing). Or: Drop ink onto paper and use a straw to blow the wet ink into spidery shapes. Or: Let watercolors spread freely on wet paper. Or: Randomly deform chunks of clay or plasticine. Or: Dye fabric with random tie-dye or batik techniques.

Contemplate the results for suggestions of imagery. With pen, paint, or colored pencils, add details to give the shapes identifiable forms. With clay: Tool the surface to represent details (if it is to be fired, hollow out the piece). With fabric: Use stitchery for details.
Materials:: For marbleizing: Artists' oil paints; turpentine; mixing pans and sticks; plastic pan or tray; disposable rubber gloves; paper; well-ventilated working area. Or: Black and/or colored inks; paper; drinking straw. Or: Watercolors; brush; paper. Or: Clay or plasticine; modeling tools. Or: 100% cotton fabric; fiber-reactive dye supplies; rubber gloves; dye pots and stirring sticks; rubber bands, string, or batiking equipment. Appropriate materials for adding detail.

\#4. CLOUDS AND ROCKS: Practice projective meaning.
Spend some time contemplating fluffy cumulus clouds; let your mind freely imagine what the forms might represent. Sketch these forms quickly, as they occur, or photograph them (use a yellow filter to increase contrast). (Sketches by John Constable and J. M. W. Turner can be helpful resources.) Later use your sketches or photographs as the basis for a painting, (soft) sculpture, or batik.

Or: Collect three or four interestingly shaped rocks. Select one and contemplate it (by yourself or with other people) for fifteen minutes or more, turning it this way and that. Allow your mind to discover faces, animals, landscapes, or other subjects. When the contemplation time is up (not before), decide on the best image and develop it on the rock with acrylic paint.
Materials: With clouds: Sketchbook and pencil or watercolors; or camera; yellow filter; film. With rocks: acrylic paint (for a weatherproof surface); brushes.

5. SILENT SIGNALS: Analyze eye contact.
For one week, keep a journal of observations of how people use eye contact to communicate: For example, when con-

versing with friends and family, while walking or sitting in public places. Try to include a wide range of situations that involve you in both observation and participation. Notice particularly how strangers or people of different ethnic groups use (or avoid) eye contact. What general principles of eye-contact communication can you formulate, based on your own observations?

6. JUNK SCULPTURE: Find new meaning in old things.
Search through a repair shop, junkyard, basement, or attic for discarded objects that—by themselves or in combination—suggest new meanings (see figure 1-3). Mount or display the object(s), adding touches of acrylic or enamel paint if desired, to make your meaning perceptually salient to a viewer.
Materials: Discarded object(s); glue or paint as needed; mounting materials.

7. ANOMALIES: How long does it take to perceive them?
Use your sense of mischief to contrive a subtle visual anomaly in an everyday situation where you can observe whether or not other people take notice of it. For example: Doctor the numbers on a calendar, the shapes or numbers on playing cards, pictures in a magazine, newspaper, or poster. How long is it before someone perceives the anomaly (if at all)? Who perceives it? Under what circumstances? What conclusions can you draw about everyday seeing?

*8. MY WORD: Compose found poetry.
Write down every seventh word from a prose passage until you have a total of thirty or more words. Then cut the words apart and play with arrangements until you create a poem that incorporates every word. Grouping the words by parts of speech can be helpful in suggesting relationships. Add punctuation freely. If you want a real challenge, create a second poem from the same words. You can use the poem as the basis for a calligraphic or typographic design project. [With a computer: Use a word processing program, and employ various fonts to create the final version.]

*9. MY STARS: Create new constellations.
Trace the locations of the stars from a star map. Study these charts and make up your own images by connecting the dots in new groupings. Name your new constellations and, if inspired, write stories or myths to accompany them.
You can turn this into a more complex project. For example, use the dot patterns to punch holes in a piece of metal foil, tin, or vellum and create a lampshade; the holes will yield pinpoints of light when the lamp is turned on. Connect the holes with tooled or painted lines. Or: Use your star patterns as the basis for a stitchery, tie-dye, or batik.
[With a computer: Transfer the star map to clear acetate and tape onto the monitor screen, enlarging or reducing the map as needed. Begin with a black screen and follow the acetate guide to create white stars with a paint/draw program. Connect the stars with a less contrasty color. This display will be quite dramatic if viewed in a completely darkened room. You can use a printout of the map as a pattern for further projects.]
Materials: Star map; tracing paper and pencil (or acetate and markers); project materials. Or: Computer (preferably with color monitor); paint/draw software.

*#10. TIME LINE: Animate human evolution
Using source material on human evolution, trace side-views of the human figure as it evolved over time from prosimians to *Homo sapiens sapiens*. With a photocopy machine, enlarge and reduce your tracings until their size relationships are accurate. Use these as key frames and construct enough intermediate steps to complete a set of twenty or more drawings. (You can also make the rate of transformation correspond to the various lengths of evolutionary time periods.)
[Flip book: Reduce the drawings to approximately two inches, and reproduce on $3'' \times 5''$ index cards.][With movie or video camera: Expose each drawing in sequence for several seconds.][With computer: Trace drawings onto an acetate guide, or digitize them. Enlarge or reduce to obtain accurate size relationships. Use an animation program to construct intermediate steps.]
Materials: Resource material on human evolution; tracing paper; pencil and eraser; light box (optional); drawing paper or $3'' \times 5''$ cards; photocopy machine with enlargement/reduction capabilities. Or: Computer: acetate and markers; draw/paint and animation software.

CHAPTER 2

*1. AFTERIMAGE: Create ghostly visions.
Create a situation or image that causes the viewer to experience an afterimage (see figure 2-14). The simplest method is to divide a piece of blank white paper in half. Place a simple design on the left half, and leave the right half blank except for a tiny dot on which the viewer can fixate. [With a computer: Divide the screen in half.] Because of Emmert's law, afterimage effects can be quite startling when the viewer fixates on a white wall or movie screen. Afterimages can be carried to sophisticated levels, as in the works of Bridget Riley (see figure 2-15).
Or: Use two images that will fuse in the afterimage. The viewer first stares at one, and then fixates on the other (for example, at a flag, and then at a pole).
Materials: White paper or posterboard; markers or construction paper; rubber cement; scissors. Or: Computer; graphics software. Or: Painting, drawing, or printmaking media.

2. EYEBALLS: Reach out and shock someone!
Paint a hollowed egg, rock, ping-pong ball, or other likely object to look like an eyeball. Place the eyeball in a dramatic setting. If the effect is to be convincing, you must be precise and scientifically accurate in your rendering: use a reference, such as a good photograph, or carefully study the appearance of your own or someone else's eye.
Materials: Round object; reference material or model; acrylic paint; fine brushes.

*3. SHIMMER: Tickle the eyes.
Create a pattern that generates an optical, shimmering appearance (like the one in figure 2-21). Neatness and precision are essential for an effective result.
Materials: Paper; pens or markers; straightedge, templates. Or: Painting surface; paint; masking tape; brushes. Or: Computer; graphics software.

*4. SPOTS: Look, look! See Spot run away!
Study figure 2-9 and other instances of elusive spots. Create an image that will produce them.

Materials: Paper; pen(s) or marker(s); straightedge; French curve; templates. Or: Other painting, drawing, or printmaking media. Or: Computer; graphics software.

*#5. MOSAIC: Explore problems in resolution.
Create a mosaic image (or translate a found image into a mosaic image), using units of a size larger or smaller than the original (see figure 2-4). The unit size can be extremely small (as in a drawing composed entirely of stippling) or quite coarse (as with ceramic, paper, or fabric tiles). [With photography: Experiment with printing, using various sizes of halftone screens.] (NOTE: Explore viewing from different distances. Art historical references such as Roman and Byzantine mosaics can be helpful.)

Materials: Colored paper; rubber cement; scissors. Or: Drawing, painting, or printmaking media. Or: Darkroom materials. Or: Ceramic tiles. Or: Fiber media (patchwork; stitchery; beadwork).

*6. CONTOUR CONTRAST: Maximize brightness or edges.
Enhance the perception of edge or contour in an abstract or representational image by rendering the contour with subtle dark-to-light shading that grades gradually outward from selected edges (as in figures 2-10, 2-12, and 2-13). Study the effect further by reversing the dark-to-light shading in a second image that is otherwise identical to the first. [With ceramics: Carve a sharp-edged relief into leather-hard clay; then gently wash the surface to graduate the transition from high to low surfaces; finish with a single, transparent glaze. (Research into Chinese porcelain techniques will add authenticity.)]

Materials: Drawing or painting media (an airbrush is especially appropriate). Or: Clay and glazes; ceramic equipment. Or: Computer; graphics software (use "dithering").

*7. ZONES OF CLARITY: Capture the visual field.
Create (or reinterpret) an image in a way that represents various zones of clarity in the visual field (see figure 2-17). [With photography: Experiment with various vignetting devices in both shooting and printing.] [With computer: Reduce the density of representational pixels outward from the center of the image.]

Materials: Drawing or painting media. Or: Photography materials. Or: Computer; graphics software.

8. INNOCENT EYE: Eye over mind.
Like the Impressionists, observe a real-life subject and attempt to reproduce only what your eyes see; that is, record the patterns of light and color before your mind interprets and identifies them. This is, of course, frustrating and impossible; however, the attempt will be enlightening.

Materials: Any drawing or painting media.

#9. INVISIBLE IMAGES: Extend vision beyond light.
Various technologies record invisible electromagnetic wavelengths, translating them into visible images (light). Examples include X-rays, sonograms, thermograms, infrared photography, and radioactive (nuclear) imaging. Research some aspect of these technologies, and use a translated image as the basis for creating an artwork or pattern design.

Materials: Research resources; drawing, painting, printmaking, fiber, or photography materials.

*10. SELECTIVE VISION: Look through alien eyes.
The eyes of different biological species (such as frogs, birds, snakes, horses, dogs, and insects) are specialized to see the world differently from the way human eyes do. Research the visual specialization of one or two species. Reinterpret a normal human visual image (for example, as represented in a photograph) as the same subject might be seen in the specialized vision of another species. [Extension: Imagine the imagery of an outer-space creature which is blind to the electromagnetic frequencies that human beings experience as light.]

Materials: Research resources; drawing or painting media. Or: Digitized image; computer; graphics software.

CHAPTER 3

*1. TRACE: Find figure/ground relationships in art.
Using reproductions of famous paintings, trace the main lines of the compositions (see figure 3-10). (Be sure to include the outside borders.) This becomes an art history game when you ask other people to identify the paintings from the tracings.

Materials: Reproductions of paintings; soft-leaded pencil; tracing paper. [With computer: Digitized reproductions.]

*#2. PERIODIC PATTERNS: Explore optical potential in repetition.
Create a design by using identical or nearly identical units repeated in a regular and predictable pattern (see figure 3-19). Aim for a design in which several different perceptual groupings can take place. [With photography: Photograph instances of periodic patterns in the environment.]

Materials: Construction paper; pencil; scissors; templates; rubber cement. Or: Pen and/or brush; india ink; paper. Or: art-gum eraser; linoleum cutting tool; printing ink; palette; brayer; paper. Or: Computer; graphics software. Or: Camera; film.

*#3. ONE PLUS ONE EQUALS THREE: Challenge your patience and precision!
Experiment with superimposing one periodic pattern on another to create a third pattern from the areas of intersection. One way to approach this is by drawing several patterns on pieces of tracing paper. Superimpose these in different combinations and positions against a window pane or on a light box. Use the best one(s) as the basis for a finished project. As an alternative, experiment with stamp-printing patterns from carved art-gum erasers.

Moiré patterns (see figure 3-20) can be done in two colors as well as in one. (NOTE: For moiré patterns to emerge, the intersecting lines must be less than 30 degrees.) [With photography: Photograph moiré patterns in the environment.]

Variations: Construct a moiré pattern in three dimensions from strips of colored paper, thread, string, monofilament fishing line, window-screening, or casement curtain cloth.

Materials: Tracing paper; ruler; french curves; templates; ball-point pen or fine-tip felt pen; paper. Or: Strips of colored paper; thread; string; monofilament fishing line; window-screening; or casement curtain cloth. Or: Printmaking media. Or: Clear acetate; acetate ink or markers. Or: Camera; film. Or: computer; graphics software with stencil capability.

*#4. HALF-GONE: Remove information but retain image.
Remove at least half of the visual information from an image or pattern; magazine photographs work best (see figure 3-17). Cut up the photo, using a pattern such that you can remove every other piece. Draw the cutting pattern on a piece of tracing paper; then place the tracing paper on the photo, and cut through both layers at the same time. Paste every other piece of the photograph onto a piece of white or colored posterboard. [With photography: When printing, mask the paper with a stencil.]

You can also cut through two pictures at once. In this case, alternate every other piece from one picture with every other piece from the other; the viewer will fill in two images. (NOTE: Be very careful to keep the cut pieces in order until you have pasted them down.)
Materials: Magazines; scissors, sharp knife, or single-edge razor blade; thin drawing paper; pencil; rubber cement; posterboard. [With computer: Digitized photographs; graphics software.]

5. ALTERNATING FIGURE/GROUND PUZZLES: Make figure and ground tangible.
Create a two-color design in which figure and ground alternate. The design can be abstract or representational, simple or complex (see figures 3-9 and 3-11). Draw the design on a thin sheet of paper; then place the drawing on top of two sheets of colored paper, and carefully cut through all three layers at the same time. You now have two puzzles in opposite colors. (NOTE: Keep an extra uncut copy of your original design. Mark the bottom side of each puzzle with an X.) Give your puzzles to two other people to assemble. You will probably be surprised at how difficult it is to put them back together.
Materials: Two sheets of colored paper; one piece of thin drawing paper; pencil; scissors, sharp knife, or single-edge razor blade.

6. NEGATIVE SPACE: Experience the power of negative thinking.
Do an observation drawing in which you draw only the spaces within and between objects. Draw the spaces as closed shapes; the objects will reappear as silhouettes. To find the shape of the negative space around the object, view it through a 1″ × 1¹/2″ hole cut in an index card that you hold at arm's length; adjust the distance to see the object(s) appear to touch the sides of the hole. Chairs are often used for this exercise.
Optional: After you finish the drawing, cut out the negative space shapes and reassemble them on a piece of dark paper, recreating the object as the spaces. Cutting out often helps people to think of negative space as something real. (For more exercises with negative space, see Edwards 1979—especially chapter 7. According to Edwards, this exercise engages the right (brain) modality.)
Materials: Drawing paper; drawing tool (soft-leaded pencil, felt-tip pen, ink and brush or pen, charcoal); black and white sheets of paper; scissors; rubber cement.

7. UPSIDE DOWN DRAWING: Trust your right brain.
Find an interesting line drawing (for example, one by Picasso or Matisse). Turn the drawing upside down, and copy it carefully. Do not hurry, and do not turn the drawings right-side up to check your progress! When you have finished, you will probably be very surprised at how well you did. (According to Betty Edwards (1979, 1987), this exercise turns off your left-brain mode, which wants to know what it is doing, so that your right-brain mode is free to copy the lines.)
Materials: Reproduction of a drawing; drawing paper; pencil.

*#8. SUBJECTIVE CONTOURS: Create a high-contrast image.
Translate a full-value-range photograph into a black-and-white image (see figure 3-15). Place a sheet of thin tracing paper over the photograph, and decide which grays should be translated into black and which into white. Using a pencil, color in the black areas so that you will not be confused later. Transfer the drawing to a fresh surface (enlarge it with a grid system, if you wish), and draw or paint the final image. Subjective contours will automatically occur; they indicate the perceptual correctness of your translation. This exercise can also be done with abstract shapes (as in figure 3-16). [With a computer: Use a black-and-white digitized photograph, and convert each shade of gray pixels to either black or white.] [With photography: Use high-contrast film and paper.]
Materials: Photographic image; tracing paper; pencil; ruler for an enlarging grid. For the final image: Any drawing or painting medium. [With abstract shapes: Colored paper; scissors; posterboard; rubber cement.] Or: camera; high-contrast film. Or: computer; digitized photograph; graphics software.

#9. IMAGE FUSION: One plus one equals one.
Find or make two images for the brain to fuse into a single image (for example, a bird-cage and a bird). The images should be approximately the same size and fairly small (less than 3 inches square). To view: Hold an ordinary index card vertically between the two images, and look at very close range. Relax your focus as if you were looking beyond the images, and experiment to find the appropriate viewing distance. An old stereopticon, of course, would be ideal.
Materials: Drawings, photographs, or pictures; one 3″ × 5″ index card.

#10. STEREO: Create three-dimensional photographs.
Take two photographs of the same scene from viewpoints 2¹/2 inches apart. View the photographs with a stereopticon.
Materials: Camera; tripod; film; stereopticon.

CHAPTER 4

1. WINDOW ON THE WORLD: How small is far?
Tape a piece of clear acetate over a window or piece of glass or Plexiglas. Fix it firmly in position, and with a marker trace what you see through the window onto the acetate. Look with one eye and hold your head absolutely still.
Materials: Clear acetate; tape; marker or grease pencil; window or piece of glass or Plexiglas.

*2. SURREAL: Play with size constancy.
Make a surrealistic collage that produces a dramatic effect by violating expected size relationships. Look for a background picture first to set the scene and suggest possibilities. By cutting slits in well-selected places in the background picture, you can insert other images to create a feeling of depth. (NOTE: Use photographic images—not drawings or paintings—because artwork is immediately identified as not real, and consequently the effect is easily lost.)
Materials: Magazines; scissors, sharp knife, or single-edge razor blade; rubber cement; posterboard. [With computer: Digitized photos; graphics software.]

3. LOOSE CANON: Explore Egyptian form constancy.
Apply ancient Egyptian formulas to depict scenes of contemporary life. Several such scenes can be combined to make a mural. (NOTE: Aztec-Mixtec-Zapotec art styles can be used in the same way.)
Materials: Resource material on Egyptian (or Aztec-Mixtec-Zapotec) art; paper; pencil; paint; brushes.

*#4. STORY: Communicate with shape/size transformations.
Design a simple abstract black-and-white story that communicates its plot by means of changes in size or shape. The story should have at least four frames, should be read from left to right (in rows from top to bottom if necessary), and should have a beginning and an ending. For example, the story of a ball coming toward you might begin with a black dot in the first frame, change to a circle in the second frame, change to a larger circle in the third frame, and end with a completely black fourth frame. (NOTE: Make only one change per frame.)
Materials: Black and white construction paper; rubber cement; scissors; pencil; paper for sketching out ideas.

*#5. UPSIDE-DOWN AND SIDEWAYS: Observe orientation.
Find familiar images that seem difficult to identify when rotated 90 or 180 degrees. Draw, cut out, or photograph them, and then mount them with the largest margin at the bottom for upside-down or sideways viewing. Conduct your own experiments to find out how long it takes people to recognize the image. For example, you might work with the outlines of continents or with photographs of well-known people.
Materials: Source material; tools for drawing or cutting/pasting; posterboard. Or: Camera; film. Or: Computer; graphics software.

6. VANISHING-POINT PERSPECTIVE: How far is small?
Find a largish magazine photograph of a scene that clearly shows vanishing-point perspective. Mount it on a piece of posterboard. Using a tracing-paper overlay, find the vanishing point(s) and trace the main converging lines. Next, look for magazine photos of people or objects to cut out and paste on the first photograph. Use the traced overlay to position the cutouts accurately onto the original photo.
Materials: Magazines; scissors; posterboard; rubber cement; tracing paper; pencil.

*#7. SILHOUETTES: Study retinal projections.
Choose a simple, familiar object (such as a teacup or a chair), and draw it carefully and accurately as a black shape (silhouette) from at least six different viewpoints, including above and below. Leave negative spaces white. Which views are easiest to identify? Which are relatively difficult? After you master the projected images of simple things, go on to more complex subjects (such as a plant or a bicycle). [With photography: Photograph different views of the same object. Overlay each photograph with translucent drafting paper, and trace the shapes.]
Materials: Drawing paper; soft-leaded pencil, conte crayon, marker, or pen (or brush) and ink. Or: Camera; film; drafting paper; pencil. Or: Computer; 3-D software.

#8. BLOW UP: Create a monument.
Make a drawing, painting or photograph in which you single out an object that is almost never seen in isolation and eliminate its usual context (see figure 4-4).
Materials: Drawing/painting media. Or: Camera; film.

#9. RELATIVITY: Experiment with context.
Choose a familiar object that normally comes in a range of sizes (for example, a pumpkin, a doll or an iron skillet), and photograph the object in a series of different contexts. Attempt to make the object appear larger and smaller by changing the surroundings, by adopting various camera viewpoints, or by using other techniques.
Materials: Camera; film.

*10. RE-VISION: Reinterpret a famous painting.
Select a painting done in conformity with size or form constancy (like figures 4-11, 4-12, 4-24, and 4-25). Redraw it, using vanishing-point or parallel perspective. Or: Choose a painting that uses vanishing-point perspective (like figures 4-14, 6-23, 7-5, 7-15 and 7-23). Redraw it, using parallel perspective or some other system that maintains size constancy (such as Oriental near-middle-far distances or the Egyptian canon).
Materials: Reproductions of appropriate paintings; drawing paper; pencil; eraser; painting materials. [With computer: Digitized reproductions; graphics software.]

CHAPTER 5

*1. THEME: Capture a mood with color.
Choose a theme (such as summer, spring, autumn, winter, a cornfield, the beach, or Times Square). Using a palette of colors strongly associated with the theme, create an abstract collage (or painting, or computer graphic) that conveys the feeling of the theme without using recognizable or realistic forms.
Materials: Various colored papers; white glue or rubber cement; scissors; backing. Or: Painting materials. Or: Computer with paint software.

2. NATURAL PIGMENTS: Make your own water-colors.
Collect various substances from your environment (for example, flower petals, leaves, seed pods, fruits, vegetables, insects, samples of earth, and charcoal). Pulverize the material (by pounding, mashing, cooking, putting in a blender, or some other method). Put the mash in a covered jar, add water, shake well, label, and let sit a day or two, shaking occasionally. Pour through a tea-strainer or several layers of cheesecloth into a clean jar, label, and refrigerate (unless you are going to use immediately).
Test for colorfastness: On a sheet of good watercolor

paper, paint a 2″ × 4″ swatch with each liquid, running the swatches in a column down the center of the paper, and labeling each. Cover one-half of the column of swatches with a piece of heavy cardboard. Tape the sheet to a south window, facing into strong sunlight. After a week, remove the sheet from the window, and take off the cardboard. Comparing the sun-exposed areas with the unexposed areas will give you an index of colorfastness. Use your most successful colors to make a watercolor painting.

Materials: Substances collected from your environment; glass jars with lids; labels; fine-mesh strainer or cheese-cloth; watercolor paper; brush; scrap cardboard; tape.

*3. PERCEPTUAL COLOR: Experiment with color effects.
Using colored papers (or computer graphics), create simple demonstrations of various perceptual color effects: afterimage; successive, simultaneous, and border contrasts; vibration; optical mixture; transparency; and so on.

Materials: Colored papers (Color-Aid papers give a range of over 200 colors); scissors or X-Acto knife; rubber cement; posterboard backing. Or: Computer and graphics software.

*4. COLOR SCHEMING: Play with color combinations.
Apply several different color-wheel schemes (monochrome, analogous, complementary, split-complementary, triad) to a single composition or design (for example to a fashion outfit and accessories, or to interior, textile, or package design). Make separate renderings, or use overlays. Collect other people's opinions on the effectiveness of the various schemes. [With computer: Create different color palettes and apply to the graphic image.]

Materials: Color-wheel reference; appropriate drawing or painting materials. Or: Computer with CAD or paint software.

5. TRANSPARENT COLOR LAYERING: Do and dye.
Layer transparent colors on fabric or clothing with successive dye baths, using batik or tie-dye techniques.

Materials: Fabric (100 percent cotton, silk, or wool); dyeing equipment and dyes (fiber-reactive dyes are light- and wash-fast).

6. REFLECTED COLOR: Create auras.
Make a construction in which color from an invisible surface casts reflected color onto a visible surface. For example, back one or more cardboard shapes with a bright color of paper or paint (treat the front any way you wish). Mount the shape(s) so that they are raised an inch or so above a white or foil-covered background, and display in good light; a soft glowing color shadow will appear on the background. Or: Use three-dimensional projecting forms (such as cubes and cones); glue them to the background along their edges or tips.

Materials: White or foil-covered background surface; two- or three-dimensional shapes/forms; bright color(s) of paint or paper; spacers for mounting the shape (such as toothpicks, small blocks, or rigid wire); white glue.

7. COPY A MASTER: Practice color mixing and matching.
Choose a reproduction (5″ × 7″ or larger) of a painting that you would like to reproduce; compositions with areas of flat color and few details (as in the works of Miro, Klee, and Matisse) work best. With care and accuracy, trace the com-position, and use carbon paper to transfer the image to your painting surface (canvas or matboard).

Carefully comparing the paint manufacturer's color chart to the reproduction, select a basic palette of colors—no more than six colors, plus black and white. To test your palette, place a piece of window glass over the reproduction and experiment with mixing and matching colors. Once you have a workable palette, copy the painting by mixing paint on the glass to match colors in the reproduction beneath. When you are finished, mat both the reproduction and your copy, and study them from a distance. Your success can be measured by the distance at which you (or an innocent observer) cannot easily tell the reproduction from the copy.

Materials: Reproduction of a painting (a good 7″ × 10″ color Xerox made from a slide is recommended); tracing paper, pencil; carbon paper; pane of window glass about 9″ × 12″; artist's tube colors (acrylic, gouache, or watercolor) and the manufacturer's color chart; palette knife; good-quality brushes; water container; painting ground (unstretched canvas or bristol board); matting materials.

#8. LIGHT AND COLOR: Create a magical image.
In a semidarkened room, shine a spotlight or strong (halogen) flashlight beam through various colors of cellophane, acetate, or stage-lighting gels. Explore how the different colors of light affect the appearance of different colors of paint or paper (for example, a same-color filter will make a color disappear, while a complementary-color filter will darken and neutralize it). Use your results to create a color composition that looks strikingly different depending on the color of the illumination. Abstract compositions are fine, but representational images can present interesting challenges—for example, a scene that changes from night to day, or one in which figures unnoticed in one color of illumination become prominent in another. [Variation: Explore the effect by viewing through colored spectacles instead of in colored light.] [With photography: Use daylight film and various color filters to photograph (or to print) the composition.]

Materials: Spotlight or strong flashlight; colored cellophane, acetate, stage gels, or colored glass (optional: black light); swatches of paint or colored papers. Or: Camera; daylight film; color filters.

9. FOUR-COLOR PRINTING: Design color separations.
Using printmaking media, produce a four-plate four-color print with yellow, magenta, cyan, and black inks (see plate C-2). This project requires careful planning; a study of Japanese woodblock printing techniques can be helpful.

Materials: Printmaking materials (such as for woodblock, lino-cut, collotype, silk-screen, or color lithography); transparent or semitransparent inks; paper.

*#10. COLOR AMBIENCE: Explore variability in natural light.
Working outdoors from observation, follow Monet's procedure of making several paintings of a single subject at various different times of day. [With photography: Photograph an outdoor subject in color at two- or three-hour intervals throughout the day; if possible, leave the camera on a tripod, so that your compositions will be identical except for changes in light and color.] [With computer: Begin with a digitized color photograph or video frame; create various

color palettes to convey impressions of different times of day or different weather conditions.]

Materials: Material to make several paintings or pastel drawings (use dark paper). Or: Camera; tripod; color film (slide film will produce the most sensitive color differences). Or: Computer; digitized photograph or video frame; graphics software.

CHAPTER 6

*1. BLIND DRAWING: Use kinesthetic clues.
Draw something from observation, without looking at the paper! Since this requires impossible self-discipline, cover your hands and paper with a loose cloth. When you finish, draw the same object in the usual way. You probably will not like the blind drawing, but nonetheless look open-mindedly for the differences in energy reflected in each drawing.

Materials: Paper; pencil, crayon, marker, or charcoal; cloth. Or: Computer; drawing software.

2. FURNITURE ARRANGEMENT: Structure other people's
   behavior.
At least twice, rearrange the furniture in your room, house, dorm, or office. Record people's reactions; note ways in which their behavior seems to be structured by the furniture.

Materials: A room and some furniture.

3. GETTING THERE FROM HERE: Collect different map-
   making styles.
Ask about ten people, one at a time, to draw you a map for getting from one place to another. Make these identical requests casually, as though you actually need the information. Can you classify the different styles of map-making? What differences did you notice in self-confidence, amount and kind of details, use of visual symbols, clarity, organization, and the like? What conclusions would you reach about cognitive styles, based on this experiment?

Materials: Notebook; pen or pencil.

#4. PEOPLE IN SPACE: Watch people interact.
This is a study in observation. As you go through your normal activities during the week, keep a journal in which you chronicle observations of people in relation to their personal space. Try to observe a wide variety of situations. Note the nonverbal signals that tell you when you are too close to someone. Describe strategies that people use to increase or decrease their distance from others. Do people change distance depending on the subject of the conversation? How do people adjust themselves to include or exclude others from their conversations? How do various seating arrangements function to define distance and relationships between people? How do people protect their personal space in crowded public places (such as elevators, buses, and subways)? Did you observe differences among different social or ethnic groups? [With photography: Keep a visual record. A telephoto lens would be useful.]

5. MENTAL IMAGERY: How do other people remember?
Tape-record a dozen individuals' responses to a common hypothetical situation involving remembering (for example, arriving at the grocery store without a list, or trying to remember how to get to someone's house). Ask each person the same what-if question(s). Analyze the responses in accordance with the seven types of mental imagery discussed in chapter 6: visual, kinesthetic, spatial, verbal, auditory, interpersonal, intrapersonal. Listen for clues in the kind of words chosen. (Be sure to ask for permission to record the answers.)

Materials: Tape recorder.

*6. BREAKDOWN: Create your own block portrait.
Overlay a black-and-white photograph of someone's face with a piece of translucent drafting paper marked with a grid that will give you at least 256 (16 × 16) squares. Study the photograph through one square of the grid; with pencil, color the square a solid gray tone that represents your estimate of the average tonality of that square area. Repeat this procedure with each square in the grid (see Figure 6-13). Then mount the drafting paper on white posterboard, and view it from a distance.* [With computer: Convert all the pixels within a grid section into a single averaged gray or color.]

Variations: Try the same approach, using other geometric patterns in place of the grid squares (for example, diamonds, triangles, or hexagons). After you have been successful with shades of gray, try the exercise with a color photograph and colored pencils.

Materials: Translucent drafting paper; photo portrait; ruler; 6H pencil to make the grid; soft-leaded pencil (or colored pencils); posterboard. [With computer: Digitized portrait photo; graphics software.]

*Adapted from Roukes, Nicholas. 1982. *Art Synectics.* Wooster, Mass.: Davis Publications Inc., p. 46.

*7. SUBJECTIVE PERSPECTIVE: Begin with yourself.
Settle into a comfortable position. On the lower edge of your paper (or computer screen), begin by drawing a picture of the top edge of your paper (or computer screen). Then draw what is next to the edge of the paper (or screen) in your visual field; then draw what appears next outward; and so on. Work systematically outward from yourself, drawing each thing in turn. (Do not at anytime skip space or draw from outward in.) Use a strong, dark contour line—no hesitant, sketchy lines! Draw slowly and carefully: spend as much time looking as you spend drawing. Continue until you reach the edges of the paper. Do not be surprised if the total distance covered does not seem like much.

Materials: Drawing paper, 18″ × 24″; soft-leaded pencil, conte crayon, ballpoint pen or felt-tip pen. Or: Computer; drawing software.

#8. FIELD AND FRAME: Program the viewer's involvement.
Experiment with producing different perceptual distances from the subject of a drawing, painting, or photograph by varying the field-and-frame relationship (from close-up to longshot).

Materials: Drawing, painting, or photography materials.

*#9. XRAY: Show the whole thing!
The perception of transparency occurs when a form is seen as complete and overlapping at the same time. Draw or paint a subject in which you show both inside and outside at the same time (see figure 6-25). The subject can be a living organism or a machine. The insides can also take on symbolic dimensions of meaning. [With photography: Use dou-

ble exposures, or combine two negatives into a single print.] [With computer: Use graphics software with transparent-brush mode.]

Materials: Drawing and/or painting media. Or: Camera and film, or darkroom materials. Or: Computer; appropriate graphics software.

#10. MOTION PARALLAX: Explore pictorial composition.
Sketch or photograph the same scene from a series of slightly different viewpoints, studying the visual relationships of objects to each other in the visual field (see figure 9-6). Good subjects for this kind of project are trees in a woods, a number of people in a room, and similar groupings. Look for changes in patterns of interposition. Why are some compositions more effective than others?

Materials: Paper; pencil. Or: Camera; film.

CHAPTER 7

*1. PHOTOTRACE: Clarify your understanding of vanishing points.
Find photographs that appear to show linear perspective. Place a piece of tracing paper over each photograph, and trace the dominant lines to their points of convergence (vanishing points). In two- or multiple-point perspective, these points usually lie outside the borders of the picture. The tracing will show how vanishing points are determined by the camera's location in space and time. (NOTE: Not all photographs will show vanishing points.)

Materials: Photographs from newspapers or magazines; tracing paper; pencil. Or: Digitized photographs or video input; computer; graphics software.

*2. GRADIENT: Create illusions of space and distance.
Create an abstract illusion of depth and distance by using one or more gradient systems (pattern, detail, sharpness, color, light, or size; see, for example, figures 7-1, 7-2).

Materials: Paper; pens or markers; templates. Or: Paint; brushes; paper or canvas. Or: Collage. Or: Scratchboard; etching; woodcut. Or: Fibers (such as stitchery or weaving). Or: Computer; graphics software. This exercise can be practiced with almost any two-dimensional medium.

3. LANDSCAPE: Create abstraction without representation.
Create an abstract landscape collage, patchwork, print, or painting—one that conveys the feeling of a landscape without showing any recognizable objects. Use torn and/or cut pieces of colored paper and/or patterned paper (or dies or fabric) for density gradients. Try to incorporate all of the following strategies:

Overlapping/interposition (continuity of outline; see chapter 6)
Vertical positioning (see chapter 6)
Size and interval gradients
Color gradients (aerial perspective; see also chapter 5)
Texture gradients (pattern, detail)

Variation: Abstract the composition of a famous painting, using (insofar as is possible) the same depth and distance system found in the painting (see, for example, figures 4-7, 6-23, and 7-15).

Materials: Variously colored and/or patterned papers; rubber cement or polymer medium; posterboard. Or: For patchwork techniques, various fabrics. Or: Printmaking media (such as monoprint, or silkscreen with paper stencils).

*#4. AERIAL: Color it far out!
Using an imagined or actual landscape, compose a painting, drawing, collage, photograph, or computer image that uses aerial perspective (gradients of color, edge, and detail) as the major means of producing an illusion of distance.

Materials: Paper; watercolor or ink washes; brushes. Or: Paper; colored pencils or pastels. Or: Tissue paper; polymer medium; posterboard. Or: Paper or canvas; acrylic paint. Or: Dyes; paper or fiber/fabric medium (such as batik or weaving). Or: Computer; graphics software; optional digitized image.

*#5. CHIAROSCURO: Color it dramatic!
Set up a still-life arrangement of common objects with plain (not patterned or textured) surfaces (for example, cardboard boxes, tin cans without labels, and draped fabric). Or: Use a life-drawing situation. To get good light/dark contrasts, place the subject near a window, or illuminate it with a bright light. Render the image with only light/dark areas and edges (no lines!). (NOTE: Squinting your eyes will help to fuzz out detail so that you can see the light and shadow patterns more easily.) [With photography: Use film and darkroom techniques to create an extremely course-grained (low-resolution) black-and-white print.]

Materials: Lithographic crayon, charcoal, India ink and brush, or airbrush (avoid linear drawing tools); rough-surfaced drawing paper (such as coquille, charcoal, or watercolor paper). Or: Lithographic crayon; lithographic equipment. Or: Camera; black-and-white film; darkroom materials. Or: Computer; graphics software (use dithering or spray can mode and only white, black, and gray pixels).

*6. VANISHING POINTS: Learn to see them in real life.
From observation, create a drawing, painting, print, or computer image of a room, building, part of a building, street scene, interior design, arrangement of boxes, or the like. (NOTE: Refer to a good book on linear perspective drawing (for example, Montague 1985); many useful references are available.)

Materials: Any drawing, painting, or printmaking medium. Or: Computer; graphics software.

*7. ANALYSIS: Find out how they did it.
Examine at least ten paintings or drawings by different artists, concentrating (if you wish) on paintings from a particular time period or culture, or on works that have subject matter in common. Carefully analyze each image to identify all the systems that are used to show space and depth, applying the following checklist:

Overlapping/interposition (continuity of outline; see chapter 6)
Position on the picture plane (see chapter 6)
Gradients of size
Gradients of detail
Gradients of color (see also chapter 5)
Gradients of sharpness (distinctness)
Gradients of light (modeling, chiaroscuro)
Linear perspective

Tracings (which can be color-coded) will help clarify how these elements relate to the overall compositions. [With computer: Working with digitized reproductions, create a separate abstraction (screen) for each method that is used to represent depth and distance.

Materials: Reproductions of paintings or drawings; tracing paper; pencil or colored pencils. Or: Digitized reproductions; computer; graphics software.

8. PLEIN AIR: Take the plunge!

Go out into the world and look at a landscape, keeping in mind illusions of depth and distance. Translate the landscape onto paper or canvas, concentrating on how the landscape looks from your point of view. This exercise must be done on the spot—that is, from life.

Materials: This is not a situation for new materials. Use any drawing or painting medium with which you are familiar and comfortable.

*9. REVISION: Redraw history.

Find a painting without linear perspective (for example, figures 4-11, 7-10, and 7-11), and recreate the composition as it might have looked if the artist had used linear perspective. Or: Do the reverse. Find a painting that uses linear perspective (see, for example, figures 7-14, 7-19, and 7-23), and recreate it as it might have looked if the artist had used other methods for portraying distance relationships. Or: Translate a vanishing-point composition into parallel perspective (see figure 4-13).

Materials: Any appropriate drawing or painting materials. Or: Computer; digitized reproductions; graphics software.

*10. ARCHITECT: Design a better building.

Imagine an original, improved design for a house or building (such as a residence, vacation house, student dorm, gas station, chapel, fast-food stand, pharmacy, office building, library, post office, or music store). Try to invent new solutions for real-life problems. Draw the exterior of the building, using either vanishing-point or parallel perspective. (NOTE: Consult a book on architectural drawing techniques.)

Materials: Technical drawing materials: T-square; ruler; triangles; hard-leaded pencils; hard-surfaced drawing paper; eraser; drawing board or drafting table. Or: Computer; graphics software.

CHAPTER 8

1. PERCEPTUAL CONTEXT: Cast images adrift in the mind of the beholder.

Select half a dozen photographs about which you have some certain knowledge of the original context (for example, photos you have taken yourself, family pictures, photojournalism). Mount each on a piece of posterboard, and show them to a dozen subjects. Ask each individual (either singly or in small groups—the dynamics are different but equally valid) to describe to you what he/she/they imagine is going on in the pictured situation, or what the people's personalities are like. Take notes or tape-record the responses; then make an analysis. What conclusions can you draw?

Materials: Photographs; rubber cement; posterboard; notebook or tape recorder.

*2. PHOTOANALYSIS: Shed new light on old family pictures.

Examine familiar family snapshots to discover ways in which feelings and relationships are visibly revealed by body language, facial expressions, and spatial relationships. You may want to exchange family photos with someone else and compare readings. [With computer: Indulge in "computherapy": Alter some digitized family photographs to emphasize your own perceptions or to express your fantasies.]

Materials: Family pictures. Or: Digitized family pictures; computer; graphics software.

*#3. PHOTOMONTAGE: Create fantastic realities.

Cut and paste photographic images to create surrealistic composite pictures (as in figure 4-6). Or: Use photoreactive dyes with textiles, or photo-decal techniques with ceramics. [With photography: Print composite images in the darkroom by combining negatives (as in figure 8-14).] [With computer: Cut and paste elements of digitized photographs or video frames.]

Materials: Photographs or photographic images from magazines or books; sharp scissors or X-Acto knife; rubber cement; posterboard backing. Or: Negatives; darkroom materials. Or: Digitized photographs or video frames; computer; graphics software.

*#4. PROJECTIONS: Play with point of view.

From observation, carefully draw the silhouette of one object (for example, a chair, bicycle, shoe, or roller-skate) as it is seen from six different viewpoints. [With photography: Photograph an object from six different viewpoints.] [With computer: Use a 3-D program to capture six different rotations of an object. Which projections are most recognizable? Why? Some such series of projections work as interactions or serial transformations that can be applied to other design projects.]

Materials: Drawing materials. Or: Camera; film. Or: 3-D CAD program; computer.

*#5. ONE IMAGE FIVE WAYS: Do a quintuple take.

Create five different images from a single negative or digitized photograph (see figure 8-18).

Materials: Negative and darkroom materials. Or: Digitized photograph; computer; graphics software.

*6. PHOTOINSPIRATION: Begin with a photograph, and move on.

Use a photograph as the basis for an artwork in another medium (painting, sculpture, textile, or some other). (If the photograph is not your own, be aware of copyright regulations.)

Materials: Any medium.

#7. PHOTODEBATE: Take both sides.

Identify a controversial condition or social problem in your community that you could safely photograph (such as a nuclear power plant, a new superhighway, homeless people, or school conditions). Pretend that you have been hired by advocates of each side of the issue to take persuasive documentary photographs. Take a series of photographs, exploring ways in which photography can be used to present biased depictions.

Materials: Camera; film.

#8. PHOTOVISION VS. ARTISTVISION: Compare eye and camera.

Make a drawn portrait of someone from observation (if you are new at this, follow the directions in Betty Edwards' book, *Drawing on the Right Side of the Brain*). When you finish, take a photograph of the person from the same viewpoint. Put the drawing away, send your model home, and wait a week. Now make a second drawn portrait, this time using the photograph as your model (do not refer to the first drawing). When you finish the second drawing, compare it with the first. What differences do you notice? Get opinions from other people as well. What conclusions can you draw? If you were to look at a drawn portrait, do you think you would be able to tell whether it was done from life or from a photograph? Why or why not?

Materials: Model; drawing materials; camera and film (Polaroid is acceptable).

9. REVISIONING: Explore pictorial alternatives.

Find a reproduction of a painting done in Renaissance-style perspective—that is, symmetrical around a central point, and encompassing an entire subject (see, for example, figures 7-14, 7-19, and 7-23). Recompose the image as if it had been conceived as asymmetrical and arbitrarily framed (see, for example, figures 8-1 and 8-2). Or: Do the reverse. Recompose an asymmetrical and arbitrarily framed composition in central-point symmetrical perspective.

Materials: Painting reproduction(s); drawing materials.

10. CAMERA OBSCURA: See the hole thing!

Make a room into a camera obscura. The room must have a window that receives strong sunlight and must be able to be completely darkened during daylight. Tape a double-convex lens onto the window, and cover the window with black paper except for the lens. Move a portable movie screen toward and away from the lens until the image is in focus. If you tape paper to the screen, you can draw the projected scene.

Materials: Appropriate room; double-convex lens; black paper, portable movie screen.

CHAPTER 9

1. ROTODISK: Go around in circles.

Create a pattern that, when rotated, will appear to move in an unexpected way (expand, contract, wobble, etc.). Use lightweight cardboard disks five to ten inches in diameter; decorate with markers or colored paper; spin on a straight-pin stuck into a pencil eraser or on a paper clip (see figure 9-5). Movement can also be generated by a lazy-Susan or bicycle wheel spun by the viewer, or by placing the disk on the shaft of a rheostatically controlled electric motor or on a variable-speed drill. If you blink your eyes, the motion will appear to stop stroboscopically. For reference, study Marcel Duchamp's *Rotoreliefs*.

Materials: Posterboard; compass; scissors; pencil; markers and/or colored papers; paper clip, straight-pin, or other mode of rotation.

2. THAUMATROPE: Look at both sides.

Design a thaumatrope disk (see figure 9-3), using two images that will blend meaningfully when spun. Use heavy cardboard; punch two holes on opposite edges of the disk and insert a loop of string in each. Spin the disk by looping string around each forefinger; then wind up the disk. Create a slight tension by spreading your fingers apart, and the disk will spin around.

Materials: Matboard disks; fine-nibbed pen, watercolors, and brushes; awl; string.

3. MOVING ART: Call on Mother Nature.

Create a project that harnesses some natural force—wind, solar heat, convection currents, gravity, magnetism, momentum, water flow, viscosity—to generate change or movement. Conventional examples include: mobiles, wind chimes, whirly-gigs, kites, weather-vanes, kaleidoscopes, Swedish Christmas chimes, and old-fashioned paper-weights. For examples of artists' works, see figures 9-29 and 9-30.

#4. SERIAL IMAGES: Go step-by-step.

Plan a serial transformation sequence of four to twelve steps. The images can be simple (like, for example, a circle getting gradually larger; a tulip emerging, blooming, and dying), or complex (Mona Lisa becoming Marilyn Monroe). Use the transformation sequence as the basis for a composition: as elements in a painting, poster image, banner, or quilt (see figures 9-15 and 9-16). [With photography: Position your camera on a tripod and shoot a gradually changing scene at predetermined time intervals (time lapse).]

Materials: For working out ideas: pencil; eraser; paper; light box (optional). Or: Camera; tripod; film.

#5. MOVING VIEWER: What a relief!

Create a relief construction in which the image changes as the viewer moves. One method is to find two magazine photographs of the same size; cut each vertically into half-inch strips (number the strips on the back to keep track of their order). Then cut a piece of lightweight cardboard the same height and twice as wide as one picture; score the cardboard at half-inch intervals and fold it accordion style. Proceeding from left to right, glue the picture strips onto the cardboard, alternating the strips from each picture. Mount the accordion relief onto a piece of matboard. When the relief is viewed from the right, one picture will be visible; when viewed from the left, the other will be. For a variation, make the folds at right angles, cutting the cardboard three times the width of one picture.

Materials: Magazines; lightweight posterboard; pencil; metal-edged ruler; sharp X-Acto knife; rubber cement. Or: Materials for another medium, such as original photographs, painted canvas, ceramic slabs, Plexiglas, tapestry weaving.

#6. VISIBLE PROCESS: Make tracks.

Experiment with "footprints" of motion that reveal information about pressure, direction, and speed of an object moving against paper. For example, coat a piece of string with printing ink or paint, and place it between two sheets of paper. Press down on the paper and, at the same time, pull out the string. The result will resemble a multiple-exposure photograph. Likewise, you can experiment with the imprints of moving objects (including your fingers). Or: Experiment with brush strokes, using different thicknesses of ink or paint, papers of various absorbencies, and changing speeds of movement. For reference, look at traditional Oriental calligraphy and ink painting (see figures 3-18, 9-

21), or Western Impressionist and Expressionist paintings (see figures 9-22, 9-23). [With photography: Experiment with photograms.]

Materials: Paper; printing ink or paint; brayer; objects. Or: Various papers; India or Chinese ink or paint, pastels, powdered chalk, or graphite; brushes. Or: darkroom; photosensitive papers and chemicals; objects.

*#7. COMPOSITE IMAGE: Use many to create one.
Using the medium of your choice, create a composite image of a single subject that incorporates different viewing positions or different phases of motion (see figures 6-11, 9-17, 9-18, 9-19, 9-20, and 9-22). [With photography: Create a photomontage or multiple exposure photograph.] [With computer: Use digitized images to create a seamless composite.] Reference sources include works by Cézanne, Hockney, Cubists, and traditional Oriental ink painters.

8. DIRECT ANIMATION: Take me to your leader.
Secure some clear 16mm film leader (or bleach-exposed movie film). Make a two-frame template to place under the leader as a guide for drawing with acetate markers directly on the leader. Or: Disregard the frame format, and simply create designs (such as long, changeable lines) on the film. Remember that twenty-four frames will be projected in one second, so keep your approach simple! Experiment with accompanying taped sound. The now-classic short films of Canadian film-animator Norman McLaren are good examples of this approach.

Materials: Clear 16mm film leader or bleached film; acetate markers; movie projector; cassette tapes and player.

*#9. ANIMATION: Create apparent motion.
Plan a film animation sequence. First draw the key frames, then create transitional steps from one key frame to the other, for a minimum total of twenty to thirty drawings. [Flip book: Place two-inch drawings on 3″ × 5″ index cards (whole or cut in half).] [With photography: Position movie or video camera on a tripod, and expose each drawing in turn for a few seconds. Or: Create a scene with collage pieces, objects, plasticine, or flexible toys. Make a series of gradual changes, shooting each change for a few seconds. Or: Shoot a few frames at predetermined time intervals (time-lapse) of a scene that changes naturally, such as clouds or a sunset (the motion will appear sped up when projected).] [With computer: Design key frames and use an animation program to generate in-between frames.]

Materials: Tracing paper; pencil and eraser; light box (optional). For flip book: 3″ × 5″ index cards. Or: Video or movie camera; tripod; film or videotape. Or: Computer and animation software.

*10. CONCEPTUAL MOTION: Use the mind's eye.
Conceive an artwork that exists only in the viewer's mind as a series of imagined actions. Convey the work through a set of written, taped, or computerized verbal or mathematical instructions that lead the viewer to visualize a process of object construction.

CHAPTER 10

1. TECHNICAL EVENTS: How frequent are they?
Choose two or more types of TV programming (for exam-

ple: documentary, soap opera, detective or adventure drama, news, situation comedy, talk show, sports). For twelve to fifteen minute program segments, measure intervals between *technical events* by counting seconds, then writing down the number. A technical event consists of a change in imagery caused by a change in camera position, camera angle, focal point, and zooming. If you miss one event, skip it and resume count with the next one. (If you use videotape, you will be able to check the accuracy of your data.) Compute the mean average by totalling your numbers for a program segment and dividing by the number of numbers. Compute the modal averages by finding the most frequently used interval for a segment; finding the second and third most frequent interval is also useful. Repeat the process with six TV ads, and with segments from movies or TV programs more than twenty years old. Are the data similar or different for contrasting types of programs? For advertising as compared to other programming? For older movies or TV programs?

Materials: TV; pencil and paper; optional: VCR.

2. BEYOND THE NAKED EYE: Find inspiration in extended vision.
Seek out images of the physical world that cannot be seen by the naked eye: thermographs, Xrays, infrared photographs, sonograms, electron microscope images. Use one of these images as the inspiration for an artwork in any medium.

3. FAMILY ALBUM: Take a sensory memory trip.
Select three family snapshots taken at different times in your life, then find a quiet place where you can remain undisturbed for about an hour. Contemplate one picture; then close your eyes, relax your mind, and in your imagination reexperience the situation in which the picture was taken. Gently guide your memory through each of the six sense modalities: sight, hearing, taste, smell, touch, and kinesthetic (or body) memory. List the sensory memories that come to you. Repeat the process with each of the other pictures, spending a minimum of twenty minutes with each. This exercise will give you some idea of the qualities of sense information that are missing from mediated images. These memories can be used as the inspiration for an artwork, poem, or story.

*4. HAND AND MOUSE: How different are they?
Make a contour-line observation drawing of a still life using a computer drawing program, then print it out. Be sensitive to your subjective experience of the drawing process, and make a list of your observations. Next, make a contour-line observation drawing of the same still life using traditional drawing materials. Again, be introspective and list what you experience. When finished, compare the lists and the drawings. What differences do you find in the subjective drawing experiences? In the drawing products? Generate some conclusions about both the processes and the products of these two drawing methods. This project will be even more informative if two or more people carry it out independently, and afterward compare observations. A second experiment can be done with "blind" contour drawings.

Materials: Traditional drawing materials; computer; drawing software; optional: printer.

5. Where are You: How does camera angle influence perception?

Rule lines to divide a piece of paper into four vertical columns and three horizontal rows. Label the columns: Public Distance (long shot); Social Distance (to knees); Personal Distance (head and upper body); Intimate Distance (face). Label the horizontal rows: Seen from above; Seen at eye level; Seen from below. Watch fifteen-minute segments of two or more contrasting types of programming (see project 10-1 above), and for each, tally the number of times you see particular kinds of shots used. Does the pattern of camera angle differ with different kinds of programs? With the tension level of the narrative? With the role of the character in the narrative? If so, how? Why?

Materials: TV; paper and pencil; optional: VCR.

6. Eyewitness Testimony: How accurate is it?

Show a group of three or four subjects a fast-paced videotape of a crime being committed (use a segment from a TV or movie crime drama, or stage your own). Ask each viewer, without conferring with the others, to write a description of the crime as if he or she were giving a bystander statement to the police. Afterwards, discuss similarities and differences in the testimony in regard to details, inferences, sequence of events and so forth. How can these be explained in perceptual terms?

Materials: VCR; appropriate videotape; paper and pencil.

*7. Digital Analysis: Try high-tech art appreciation.

Digitize art images, and use a computer paint/draw program to analyze compositional relationships or to compare style characteristics. For example: Draw lines to reveal underlying geometric structure; convert color values or positive and negative spaces to black, white, and gray to expose compositional patterns; analyze the locations of various pixel colors to discover patterns of color distribution; cut and paste together parts of different images to discover similarities and differences (see figure 10-13).

Materials: Digitized art images; computer with color monitor; draw/paint software.

#8. Independent Productions: Experiment with journalistic truth.

This project needs two or more people. Have each person independently produce a factual documentary videotape or photo-essay of the same subject (for example: a profile of your school; life in a particular area of your city; a sports event; a local social problem). Afterward, view and compare the videotapes or photos. How do they differ in content? How does the perceptual information differ? What differences in meaning are conveyed? What specific techniques have created these differences (for example, choice of camera viewpoint, image sequence, field and frame relationships, soundtrack, and so forth). Can you say that one is more truthful than the other(s)?

Materials: VCR and videotape, or camera and film.

CHAPTER 11

1. One-Foot Drawing: Concentrate on details.

On a piece of drawing paper, draw a six-inch circle. Then tie together the ends of a one-foot length of string and lay the circle of string on the ground, for example, or on a cluttered desk top. Create a detailed pen or pencil drawing of what you see inside the string.

Materials: Twelve-inch length of string; drawing paper; compass; pencil and eraser; fine-nibbed drawing pen (optional).

*2. Thumbnails: Try visual brainstorming.

On a sheet of newsprint, draw ten small rectangles about 2″ × 3″. Use these to brainstorm compositions of a single subject for a painting, poster, or other illustration project. The first three or four sketches are apt to come easily, but more creative thoughts will begin to arise as you become increasingly pressed to finish the series. After completing all ten sketches, take time out to incubate. Return to them later, with a fresh mind. Choose two or three to develop more fully, and from these choose one for your final project.

Materials: Newsprint paper; pencil and eraser. Or: Computer; drawing software.

3. Famous People: How did they use the creative process?

Using biographies or writings on creativity, compile a series of descriptions of how some well-known creative artists, writers, and scientists experienced their creative thought processes. How do these descriptions agree (or disagree) with the discussion of the creative process in chapter 11?

4. Mystery Art: Does knowledge change perception?

From a museum collection, art history book, or postcard display, choose at random three artworks you know nothing about. For each, list your initial perceptions and attitudes toward the piece. Then set about to uncover information about the works (for example, artist, culture, historical period; stylistic characteristics; critical opinions). Use several different sources for each piece in order to give breadth to your research.

After completing your investigation, again contemplate each work and list your perceptions and attitudes toward each. Compare your before and after lists. Have your perceptions changed: If so, how? Have your tastes toward the works changed? If so, how?

5. Preferences: Take your own survey.

Assemble a collection of twenty same-sized color reproductions of artworks (such as postcards sold in museum shops). Arrange them in a sequence from simplicity, order, and symmetry to complexity, disorder, and asymmetry (see figure 1-7). Then select the ten that best represent even degrees of difference between the extremes; number them from 1–10 on the backs, and then shuffle the cards.

Select ten or more people you can survey on an individual basis. First, ask a subject to rate his or her general creativity on a scale from 1 to 5 (5 being most creative). Then ask him or her to arrange the reproductions in a sequence from least to most liked (or to sort into two piles: liked and not liked). Record the subject's preference sequence (or grouping).

After you have completed your survey, analyze the results. What relationship (if any) do you find between subjects' own ratings of their creativity and their preferences in art imagery? Based on your personal knowledge of these individuals, do you find any additional factors to consider (for example, age, educational level, knowledge of art, and so forth)?

*6. WHOLE AND PART: Experiment with relationships. Using a computer and digitized color reproductions of fine artworks, experiment with changing the relationships of parts to the whole composition. (Be sure to save the original pictures in memory.) For example: Change sizes, locations, or spaces between elements; field and frame relationships; relationships of value, color, or density of detail. How do these manipulations change your perception of the whole?

Show the original pictures and your best modifications to some other people. Ask them to guess which are the originals, and to discuss the reasons for their choices.

Materials: Digitized color reproductions of artworks; computer with color monitor; paint software.

(For additional exercises in the creative process, see chapter 1 projects: 3 (DESIGN BY ACCIDENT), 4 (CLOUDS AND ROCKS), 6 (JUNK SCULPTURE), 8 (MY WORD), and 9 (MY STARS).

Bibliography

Note: Entries marked ** are recommended for classroom use. Entries marked * are recommended for general readers. Other entries are of a more specialized or technical nature.

**Akeret, Robert U. 1973. *Photoanalysis: How to Interpret the Hidden Psychological Meaning of Personal Photos.* New York: Simon and Schuster.

Albers, Josef. 1971. *The Interaction of Color.* New Haven, Conn.: Yale University Press.

Arnheim, Rudolf. 1954. *Art and Visual Perception.* Berkeley: University of California Press.

_____. 1969. *Visual Thinking.* Berkeley: University of California Press.

Asch, Solomon E., 1956. "Opinions and Social Pressure: Summary Report," *Psychological Abstracts* No. 8022.

*Barron, Frank. 1958. "The Psychology of Imagination," *Scientific American* (September): 150–66.

Becker, Henry Jay. 1987. "Using Computers for Instruction," *Byte* (February): 149–62.

**Berger, John. 1972. *Ways of Seeing.* New York: Penguin Books.

*Birdsell, J. B. 1981. *Human Evolution.* Boston: Houghton Mifflin.

Birren, Faber. 1965. *History of Color in Painting.* New York: Van Nostrand Reinhold.

Block, Ned, ed. 1981. *Imagery.* Cambridge, Mass.: MIT Press.

*Bonner, John Tyler. 1980. *The Evolution of Culture in Animals.* Princeton, N.J.: Princeton University Press.

Bower, T.G.R., 1974. *Developoment in Infancy.* San Francisco: W.H. Freeman and Company

Brou, Philippe; Sciascia, Thomas R.; Linden, Lynette, and Lettvin, Jerome Y. 1986. "The Colors of Things," *Scientific American* (September): 84–91.

*Bruce, Vicki. 1988. *Recognising Faces.* Hillsdale, N.J.: Lawrence Erlbaum Associates.

Bruner, J. S., and Postman, Leo. 1949. "On the Perception of Incongruity: A Paradigm," *Journal of Personality* 18: 206–23. Cited in Kuhn 1970.

*Burnham, David. 1983. *The Rise of the Computer State.* New York: Vintage Books.

Bush, Susan and Shih, Hsio-yen. 1985. *Early Chinese Texts on Painting.* Cambridge, Mass.: Harvard University Press.

Campbell, Bernard G. 1979. *Humankind Emerging.* Boston: Little, Brown.

*Capra, Fritjof. 1975. *The Tao of Physics.* Boulder, Colo.: Shambala.

*Clark, Linda A. 1975. *The Ancient Art of Color Therapy.* Old Greenwich, Conn.: Devin-Adair Co.

*Cole, Michael, and Scribner, Sylvia. 1974. *Culture and Thought: A Psychological Introduction.* New York: John Wiley & Sons.

Collins, Allan, and Gentner, Dedre. 1987. "How People Construct Mental Models," in Holland and Quinn 1987.

**Cook, Olive. 1963. *Movement in Two Dimensions: A Study of the Animated and Projected Pictures Which Preceded the Invention of Cinematography.* London: Hutchinson.

*da Costa Nunes, Jadviga M. 1988. "O. G. Rejlander's Photographs of Ragged Children: Reflections on the Idea of Urban Poverty in Mid-Victorian Society." Unpublished paper.

**de Grandis, Luigina. 1984. *Theory and Use of Color.* New York: Harry N. Abrams.

*de la Croix, Horst, and Tansey, Richard G. 1975. *Gardner's Art Through the Ages,* 6th ed. New York: Harcourt Brace Jovanovich.

*DeMatteo, Bob. 1986. *Terminal Shock: The Health Hazards of Video Display Terminals.* Toronto: NC Press Limited.

_____. 1989. Interview with Joe Graedon on *The People's Pharmacy,* WUNC-FM, January 28.

Deregowski, Jan B. 1972. "Pictorial Perception and Culture," *Scientific American* (November): 82–88.

**Dubery, Fred, and Willats, John. 1983. *Perspective and Other Drawing Systems.* New York: Van Nostrand Reinhold.

*Edgerton, Samuel Y., Jr. 1975. *The Renaissance Rediscovery of Linear Perspective.* New York: Basic Books.

**Edwards, Betty, 1979. *Drawing on the Right Side of the Brain; A Course in Enhancing Creativity and Artistic Confidence.* Los Angeles: J. P. Tarcher.

*_____. 1986. *Drawing on the Artist Within.* New York: Simon and Schuster.

*Elliott, George P. 1966. *Dorothea Lange.* New York: Museum of Modern Art.

Fantz, Robert L. 1961. "The Origin of Form Perception," *Scientific American* 204 (5): 66-72.

**Fineman, Mark B. 1981. *The Inquisitive Eye.* New York: Oxford University Press.

Foster, Kenneth R., and Guy, Arthur W. 1986. "The

Microwave Problem," *Scientific American* (September): 32–39.

Foucault, Michel. 1963. *The Birth of the Clinic: An Archaeology of Medical Perception*. New York: Vintage Books.

_____.1973. *This Is Not a Pipe*. Berkeley: University of California Press.

Freeman, N. H., and Cox, M. V., eds. 1985. *Visual Order: The Nature and Development of Pictorial Representation*. New York: Cambridge University Press.

*Galassi, Peter. 1981. *Before Photography: Painting and the Invention of Photography*. New York: Museum of Modern Art.

*Gardner, Howard. 1980. *Artful Scribbles: The Significance of Children's Drawings*. New York: Basic Books.

*_____. 1983. *Frames of Mind: The Theory of Multiple Intelligences*. New York: Basic Books.

Ghiselin, Brewster, ed. 1955. *The Creative Process*. New York: New American Library.

Gibson, Eleanor J., and Walk, Richard D. 1960. "The 'Visual Cliff,' " *Scientific American* (April): 64 ff.

Gibson, James J. 1950. *The Perception of the Visual World*. Boston: Houghton Mifflin.

_____. 1966. *The Senses Considered as Perceptual Systems*. Boston: Houghton Mifflin.

_____. 1979. *The Ecological Approach to Visual Perception*. Boston: Houghton Mifflin.

Gladwin, T. 1970. *East Is a Big Bird: Navigation and Logic in Puluwat Atoll*. Cambridge, Mass.: Harvard University Press.

*Gleick, James. 1987. *Chaos: Making a New Science*. New York: Penguin Books.

Glickstein, Mitchell. 1988. "The Discovery of the Visual Cortex," *Scientific American* (September): 118–27.

Gombrich, Ernest. 1960. *Art and Illusion*. New York: Pantheon Books.

**Goodman, Cynthia. 1987. *Digital Visions: Computers and Art*. New York: Harry N. Abrams.

Goodman, Nelson. 1968. *Languages of Art*. Indianapolis: Bobbs-Merrill.

Greenfield, George B., and Hubbard, Lincoln B. 1984. *Computers in Radiology*. New York: Churchill Livingston.

Greenhalgh, Michael, and MeGaw, Vincent, eds. 1978. *Art in Society: Studies in Style, Culture and Aesthetics*. New York: St. Martin's Press.

**Gregory, R. L. 1966. *Eye and Brain*. New York: McGraw-Hill.

*Griffin, Donald R. 1981. *The Question of Animal Awareness: Evolutionary Continuity of Mental Experience*. Los Altos, Cal.: William Kaufmann.

Guzelimian, Vahe; Kuhnert, Norbert K.; and Rozells, Gia L. 1987. *Becoming an Amiga Artist*. Glenview, Ill.: Scott, Foresman.

Haber, Ralph Norman. 1969. "Eidetic Images," *Scientific American* (April): 70–82. Reprinted in Held 1974.

*Hall, Edward T. 1966. *The Hidden Dimension*. Garden City, N.Y.: Doubleday.

**Hampden-Turner, Charles. 1981. *Maps of the Mind*. New York: Collier Books/Macmillan.

Harmon, Leon D. 1973. "The Recognition of Faces," *Scientific American* (November): 70–82.

Held, Richard, ed. 1974. *Image, Object, and Illusion*. San Francisco: W. H. Freeman.

Held, Richard, and Richards, Whitman, eds. 1972. *Perception: Mechanisms and Models*. San Francisco: W. H. Freeman.

*Hibbard, Howard. 1983. *Caravaggio*. New York: Harper & Row.

Holland, Dorothy and Quinn, Naomi, eds. 1987. *Cultural Models in Language and Thought*. New York: Cambridge University Press.

**Instituto Geografico de Agostini. 1956. *Leonardo da Vinci*. New York: Reynal.

**International Paper Company. 1979. *Pocket Pal: A Graphic Arts Production Handbook*. New York: International Paper.

Janson, H. W. 1968. *History of Art*. Englewood Cliffs, N.J.: Prentice-Hall.

**Jussim, Estelle, and Kayafas, Gus, 1987. *Stopping Time: The Photographs of Harold Edgerton*. New York: Harry N. Abrams.

**Kavner, Richard S., and Dusky, Lorraine. 1978. *Total Vision*. New York: A & W Publishers.

**Knobler, Nathan. 1967. *The Visual Dialogue: An Introduction to the Appreciation of Art*. New York: Holt, Rinehart & Winston.

**Koningsberger, Hans. 1967. *The World of Vermeer: 1632–1675*. New York: Time, Inc.

*Konner, Melvin. 1972. *The Tangled Wing: Biological Constraints on the Human Spirit*. New York: Holt, Rinehart & Winston.

*Kosslyn, S. 1980. *Image and Mind*. Cambridge, Mass.: Harvard University Press.

_____. 1985. "Stalking the Mental Image," *Psychology Today* (May): 22–28.

Kubovy, Michael. 1986. *The Psychology of Perspective and Renaissance Art*. Cambridge: Cambridge University Press.

**Kueppers, Harald. 1980. *The Basic Law of Color Theory*. Woodbury, N.Y.: Barron's Educational Series.

*Kuhn, Thomas S. 1970. *The Structure of Scientific Revolutions*, 2d ed. Chicago: University of Chicago Press.

Land, Edwin H. 1959. "Experiments in Color Vision," *Scientific American* (May): 84–99.

_____. 1977. "The Retinex Theory of Color Vision," *Scientific American* (December): 108–28.

Lavroff, Nicholas. 1986. *Deluxe Paint II: Manual*. San Mateo, Cal.: Electronic Arts.

*Leakey, Richard E. 1981. *The Making of Mankind*.

New York: E. P. Dutton.

*Leakey, Richard E., and Lewin, Roger. 1977. *Origins*. New York: E. P. Dutton.

*_____. 1978. *People of the Lake: Mankind and Its Beginnings*. Garden City, N.Y.: Anchor Press/Doubleday.

Liebert, Robert M., and Sprafkin, Joyce. 1988. *The Early Window,* 3d ed. New York: Pergamon Press.

*Links, J. G. 1982. *Canaletto*. Ithaca, N.Y.: Cornell University Press.

Lovejoy, C. Owen. 1988. ''Evolution of Human Walking,'' *Scientific American* (November): 118–25.

Lowe, Donald M. 1982. *History of Bourgeois Perception*. Chicago: University of Chicago Press.

**Lunde, Anders S. 1983. *Whirligigs: Design and Construction*. Hendersonville, N.C.: Mother Earth News.

**_____. 1984. *More Whirligigs: Large-Scale and Animated Figures*. Hendersonville, N.C.: Mother Earth News.

Luscher, Max. 1969. *The Luscher Color Test*. New York: Random House.

*Mander, Jerry. 1978. *Four Arguments for the Elimination of Television*. New York: William Morrow.

Miller, W. H.; Ratliff, Floyd; and Hartline, H. K. 1961. ''How Cells Receive Stimuli,'' *Scientific American* (September): 222–38. Reprinted in Held and Richards 1972.

**Millerson, Gerald. 1985. *The Technique of Television Production*, 11th ed. Boston: Focal Press.

*Minninger, Joan. 1984. *Total Recall: How to Boost Your Memory Power*. Emmaus, Pa.: Rodale Press.

Mitchell, W. J. T. 1986. *Iconology: Image, Text, Ideology*. Chicago: University of Chicago Press.

Moir, Alfred. 1967. *The Italian Followers of Caravaggio*. Cambridge, Mass.: Harvard University Press.

**Montague, John. 1985. *Basic Perspective Drawing: A Visual Approach*. New York: Van Nostrand Reinhold.

**Mortier, R. Shamms. 1989. ''How May I Animate Thee? Let Me Count the Ways . . . ,'' *Amazing Computing* (January): 10–12.

**Muybridge, Eadweard. c. 1908 *The Human Figure in Motion*. Reprint. New York: Dover, 1955.

**_____. *Animals in Motion*. Reprint. New York: Dover, 1957

**Naiman, Arthur. 1983. *Computer Dictionary for Beginners*. New York: Ballantine.

Nathaus, Jeremy. 1989. ''The Genes for Color Vision,'' *Scientific American* (February): 42–49.

**Newhall, Beaumont. 1978. *The History of Photography*, 4th ed. New York: Museum of Modern Art.

Noll, A. Michael 1966. ''Human or Machine: A Subjective Comparison of Piet Mondrian's *Composition with Lines* (1917) and a Computer-generated Picture,'' *Psychological Record* 16: 1–10.

Noton, David, and Stark, Lawrence. 1971. *Eye Movement and Vision*. New York: Plenum.

O'Doherty, Brian. 1964. ''Portrait: Edward Hopper,'' *Art in America* 52(6): 77.

**Ornstein, Robert, and Thompson, Richard F. 1984. *The Amazing Brain*. Boston: Houghton Mifflin.

*Ott, John. 1973. *Health and Light*. New York: Pocket Books.

*Paige, Ken N. 1988. ''The Wiliest Wildflower in the West,'' *Natural History* (June): 49–52.

*Panofsky, Erwin. 1955. *The Life and Art of Albrecht Dürer*, 4th ed. Princeton, N.J.: Princeton University Press.

*Peterson, Dale. 1983. *Genesis II: Creation and Recreation with Computers*. Reston, Va.: Reston Publishing.

*Piaget, Jean. 1954. *The Construction of Reality in the Child*. New York: Ballantine Books.

Pirenne, M. H. 1970. *Optics, Painting and Photography*. New York: Cambridge University Press.

Price-Williams, Douglass R. 1975. *Explorations in Crosscultural Psychology*. San Francisco: Chandler & Sharp.

Pritchard, Roy M. 1961. ''Stabilized Images on the Retina,'' *Scientific American* (June): 72–78. Reprinted in Held and Richards 1972.

**Rainwater, Clarence. 1971. *Light and Color*. New York: Golden Press.

Ratliff, Floyd. 1972. ''Contour and Contrast,'' *Scientific American* (June): 90–101. Reprinted in Held 1974.

Reichel-Dolmatoff, G. 1978. ''Drug-induced optical sensations and their relationship applied to art among some Colombian Indians.'' In Greenhalgh and MeGaw 1978.

Reiss, Timothy. 1982. *The Discourse of Modernism*. Ithaca, N.Y.: Cornell University Press.

*Restak, Richard M. 1984. *The Brain*. New York: Bantam Books.

**Rewald, John. 1962. *Post-Impressionism from Van Gogh to Gauguin*. New York: Museum of Modern Art.

**_____. 1973. *The History of Impressionism*, 4th rev. ed. New York: The Museum of Modern Art.

**Richardson, John Adkins; Coleman, Floyd W.; and Smith, Michael J. 1984. *Basic Design: Systems, Elements, Applications*. Englewood Cliffs, N.J.: Prentice-Hall.

*Rivlin, Robert, and Gravelle, Karen. 1984. *Deciphering the Senses*. New York: Simon and Schuster.

Rock, Irvin. 1975. *An Introduction to Perception*. New York: Macmillan.

Rosenthal, Robert, and Jacobson, Lenore F. 1968. *Pygmalion in the Classroom: Self-fulfilling Prophecies and Teacher Expectations*. New York: Holt, Rinehart & Winston.

Rosenzweig, Mark R.; Bennett, Edward L.; and Diamond, Marion Cleevers. 1972. ''Brain Changes in Response to Experience,'' *Scientific American* (February): 22–29. Cited in Ornstein and Thompson 1984.

Roukes, Nicholas. 1982. *Art Synectics*. Worcester, Mass.: Davis Publications.

Schnapf, Julie L., and Baylor, Denis A. 1987. "How Photoreceptors Respond to Light," *Scientific American* (April): 40–47.

*Schwarz, Heinrich. 1946-66. *Art and Photography: Forerunners and Influences*, ed. by William E. Parker. Layton, Ut.: Gibbs M. Smith, 1985.

Sebeok, Thomas A. and Rosenthal, Robert. 1981. *The Clever Hans Phenomenon*. New York: Annals of The New York Academy of Science, vol. 364.

Segall, Marshall H.; Campbell, Donald; and Herskovits, Melville J. 1966. *The Influence of Culture on Visual Perception*. Indianapolis: Bobbs-Merrill.

*Sommer, Robert, 1969. *Personal Space: The Behavioral Basis of Design*. Englewood Cliffs, N.J.: Prentice-Hall.

*Sontag, Susan. 1977. *On Photography*. New York: Delta Books/Dell.

*Thomas, Ann Wall. 1980. *Colors from the Earth*. New York: Van Nostrand Reinhold.

**Time-Life Books. 1970–72. *Life Library of Photography: Documentary Photography*, 1972. *Frontiers of Photography*, 1972. *Great Photographers*, 1971. *Travel Photography*, 1972. *Photojournalism*, 1971. *Color*, 1970. *Photography as a Tool*, 1970. *The Print*, 1970. New York: Time, Inc.

*Turnbull, Colin M. 1962. *The Forest People: A Study of the Pigmies of the Congo*. New York: Simon and Schuster.

Turner, Victor W. 1962. "Three Symbols of *Passage* in Ndembu Circumcision Ritual: An Interpretation," in M. Gluckman, ed., *Essays in the Ritual of Social Relations*. Manchester University Press.

**Upton, Barbara, and Upton, John. 1976. *Photography*. Boston: Educational Associates/Little, Brown.

van Hoorn, Willem. 1972. *As Images Unwind: Ancient and Modern Theories of Visual Perception*. Amsterdam: University Press.

**Vinroot, Sally and Crowder, Jennie. 1981. *The New Dyer*. Loveland, Co.: Interweave Press.

Wald, George. 1950. "Eye and Camera," *Scientific American* (August): 32–41. Reprinted in Held and Richards 1972.

White, John. 1967. *The Birth and Rebirth of Pictorial Space*, 2d ed. Boston: Boston Book and Art Shop.

*Williams, Raymond. 1977. *Marxism and Literature*. New York: Oxford University Press.

*_____. 1983. *Keywords: A Vocabulary of Culture and Society*, rev. ed. New York: Oxford University Press.

*Williams, Tannis Macbeth, ed. 1986. *The Impact of Television: A Natural Experiment in Three Communities*. New York: Academic Press/Harcourt Brace Jovanovich.

*Winn, Marie. 1985. *The Plug-in Drug*, rev. ed. New York: Viking.

Witkin, H.A. 1949. "Perception of Body Position and the Position of the Visual Field," *Psychological Monographs* 63: 7.

Wober, M. 1967. "Adapting Witkin's Field-independence Theory to Accommodate New Information from Africa," *British Journal of Psychology* 58: 29–38. Cited in Cole and Scribner 1974.

ADDITIONAL CHAPTER REFERENCES (NOT CITED IN TEXT)

Chapter 1: Seboek and Rosenthal 1981; Griffin 1981; Birdsell 1981; Bonner 1980; Campbell 1979; Gardner 1983; Barron 1958; Gibson 1979, 1966; Konner 1972; Leakey 1981; Leakey and Lewin 1978, 1977; Lovejoy 1988; Ornstein and Thompson 1984; Bruce 1988; Harmon 1973; Fantz 1961; Bower 1974.

Chapter 2: Schnapf and Baylor 1987; Wald 1950; Ratliff 1972; Miller, Ratliff, and Hartline 1961; Pritchard 1961; Haber 1969.

Chapter 3: Ornstein and Thompson 1984; Restak 1984; Rock 1975; Glickstein 1988; Birdsell 1981; Campbell 1979; Leakey and Lewin 1978; Minninger 1984; Gregory 1966; Cole and Scribner 1974; Price-Williams 1975; Segall 1966.

Chapter 4: Rock 1975; Gibson 1966; Freeman and Cox 1985; Bower 1974.

Chapter 5: de Grandis 1986; Brou et al. 1986; Richardson et al. 1984; Kueppers 1980; Rainwater 1971; International Paper Company 1979; Vinroot and Crowder 1981; Newhall 1978; Upton and Upton 1976; Time-Life Books 1970a, 1970b, 1970c; Kavner and Dusky 1978; Ott 1973; Nathaus 1989, Clark 1975; Paige 1988.

Chapter 6: Bower 1974; Gibson 1966, 1979; Rock 1975; Campbell 1979; Birdsell 1981; Leakey and Lewin 1977; Sommer 1969; Deregowski 1972; Gladwin 1970.

Chapter 7: Gibson 1966; Edgerton 1975; Goodman 1968; Panofsky 1955; Kubovy 1986; Foucault 1963; Dubery and Willats 1983; White 1967; Pirenne 1970; Hibbard 1983; Moir 1967; Mitchell 1986; Reiss 1982; Capra 1975; Kuhn 1970.

Chapter 8: Galassi 1981; Links 1982; Koningsberger 1967; Upton and Upton 1976; Newhall 1978; Time-Life 1971; Mander 1978; da Costa Nunes 1988; Pirenne 1970; Sontag 1977; Schwarz 1949-66.

Chapter 9: Fineman 1981; Rock 1975; Gibson 1979; Cook 1963; Lunde 1984; Newhall 1978; Jussim and Kayafas 1987; Ott 1973.

Chapter 10: Burnham 1985; Naiman 1983; Mander 1978; Millerson 1985; Winn 1985; C. Goodman 1987; Guzelimian et al. 1987; Lavroff 1986; Mortier 1989; Peterson 1983; Gleick 1987; Foster and Guy 1986; Becker 1987.

Chapter 11: Barron 1958; Edwards 1986.

Index

(Page numbers in italics refer to a figure only.)

242